LAW

AND

SOCIETY

Second Edition

STEVEN VAGO

Saint Louis University

Prentice Hall, Englewood Cliffs, New Jersey 07632

Library of Congress Cataloging-in-Publication Data

VAGO, STEVEN
  Law and Society.

  Bibliography.
  Includes index.
  1. Sociological jurisprudence. I. Title.
K370.V33 1988   340'.115   87-111454
ISBN 0-13-526492-8

Editorial/production supervision
  and interior design: Jan Stephan
Cover design: Ben Santora
Manufacturing buyer: Margaret Rizzi and Carol Bystrom

Printed in the United States of America

10 9 8 7 6 5 4 3 2 1

ISBN 0-13-526492-8   01

PRENTICE-HALL INTERNATIONAL (UK) LIMITED, *London*
PRENTICE-HALL OF AUSTRALIA PTY. LIMITED, *Sydney*
PRENTICE-HALL CANADA INC., *Toronto*
PRENTICE-HALL HISPANOAMERICANA, S.A., *Mexico*
PRENTICE-HALL OF INDIA PRIVATE LIMITED, *New Delhi*
PRENTICE-HALL OF JAPAN, INC., *Tokyo*
PRENTICE-HALL OF SOUTHEAST ASIA PTE. LTD., *Singapore*
EDITORA PRENTICE-HALL DO BRASIL, LTDA., *Rio de Janeiro*

TO KATHE, AS ALWAYS

Contents

5 Law and Social Control   142

6 Law as a Method of Conflict Resolution   179

7 Law and Social Change   219

8 The Profession and Practice of Law   253

9 Sociological Research of Law in Society   296

Index   322

Preface

The second edition of this book follows the same basic format as the first edition. I have substantially reworked large parts of the text and incorporated new developments, concerns, and controversies in the study of law and society. In revising the book, I have sought to provide a text that will be pedagogically sound, enjoyable and informative to read, and distinctive. Although intended for undergraduate students, this book is not limited to them. Anyone with an interest in the relationship between law and society will find this book instructive and provocative.

All textbooks are selective of the topics they address and, of course, this book is no exception. I have included topics that are absent from other law and society texts. Unlike other texts, this one balances the discussion of criminal law and civil law. It also considers administrative law, which is rarely analyzed by sociologists. The very nature of the subject matter also requires that an unusually diverse range of topics and issues be included in this text. Consequently, much of the material is based not only on sociology, but to some extent on anthropology, psychology, political science, and jurisprudence.

The book is designed for a one-term course. The materials are organized so that each chapter builds on the previous one. However, if an instructor should wish to utilize a different organization, it would not seriously detract from the value of the text. Depending on an instructor's preference, Chapter Nine on sociological research of law in society can be discussed after the introductory chapter or Chapter Two which deals with theoretical perspectives. To gain an overview of the subject matter, some readers may wish to refer to the detailed chapter summaries before reading the chapter.

A considerable amount of new material has been added to this revision and much has been deleted from the first one. The additions include discussions on scientific jury selection, lobbyists, the debate over death penalty, alternative dispute resolution forums, eyewitness identification, legal aspects of drug abuse, and the critical legal studies movement. I have also expanded and updated the coverage on lawyers and legal education, law enforcement, the role of law in social control and dispute resolution, and law making. To make the book livelier, I have incorporated a number of cross-cultural illustrations and lightened by writing style at the expense of sociological and legal jargon.

The study of the relationship between law and society is naturally eclectic. Knowledge about it has accumulated haphazardly. Sociological investigations of law and society are influenced by a number of theoretical perspectives, resulting in a variety of strains of thought and research. In a sense, more questions will be raised than can be answered in this volume. One of the fascinating aspects of the study of law and society is that there are so many unanswered questions, so many ways of considering the subject, and so much yet to be learned. It is hoped that this revision will serve as a useful point of departure for the further study of the complex interplay between law and society.

I am grateful to many colleagues for assistance, criticism, and their support throughout this project. To Clement S. Mihanovich I owe a very special and substantial debt for his critical comments, thoughtful suggestions, wise counsel, and encouragement. Many thanks, too, to Steven Puro whose encyclopedic knowledge of legal procedures helped me to improve considerably several chapters. Several anonymous reviewers are due credit for making valuable suggestions for the second edition. I also wish to thank the many students who during the years read and commented on the many versions of the manuscript for their invaluable feedback and unwillingness to take things for granted. At Prentice Hall, my thanks go to Jan Stephan for her superb editing of the manuscript, to Bill Webber for his unfaltering support, and to Sallie Steele and Steve Katigbak for expertly preparing the index. Finally, this project could not have been completed without the generous financial support of the Vago Foundation which magnanimously covered all expenses incurred in the preparation of this manuscript.

Steven Vago
St. Louis

1

Introduction:
Basic Concerns,
Concepts, and Controversies

Law permeates all realms of social behavior. Its pervasiveness and social significance are felt in all walks of life. In subtle and, at times, not so subtle ways a complex and voluminous set of laws governs our every action. It determines registration at birth and the distribution of possessions at death. Laws regulate prenuptial agreements, marriage, divorce, and the handling of dependent children. It sets the speed limit and the length of school attendance. Laws control what we eat and where, and what we buy and when. Laws protect ownership and define the parameters of private and public property. Laws regulate business, raise revenue, provide for redress when agreements are broken, and uphold certain institutions, such as the family. Laws are also designated to protect the legal and political system by defining power relationships, thus establishing who is superordinate and who is subordinate in any given situation. Laws maintain the *status quo* but also provide for necessary changes. Finally, laws, in particular criminal laws, not only protect private and public interests, but also preserve order. There is no end to the ways in which the law has a significant effect upon our lives.

The principal mission of this book is to serve as a text in undergraduate courses on law and society. The relatively large number of references cited also makes the text a valuable source for both graduate students engaging in research on the sociology of law and instructors who may be teaching this subject for the first time. Since this book has been written primarily for the undergraduate student, no one particular approach to law and society has been taken, nor a particular ideology or theoretical stance embraced. To have done so would have been too limiting for a text, since important contributions would have been excluded or would have been considered out of context. Consequently, the book does not propound a single thesis; instead, it attempts to expose the reader to a variety of sociological methods and theoretical perspectives used to explain the interplay between law and society in the social science literature.

OVERVIEW

All societies have mechanisms for declaration, administration, and enforcement of the rules by which their members live. Not all societies, however, utilize a formal legal system (courts, judges, lawyers, and law enforcement agencies), to the same degree. Traditional societies, for example, may rely almost exclusively on custom as the source of legal rules and resolve disputes through conciliation or mediation by village elders, or by some other moral or divine authority. As for law, such societies need little of it. Traditional societies are more homogeneous than modern industrial societies. Social relations are more direct and intimate, interests are shared by virtually everyone, and there are fewer things to quarrel about. Since relations are more direct and intimate, nonlegal mechanisms of social control are generally more effective.

As societies become larger, more complex, and modern, homogeneity gives way to heterogeneity. Common interests decrease in relation to special interests. Face-to-face relations become progressively less important, as do kinship ties. Access to material goods becomes more indirect with a greater likelihood for unequal allocation, and the struggle for available goods becomes intensified. The potentialities for conflict and dispute within the society consequently increase. The need for explicit regulatory and enforcement mechanisms becomes increasingly evident. The development of trade and industry requires a system of legal rules dealing with business organizations and commercial transactions, subjects which normally are not part of customary or religious law. Such commercial activity also requires a more effective method of settling disputes than trial by ordeal, trial by combat, or decision by a council of elders. As one commentator has noted: "The paradox ... is that the more civilized man becomes, the greater is man's need for law, and the more law he creates. Law is but a response to social needs" (Hoebel, 1954:292).

"The law embodies the story of a nation's development through many centuries" (Holmes, 1881:5), and every legal system stands in close relationship to the ideas, aims, and purposes of society. Law reflects the intellectual, social, economic, and political climate of its time. It also reflects the particular ideas, ideals, and ideologies which are part of a distinct "legal culture"—those attributes of behavior and attitudes that make the law of one society different from that of another, that make, for example, the law of the Eskimos different from the law of the French (Friedman, 1984:6).

In sociology, the study of law touches a number of well-established areas of inquiry. Sociology is concerned with values, interaction patterns, and ideologies that underlie the basic structural arrangements in a society, many of which are embodied in law as substantive rules. Both sociology and law are concerned with norms, rules that prescribe the appropriate behavior for people in a given situation. The study of conflict and conflict resolution are central in both disciplines. Both sociology and law are concerned with the nature of legitimate authority, the mechanisms of social control, issues of civil rights, power arrangements, and the relationship between public and private spheres (Selznick, 1968:50).

From an historical perspective, the rapprochement of sociology and law is not novel. Early American sociologists, after the turn of the century, emphasized the various facets of the relationship between law and society. E. A. Ross (1922:106) considered law as "the most specialized and highly furnished engine of control employed by society." Lester F. Ward (1906:339), who believed in governmental control and social planning, predicted a day when legislation would endeavor to solve "questions of social improvement, the amelioration of the conditions of all the people, the removal of whatever privations may still remain, and the adoption of means to the positive increase of the social welfare, in short, the organization of human happiness."

The writings of these early sociologists have greatly influenced the development of the school of legal philosophy that became a principal force in American sociological jurisprudence. (Sociological jurisprudence is based on a comparative study of legal systems, legal doctrines, and legal institutions as social phenomena, and considers law as it actually is—the "law in action" as distinguished from the law as it appears in books.) Roscoe Pound, the principal figure in sociological jurisprudence, relied heavily on the findings of early sociologists in asserting that law should be studied as a social institution. For Pound (1941:18), law was a specialized form of social control that exerts pressure on a person "in order to constrain him to do his part in upholding civilized society and to deter him from anti-social conduct, that is, conduct at variance with the postulates of social order."

Interest in law among sociologists grew rapidly after the Second World War. In the United States some sociologists became interested in law almost by accident. As they investigated certain problems, such as race relations, they found law to be relevant. Others became radicalized in the mid- and late 1960s, during the period of the Vietnam War, and their work began to emphasize social conflict and the functions of stratification in society. It became imperative for sociologists of the left to dwell on the gap between promise and performance in the legal system. By the same token, those sociologists defending the establishment were anxious to show that the law dealt with social conflict in a legitimate fashion.

But interest in law and society is not confined to the United States. Adam Podgorecki, a Polish sociologist, has analyzed a number of distinct national styles in social science work related to law. Scandinavian scholars have emphasized the social meaning of justice. In particular, they have investigated knowledge of the law and attitudes toward it. Italian social scientists have been concerned with empirical investigations of judges and with the process of judging. Sociologists in both East and West Germany have been interested in comparing the impact of socialistic and capitalistic systems on the way the Eastern and Western legal systems function. Latin American scholars, particularly those in Chile and Peru, have investigated the operations of their legal institutions, most notably in the area of agrarian reform. There is a flourishing interest in law and society in Japan, initiated by the many problems Japan experienced with the reception of European law. Both nationally and internationally, a number of organizations have been formed, and centers established, to study the multifaceted interaction between law and society (Rehbinder, 1975:13–48).

Few sociologists concerned with the study of law and society would question Eugen Ehrlich's oft quoted dictum that the "center of gravity of legal development lies not in legislation, nor in juristic science, nor in judicial decision, but in society itself" (Ehrlich, 1975: Foreword). I share I. D. Willock's (1974:7) position that "in so far as jurisprudence seeks to give law a location in the whole span of human affairs it is from sociology that it stands to gain most." Sociological knowledge, perspectives, theories, and methods are not only useful, but are essential for the understanding and possible improvement of law and the legal system in society.

But the sociological study of law is somewhat hampered by difficulties of interaction between sociologists and lawyers. As Edwin M. Schur correctly notes, "In a sense ... lawyers and sociologists 'don't talk the same language,' and this lack of communication undoubtedly breeds uncertainty in both professions concerning any involvement in the other's domain, much less any cooperative interdisciplinary endeavors." He goes on to say: "Sociologists and lawyers are engaged in quite different sorts of enterprises," and notes that "the lawyer's characteristic need to make decisions, here and now, may render him impatient with the sociologist's apparently unlimited willingness to suspend final judgment on the issue ... " (Schur, 1968:8). The complexity of legal terminology further impedes interaction. Law has its own vocabulary, terms like *subrogation* and *replivin* and *respondeat superior* and *chattel lien* abound. Lawyers use a special arcane writing style, at times replete with multiple redundancies such as *null and void* or *in full force and effect*. Not surprisingly, "Between specialized vocabulary and arcane style, the very language of the law defies lay understanding" (Chambliss and Seidman, 1982:119).

Problems of interaction are also brought about and reinforced by the differences in professional cultures (Davis, 1962). Lawyers are advocates, they are concerned with the identification and resolution of the problems of their clients. Sociologists consider all evidence on a proposition and approach a problem with an open mind. Lawyers to a great extent are guided by precedents, and past decisions control current cases, as contrasted to sociologists who emphasize creativity, theoretical imagination, and research ingenuity. The pronouncements of the law are predominantly prescriptive: They tell people how they should behave and what will happen to them if they do not. In sociology, the emphasis is on description, on understanding the reasons why certain groups of people act certain ways in specific situations. The law *reacts* to problems most of the time; the issues and conflicts are brought to its attention by clients outside the legal system. In sociology, issues, concerns, and problems are *generated* within the discipline on the basis of what is considered intellectually challenging, timely, or of interest to funding agencies.

These differences in professional cultures are, to a great extent, due to the different methods lawyers and sociologists use in searching for "truth." Legal thinking, as Vilhelm Aubert (1973:50–53) explains, is different from scientific thinking for the following reasons:

1. Law seems to be more inclined toward the particular than toward the general (e.g., what happened in a specific case).
2. Law, unlike the physical and social sciences, does not endeavor to establish dramatic connections between means and ends (e.g., the impact the verdict has on the defendant's future conduct).
3. Truth for the law is normative and non-probabilistic; something either has happened or it has not. A law is either valid or invalid (e.g., did a person break a law or not?).
4. Law is primarily past and present oriented and is rarely concerned with future events (e.g., what happens to the criminal in prison).
5. Legal consequences may be valid even if they do not occur; that is, their formal validity does not inevitably depend on compliance (e.g., the duty to fulfill a contract. If it is not fulfilled, it does not falsify the law in question).
6. A legal decision is an either/or, all or nothing process with little room for a compromise solution (e.g., a litigant either wins or loses a case).

These generalizations, of course, have their limitations. They are simply indicative of the fact that law is an authoritative and reactive problem-solving system which is geared to specific social needs. Since the emphasis in law is on certainty—or predictability or finality—its implementation often requires the adoption of simplified assumptions about the world. The lawyer generally sees the law as an instrument to be wielded, and he or she is more often preoccupied with the practice and pontification of the law than with its consideration as an object of scholarly inquiry.

Perhaps the question most frequently asked of any sociologist interested in law is, "What are you doing studying law?" Unlike the lawyer, the sociologist needs to "justify" any research in the legal arena and often envies colleagues in law schools who can carry out such work without having to reiterate its relevance or their own competence. Yet, this need for justification is not an unmixed evil since it serves to remind the sociologist that he or she is not a lawyer but a professional with special interests. Yet, like the lawyer, the sociologist may be concerned with the understanding, prediction, and perhaps even the development of law. Obviously, the sociologist and the lawyer lack a shared experience, a common quest. At the same time, increasingly, sociologists and lawyers work together on problems of mutual interests (such as, research on delinquency, crime, consumer problems, and so forth) and are beginning to see the reciprocal benefits of such endeavors. Sociologists also recognize that their research has to be adopted to the practical concerns of lawyers if it is to capture their interest. In view of the vocational orientation of law schools and the preoccupation of lawyers with legal doctrine, it is unlikely that research aimed at theory building will attract or retain the attention of most law students and professors (Posner, 1985:327–330).

WHAT IS LAW?

In everyday speech, the term "law" conjures up a variety of images. For some, law may mean getting a parking ticket, the inability to get a drink if under age, or registration for the draft. For others, law is paying income tax, being evicted, or going to prison for growing marijuana. For still others, law is concerned with what legislators enact or judges declare. Law means all these and more. Even among scholars, there is no agreement on the term. The purpose here is to introduce some of the classic and contemporary conceptualizations of law to illustrate the diverse ways of defining it.

The question, "What is law?" haunts legal thought, and probably more scholarship has gone into defining and explaining the concept of law than into any other concept still in use in sociology and in jurisprudence. Reviews of the literature by Ronald L. Akers and Richard Hawkins (1975:5–15), and Robert M. Rich (1977), indicate that there are almost as many definitions of law as there are theorists. E. Adamson Hoebel (1954:18) comments that "to seek a definition of the legal is like the quest for the Holy Grail." He cites Max Radin's warning that "Those of us who have learned humility have given over the attempt to define law." In spite of these warnings, law *can* be defined. In any definition of law, however, we must keep Julius Stone's (1964:177) admonition in mind that " 'law' is necessarily an abstract term, and the definer is free to choose a level of abstraction; but by the same token, in these as in other choices, the choice must be such as to make sense and be significant in terms of the experience and present interest of those who are addressed."

In our illustrative review of the diverse conceptualizations of law, let us first turn to two great American jurists, Benjamin Nathan Cardozo and Oliver Wendell Holmes. Cardozo (1924:52) defines law as "a principle or rule of conduct so established as to justify a prediction with reasonable certainty that it will be enforced by the courts if its authority is challenged." Holmes (1897:461) declares that "The prophecies of what the courts will do in fact, and nothing more pretentious, are what I mean by the law." For Holmes, judges make the law on the basis of past experience. In both of these definitions the courts play an important role. These are pragmatic approaches to law as revealed by court rendered decisions. Although implicit in these definitions is the notion of courts being backed by the authoritative force of a political state, these definitions of law seem to have a temporal character: What is the law at this time?

Anthropologists have taken a somewhat different approach to the notion of law than legal scholars. In his classic study on primitive law, Bronislaw Kasper Malinowski views the essence of law to be embodied in the principle of reciprocity. In his words:

> The rules of law stand out from the rest in that they are felt and regarded as the obligations of one person and the rightful claims of another. They are sanctioned not by a mere psychological motive, but by a definite social ma-

chinery of binding force, based . . . upon mutual dependence, and realized in the equivalent arrangement of reciprocal services . . . (Malinowski, 1926:55).

For him: "Law is the specific result of the configuration of obligations, which makes it impossible for the native to shirk his responsibility without suffering for it in the future" (1926:49). Malinowski's analysis of law implies that law operates not only in conflict or dispute situations, but also in the realm of common everyday activities. One of the criticisms frequently made of Malinowski's work is that he fails to differentiate adequately between law and customs. Perhaps because of this, many other theorists went through great pains to separate the two, usually in terms of the source of sanctions and enforcement (group or individual sanctions in the case of customs and centralized authority in the case of society dealing with law). Other anthropologists, as a result, began to see law as the administration of state power. This orientation is reflected, for example, in Radcliffe-Brown's notion of law as "the maintenance or establishment of social order, within a territorial framework, by the exercise of coercive authority through the use, or the possibility of use, of physical force" (Radcliffe-Brown, cited by Hoebel, 1954:26). Similarly, E. Adamson Hoebel (1954:28) argues in his influential formulation of law that "A social norm is legal if its neglect or infraction is regularly met, in threat or in fact, by the application of physical force by an individual or group possessing the socially recognized privilege of so acting."

An objection that has been raised regarding Radcliffe-Brown's and Hoebel's definitions is that they fail to distinguish between law and government. This approach to law makes it difficult to make this separation for analytical purposes and renders meaningless the notion that government is subject to law (Schur, 1968:75). These are, however, meager objections. Law and government are fundamentally inseparable. Governments not only create and enforce their own laws, but law gives them the authority to do so. No government could exist without law, and without some form of government law would be meaningless. Richard Quinney (1970:13) succinctly supports this argument in stating: "Law is the creation and interpretation of specialized rules in a politically organized society."

From a sociological perspective, one of the most influential conceptualizations of law is that of Max Weber. Starting with the idea of an *order* characterized by legitimacy, he suggests: "An order will be called *law* if it is externally guaranteed by the probability that coercion (physical or psychological), to bring about conformity or avenge violation, will be applied by a *staff* of people holding themselves specially ready for that purpose" (Weber, 1954:5). Weber argues that law has three basic features which, taken together, distinguish it from other normative orders, such as custom or convention. First, pressures to comply with the law must come externally in the form of actions or threats of action by others regardless of whether a person wants to obey the law or does so out of habit. Second, these external actions or threats always involve coercion or force. Third, those who implement the coercive threats are individuals whose official role is to enforce the law. Weber refers to "state" law when the persons who are charged to enforce the law are part of an agency of political authority.

Weber contends that customs and convention can be distinguished from law because they do not entail one or more of these features. Customs are rules of conduct in defined situations that are of relatively long duration and are generally observed without deliberation and "without thinking." Customary rules of conduct are called usages, and there is no sense of duty or obligation to follow them. Conventions, by contrast, are rules for conduct and they involve a sense of duty and obligation. Pressures, which usually include expressions of disapproval, are exerted on individuals who do not conform to conventions. Weber (1954:27) points out that unlike law, a conventional order "lacks specialized personnel for the implementation of coercive power."

Although a number of scholars accept the essentials of Weber's definition of law, they question two important points. First, some contend that Weber places too much emphasis on coercion and ignores other considerations that may induce individuals to obey the law. For example, Philip Selznick (1968; 1969:4–8) argues that the authoritative nature of legal rules brings about a special kind of obligation which is not dependent on the use or threat of coercion or force. Many laws are obeyed because people feel it is their duty to obey. The second point is concerned with Weber's use of a special staff. Some scholars claim that Weber's definition limits the use of the term "law" in cross-cultural and historical contexts. They argue that the word "staff" implies an organized administrative apparatus which may not exist in certain illiterate societies. E. Adamson Hoebel (1954:28), for instance, proposes a less restrictive term by referring to individuals possessing "a socially recognized privilege," and Ronald L. Akers (1965:306) suggests a "social authorized third party." Of course, in modern societies law provides for a specific administrative apparatus. Still, these suggestions should be kept in mind while studying the historical developments of law or of primitive societies (see, for example, Pospisil, 1971; 1978).

From a different perspective, sociologist Donald Black (1976:2) contends that law is essentially governmental social control. In this sense, law is "the normative life of a state and its citizens, such as legislation, litigation, and adjudication" (Black, 1976:2). He maintains that several styles of law may be observed in a society, each corresponding to a style of social control. Four styles of social control are represented in law: the penal, compensatory, therapeutic, and conciliatory. In the penal style, the deviant is viewed as a violator of a prohibition, an offender to be subjected to condemnation and punishment, for example, a drug pusher. In the compensatory style, a person is considered to have a contractual obligation and, therefore, owes the victim restitution, for example, a debtor failing to pay the creditor. Both these styles are accusatory where there is a complainant and a defendant, a winner and a loser. According to the therapeutic style, the deviant's conduct is defined as abnormal, the person needs help, such as treatment by a psychiatrist. In the conciliatory style, deviant behavior represents one side of a social conflict in need of resolution without consideration who is right or wrong, for example, as in marital disputes. These last two are remedial

styles, designed to help people in trouble and ameliorate a bad social situation.

Elements of two or more of these styles may appear in a particular
instance, for example, when a drug addict is convicted of possession and
is granted probation contingent upon his or her participation in some kind
of therapy program.

The above definitions illustrate some of the alternative ways of looking at law. It is the law's specificity in substance, its universality of applicability, and the formality of its enactment and enforcement that set it apart
from other devices for social control. Implicit in these definitions of law is
the notion that law can be analytically separated from other normative systems in societies with developed political institutions and specialized lawmaking and law enforcing agencies. The principal function of law is to
regulate and constrain the behavior of individuals in their relationships
with one another. Ideally, law is to be employed only when other formal
and informal social control mechanisms fail to operate or are inadequate
for the job. Finally, law can be distinguished from other forms of social
control primarily in that it is a formal system embodying explicit rules of
conduct, the planned use of sanctions to insure compliance with the rules,
and a group of authorized officials designated to interpret the rules and
apply sanctions to violators (Davis, 1962:39–63). From a sociological perspective, the rules of law are simply a guide for action. Without interpretation and enforcement, law would remain meaningless. As Henry M. Hart
(1958:403) points out, law can be analyzed sociologically as a "method" of
doing something. In this context, law can be studied as a social process,
implemented by individuals during social interaction. Sociologically, law
consists of the behaviors, situations, and conditions for making, interpreting, and applying legal rules which are backed by the state's legitimate coercive apparatus for enforcement.

TYPES OF LAW

The content of law may be categorized as *substantive* or *procedural*. *Substantive*
laws consist of rights, duties, and prohibitions administered by courts—
which behaviors are to be allowed and which are prohibited (such as prohibition against murder or the sale of narcotics). *Procedural* laws are rules
concerning just how substantive laws are to be administered, enforced,
changed, and used in the mediation of disputes (such as filing charges or
presenting evidence in court).

At times a distinction is made between *public* law and *private* law (Johnson, 1977:59–60). *Public* law is concerned with the structure of government,
the duties and powers of officials, and the relationship between the individual and the state. "It includes such subjects as constitutional law, administrative law, regulation of public utilities, criminal law and procedure,
and law relating to the proprietary powers of the state and its political sub-
divisions" (Davis, 1962:51). *Private* law is concerned with both substantive
and procedural rules governing relationships between individuals (such as

the law of torts or private injuries, contracts, property, wills, inheritance, marriage, divorce, adoption, and the like).

A more familiar distinction is between *civil* law and *criminal* law. As noted, *civil* law, as private law, consists of a body of rules and procedures intended to govern the conduct of individuals in their relationships with others. Violations of civil statutes, called *torts,* are private wrongs for which the injured individual may seek redress in the courts for the harm he or she experienced. In most cases, some form of payment is required from the offender to compensate for the injury he or she has caused. Similarly, one company may be required to pay another a sum of money for failing to fulfill the terms of a business contract. The complainant firm is thus "compensated" for the loss it may have suffered as a result of the other company's neglect or incompetence. *Criminal law* is concerned with the definition of crime and the prosecution and penal treatment of offenders. Although a criminal act may cause harm to some individual, crimes are regarded as offenses against the state or "the people." A crime is a "public" as opposed to an "individual" or "private" wrong. It is the state, not the harmed individual, that takes action against the offender. Furthermore, the action taken by the state differs from that taken by the plaintiff in a civil case. For example, if the case involves a tort or civil injury, compensation equivalent to the harm caused is levied. In the case of crime, some form of punishment is administered. Henry M. Hart suggests that a crime " ... is not simply antisocial conduct which public officers are given a responsibility to suppress. It is not simply any conduct to which a legislature chooses to attach a 'criminal' penalty. It is a conduct which, if duly shown to have taken place, will incur a formal and solemn pronouncement of the moral condemnation of the community" (1958:404). In Hart's view, both the condemnation and the consequences that follow may be regarded as constituting the punishment.

A distinction can also be made between *civil law* and *common law.* In this context, civil law refers to legal systems whose development was greatly influenced by Roman law, a collection of codes compiled in the *Corpus Juris Civilis* (Code Civil). Civil law systems are codified systems and the basic law is found in codes. These are statutes that are enacted by national parliaments. France would be an example of a civil law system. The civil code of France first appeared in 1804, is called the Code Napoleon, and embodies the civil law of the country. By contrast, *common law* resisted codification. Law is not based on acts of parliament but on *case law,* which relies on precedents set by judges to decide a case (Friedman, 1984:16). Thus, it is "judge-made" law as distinguished from legislation or "enacted law."

Law may be further divided into the following categories: constitutional law, case law, statutory law, executive orders, and administrative law. *Constitutional law* is a branch of public law. It determines the political organization of the state and its powers, while also setting certain substantive and procedural limitations on the exercise of governing power. Constitutional law consists of the application of fundamental principles of law based on that document, as interpreted by the Supreme Court. *Case law* is enacted by judges in cases that are decided in the appellate courts. *Statutory law* is legislated law—law made by legislatures. *Executive orders* are regulations issued by the executive branch of the government at the federal and state levels. Finally, *administrative* law is a body of law created by administrative agencies in the form of regulations, orders, and decisions. These various categories of laws will be discussed and illustrated later in the text.

FUNCTIONS OF LAW

Why do we need law and what does it do for society? More specifically, what functions does law perform? As with the definition of law, there is no agreement among scholars of law and society on the precise functions, nor is there consensus on their relative weight and importance. A variety of functions are highlighted in the literature (see, for example, Aubert, 1969:11; Bredemeier, 1962:74; Mermin, 1973:5–10; Nader and Todd, 1978:1; and Pollack, 1979:669), depending on the conditions under which law operates at a particular time and place. The recurrent themes include social control, dispute settlement, and social engineering. I shall now consider them briefly. These functions of the law will be examined in detail in the chapters dealing with social control, conflict resolution, and social change.

Social Control

In a small, homogeneous society, behavioral conformity is insured by the fact that socializing experiences are very much the same for all members. Social norms tend to be consistent with each other and are strongly supported by tradition. Social control in such a society is primarily dependent upon self-sanctioning. Even on those occasions when external sanctions are required, they seldom involve formal punishment. Deviants are subjected to informal mechanisms of social control, such as gossip, ridicule, or humiliation.

Even in a complex, heterogeneous society, such as the United States, social control rests largely on the internalization of shared norms. Most individuals behave in socially acceptable ways, and, as in simpler societies, fear of disapproval from family, friends, and neighbors is usually adequate to keep potential deviants in check. Nevertheless, the great diversity of the population, the lack of direct communication between various segments, the absence of similar values, attitudes, and standards of conduct, and the competitive struggles between groups with different interests, have all led to an increasing need for formal mechanisms of social control. Formal social control is characterized by "(1) explicit rules of conduct, (2) planned use of sanctions to support the rules; and (3) designated officials to interpret and enforce the rules, and often to make them" (Davis, 1962:43).

In modern societies there are many methods of social control, both formal and informal. Law is considered one of the forms of formal social control. In the words of Roscoe Pound (1941:249): "I think of law as in one sense a highly specialized form of social control in a developed politically organized society—a social control through the systematic and orderly application of the force of such a society."

Lawrence M. Friedman calls attention to two ways in which law plays an important role in social control:

> In the first place, legal institutions are responsible for the making, care and preservation of those rules and norms which define deviant behavior; they announce (in a penal code, for example) which acts may be officially punished and how and which ones may not be punished at all. In the second place, the legal system carries out many rules of social control. Police arrest burglars, prosecutors prosecute them, juries convict them, judges sentence them, prison-guards watch them, and parole boards release them (1977:11).

Of course, as we shall see, law does not have a monopoly on formal mechanisms of social control. Other types of formal mechanisms (such as firing, promotion, demotion, and so forth) are found in industry, academe, government, business, and in various private groups (Selznick, 1969).

Dispute Settlement

As Karl N. Llewellyn so aptly put it:

> What, then, is this law business about? It is about the fact that our society is honeycombed with disputes. Disputes actual and potential, disputes to be set-tled and disputes to be prevented; both appealing to law, both making up the business of law ... This doing of something about disputes, this doing of it reasonably, is the business of law (1960:2).

By settling disputes through an authoritative allocation of legal rights and obligations, the law provides an alternative to other methods of dispute resolution. Increasingly, people in all walks of life let the courts settle matters that were once resolved by informal and nonlegal mechanisms, such as negotiation, mediation, or forcible self-help measures. It should be noted, however, that law only deals with disagreements that have been translated into legal disputes. A legal resolution of conflict does not necessarily result in a reduction of tension or antagonism between the aggrieved parties. For example, in a case of employment discrimination on the basis of race, the court may focus on one incident in what is a complex and often not very clear-cut series of problems. It results in a resolution of a specific legal dispute but not in the amelioration of the broader issues that have produced that conflict.

Social Engineering

Many scholars contend that a major function of law in modern society is social engineering. It refers to purposive, planned, and directed social change initiated, guided, and supported by the law. Roscoe Pound captures the essence of this function of law in stating:

For the purpose of understanding the law of today I am content to think of law as a social institution to satisfy social wants—the claims and demands involved in the existence of civilized society—by giving effect to as much as we need with the least sacrifice, so far as such wants may be satisfied or such claims given effect by an ordering of human conduct through politically organized society. For present purposes I am content to see in legal history the record of a continually wider recognizing and satisfying of human wants or claims or desires through social control; a more embracing and more effective securing of social interests; a continually more complete and effective elimination of waste and precluding of friction in human enjoyment of the goods of existence—in short, a continually more efficacious social engineering (1959:98–99).

In many instances law is considered a "desirable and necessary, if not a highly efficient means of inducing change, and that, wherever possible, its institutions and procedures are preferable to others of which we are aware" (Grossman and Grossman, 1971:2). Although some sociologists disagree with this contention (for example, Quinney, 1974), law is often used as a method of social engineering, a way of bringing about planned social change by the government. Social engineering is a prominent feature of modern welfare states. For example, part of the taxes a government collects goes to the poor in the form of cash, food stamps, medical and legal benefits, and housing (Friedman, 1984:10). I shall return to this social engineering function of the law in the discussion of law and social change in Chapter Seven.

DYSFUNCTIONS OF LAW

Although law is an indispensable and ubiquitous institution of social life, it possesses—like most institutions—certain dysfunctions which, if they are not seriously considered, may evolve into serious operational difficulties. These dysfunctions stem in part from the law's conservative tendencies, in part from the rigidity inherent in its formal structure, and in part from the restrictive aspects connected with its control functions.

Hans Morgenthau (1967:418) suggests that "a given status quo is stabilized and perpetuated in a legal system" and that the courts, being the chief instruments of a legal system, "must act as agents of the status quo." Although this observation does not fully consider the complex interplay between stability and change in the context of law, it still contains an important ingredient of truth. By establishing a social policy of a particular time and place in constitutional and statutory precepts, or by making the precedents of the past binding, the law exhibits a tendency towards conservatism. Once a scheme of rights and duties has been created by a legal system, continuous revisions and disruptions of the system are generally avoided in the interests of predictability and continuity. Social changes often precede changes in the law. In times of crisis, the law can break down, providing an opportunity for discontinuous and sometimes cataclysmic adjustments. Illustrations of this would include the various first aid legal measures used during an energy crisis, such as the establishment of maximum or minimum limits for gasoline purchases.

Related to these conservative tendencies of the law is a type of rigidity inherent in its normative framework. Since legal rules are couched in general, abstract, and universal terms, they sometimes operate as strait-jackets in particular situations. An illustration of this would be the failure of law to consider certain extenuating circumstances for a particular illegal act, for example, stealing because one is hungry or stealing for profit.

A third dysfunction of the law stems from the restrictive aspects of normative control. Norms are shared convictions about the patterns of behavior that are appropriate or inappropriate for the members of a group. Norms are designed to, and serve to, combat and forestall anomie (a state of normlessness) and social disorganization. Law can overstep its bounds, and regulation can turn into over-regulation, in which situation control may become transformed into repression. For example, in nineteenth-century America, public administration was sometimes hampered by an overrestrictive use of the law which tended to paralyze needed discretionary exercises in governmental power (Pound, 1914:12–13).

Obviously, the list of dysfunctions of the law is incomplete. One may add to this list a variety of procedural inefficiencies, administrative delays, and archaic legal technologies. One may also include the cost of justice to the middle class, its unavailability to the poor, to the consumer, to minority group members. Questions can also be raised about the narrowness of legal education and the failure of ethical indoctrination, of laws being out-of-date, inequitable criminal sentencing, lack of clarity of some laws resulting in loopholes and diverse interpretations, and the dominating use of law by one class against another (Rostow, 1971; Strick, 1977). Finally, critics of the law point to the current rage for procedure and to "government by judges" as being particularly dysfunctional in a world as complex as ours (Crozier, 1984:116–117).

TWO MODELS OF SOCIETY

Sociological discussion of law in society are generally grounded in one of two ideal conceptions of society: the *integration-consensus* and the *conflict-coercion* perspectives. The former describes society as a functionally integrated, relatively stable system held together by a basic consensus of values. Social order is considered as more or less permanent, and individuals can best achieve their interests through cooperation. Social conflict is viewed as the needless struggle among individuals and groups who have not yet attained sufficient understanding of their common interests and basic interdependence. This perspective stresses the cohesion, solidarity, integration, cooperation, and stability of society, which is seen as united by a shared culture, and by agreement on its fundamental norms and values.

The *conflict-coercion* perspective, in direct opposition, considers society as consisting of individuals and groups characterized by conflict and dissension, and held together by coercion. Order is temporary and unstable because every individual and group strives to maximize its own interests in a world of limited resources and goods. Social conflict is considered as intrinsic to the interaction between individuals and groups. In this perspective, the maintenance of power requires inducement and coercion, and law is an instrument of repression perpetuating the interests of the powerful at the cost of alternative interests, norms, and values.

But, as Ralf Dahrendorf aptly points out, it is impossible to choose empirically between these two sets of assumptions: "Stability and change, integration and conflict, function and 'dysfunction,' consensus and constraint are, it would seem, two equally valid aspects of every imaginable society" (1958:174–175). When law in society is viewed in one of these two perspectives, not surprisingly, quite disparate conceptions of its basic role emerge. Let us examine in some detail the role of law in these two perspectives.

The Integration-Consensus Perspective

The integration-consensus perspective considers law as a neutral framework for maintaining societal integration. One of the best known and most influential legal scholars, Roscoe Pound (1943, 1959), views society as composed of diverse groups whose interests often conflict with one another, but which are in basic harmony. He considers certain interests as essential for the well-being of society and maintains that the reconciliation between the conflicting interests of the diverse groups in society is essential in order to secure and maintain social order. In his words, law:

> is an attempt to satisfy, to reconcile, to harmonize, to adjust these overlapping and often conflicting claims and demands, either through securing them directly and immediately, or through securing certain individual interests, or through delimitations or compromises of individual interests, so as to give effect to the greatest total of interests or to the interests that weigh most in our civilization, with the least sacrifice of the scheme of the interests as a whole (Pound, 1943:39).

In Pound's view, law in a heterogeneous and pluralistic society such as the United States, is best understood as an effort at social compromise with an emphasis on social order and harmony. Pound argues that the historical development of law demonstrates a growing recognition and satisfaction of human wants, claims, and desires through law. Over time, law has concerned itself with an ever wider spectrum of human interests. Law has more and more come to provide for the common good and the satisfaction of social wants (Pound, 1959:47). He considers law a form of "social engineering" directed toward achieving social harmony. Pound argues that the purpose of law is to maintain and to ensure those values and needs essential to social order, not by imposing one group's will on others, but by controlling, reconciling, and mediating the diverse and conflicting interests of individuals and groups within society. In brief, the purpose of law is to control interests and to maintain harmony and social integration.

Talcott Parsons (1962:58) concurs with this view by suggesting that

" . . . the primary function of a legal system is integrity. It serves to mitigate potential elements of conflict and to oil the machinery of social inter-course." Other sociologists, such as Harry C. Bredemeier (1962), accept this perspective and believe that it is necessary for society to supplement in-formal with formal mechanisms for generating and sustaining interper-sonal cooperation. Proponents of the integration-consensus perspective further advocate that law exists to maintain order and stability. Law is a body of rules enacted by representatives of the people in the interests of the people. Law is essentially a neutral agent, dispensing rewards and pun-ishments without bias. A fundamental assumption of this perspective is that the political system is pluralistic; that society is composed of a number of interest groups of more or less equal power. The laws reflect compromise and consensus among these various interest groups and the values that are fundamental to the social order (Chambliss, 1976:4).

The Conflict-Coercion Perspective

In marked contrast to the integration-consensus perspective, the conflict-consensus view considers law as a "weapon in social conflict" (Turk, 1978) and an instrument of oppression "employed by the ruling classes for their own benefit" (Chambliss and Seidman, 1982:36). From this perspec-tive, the transformation of society from a small, relatively homogeneous social group to a network of specialized groups is brought about by the evolution of both distinct sets of interests and differences in real power between groups. When diverse groups come into conflict, they compete in order to have their interests protected and perpetuated through the for-malization of their interests into law. On the basis of this idea, Richard Quinney argues that rather than being a device to control interests, law is an expression of interests, an outgrowth of the inherent conflict of interests characteristic of society. According to Quinney:

> Society is characterized by diversity, conflict, coercion, and change, rather than by consensus and stability. Second, law is a *result* of the operation of interests, rather than an instrument that functions outside of particular in-terests. Though law may control interests, it is in the first place *created* by interests of specific persons and groups; it is seldom the product of the whole society. Law is made by men, representing special interests, who have the power to translate their interests into public policy. Unlike the pluralistic con-ception of politics, law does not represent a compromise of the diverse in-terests in society, but supports some interests at the expense of others (1970:35).

Proponents of the conflict-coercion perspective believe that law is a tool by which the ruling class exercises its control. Law both protects the property of those in power and serves to repress political threats to the position of the elite. Quinney (1975:285) writes that while the state, con-trary to conventional wisdom, is the instrument of the ruling class, "Law is the state's coercive weapon, which maintains the social and economic order," and supports some interests at the expense of others, even when those interests are that of the majority.

But advocates of this position overstate their case. Not all laws are created and operated for the benefit of the powerful ruling groups in society. Laws prohibiting murder, robbery, arson, incest, and assault benefit all members of society, regardless of their economic position. It is too broad an assumption that powerful groups dictate the content of law and its enforcement for the protection of their own interests. As we shall see in Chapter Four, all kinds of groups are involved in lawmaking, although the powerful groups do have substantial input into the lawmaking process.

These two perspectives—integration-consensus and conflict-coercion—of society are ideal types (that is, abstract concepts used to describe essential features of a phenomenon). Considering the operation of legal systems in society, there may be an element of truth in both. Sociologists who are influenced by Karl Marx, Georg Simmel, Lewis Coser, and Ralf Dahrendorf generally tend to embrace the conflict-coercion perspective of law in society. One of their justifications for taking this theoretical stance is that this approach emphasizes the role of special interest groups in society. For example, the power of economic and commercial interests to influence legislation is illustrated by William J. Chambliss in his study of vagrancy statutes. He notes that the development of vagrancy laws paralleled the need of landowners for cheap labor during the period in England when the system of serfdom was collapsing. The first of these statutes, which came into existence in 1349, threatened criminal punishment for those who were able-bodied and yet unemployed—a condition that existed when peasants were in the process of moving from the land into the cities. The vagrancy law served "to force laborers (whether personally free or unfree) to accept employment at a low wage in order to insure the landowner an adequate supply of labor at a price he could afford to pay" (Chambliss, 1964:69). Subsequently, vagrancy statutes were modified to protect the commercial and industrial interests and to insure safe commercial transportation. In the late nineteenth and early twentieth centuries in the United States, vagrancy laws were used again to serve the interests of the wealthy. Agricultural states during harvest time enforced vagrancy laws to push the poor into farm work. In periods of economic depression, similar laws were used to keep the unemployed from entering the state (Chambliss and Seidman, 1982:182). This is just one illustration to show how law came to reflect the particular interests of those who have power and influence in society. I shall return to the role of interest groups in Chapter Four dealing with decision making processes in the context of lawmaking.

CONTROVERSIES OVER THE ROLE
OF SOCIOLOGISTS IN THE STUDY OF LAW AND SOCIETY

As with the approaches to the study of law and society, divergencies of opinion also characterize the question of what role sociologists should play in such endeavors. This question, to a substantial degree, polarized the discipline. Some sociologists consider their role primarily as objectively describing and explaining social phenomena. They are concerned with the understanding of social life and social processes, and they go about their research in an alleged value-neutral and empirical fashion. They accept as scientific only those theoretical statements whose truth can be proven empirically. They are guided by Max Weber's notion of sociology as "a science which seeks to understand social action interpretively, and thereby to explain it causally in its course and its effects" (Weber, 1968:3). They believe that the discovery of causal laws is the ultimate goal of sociology, but understanding of people's motives is central.

Others, however, go beyond the notion of *verstehen* (understanding). Sociologists who claim to be dialectical and critical in their orientation do not merely seek to describe and to explain social events. They, as scientists, assert their right to criticize. The standards of evaluation upon which their criticism is based, and which these sociologists deduce from the nature of human beings and from considerations about social development, cannot always be empirically tested. To them, empirical research is necessary insofar as it provides and explains the data, but it is, so to speak, only a first step toward the essential criticism. They believe that the task of sociology is to account for human suffering. They aim at demystifying the world, to show people what constrains them and what are their routes to freedom. Their criticisms are prompted by their belief that human condition and the social order have become unbearable. These critics believe that they have a responsibility not only to identify the factors that have precipitated a deleterious condition, but also to provide, through theoretical and empirical efforts, ways of rectifying or redressing it. In the context of law and society studies, illustrations of such attempts would include Jerold S. Auerbach's *Unequal Justice* (1976), Leonard Downie's *Justice Denied* (1972), Richard Quinney's *Critique of Legal Order* (1974), and Anne Strick's *Injustice For All* (1977).

Finally, for some sociologists, criticism is interconnected with practice. They endorse the role of being simultaneously a student and an agent of social action. They are guided by *praxis,* or the wedding of theory and action. Because of their knowledge of social conditions, they are obligated to take action. This position is associated with a Marxist tradition. It is based on the notion that knowledge generated from an analysis of a specific historical situation may be used as an argument for intervention. Sociologists in such situations try to demystify, clarify, and show individuals the source of their misery and the means of overcoming it. In a Marxian context, praxis means what people do, as contrasted to what they think. "Praxis is a revolutionary form of social practice (i.e., it contributes to the humanization of people by transforming reality from alienation to hopefully better future). The concept is both a means of consciously shaping historical conditions and a standard for evaluating what occurs in any historical order. Marx maintains that a dialectical relationship exists between theory and praxis" (Reasons and Rich (1978:431). Thus, sociologists of this perspective actively advocate changes in law and legal institutions wherever needed and work for the reformation of both the criminal system and the criminal law when warranted (Krisberg, 1978).

These controversies beset the "proper" role of sociologist in the discipline. Based on one's values, ideologies, conception of sociology, and a plethora of other considerations, one may prefer to be a detached observer of social life, a critic of the social order, or an active agent of change. These roles, fortunately, are not mutually exclusive. Depending on the nature of the issue under consideration, the degree of commitment to and involvement in that issue, one may freely select among these alternatives. As an intellectual enterprise, sociology is flexible enough to accommodate these diverse positions. In a sense, they contribute to a greater understanding of the complicated interplay between law and society.

SUMMARY

In sociology, the study of law touches a variety of well-established areas of inquiry. It incorporates values, ideologies, social institutions, norms, power relations, and social processes. Since World War II, there has been a growing interest in law among sociologists both in the United States and abroad. Some of the examples of the study of law and society include the effectiveness of law, the impact of law on society, methods of dispute resolution, and research on judicial, legislative, and administrative processes. However, there are still some obstacles to interaction between sociologists and lawyers as a consequence of differences in terminology, perception of the role of law in society, methodology, and professional culture. Yet, in spite of these difficulties, collaboration is on the increase between members of the two professions.

Scholarly debate over a proper definition of law has long preoccupied scholars in jurisprudence and in the social sciences. In our illustrative definitions, it was noted that law is a form of social control with explicit sanctions for noncompliance, and it consists of the behaviors, situations, and conditions for creating, interpreting, and applying legal rules.

The content of law may be considered as substantive or procedural. A distinction is made also between public law and private law, as well as between civil law and criminal law. Common law generally refers to "judge-made" law or "case" law, as differentiated from statutory or enacted law.

Law performs a multitude of functions in society. It is difficult to arrive at a satisfactory and meaningful list of functions. Still, there seems to be a great deal of emphasis in the literature on the recurrent social control, dispute settlement, and social engineering functions of law. But law, like other social institutions, possesses certain dysfunctions as a result of law's conservative tendencies, the rigidity inherent in its formal structure, and the restrictive aspects connected with its social control functions.

Sociological analyses of law and society are generally based on two ideal views of society—the integration-consensus and the conflict-coercion perspectives. The former considers society as a functionally integrated, relatively stable system held together by basic consensus of values. The latter conceives of society as consisting of groups characterized by conflict and dissensus on values and held together by some members who coerce others. These dialectic models of society are ideal types. Taken toward the operation of the lawmaking organizations, there may be an element of truth in both. In this context, perhaps an eclectic approach is best.

In addition to divergences in the way of studying law in society, controversies also beset the "proper" role sociologists should play in the study of law and society. Some sociologists maintain that their role is to try to understand, describe, and empirically analyze social phenomena in a more or less value-free context. Others argue that it is a responsibility of social scientists to criticize malfunctioning components of, and processes in, a social system. Still others are guided by the notion of *praxis;* they seek to combine theory with practice, and their objective is to try to redress deleterious social conditions by means of legal action. Of course, these divergent positions are not mutually exclusive, and an awareness of these perspectives on the role of sociologists can contribute to a greater understanding of the intricate interplay between law and society.

SUGGESTED FURTHER READINGS

JAMES E. DUKE, *Conflict and Power in Social Life.* Provo, Utah: Brigham Young University Press, 1976. A detailed review of the influential and important conflict theories in sociology. It provides several ramifications of the conflict-coercion model of society.

LAWRENCE M. FRIEDMAN, *Total Justice.* New York: Russell Sage Foundation, 1985. A short and highly readable book on law and the legal system in the United States.

E. ADAMSON HOEBEL, *The Law of Primitive Man, A Study in Comparative Legal Dynamics.* Cambridge, Massachusetts: Harvard University Press, 1954. A highly influential treatise on the cross-cultural study of the dynamics of law. A must for students interested in law from an anthropological perspective.

HERBERT JACOB, *Law and Politics in the United States.* Boston: Little, Brown and Company, 1986. An overview of the components and processes of the American legal system. See Chapter Two on the various ways of looking at law.

MITCHELL S. G. KLEIN, *Law, Courts, and Policy.* Englewood Cliffs, NJ: Prentice-Hall, Inc., 1984. See in particular Chapter One, which is a good overview of law and society from the perspective of political science.

RICHARD LEMPERT and JOSEPH SANDERS, *An Invitation to Law and Social Science.* New York: Longman, 1986. An interdisciplinary analysis of law and the legal system written by two law professors for students in both law and the social sciences.

PHILLIPPE NONET and PHILIP SELZNICK, *Law and Society in Transition, Toward Responsive Law.* New York: Octagon Books, 1978. A provocative essay on repressive, autonomous, and responsive laws.

REFERENCES

AKERS, RONALD L. 1965. "Toward a Comparative Definition of Law," Journal of Criminal Law, Criminology, and Police Science 56 (September): 301–306.

AKERS, RONALD L., and RICHARD HAWKINS, eds. 1975. *Law and Control in Society.* Englewood Cliffs, NJ: Prentice-Hall.

AUBERT, VILHELM, ed. 1969. Sociology of Law. "Introduction." Pp. 9–14. Harmondsworth, England: Penguin; 1973. "Researches in the Sociology of Law," Pp. 48–62. In Michael Barkun (ed.), Law and the Social System. New York: Lieber-Atherton.

AUERBACH, JEROLD S. 1976. *Unequal Justice.* New York: Oxford University Press.

BLACK, DONALD. 1976. *The Behavior of Law.* New York: Academic Press.

BREDEMEIER, HARRY C. 1962. "Law as an Integrative Mechanism," Pp. 73–90 in William J. Evan (ed.), Law and Sociology: Exploratory Essays. New York: Free Press.

CARDOZO, BENJAMIN NATHAN. 1924. *The Growth of the Law.* New Haven: Yale University Press.
CHAMBLISS, WILLIAM J. 1964: "A Sociological Analysis of the Law of Vagrancy," Social Problems, 12 (1) (Summer): 67–77; 1976. "Functional and Conflict Theories of Crime: The Heritage of Emile Durkheim and Karl Marx." Pp. 1–28 in William J. Chambliss and Milton Mankoff, eds., Whose Law? What Order? A Conflict Approach to Criminology. New York: John Wiley.
CHAMBLISS, WILLIAM and ROBERT SEIDMAN. 1982. *Law, Order, and Power.* 2nd ed. Reading, MA: Addison-Wesley Publishing Company.
CROZIER, MICHEL. 1984. *The Trouble with America.* Translated by Peter Heinegg. Berkeley: University of California Press.
DAHRENDORF, RALF. 1958. "Toward a Theory of Social Conflict," Journal of Conflict Resolution, (2)(June):170–183.
DAVIS, F. JAMES. 1962. "Law as a Type of Social Control." Pp. 39–63 in F. James Davis, et al. (eds.), Society and the Law: New Meanings for an Old Profession. New York: The Free Press of Glencoe.
DOWNIE, LEONARD. 1972. *Justice Denied.* Baltimore: Penguin.
EHRLICH, EUGEN. 1975. *Fundamental Principles of the Sociology of Law,* Foreword. New York: Arno Press, Walter L. Mall, trans. Originally published by Harvard University Press, 1936.
FRIEDMAN, LAWRENCE M. 1975. *The Legal System, A Social Science Perspective.* New York: Russell Sage Foundation; 1977. *Law and Society, An Introduction.* Englewood Cliffs, NJ: Prentice-Hall; 1984. American Law: An Introduction. New York: W. W. Norton and Company.
GROSSMAN, JOEL B., and MARY H. GROSSMAN, eds. 1971. "Introduction." Pp. 1–10, Law and Change in Modern America. Pacific Palisades, CA: Goodyear.
HART, HENRY M., Jr. 1958. "The Aims of the Criminal Law," Law and Contemporary Problems. (23)(Summer):401–441.
HOEBEL, E. ADAMSON. 1954. *The Law of Primitive Man, A Study of Comparative Legal Dynamics.* Cambridge, MA: Harvard University Press.
HOLMES, OLIVER WENDELL. 1897. "The Path of the Law," Harvard Law Review. (10)(March): 457–461; 1963. *The Common Law.* Cambridge, MA: Harvard University Press, Mark D. Howe, ed. Originally published in 1881.
JOHNSON, ALAN V. 1977. "A Definition of the Concept of Law," Mid-American Review of Sociology 2(1)(Spring):47–71.
KRISBERG, BARRY. 1978. "The Sociological Imagination Revisited." Pp. 455–470 in Charles E. Reasons and Robert M. Rich, eds., The Sociology of Law, A Conflict Perspective. Toronto: Butterworths.
LLEWELLYN, KARL N. 1960. *The Bramble Bush.* Dobbs Ferry, NY: Oceana Publications, Inc. Originally published in 1930.
MALINOWSKI, BRONISLAW. 1959. *Crime and Custom in Savage Society.* Patterson, NJ: Littlefield. Originally published in 1926.
MERMIN, SAMUEL. 1973. *Law and the Legal System, An Introduction.* Boston: Little, Brown.
MORGENTHAU, HANS. 1967. *Politics Among Nations,* 4th ed. New York: Knopf.
NADER, LAURA, and HARRY F. TODD, JR., eds. 1978. "Introduction." Pp. 1–40. The Disputing Process—Law in Ten Societies. New York: Columbia University Press.
PARSONS, TALCOTT. 1962. "The Law and Social Control." Pp. 56–72 in William M. Evan, ed., Law and Sociology: Exploratory Essays. New York: Free Press.
POLLACK, ERVIN H. 1979. *Jurisprudence, Principles and Applications.* Columbus: Ohio State University Press.
POSNER, RICHARD A. 1985. *The Federal Courts: Crisis and Reform.* Cambridge, MA: Harvard University Press.
POSPISIL, LEOPOLD J. 1971. *Anthropology of Law, A Comparative Theory.* New York: Harper & Row, Pub.; 1978. *The Ethnology of Law,* 2nd ed. Menlo Park, CA: Cummings Publishing Company.
POUND, ROSCOE. 1914. "Justice According to Law," Columbia Law Review. 14(1):1–26; 1941. *In My Philosophy of Law.* St. Paul, MN: West Publishing Company; 1943. "A Survey of Social Interests," Harvard Law Review. (57)(October):1–39; 1959. *An Introduction to the Philosophy of Law.* New Haven: Yale Univesity Press.
QUINNEY, RICHARD. 1970. *The Social Reality of Crime.* Boston: Little, Brown; 1974. *Critique of Legal Order: Crime Control in Capitalist Society.* Boston: Little, Brown; 1975. *Criminology, Analysis and Critique of Crime in America.* Boston: Little, Brown.

REASONS, CHARLES E., and ROBERT M. RICH, eds. 1978. *The Sociology of Law, A Conflict Perspective.* Toronto: Butterworths.

REHBINDER, MANFRED. 1975. *Sociology of Law, A Trend Report and Bibliography.* The Hague: Mouton.

RICH, ROBERT M. 1977. *The Sociology of Law: An Introduction to Its Theorists and Theories.* Washington, DC: University Press of America.

ROSS, E. ADAMSON. 1922. *Social Control.* New York: Macmillan. Originally published in 1901.

ROSTOW, EUGENE V., ed. 1971. *Is Law Dead?* New York: Simon & Schuster.

SCHUR, EDWIN M. 1968. *Law and Society, A Sociological View.* New York: Random House.

SELZNICK, PHILIP. 1968. "Law: The Sociology of Law," International Encyclopedia of the Social Sciences. (9):50–59. New York: Free Press; 1969. *Law, Society and Industrial Justice.* New York: Russell Sage Foundation.

STONE, JULIUS. 1964. *Legal System and Lawyers' Reasonings.* Stanford: Stanford University Press.

STRICK, ANNE. 1977. *Injustice for All.* New York: Penguin.

TURK, AUSTIN T. 1978. "Law as a Weapon in Social Conflict." Pp. 213–232 in Charles E. Reasons and Robert M. Rich, eds., The Sociology of Law: A Conflict Perspective. Toronto: Butterworths.

WARD, LESTER F. 1906. *Applied Sociology.* Boston: Ginn.

WEBER, MAX. 1954. *Law in Economy and Society,* ed. Max Rheinstein and trans. Edward Shils, and Max Rheinstein. Cambridge, MA: Harvard University Press.

WEBER, MAX. 1968. *Economy and Society.* Trans. Guenther Roth and Claus Wittich. New York: Bedminster Press.

WILLOCK, I. D. 1974. "Getting on With Sociologists," British Journal of Law and Society, 1 (1):3–12.

2

Theoretical Perspectives on Law and Society

This chapter explores the development of legal systems and reviews some of the major classical and contemporary theories of the relationship between law and society. There is no single, widely accepted, comprehensive theory of law and society. The field is enormously complex and polemical, and individual explanations have thus far failed to capture fully this complexity and diversity. This is, of course, not due to lack of effort. On the contrary, sociological theories of law abound (Rich, 1978). Of the vast amount of literature, this chapter deals briefly with only a few of the important classical and contemporary theories of law and society. This approach serves certain purposes. It provides the reader with some conception of the development and content of these different theories and how they relate to one another. While the discussion of these theories clearly shows the complex and multifaceted nature of the relationship between law and society, it also serves as a means of differentiating, organizing, and understanding a great mass of material. Thus, although the concern is to suggest the magnitude and diversity of the field, an attempt is made also to lend order to that magnitude and diversity.

A cautionary note is in order with regard to the procedures followed in this chapter for grouping various theories. It will become clear that many theories of law and society tend to overlap. For example, the reader may find that a theory which has been placed under the heading of "The European Pioneers" will contain similar elements to those embodied in "Influential Sociological Theorists." Any such effort at classification of theories should be viewed as essentially an heuristic device to facilitate discussion, rather than to reflect the final status of the theories considered.

There are, of course, many ways of categorizing law and society theories. They may be considered from the disciplinary perspectives of jurisprudence, philosophy of law, sociology of law, and anthropology of law. They can also be listed under the headings of sociology of civil law, sociology of criminal law, sociological jurisprudence, and anthropology of law (Rich, 1978), or grouped by various theoretical trends, such as natural law, historical and analytical jurisprudence, utilitarianism, positivism, and legal realism (Bodenheimer, 1974; Pollack, 1979). Any attempt to categorize theories under particular labels is open to question. The present effort should not be an exception. The categories used are in some ways arbitrary, since they can be increased or decreased depending on one's objectives. These categorizations simply provide some semblance of order for the principal theoretical approaches to law and society. In the schema employed, the diverse theories are presented in a chronological order with an emphasis on influential classical and contemporary theories.

THE DEVELOPMENT OF LEGAL SYSTEMS

In the sociological literature, there is substantial consensus that formal codified law emerges when the social structure of a given society becomes so complex that regulatory mechanisms and methods of dispute settlement can no longer be dependent on informal customs and social, religious, or moral sanctions. Formal and institutionalized regulatory mechanisms come into being when other control devices are no longer effective. Changes in the organization of a society from kinship and tribe to territorially based political organization inevitably result in changes in the legal system. As the economy grows more complex and diversified, as industrialization increases, as social institutions become more stratified and specialized, the basic content of the law and legal system will concomitantly become more complex, specialized, and statutory.

Historically, legal development and industrialization, urbanization, and modernization are closely intertwined. In a small, homogeneous society with little division of labor and a high degree of solidarity, informal sanctions are sufficient to keep most behavior in line with the norms. An ideal example is the community on Tristan da Cunha, an isolated island in the middle of the South Atlantic Ocean. A few hundred people live there, growing potatoes and catching fish. When visited by social scientists in the 1930s, they were amazed to see how "law abiding" these people were even though they had nothing resembling law as we know it. There was no serious crime on the island that anyone could recall, no police, courts, jails, or judges. There was no need for them. People in the community relied on informal mechanisms of social control such as shaming and open disapproval which can be effective and severe in their own way. Such forms of control work in small, homogeneous, face-to-face communities (Friedman, 1984:31).

But in a modern, heterogeneous, and complex society, formal norms and sanctions are necessary to control behavior so that society can continue to function in an orderly and predictable fashion. The presence of law and a legal system is essential to the maintenance of social order.

The reciprocal relationships between society and the legal system during their parallel development are perplexing issues which have been vaguely conceptualized in the literature. Jonathan H. Turner points out that

> ... linkages between law and society are often left implicit; change in the relative importance of these linkages is frequently not discussed; and there is a tendency to place too heavy an emphasis on single variables and thereby ignore the multiplicity of institutional influences on legal development (1974:3).

Turner (1972:242) views legal development as a form of institutional adjustment to the ubiquitous problems of control and coordination facing modernizing society and reasons that modernization inevitably generates conflict, tension, strains, and disjunctures which can force the modernization of law in society. It should be noted, however, that while there is some overall pattern of legal development, the specifics vary from society to society as a result of unique conditions, such as geographical location, historical events, conquest, and prevailing political and social forces. As a result, it is impossible to trace legal development from a primitive to a modern profile for one society because changes in geographical boundaries, wars, and other events would obscure unilineal development. For instance, a highly developed system of Roman law was imposed upon primitive legal systems during the expansion of the Empire, "with the result that a developmental jump occurred in these primitive legal systems" (Turner, 1972: 242).

Developmental models, although controversial, have been applied with varying success in virtually every field of social science. The justification for the use of developmental models lies in the attempt to make sense of institutional history which seems to require an appreciation of directionality, growth, and decay (Nonet and Selznick, 1978:19). The early sociologists all believed in the progressive development of social patterns over long periods of time. This is also found in psychology, in, for example, the stages of growth to psychological maturity in Freudian theory, or the development of personality in the theories of Piaget (1932). Similarly, in economics, Walt W. Rostow (1961) talks about the stages of economic growth. In the same vein, students of modern organization talk rather freely of three stages: prebureaucratic, bureaucratic, and postbureaucratic (Bennis, 1966:3–15). Developmental models can deal with transformations at various levels in society, such as individual, group, community, organization, or social institutions, or they may deal with the transformation of entire societies. The underlying theme in developmental models is the identification of forces that, having been set in motion at one stage, produce a characteristic outcome in another stage.

Thus, it is not surprising that Pound (1959:366), among others, finds it "convenient to think of ... stages of legal development in systems which have come to maturity." The law and society literature suggests that the more complex the society, the more differentiated is the legal system (Schwartz and Miller, 1975). Underlying this proposition is the notion that legal development is conditioned by a series of integrative demands stemming from society's economic, political, educational, and religious institutions. Based on the complexity and magnitude of the interplay among these institutions and between these institutions and the law, several types of legal systems may be identified in the course of societal development. There is practically no limit to the variability of legal systems, and many scholars have developed typologies to capture this diversity (such as Diamond, 1971; Pospisil, 1971:97–126; Wormser, 1962). These typologies seldom correspond fully to the real world, but they are essential in an analytical discussion dealing with the types of legal systems. From a developmental perspective, some general types can be isolated, and following Turner's discussion (1972:216–230), the primitive, transitional, and modern legal systems will be examined.

Primitive Legal Systems

Primitive legal systems are characteristic of hunting and gathering, and simple agrarian societies. The laws are not written or codified; they are permeated by customs, tradition, religious dogmas, and values. Primitive laws often coexist with ancient norms, and are also comparatively undifferentiated. There is, however, some distinction between *substantive* and *procedural* laws. Substantive laws consist of rights, duties, and prohibitions concerning what is right, wrong, permissible, and unpermissible. Procedural laws are rules regarding just how substantive law is to be administered, enforced, changed, and used in the mediation of disputes. Subsequent differentiation of types at later stages of legal evolution can be encompassed under these two general types of law.

The functions of law in primitive societies are essentially the same as those in more advanced societies. Laws preserve important cultural elements; they coordinate interaction, settle disputes, check deviance, and regularize exchanges. Laws also legitimize existing inequalities, and: "By codifying, preserving, and enforcing certain key kinship rules (usually descent and authority), religious rituals and dogmas, and the chief's right to enact laws, differences in power and privilege are preserved and made to seem appropriate" (Turner, 1972:220).

In primitive societies, there are no well-developed political subsystems, and the polity is composed of kin leaders, councils of elders or chiefs, and various religious leaders. Legislators are political bodies and, as such, do not formally exist in primitive societies. In such societies, judges and political leaders (elders, etc.) are one and the same. The emphasis is on court enacted law (common law) rather than legislative law enacted by political bodies (statutory law). Although the distinction between the two in primitive societies does not exist, since courts are political and their decisions constitute legislation, chiefs or elders can enact both substantive and procedural laws. Because there are no written laws, the chief-legislator can strike, rescind, or change old laws more easily than the modern legislator; and if such action appears reasonable, little resistance is offered. Obviously, getting old laws off the books in modern societies is rarely this easy.

Courts, like the police force, in primitive societies are temporarily assembled and then dispersed as disputes arise and are settled. Although they are provisional, the courts comprise at least two clearly differentiated roles: that of the judges who hear evidence and make decisions in accordance with laws, and that of litigants who have to abide by the judges' decision. Occasionally, a third role can be identified in such courts, that of a representative "lawyer" who pleads the case for a litigant. As the legal system develops, these roles become more clearly differentiated. In primitive societies, however, these three procedures are sufficient to maintain a high degree of societal integration and coordination.

Transitional Legal Systems

Transitional legal systems are characteristic of advanced agrarian and early industrial societies where the economic, educational, and political subsystems are increasingly differentiated from kinship relationships. As a result of increases in integrative problems, the legal subsystem becomes more complex and extensive, as evidenced by a clear-cut differentiation in basic legal elements—laws, courts, enforcement agencies, and legislative structures. In the transitional stage, most of the features of the modern legal system are present, but not to the same degree. Law becomes more differentiated from tradition, customs, and religious dogma. There is a distinction between *public* and *private* law. The former is concerned with the structure of government, the duties and powers of officials, and the relationships between the individual and the state, while the latter regulates relations among nonpolitical units. *Criminal* law also becomes distinguishable from *torts*. Criminal law denotes wrongs against the state, community, and public. Torts are laws pertaining to private wrongs of parties against each other rather than against the state or public. There is, similarly, a clearer differentiation between procedural and substantive laws, and as the types of laws increase, laws become systems of rules (Friedman, 1975:291–309).

The increased differentiation of laws is reflected in the increased complexity of the courts. Accompanying this differentiation is the emergence of at least five distinct types of statuses: judge; representative or lawyer; litigant; court officials and administrators; and jurors. The roles of judges and lawyers become institutionalized, requiring specialized training. In transitional legal systems, written records of court proceedings become more common, contributing to the emergence of a variety of administrative roles, which in turn, leads to the initial bureaucratization of the court.

With the development of clearly differentiated, stable, and autonomous courts, legal development accelerates for the following reasons:

> (1) Laws enacted by the growing legislative body of the polity can be applied systematically to specific circumstances by professionals and experts. This means that laws enacted by the centralizing polity have institutional channels of application. (2) Where political legislation of laws is absent, an established court can enact laws by handing down common-law precedents. Such common laws tend to fit nicely the structural conditions in a society, since they emerge out of attempts to reconcile actual and concrete conflicts (Turner, 1972:222).

Initially, courts are localized and characterized by common law decisions. In time, their conflicting and overlapping rules provide an impetus
for the unification of a legal system eventually leading to a more codified
system of laws.

There is also the emergence of explicit, relatively stable, and somewhat autonomous police roles in transitional legal systems. Concomitant
with the development of police roles is the emergence of legislative structures. This results in a clear differentiation of legislative statuses from judicial (courts) and enforcement (police) statuses. Legislating new laws or
abolishing old ones is no longer a matter of a simple decree. In transitional
legal systems, a small cluster of statuses, whether organized in a forum, senate, or royal council, can enact laws. Initially, these laws are dominated by
a political elite and are responsive to its demands. Later on, legislative
changes become more comprehensive, involving a group of laws pertaining
to general problem areas. With the enactment of more comprehensive statutes and codes, a system of civil law begins to emerge in order to supplement common law. The development of civil codes is stimulated by an established court system and police force, a pool of educated lawyers and
judges, a background of common law, and a degree of political and national
unity. The functions of law in transitional legal institutions are essentially
similar to those in primitive systems—perhaps a bit more complex, and at
the same time, less successful in resolving integrative problems. Structural
differentiation becomes more complex. Political development increases,
bringing with it inequities in power and wealth. Civil law in such situations
tends to legitimize these inequalities.

Modern Legal Systems

In modern legal systems we find all the structural features of transitional systems present, but in greater and more elaborate arrangements.
Turner notes: "Laws in modern legal systems are extensive networks of local
and national statutes, private and public codes, crimes and torts, common
and civil laws, and procedural and substantive rules" (1972:225). A distinctive feature of modern legal systems is the proliferation of public and procedural laws, referred to as *administrative* law. Another aspect is the increasing proportion of statutory law over common law. Legislation, as a result
of political development, becomes a more acceptable method of adjusting
law to social conditions. There are also clear hierarchies of laws ranging
from constitutional codes to regional and local codes.

Courts in modern legal systems have an important role in mediating
and mitigating conflict, disputes, deviance, and other sources of malinte-
gration. The roles of lawyers and judges become highly professionalized
with licensing requirements and formal sanctions. The various administrative statuses—clerks, bailiffs, and public prosecutors—specialize, proliferate, and become heavily bureaucratized. The jurisdictions of courts are
specified with clearly delineated appeal procedures. Cases unresolved in
lower courts can be argued in higher courts which have the power to reverse lower court decisions.

In modern legal systems, laws are enforced and court decisions are carried out by clearly differentiated and organized police forces, which are organized at the local, state, and federal levels. Each force possesses its own internal organization, which becomes increasingly bureaucratized at the higher levels. In addition to police forces, regulatory agencies, such as the Federal Trade Commission and the Federal Aviation Administration, regularly enforce and oversee conformity to laws. Administrative agencies, as we shall see in Chapters Three and Four, also make and interpret laws in the context of their own mandates.

Legislative bodies at various levels proliferate in modern legal systems. There is a greater emphasis on integrative problems and on an effort to enact comprehensive laws. Accompanying the emergence of a stable legislature, well-planned and comprehensive law enactment can become an effective mechanism of social change.

Inherent in modern legal systems is the notion of "modern" law. Marc Galanter (1977) sets forth a comprehensive conceptualization of modern law. His model, not a description, includes eleven salient features that characterize the legal systems of the industrial societies of the last century, and many of them can be found in modern societies as well. He argues that "modern law consists of rules that are uniform and unvarying in their application" (1977:1047). The same rules and regulations are applicable to everyone. Modern law is also "transactional." Rights and duties stem from "transactions." They are not "aggregated in unchanging clusters" prescribed to an individual by ascribed status. Galanter insists that modern legal norms are "universalistic," that is, their application is predictable, uniform, and impersonal. Further, the system, to be uniform and predictable, operates on the basis of written rules and has a regular chain of command. The system is "rational" in the Weberian sense and "Rules are valued for their instrumental utility in producing consciously chosen ends, rather than for their formal qualities" (1977:1048). Such a system is run by full time professionals whose "qualifications come from mastery of the techniques of the legal system itself, not from possession of special gifts or talents or from eminence in some other area of life" (1977:1048). Professionals run the law, lawyers replace "mere general agents" as the legal system grows more complex. The system is "amendable." It can be changed and it does not have "sacred fixity." Says Galanter: "Legislation replaces the slow reworking of customary law" (1977:1048). It is also "political," that is, tied to the state which has a monopoly on law. Finally, legislative, judicial, and executive functions are "separate and distinct" in modern law.

Thus far we have identified some of the preconditions necessary for the development of modern legal systems. Let us now consider some of the theories accounting for these developments.

THEORIES OF LAW AND SOCIETY

The preceding section dealt with some general types of legal systems as they correspond to various stages of modernization and social development. The present section addresses two questions emerging from the previous discussion. Why did changes in the legal system take place? What factors contributed to legal development from an historical perspective? In attempting to answer these questions, two general issues can be distinguished. The first is the issue of legal development in any society. The second is concerned with forces that produce or thwart change in the legal system.

Theorists of law and society have long been preoccupied with efforts to describe the broad historical course of legal development and to analyze the factors that influence legal systems. The literature is extensive, going back several centuries. The investigation of legal development has traditionally been the concern of scholars in a variety of fields. In view of the limits set for this study, no attempt is made here to provide a comprehensive and systematic review of major theories and schools. Certain major theorists will, however, be considered.

Among the theorists to be presented, there is more or less general agreement that societal and legal complexities are interrelated. Beyond that, there is little consensus. The particular theorists differ as to detail and interpretation of the general relationship between legal change and social change. It is hoped that the following sample of theorists from various disciplines, historical periods, and countries will provide a better understanding of the diverse issues involved in the investigation of the multifaceted relations between law and other major institutions of society.

The European Pioneers

For centuries, law has been considered by Europeans as an absolute and autonomous entity unrelated to the structure and function of the society in which it existed. The idea of natural law constitutes the basis for this conception of law. The origins of natural law can be traced back to ancient Greece. Aristotle maintains that natural law has a universal validity and is based on reason that is free from all passion. St. Thomas Aquinas argues that natural law is part of human nature, and through natural law, human beings participate as rational beings in the eternal laws of God.

The idea of natural law is based on the assumption that through reason the nature of human beings can be known, and that this knowledge can provide the basis for the social and legal ordering of human existence (Marske, Kofron, Vago, 1978). Natural law is considered superior to enacted law. It is "the chief tenet of natural law that arbitrary will is not legally final" (Selznick, 1961:100). An appeal to higher principles of justice is always permissible from the decrees of a lawmaker. When enacted law does not coincide with the principles of natural law, it is considered unjust. For example, proponents of pro-life maintain that laws providing for abortion on demand are contrary to the tenets of natural law.

Under the influence of natural law, many European thinkers believed that law in any given society was a reflection of a universally valid set of legal principles based on the idea that, through reason, the nature of man can be ascertained. This knowledge could then become the basis for the social and legal order of human existence. From the middle of the nineteenth century, however, the idea of natural law was largely displaced by historical and evolutionary interpretations of law, and by legal positivism, which considered the legal and the moral to constitute two quite separate realms. These two views of the law sought to explain the law causally in terms of ethnological factors, or by reference to certain evolutionary forces which pushed the law forward along a predetermined path. Many scholars sought to discourage philosophical speculation about the nature and purposes of law and concentrated on the development and analysis of positive law laid down and enforced by the state. The most notable among these scholars include Baron de Montesquieu in France, Friedrich Karl von Savigny in Germany, Herbert Spencer, and Sir Henry Sumner Maine in England. I shall now consider their theories in some detail.

Baron de Montesquieu (1689–1755) Montesquieu challenges the underlying assumptions of natural law by presenting a radically different conceptualization of law and society. He considers law an integral part of a particular people's culture. The central thesis of his *Spirit of Laws* (1886) is that laws are the result of a number of factors in society such as customs, physical environment, and antecedents, and that laws can only be understood in the context of particular societies. He further posits that laws are relative, and that there are no "good" or "bad" laws in the abstract, a proposition that ran contrary to the opinions of the day. Each law, Montesquieu maintains, must be considered in relation to its background, its antecedents, and its surroundings. If a law fits well into this framework, it is a good law; if it does not, it is bad.

But Montesquieu's fame rests above all on his political theory of the separation of powers. According to this theory, a constitution is comprised of three different types of legal powers: legislative, executive, and judicial, each vested in a different body or person. The role of the legislature is to enact new laws; of the executive, to enforce and administer the laws as well as to determine policy within the framework of those laws; and of the judiciary, simply to interpret the laws established by the legislative power. This neat classification had considerable influence on the form of constitution subsequently adopted by the newly created United States of America after the Declaration of Independence (Bodenheimer, 1974:49).

Leopold Pospisil (1971:138), in his analysis of Montesquieu's contributions, aptly remarks: "With his ideas of the relativity of law in space as well as in time, and with his emphasis on specificity and empiricism, he can be regarded as the founder of the modern sociology of law in general and of the field of legal dynamics in particular."

Friedrich Karl von Savigny (1779–1861) The natural law philosophers of the seventeenth and eighteenth centuries had looked to reason as a guide for discerning the most perfect form of law. They were interested in the purposes of the law, not in its history and growth. They sought to construct a new legal order based on certain principles of liberty and equality which they proclaimed to be eternal postulates of reason and justice.

The age of rationalism and natural law in Europe culminated in the French Revolution of 1789. When this revolution failed to reach its objectives in its doctrinaire way, and thus had to be content with partial results, a certain reaction against its rationalistic premises pervaded Europe. In Germany and England—which resisted most of the ideas of the French Revolution—a movement against the unhistorical rationalism of the antecedents of the revolution became quite powerful. Conservative ideas based on history and tradition were emphasized and propagated. In the sphere of law this meant an emphasis on legal history and legal tradition as against the speculative attempts to establish a law of nature. This was the period in which scientific research into the forces shaping the law began to replace the rationalistic inquiries into the ideal nature, purposes, and social objective of the law. This resulted in the emergence of a school of "historical jurisprudence" of which Savigny, a German jurist, is considered the founder.

Savigny's view of the law was first presented in his famous pamphlet, "Of the Vocation of Our Age for Legislation and Jurisprudence" (1975). He argues that law has no abstract origin in nature or in mind, but is organically connected with the people of a particular nation and is an expression of its *Volksgeist* or national spirit. In his view, the law is not something that should be made arbitrarily and deliberately by a lawmaker. Fundamentally, he contends that law is formed by custom and popular faith, "by internal, silently-operating forces" (1975:30), not by the arbitrary will of a lawgiver. The real law is always the proper will of the people. Like language and manners, law has movement and development. It grows with a people and dies with them.

In earliest historical times, Savigny claims that law was no more separable from a people than were its language or manners. Rights and duties were created and extinguished by symbolic acts which were the "true grammar" of law in this period. As social life became more complex and sophisticated, law started to be expressed in abstract forms. Jurists became a professional class, and law perfected its language and took a scientific direction. Law thus became an expression of "national spirit." He was well aware of the fact that, in modern legal systems, legal scholars, judges, and lawyers play an active part in the shaping of legal institutions.

Savigny's recognition that the development of different types of legal systems in different societies is brought about by diverse modernization forces, and his view that laws have no universal validity or applicability, constitute an important historical step toward the development of sociology of law. However, his idea of *Volksgeist* (national spirit) became one of the more important ingredients of Hitler's notion of race and nation and provided a justification for the doctrines of Nazism.

Herbert Spencer (1820-1903)   Contrary to the doctrines of natural law, in nineteenth-century England, Herbert Spencer provides the philosophical underpinnings for the theory of unregulated competition in the economic sphere. Strongly influenced by Charles Darwin, he draws a picture of the evolution of civilization and law in which natural selection and the survival of the fittest are the major determining factors. Evolution for Spencer consists of growing differentiation, individuation, and increasing division of labor. Civilization is the progress of social life from primitive homogeneity to ultimate heterogeneity. He identifies two main stages in the development of civilizations: a primitive or military form of society, with war, compulsion, and status as regulatory mechanisms, and a higher or industrial form of society, with peace, freedom, and a contract as the controlling devices.

Spencer is convinced that in his second stage, human progress is marked by a continual increase in individual liberty and a corresponding decrease in governmental activities. Government, he believes, would gradually confine its field of action to the enforcement of contracts and the protection of personal safety. He strongly opposes public education, public hospitals, public communications, and any governmental programs designed to alleviate the plight of the economically weaker groups in society. He was convinced that social legislation of this type is an unwarranted interference with the laws of natural selection (Spencer, 1899).

Spencer's ideas on law influenced a number of early sociologists in the United States. For example, William Graham Sumner advocates a position essentially similar to that of Spencer. He, too, sees the function of the state limited to that of an overseer who guards the safety of private property and sees to it that the peace is not breached. He favors a regime of contract in which social relations are regulated primarily by mutual agreements, not by government-imposed legal norms. He argues that society does not need any supervision. Maximum freedom of individual action should be promoted by law. He considers attempts to achieve a greater social and economic equality among men ill-advised and unnatural.

> Let it be understood that we cannot go outside of this alternative: liberty, inequality, survival of the fittest; not liberty, equality, survival of the unfittest. The former carries society forward and favors all its best members; the latter carries society downward and favors all its worst members (Sumner, 1940:25).

To a great extent, the *laissez-faire* doctrines of courts and legislatures in the United States for decades, perhaps consciously or unconsciously, reflected the economic and social philosophy of Spencer and Sumner. Up until recently, for example, legislative policies designed to equalize the bargaining power of management and labor, to protect the health and subsistence of marginal groups, or to interfere with that freedom of contract which was considered the true birthmark of an advancing civilization, appeared to be widespread. In part, these are still discernible in attitudes which place the rights of wealthier groups above those of the disfavored members of society.

Sir Henry Sumner Maine (1822–1888)   The founder and chief proponent of the English historical school of law is Sir Henry Sumner Maine. He was strongly influenced by Savigny's historical approach to the problems of jurisprudence, but he goes beyond this philosopher in undertaking broad comparative studies of the growth of legal institutions in primitive as well as progressive societies. These studies led him to the conviction that the legal history of people shows patterns of evolution which recur in different societies and in similar historical circumstances. He argues that there do not exist infinite possibilities for building and managing human societies; certain political, social, and legal forms reappear in seemingly different garb, and if they reappear, they manifest themselves in certain typical ways. For example, Roman feudalism produced legal rules and legal institutions strikingly similar to English feudalism, although differences can also be demonstrated.

One of his general laws of legal evolution is set forth in his classical treatise, *Ancient Law:*

> The movement of the progressive societies has been uniform in one respect. Through all its course it has been distinguished by the gradual dissolution of family dependency and the growth of individual obligation in its place. The Individual is steadily substituted for the Family, as the unit of which civil laws take account. The advance has been accomplished at varying rates of celerity, and there are societies not absolutely stationary in which the collapse of the ancient organization can only be perceived by careful study of the phenomena they present. But, whatever its pace, the change has not been subject to reaction or recoil, and apparent retardations will be found to have been occasioned through the absorption of archaic ideas and customs from some entirely foreign source. Nor is it difficult to see what is the tie between man and man which replaces by degrees those forms of reciprocity in rights and duties which have their origin in the Family. It is Contract. Starting, as from one terminus of history, from a condition of society in which all the relations of Persons are summed up in the relations of Family, we seem to have steadily moved towards a phase of social order in which all these relations arise from the free agreement of Individuals (1861:170).

Thus, Maine arrives at his often quoted dictum that "the movement of the progressive societies has hitherto been a movement from Status to Contract" (1861:170). Status is a fixed condition in which an individual is without will and without opportunity. Ascribed status prevails, legal relations depend on birth or caste. It is indicative of a social order in which the group, not the individual, is the primary unit of social life. Every individual is enmeshed in a network of family and group ties. With the progress of civilization, this condition gradually gives way to a social system based on contract. Maine argues that a progressive civilization is manifested by the emergence of the independent, free, and self-determining individual, based on achieved status, as the primary unit of social life. He suggests that the emphasis on individual achievement and voluntary contractual relations set the conditions for a more mature legal system which uses legislation to bring society and law into harmony. In essence, his argument is that in modern societies legal relations are not conditioned by one's birth but they depend on voluntary agreements.

Influential Sociological Theorists

Early sociologists have recognized the essential interrelation between legal institutions and the social order. In this section, the influential theoretical explanations of law and society of Karl Marx, Max Weber, Eugen Ehrlich, and Emile Durkheim are explored.

Karl Marx (1818–1883)   Of all the social theorists, few are as important, brilliant, or original as Karl Marx. Part philosopher, part economist, part sociologist, and part historian, Marx combines political partisanship with deep scholarship. Marx, and the subsequent ideology of Marxism, may have caused more social change than any other force in the modern world, in both developed and developing societies (Barber, 1971:260).

Marx postulates that every society, whatever its stage of historical development, rests on an economic foundation. He calls this "mode of production" of commodities, which has two elements. The first is the physical or technological arrangement of economic activity. The second is "the social relations of production," or the indispensable human attachments that people must form with one another when engaged in economic activity. In his words:

> The sum total of these relations of production constitutes the economic structure of society—the real foundation, on which rise legal and political superstructures and to which correspond definite forms of social consciousness (Marx, 1959:43).

For Marx the determinant variable is the mode of production. Changes in this produce changes in the way in which groups are attached to production technology. This economic determinism is reflected in Marx's theory of law.

Marx's theory of law, which has greatly influenced social and jurisprudential thinking throughout the world, may be summarized in three principal assumptions: (1) Law is a product of evolving economic forces; (2) Law is a tool used by a ruling class to maintain its power over the lower classes; and (3) In the communist society of the future, law as an instrument of social control will "wither away" and finally disappear.

The idea that law is a reflection of economic conditions is an integral part of the doctrine of "dialectical materialism." According to this doctrine, the political, social, religious, and cultural order of any given epoch is determined by the existing system of production and forms a "superstructure" on top of this economic basis. Law, for Marx, is part of this superstructure whose forms, content, and conceptual apparatus constitute responses to economic developments. This view maintains that law is nothing more than a function of the economy but without any independent existence.

In societies with pronounced class distinctions, the means of production are owned and controlled by the ruling class. Marx's theory of law is the characterization of law as a form of class rule. While addressing the bourgeoisie of his day in his *Communist Manifesto,* Marx (1955:47) writes, "Your jurisprudence is but the will of your class made into a law for all, a will whose essential character and direction are determined by the economic conditions of existence of your class." Marx further argues that law, as a form of class rule, is sanctioned by public authority which, through the use of armed bodies, has the power of enforcement.

Finally, Marx suggests that after the revolution when class conflict is resolved and the institution of private property is replaced by a communist regime, law and the state, hitherto the main engines of despotism and oppression, will "wither away." There will be no need for coercion since everyone's needs will be fulfilled, and universal harmony will thus prevail. According to this view, there will be no need for law in the future—a future which will be the final stage of humanity's evolution because stateless and lawless communism shall exist forever.

As yet, however, we are far from this "withering away" idea of law. Law still persists in the dictatorship of proletariats, first established in Russia in 1917. This idea prevailed for a short time in the late 1920s in the Soviet Union, as Rostow (1952:103) notes: "Since 1936 the teaching and practice of law has been rehabilitated, new codes have been promulgated, and a tone of positive legalism has suffused Soviet society." After the rehabilitation of the law and the emphasis on its benefits, which is called "socialist legality" (Kerimov, 1964), the "withering away" doctrine was not entirely abandoned, but its realization was deferred to a distant future. Still, some "Western scholars are surprised by the fact that state and law are growing in Russia rather than withering away; or by the fact that Soviet legal devices for controlling a growingly complex economically organised society, resemble those in a similar 'capitalist' society" (Stone, 1966:505). I shall return in this chapter to Marx's ideas of law and his influence on contemporary theorists in the discussion on conflict and Marxist approaches to law.

Max Weber (1864–1920)   The German sociologist and lawyer, Max Weber, played a crucial role in the development of sociology. His significance is not merely historical; he remains an ever present force in contemporary sociology. He occupies a central position among the law and society theorists.

Weber's typology of legal systems is based on two fundamental distinctions (1954:63). First, legal procedures are rational or irrational. *Rational* procedures involve the use of logic and scientific methods to attain specific objectives. *Irrational* procedures rely on ethical or mystical considerations such as magic or faith in the supernatural. Second, legal procedures can proceed, rationally or irrationally, with respect to formal or substantive law. *Formal* law refers to making decisions on the basis of established rules, regardless of the notion of fairness. *Substantive* law takes the circumstances of individual cases into consideration along with the prevailing notion of justice. These two distinctions create four ideal types which are seldom, if ever, attained in their pure form in specific societies.

1. *Substantive irrationality.* This exists when a case is decided on some unique religious, ethical, emotional, or political basis instead of by general rules. An example of this would be when a religious judge makes a decision without any recourse to explicit rules or legal principles.

2. *Formal irrationality.* This involves rules based on supernatural forces. It is irrational because no one tries to understand or clarify why it works and formal because strict adherence is required to the procedures. The Ten Commandments, for example, were enacted in a formally irrational way: Moses, claim-

ing direct revelation, presented the tablets and announced, "This is the Law." Other examples would include the use of ordeals and oaths.

3. *Substantive rationality.* This is based on the application of rules from nonlegal sources such as religion, ideology, or science. It is rational because rules are derived from specific and accepted sources and substantive because there is a concern for justness of outcomes in individual cases. The efforts of Ayatollah Khomeini in Iran to make decisions on the basis of the Koran would be an example of substantive rationality.

4. *Formal rationality.* This involves the use of consistent, logical rules independent of moral, religious, or other normative criteria which are applied equally to all cases. An example of this is modern American or western law.

While referring to both formal and substantive rationality, Weber identifies three types of administration of justice: (1) *Kahdi* justice; (2) empirical justice; and (3) rational justice. *Kahdi* justice is dispensed by the judge of the Islamic *Sharia* Court. It is based on religious precepts and is so lacking in procedural rules as to seem almost completely arbitrary. The *Koran* contains the revealed word of God, and this bible forms the heart of the Islamic legal system in such countries as Iran or Pakistan. Empirical justice, the deciding of cases by referring to analogies and by relying on and interpreting precedents, is more rational than *Kahdi* justice, but notably short of complete rationality. Weber argues that modern law is rational while traditional and primitive laws were irrational, or at least, less rational. Rational justice is based on bureaucratic principles. The rational legal system is basically universalistic; the irrational is particularistic. The rational legal system looks toward contract, not toward status (Parsons, 1964:339). Rationality can be further based on adherence to "eternal characteristics" (observable concrete features) of the facts of the case. However, Weber perceives that Western law, with its specialized professional roles of judges and lawyers, is unique in that it is also reliant on the "logical analysis of meaning" of abstract legal concepts and rules.

Modern society differs from its past in many ways which Max Weber sums up in a single concept: the *rational.* Modern society is in pursuit of the rational. Weber contends that the modern law of the West has become increasingly institutionalized through the bureaucratization of the state. He points out that the acceptance of the law as a rational science is based on certain fundamental and semi-logical postulates, such as, that the law is a "gapless" system of legal principles, and that every concrete judicial decision involves the application of an abstract legal proposition to a concrete situation. There is little doubt that Weber captures, in his idea of rationality, a crucial feature of modern legal systems. It is rather ironic that soon after Max Weber's death in 1920, rational law in Germany was in part replaced by a faith in the intuition of a charismatic leader—Adolph Hitler.

Eugen Ehrlich (1862–1922)   The Austrian jurist and sociologist, Eugen Ehrlich, a contemporary of Max Weber, is often referred to as the founder of "sociological jurisprudence." In fact, his major work is entitled, *Fundamental Principles of the Sociology of Law* (1975). His main objective is to penetrate behind the screen of formal rules, hitherto treated as synonymous with the law itself, to those actual social norms which govern society in all its aspects, and which he describes as "the living law." The "living law" is conceived by Ehrlich (1975:37) as "the inner order of associations," that is, the law practiced by society, as opposed to the law enforced by the state. In his words:

> The living law is the law which dominates life itself even though it has not been posited in legal propositions. The source of our knowledge of this law is, first, the modern legal document; secondly, direct observation of life, of commerce, of customs and usages, and of all associations, not only of those the law has recognized but also those that it has overlooked and passed by, indeed even of those that it has disapproved (Ehrlich, 1975:493).

Ehrlich argues that a court trial is an exceptional occurrence in comparison to the innumerable contracts and transactions which are consummated in the daily life of the community. He points out that only small morsels of real life come before the officials charged with the adjudication of disputes. To study the living body of law, one must turn to marriage contracts, leases, contracts of purchase, wills, the actual order of succession, partnership articles, and the bylaws of corporations (Ehrlich, 1975:495).

He contrasts the "norms of decision" laid down for the adjudication of disputes with the "norms of organization," which originate in society and determine the actual behavior of the average person who becomes enmeshed in innumerable legal relations. With some exceptions, he or she will quite voluntarily perform the required duties. One performs one's duties as father and son, or as husband and wife. One pays one's debts and renders to one's employer the performance that is due. It is not, in Ehrlich's view, the threat of compulsion by the state that normally induces a person to perform these duties (1975:21). Rather, the performance of legal duties is conditioned by the environment and reinforced by the internalization of normative expectations.

Ehrlich further suggests that law is subjugated to social forces and could not, by itself, be effective, because order in society is based on the social acceptance of law, and not on official proclamations by the state. Social order for Ehrlich is based on the fact that, in general, acceptance of law is based on social rules and regulations which the legal system tends to reflect. Consequently, Ehrlich states that those who are responsible for developing the legal system need to be in close touch with the prevailing ethical values in society. This awareness is a requirement for members of the legal profession who are instrumental both in developing the living law itself, and in determining what is to be the true scope of the rules of positive law and their correlation with the living law.

Emile Durkheim (1858–1917)   The French sociologist, Emile Durkheim, outlines his thesis on law in society in his influential work, *The Division of Labor in Society* (1964). While tracing the development of social order through social and economic institutions, Durkheim sets forth a theory of legal development by elucidating the idea that law is a measure of the type of solidarity in a society. Durkheim maintains that there are two types of solidarity: *mechanical* and *organic*. Mechanical solidarity prevails in relatively simple and homogeneous societies where unity is ensured by close interpersonal ties, similarity of habits, ideas, and attitudes. Organic solidarity is characteristic of modern societies which are heterogeneous and differentiated by a complex division of labor. The grounds for solidarity are the interdependence of widely different persons and groups performing a variety of functions.

Corresponding to these two forms of solidarity are two types of law: repressive and restitutive. Mechanical solidarity is associated with repressive and penal law. In a homogeneous, undifferentiated society, a criminal act offends the collective conscience, and punishment is meant to protect and preserve social solidarity. Punishment is a mechanical reaction. The wrongdoer is punished as an example to the community that deviance will not be tolerated. There is no concern with the rehabilitation of the offender.

In modern heterogeneous societies, repressive law tends to give way to restitutive law with an emphasis on compensation. Punishment deals with restitution and reparations for harm done to the victim. Crimes are considered acts that offend others and not the collective conscience of the community. Punishment is evaluated in terms of what is beneficial for the offender and is used for rehabilitation.

Stated concisely, Durkheim's position is that penal law reflects mechanical solidarity. Modern society is bound together by organic solidarity—interdependence and division of labor flowing out of voluntary acts. Society is complex—its parts are highly specialized. Through contracts, which are the main concern of modern law, people arrange their innumerable, complex relationships. Contracts and contract laws are central to modern society and influence the course of societal development through the regulation of relationships.

Although Durkheim's concern is not with the elaboration of a general framework or methodology for the sociological analysis of law, his interest in law "resulted in the school that formed around him developing a considerable interest in the study of law as a social process" (Hunt, 1978:65). His ideas on law also provided an important background to subsequent discussions concerning the nature of primitive law and the nature of crime. Although it may be questionable that "he made a serious contribution to the development of systematic legal sociology" (Gurvitch, 1942:106), he certainly made an important contribution to our understanding of the relationship between law and social solidarity.

Socio-Legal Theorists

The theorists that will be considered in this section argue that law cannot be understood without regard for the realities of social life. Since the beginning of the twentieth century, scholars of jurisprudence and of related disciplines on both sides of the Atlantic reflected the influence of the social sciences in their analysis of legal development. The more prominent ones that shall be included in our analysis are Albert Venn Dicey, Justice Oliver Wendell Holmes, Roscoe Pound, Karl N. Llewellyn, and E. Adamson Hoebel.

Albert Venn Dicey (1835-1922)   Albert Venn Dicey (1905), an English legal scholar, offers what has become a classic theory on the influence of public opinion on social change in his lectures given at Harvard Law School in 1898. He traces the growth of statutory lawmaking and the legal system in terms of the increasing articulateness and power of public opinion. He notes that the process begins with a new idea which "presents itself to some one man of originality or genius." He has in mind such individuals as Adam Smith or Charles Darwin. Next, the idea is adopted by supporters who "preach" it to others. As time passes, "the preachers of truth make an impression, either directly upon the general public or upon some person of eminence, say a leading stateman, who stands in a position to impress ordinary people and thus to win the support of the nation" (Dicey, 1905:23). As Dicey points out, however, something must happen so that people will listen to a truly new idea and change their values. He talks of "accidental conditions" which enable popular leaders to seize the opportunity. As an example he gives the Irish famine which enabled Cobden and Bright to gain acceptance of Adam Smith's doctrine of free trade.

Public opinion for Dicey is "the majority of those citizens who have at a given moment taken an effective part in public life" (1905:10). Dicey talks of the "gradual, or slow, and continuous" (1905:27) developments of tides of public opinion in England. Generally, he maintains there are few abrupt changes. Ideally, legislators should reflect and act upon public opinion, but judges, even more than legislators, lag behind public opinion. Dicey concedes that although judges are "guided to a considerable extent by the dominant current of public opinion" (1905:363), "they are also guided by professional opinions and ways of thinking which are, to a certain extent, independent of and possibly opposed to the general tone of public opinion" (1905:364). He then concludes, "they are men advanced in life. They are for the most part persons of a conservative disposition" (1905:364).

Dicey is also known for his famous doctrine of "the rule of law." The doctrine has three aspects: First, no one is punishable except for a distinct breach of law and, therefore, the rule of law is not consistent with arbitrary or even wide discretionary authority on the part of the government. Second, the rule of law means total subjection of all classes to the law of the land, as administered by the law courts. Third, individual rights derive from court precedents rather than from constitutional codes.

From a sociological perspective, Dicey's most crucial contribution to law and society is the recognition of the importance of public opinion in legal development. As Lord Tangley (1965:48) observes: "We are indebted to Professor Dicey for many things—he established for all time the relationship between public opinion and law reform and traced its course through the nineteenth century."

Oliver Wendell Holmes (1841-1935)   The distinguished American judge, Oliver Wendell Holmes, is considered one of the founders of the school called "legal realism." This is based on the conception of the judicial process whereby judges are responsible for formulating law, rather than merely finding it in law books. The judge always has to exercise choice when making a decision. He has to decide which principle will prevail and which party will win. According to the legal realists' position, judges make decisions on the basis of their conceptions of justness prior to resorting to formal legal precedents. Such precedents can be found or developed to support almost any outcome. The real decisions are based on the judge's notion of justness, conditioned, in part, by values, personal background, predilections, and so forth. They are then rationalized in the written opinion.

Holmes stresses the limits that are set to the use of deductive logic in the solution of legal problems. He postulates that the life of law has been experience and not logic and maintains that only a judge or lawyer who is acquainted with the historical, social, and economic aspects of the law will be in a position to fulfill his or her functions properly.

Holmes assigns a large role to historical and social forces in the life of law, while deemphasizing the ethical and ideal elements. He considers law largely as a body of edicts representing the will of dominant interests in society, backed by force. Although he admits that moral principles are influential in the initial formulation of the rules of law, he is inclined to identify morality with the taste and value preferences of shifting power groups in society. Schwartz notes: "Holmes was part of the generation that had sat at the feet of Darwin and Spencer and he could never shed his Darwinist outlook" (1974:151). His basic philosophy is that life is essentially a Darwinian struggle for existence and that the goal of social effort was to "build a race" rather than to strive for the attainment of humanitarian ethical objectives.

In his often quoted essay, "The Path of the Law," Holmes (1897:458) outlines some of his basic propositions and states that "a legal duty so called is nothing but a prediction that if a man does or omits certain things he will be made to suffer in this or that way by judgment of a court." A pragmatic approach to law, he declares, must view the law from the point of view of the "bad man." Such a person does not care about the general moral pronouncements and abstract legal doctrines. What is important, is simply what the courts are in fact likely to do.

He argues that any sense of absolute certainty about the law was bound to be illusory.

> Behind the logical forms lies a judgment as to the relative worth and importance of competing legislative grounds, often an inarticulate and unconscious judgment, it is true, and yet the very root and nerve of the whole proceeding. You can give any conclusion a logical form (Holmes, 1897:465–466).

Lawyers and judges should be aware of this and should "consider the ends which the several rules seek to accomplish, the reasons why those ends are desired, what is given up to gain them, and whether they are worth the price" (Holmes, 1897:476).

Roscoe Pound (1870–1964)   Roscoe Pound is considered the founder of American sociological jurisprudence. Working on the foundations laid by the German sociological jurists, he introduces a new and distinctly American flavor to the study of law in society. The rise of technology in modern times and its impact on humanity's social and economic life led Pound, as noted in Chapter One, to explain the legal process as a form of "social engineering."

Pound considers the object of law in terms of achieving a maximum limit of satisfaction of wants. He points out that during the nineteenth century the history of law was largely a record of a continually increasing recognition of individual rights, often regarded as "natural" and absolute. In the twentieth century, he proposes that this history should be rewritten in terms of a continually wider recognition of wants, demands, and social interests.

Pound's theory of interests lies at the very heart of sociological jurisprudence. Pound (1942:66) defines an interest as "a demand or desire which human beings, either individually or through groups or associations or in relations, seek to satisfy." He distinguishes between *individual interests, public interests,* and *social interests* (Pound, 1943:1–2). In the last category he includes, among others, the interests in the general security, the individual life, the protection of morals, the conservation of social and physical resources, and the interest in economic, political, and cultural progress.

Pound notes that justice may be administered with or without law. Justice, according to the law, means "administration according to authoritative precepts or norms (patterns) or guides, developed and applied by an authoritative technique, which individuals may ascertain in advance of controversy and by which all are reasonably assured of receiving like treatment. It means an impersonal, equal, certain administration of justice so far as these may be secured by means of precepts of general application" (Pound, 1959:374–375). Justice without law, on the other hand, is administered according to the will or intuition of an individual who, in making this decision, has a range of discretion, and is not bound to observe any fixed and general rules. The first form of justice is of a judicial character, the second is of an administrative character. Pound suggests that elements of both of these forms of justice are to be found in all legal systems. He observes that the history of law shows a constant oscillation between wide discretion and strict, detailed rules. He concludes that the problem of the future is the achievement of a workable balance between the judicial and the administrative elements and justice.

Karl N. Llewellyn (1893–1962)   Karl Llewellyn considers the development of law in the context of the relation between legal rulings and the changing social situation. Law, he argues, is a part of the culture—the habits, attitudes, and ideals that are transmitted from one generation to another. More precisely, it is an aspect of the institutionalized part of the culture. Social institutions are organized, and their expectations are stated as explicit rules that are obligatory and that are supported by specialists (Llewellyn, 1949).

Llewellyn suggests that law can be analyzed from the institutional perspective. It thus will be understood by both legal and sociological theorists. A legal institution may be analyzed by examining its interaction, norms, and standards. He describes the function of the legal institution in terms of what he calls "law jobs." There are four such law jobs: (1) cleaning up of trouble cases; (2) channeling of conduct, habit, and expectation in order to prevent or reduce the emergence of such trouble cases; (3) rechanneling conduct, creating new habits and expectations appropriate to changing conditions of personal or group life without creating new trouble cases; and (4) allocating the authoritative power and regulating it in case of emergency or of doubt or of innovation (Llewellyn, 1962:358–360).

Influenced by Weber's notion of bureaucracy, Llewellyn feels that the concept of craft should be used as a working tool in legal institutions. He maintains that a law-craft is a recognizable line of work. Law-work is a broader concept that he uses to describe the fact that a particular lawyer may practice more than one law-craft in legal institutions, for example, that of advocate, judge, counselor, and legislator. He has also, consistent with the postulate of sociological jurisprudence, sought to explore the relations and context between the law and the other social sciences, concluding that lawyers, as well as the social scientists, had thus far failed to make an "effective effort at neighborliness."

E. Adamson Hoebel (1906–   )   The leading American scholar in the field of anthropology of law was much influenced by Llewellyn with whom he collaborated on an analysis of the "law ways" in traditional Cheyenne society. The emphasis on the "law-jobs" having both a "pure survival" or "bare bones" aspect for the society and a "questing" or "betterment" value as well (Llewellyn and Hoebel, 1941:Ch. 3) contributed significantly to the development of a modern functional approach to the legal system. I shall return to this point in the discussion on the functionalist approach later in this chapter.

Hoebel's (1954:288–333) views on the development of legal systems are presented in the concluding chapter entitled "The Trend of the Law" in his book, *The Law of Primitive Man*. Hoebel (1954:288) notes that: "There has been no straight line of development in the growth of law." His description of trends in legal development is based on the assumption that cultures of contemporary primitive societies exhibit characteristics that are similar "to those that presumably prevailed in the early cultures of the infancy of mankind" (1954:290). He considers law and the legal system as a property of a specific community or subgroup of a society, and states: "Without the sense of community there can be no law. Without law there cannot be for long a community" (1954:332). Consequently, law exists to some extent even in the simplest societies.

Hoebel begins his description of the trend of law with a discussion of the "lower primitive societies"—the hunters and gatherers, such as the

Shoshone Indians or the Andaman Islanders. Almost all relations in such a society are face-to-face and intimate. The demands imposed by culture are relatively few. Ridicule is a potent mechanism of social control. Taboo and the fear of supernatural sanctions control a large area of behavior. Special interests are few, for there is little accumulated wealth. Conflict arises mostly in interpersonal relations. Repetitive abuse of the customs and codes of social relations constitutes a crime, and the offender may be beaten or even killed by the members of the community. Hoebel writes: "Here we have law in the full connotation of the word—the application, in threat or in fact, of physical coercion by a party having the socially recognized privilege—right of so acting. First the threat—and then, if need be, the act" (1954:300).

Among the more organized hunters, the pastoralists and the rooter-gardening peoples, such as the Cheyenne, Comanche, Kiowa, and Indians of the northwest coast of North America, the size of the group and the increased complexity of the culture make possible a greater divergence of interests between the members of society. Conflict of interests grow and the need arises for legal mechanisms for settlement and control of the internal clash of interests. Private law emerges and spreads, although much of the internal social control problems are handled on other than a legal basis.

In the tribes, a more formalized chieftanship develops, with a tendency toward hereditary succession (Hoebel, 1954:309–310). Although homicide and adultery still represent major difficulties, the development of criminal law remains weak.

"The real elaboration of law begins with the expansion of the gardening-based tribes," such as the Samoans or the Ashanti (Hoebel, 1954:316). The gardening activity provides an economic foundation for the support of larger populations which can no longer maintain face-to-face relationships. With the formation of more communities: "The pressures to maintain peaceful equilibrium between the numerous closely interacting communities become intensified. The further growth of law and a more effective law is demanded" (1954:316). The attempt to establish the interest of the society as superior to the interests of kinship groups is the prime mover of law in this type of society. Allocation of rights, duties, privileges, powers, and immunities with regard to land becomes important and "The law of things begins to rival the law of persons" (1954:316). "Clear-cut crimes" (1954:319) are established in the legal systems of these societies, and action for damages becomes even more frequent than on the preceding level.

For Hoebel, the "trend of law" is one of increasing growth and complexity in which the tendency is to shift the privilege-right of prosecution and imposition of legal sanctions from the individual and the kinship group to clearly defined public officials representing the society as such. Hoebel notes: "Damages have generally replaced death as penalties in civil suits" (1954:329). Hoebel maintains that this is how law developed in human societies through the ages, but the laws of particular societies have not followed a single line of development through fixed, predetermined, and universal stages. The development of legal systems in particular societies is characterized by a trend that only in general exhibits the features described here.

Contemporary Theorists of Law and Society

A brief explanation is warranted for the selection of the particular contemporary theorists discussed here. Comprehensive theoretical studies on law and society are limited. My intention in this section is to describe influential (and possibly controversial) theoretical developments that have taken place since the 1970s. The rationale for this preference is to illustrate some of the relatively recent advances in socio-legal theorizing on law and society. There are, of course, a number of other theorists (who will be alluded to in specific contexts) who could have been discussed. They include, among others, the works of William Chambliss and Robert Seidman (1982), *Law, Order, and Power;* Hyman Gross (1979), *A Theory of Criminal Justice;* Philippe Nonet and Philip Selznick (1978), *Law and Society in Transition, Toward Responsive Law;* Harold E. Pepinsky (1976), *Crime and Conflict, A Study of Law and Society;* and Charles E. Reasons (1974), *The Criminologist: Crime and the Criminal.* As illustrations of contemporary theorists, these and similar works tend to be limited in scope. By contrast, the authors chosen for examination attempt to account for law and society in their treatises from different, but at the same time, complementary perspectives. Their alternative viewpoints are also broad enough to include both the older theoretical perspectives, as well as the more contemporary, specialized advancements.

Donald Black   In *The Behavior of Law,* Donald Black (1976) sets forth a theory of law that he contends explains variations in law from a cross-national perspective, as well as among individuals within societies. As noted in Chapter One, he considers law as governmental social control, which makes use of legislation, litigation, and adjudication. He distinguishes between behavior that is controlled by these means from behavior that is subject to other forms of social control, such as etiquette, custom, and bureaucracy.

Black contends that law is a quantitative variable that can be measured by the frequency by which, in a given social setting, statutes are enacted, regulations are issued, complaints are made, offenses are prosecuted, damages are awarded, and punishment is meted out. Consequently, the quantity of law varies from society to society and from one historical period to another in a given society. Different organizations in a society may have more or less law both for themselves and in regard to other groups and organizations.

The direction of law (that is, the differential frequency and success of its application by persons in different social settings) also varies. So is the style of law which, as I mentioned earlier, may be accusatory (with penal or compensatory consequences), or remedial (with therapeutic or conciliatory consequences).

Next, Black develops a number of propositions that explain the quantity, direction, and style of law in regard to five measurable variables of social life: stratification, morphology, culture, organization, and social control. *Stratification* (inequality of wealth) can be measured in such ways as differences in wealth and rates of social mobility. *Morphology* refers to those aspects of social life that can be measured by social differentiation or the degree of interdependence (for example, the extent of division of labor). *Culture* can be measured by the volume, complexity, and diversity of ideas, and by the degree of conformity to the mainstream of culture. *Organization* can be measured by the degree to which the administration of collective action in political and economic spheres is centralized. Finally, the amount of nonlegal *social control* to which people are subjected is a measure of their respectability, and differences between people indicate normative distance from each other.

On the basis of sociological, historical, and ethnographic data, Black arrives at a number of conclusions. He points out that the quantity of law varies directly with stratification rank, integration, culture, organization, and respectability, and inversely with other forms of social control. Thus, stratified societies have more law than simple ones, wealthy people have more law among themselves than poor people, and the amount of law increases with the growth of governmental centralization.

The relationships between the quantity of law and the variables of differentiation, relational distance, and cultural distance are curvilinear. Law is minimal at either extreme of these variables and accumulates in their middle ranges. For example, law relating to contractual economic transaction is limited in simple societies where everyone engages in the same productive activity, and in the business world where manufacturers operate in a symbiotic exchange network.

The style of law varies with its direction: In relation to stratification, law has a penal style in its downward direction, a conpensatory or a therapeutic style in its upward direction, and a conciliatory style among people of equal rank. In regard to morphology, law tends to be accusatory among strangers and therapeutic or conciliatory among intimates. Less organized people are more vulnerable to penal law and more organized people can count on compensatory law.

These patterns of stylistic variation explain, for example, why an offense is more likely to be punished if the rank of the victim is higher than that of the offender, but is more likely to be dealt with by compensation if their ranks are reversed, why accusatory law replaces remedial law in societies undergoing modernization, why members of subcultures are more vulnerable to law enforcement than conventional citizens, and why organizations usually escape punishment for illegal practices against individuals.

Black's theory of law has been referred to as a "crashing classic" (Nader cited by Gottfredson and Hindelang, 1979:3), and "as the most important contribution ever made to the sociology of law. It is that and more" (Sherman, 1978:11). At the same time, it is criticized as "circular" (Michaels, 1978:11). Others, such as Michael R. Gottfredson and Michael J. Hindelang (1979:3–18), contend that some of the propositions derived from Black's theory do not stand up well to the rigors of empirical testing. Regardless of these and other criticisms, it is apparent that Black's theory of law will

be the stimulus for a great deal of research in coming years. His propositions are likely to be further subjected to rigorous examinations, criticisms,
and possible revisions and reformulations. But, as Sherman notes, "whatever the substance or method, social research on law cannot ignore Black"
(1978:15).

Roberto Mangabeira Unger   In *Law in Modern Society*, Unger revives the
sweeping scope of Max Weber's theorizing on law and places the development of rational legal systems within a broad historical and comparative
framework. Unger locates the study of law within the major questions of
social theory in general: the conflicts between individual and social interests, between legitimacy and coercion, and between the state and society.
His main thesis is that the development of the rule of law, law which is
committed to general and autonomous legal norms, could only take place
when competing groups struggle for control of the legal system and when
there are universal standards which can justify the law of the state.

Unger's analysis emphasizes the historical perspective. His goal is an
understanding of modern law and society. He examines the nature of society, and compares rival systems (for example, the Chinese), with the Western tradition with the scope of special types of law—customary or interactional law, regulatory law, and autonomous legal order. Customary or
interactional law is "simply any recurring mode of interaction among individuals and groups, together with the more or less explicit acknowledge-
ment by these groups and individuals that such patterns of interaction produce reciprocal expectations of conduct that ought to be satisfied" (1976:49).
Bureaucratic or regulatory law for Unger "consists of explicit rules established and enforced by an identifiable government" (1976:50). This type of
law is not a universal characteristic of social life: "It is limited to situations
in which the division between state and society has been established and
some standards of conduct have assumed the form of explicit prescriptions,
prohibitions, or permissions, addressed to more or less general categories
of persons and acts" (1976:51). Unger calls the third type of law the legal
order or legal system, which is both general and autonomous, as well as
public and positive (1976:52). From an evolutionary perspective, these different types of law turn out to be stages, for they build upon one another,
regulatory law upon customary law, the autonomous legal order upon regulatory law.

For Unger, law is indicative of the normative structure of social life.
He contends that there are two competing forms of normative integration:
consensual and instrumental. "Consensual law expresses the shared values
of a group or community and manifests the stable structure in recurring
interactions. Regulatory law is instrumental social control by political institutions through positive and public rules" (Eder, 1977:142). Unger considers autonomous law as both instrumental and consensual.

Unger accounts for these different types of law in an evolutionary
context. The change of customary law into bureaucratic law is characterized
by an extension of instrumental rules which have normative quality (state
law, governmental sanctions). This extension of the instrumental rule is de-

pendent upon the recognition of the consensual basis of law. Unger argues that sacred and natural law can provide the cultural context within which instrumental norms can be legitimized. The development of an autonomous legal order brings about a further extension of instrumental rules to everybody. Everyone can pursue their personal objectives as long as these do not infringe upon those of others. Laws set these limits. He notes, however, that this situation requires a further legitimation of the principles of law, and consensus must be generated by social contract and by agreement upon the criteria of substantive justice.

Unger makes an important contribution to the understanding of social theory and the nature of law in modern society. His theory of law is useful for the analysis of changes in law. He has generated enough testable propositions to enable sociologists to study law on two levels: "a synchronic structural description of forms of normative order and a diachronic social-historical analysis of the factors that produce structural transformations of law" (Eder, 1977:143).

Adam Podgorecki   The best known and perhaps most influential theorist of the middle range is the Polish sociologist, Adam Podgorecki. As the founder, in 1962, of the Research Committee on Sociology of Law of the International Sociological Association, he is well known among scholars interested in law and society on both sides of the Iron Curtain. Although few of his publications are available in English translation, Podgorecki's (1974) major ideas can be found in his *Law and Society.*

In order to make sociological studies of law a viable enterprise in Eastern European countries, which are under the influence of Marxist-Leninist theories of law and state, it was necessary to eliminate all stereotypes. In these countries, the end of the Second World War was marked by an abrupt overthrow of the bourgeois regimes and bourgeois values, which were replaced by socialist states in the Soviet pattern. These overthrows were accompanied by significant changes in the relationship between law and society and by the introduction of a new jurisprudence based on the Marxist-Leninist theory of state and law, which describes and explains the functioning of law in society in the context of dialectical materialism (Antalffy, 1974). This approach posits a necessary relationship between law in a society at a given point in time as well as the development of a class state. In such a state, the ruling class must use the law to retain its power and to protect its interests. With the successful completion of class struggles, a classless society would emerge following the transition from socialism to communism. This macrosociological approach to the theory of state and law still offers normative guidelines for political action and for scientific inquiry. The solution adopted by Eastern European sociologists was that legal sociological inquiries were explained theoretically and were based on theories of the middle range (attempts to interrelate a small number of empirical generalizations), which could exist on good terms with the all-comprising philosophical base of dialectical materialism.

Podgorecki's theory of law is based on four general postulates. First is the idea that empirical sociology of law is the preeminent legal science which should replace traditional jurisprudence. Second, the task of the sociology of law is to provide the basis for efficient laws by determining the most effective instruments for "remolding political attitudes, economic relationships, or human interaction . . . " (1974:7). Third, the sociology of law is the theoretical base for a new science of legal policy. Fourth, the sociology of law includes, within its domain, the responsibility for making definitive theoretical statements about the law.

Podgorecki argues that the Marxist theory of state and law cannot really provide a good explanation of how law functions in society. He advocates research into the social reality of law to overcome the myth "that existing law is efficient merely because it exists" (1974:24). He contends that the aim of a realist legal theory is to reveal:

> as fully as possible the conditions for the efficiency of the working of law; it must be disclosed how the existing law interacts with various social and economic factors, enhancing or impeding or even sometimes losing, its own effectiveness in the process (Podgorecki, 1974:24–25).

Traditional speculative jurisprudence is limited as a legal science by its allegiance to the state and law theory and by the absence of a satisfactory means of verification. In contrast, an empirical sociology of law can provide a theoretical base for scientific legal policy and expert advice for social engineering. Podgorecki (1974:47) concludes that the sociology of law "in its mature version, would be an empirical replacement of jurisprudence."

Podgorecki rejects judicial definitions of legal norms and seeks a "synthetic" definition based on the generalization of data generated from sociological experience by which to examine the distinguishing features of legal, moral, and other social norms. He contends that between a law and the type of behavior it aims to regulate, three variables enter to produce the final behavioral result, that is, the acceptance of a law: (1) the type of socioeconomic system into which the law fits; (2) the subculture which characterizes that part of the system into which the law enters (linking the demands of law with the characteristic behavior of those bound by it); and (3) the types of individual personalities of those in the social system. He points out that law is accepted for several reasons: as a matter of principle, as a means to obtain personal or social objectives, or as an authoritarian device. Podgorecki states:

> if law is accepted as a matter of principle the view is that it has an autonomous value; if law is generally accepted by well-adjusted people the idea is that law can be an effective means of controlling others, as well as oneself; obedience to law expressed by respect for superiors is the attitude of people with authoritarian propensities, who are apt to be afraid of power or, to release anxiety, are likely to identify themselves with power (1974:208).

Podgorecki then raises questions about the effectiveness of law as a regulator of social behavior and the factors that determine the relationships legal prescription and conduct. He finds, not surprisingly, that new laws, enjoying substantial preexistent support in the informal normative patterns of the population, are likely to be effective with a minimum of dysfunctional and unintended consequences. But he firmly believes that law can lead as well as follow. He finds that new laws designed to regulate behavior for efficiency's sake carry with them a sense of moral obligation. Podgorecki is committed to the use of law for social engineering. For him, legal policy provides the principles of effective legislation for directing social change, while sociology has the complementary task of providing the theoretical ground for legal policy.

The major value of Podgorecki's contribution can be identified as the unification of diverse concepts in the study of law and society, the useful applications of sociological concepts to social policy, and the use of law as a means of social engineering once sufficient scientific knowledge about its operation has been gained. Podgorecki's ideas, however, have limited impact on Western European theorists of law and society. Klaus A. Ziegert (1977:175–176) attributes this lack of impact to three factors. First, the ideological significance of the relationship between law and society in the West is less problematic than in the East, and as a result, socio-technical (social engineering) matters concerning legal policy in the context of law and society are unusual and marginal. Second, Western sociologists are primarily preoccupied with the democratization of the law, which is quite different from Podgorecki's concern with the acceptance of law. Third, Podgorecki's approach to law does not seem to be adequate for a full understanding of the relationship between law and society.

CURRENT TRENDS IN THE STUDY
OF LAW IN SOCIETY

As I have shown in Chapter One, sociological discussions of the role of law in society generally take place in the context of two ideal conceptions of society: the integration-consensus and conflict-coercion perspectives. The integration-consensus perspective is grounded in the functionalist approach, and the conflict-coercion perspective in the conflict and Marxist approaches to the study of law in society. These are the two prevailing approaches in the sociological literature. Most sociologists opt for either a version of the functionalist or the conflict and Marxist approaches to law and the legal system.

Functional analysis examines social phenomena in terms of their consequences for the broader society. Proponents of this approach ask specific questions such as: What does a kinship system do for society? What does law do for society? What are the "functions" of government, of social classes, or of any social phenomenon? In the context of the analysis of law, functionalists are concerned with the identification of the characteristics of legal phenomena, as well as indicating how legal institutions fit into the workings of the overall structure. Theorists embracing conflict and Marxist approaches emphasize the structuring of economic relations which provide, for them, the foundation for various specific studies of legal trends. I shall now consider these two approaches in some detail.

The Functionalist Approach   "Functionalism is," writes Robert A. Nisbet (1969:228), "without any doubt, the single most significant body of theory in the social sciences in the present century. It is often thought to be essentially a theory of order, of stability, of how society is possible." Historically, functionalism was brought into sociology by borrowing directly, and developing analogies for, concepts in the biological sciences. Biology, since the middle of the nineteenth century, frequently referred to the "structure" of an organism, meaning a relatively stable arrangement of relationships between the different cells, and to the "function" of the organism which considered the consequences of the activity of the various organs in the life process. The principal consideration of this organic analogy was how each part of the organism contributed to the survival and maintenance of the whole.

Sociologists distinguish between the manifest and latent functions (Merton, 1957:19–84). Manifest functions are those that are built into a social system by design. They are well understood by group members. Latent functions are, by contrast, unintentional and often unrecognized. They are unanticipated consequences of the system that have been set up to achieve other ends. For example, the minimum wage law was enacted to provide unskilled laborers with an income slightly above poverty level. Unintentionally, however, this law contributed to the increase in teenage unemployment, particularly among black youths (Herbers, 1979), and reduced job prospects of low wage earners. When the minimum wage increased, employers tended to hire more part-time than full-time workers, and the overall level of hiring was lower.

The basic tenets of functionalism are summarized in the following key assumptions (Van der Berghe, 1967:294–295):

1. Societies must be analyzed "holistically as systems of interrelated parts."
2. Cause and effect relations are "multiple and reciprocal."
3. Social systems are in a state of "dynamic equilibrium," such that adjustment to forces affecting the system is made with minimal change within the system.
4. Perfect integration is never attained, so that every social system has strains and deviations, but the latter tend to be neutralized through institutionalization.
5. Change is fundamentally a slow adoptive process, rather than a revolutionary shift.
6. Change is the consequence of the adjustment of changes outside the system, growth by differentiation, and internal innovations.
7. The system is integrated through shared values.

In sociology, functional analysis is as old as the discipline. Comte, Spencer, Durkheim, Malinowski, Radcliffe-Browne, Merton, and Parsons, to name a few, have engaged in the functional analysis of the social world (Turner and Maryanski, 1979:XI).

Ever since the classical sociological theorist Emile Durkheim postulated the notion that deviance could serve certain social functions in a society, sociologists have looked for evidence to support this contention.

Durkheim had in mind the idea that a society needed deviance in order to continually reaffirm its boundaries of propriety. Functional arguments for the importance of deviance are intriguing. They provide a novel way of showing how certain institutions in a society, if not the society itself, continue to operate. Durkheim points out, for example, that without the existence of sinners, a church could not exist. Their very existence provides the opportunity for believers to reaffirm the faith that has been offended by the sinner. Thus, the worst thing that could happen to a church is to completely eliminate sin from the world and completely propagate the faith to society.

Functionalism is also present in legal anthropology. For example, in *The Cheyenne Way*, Karl N. Llewellyn and E. Adamson Hoebel (1941) outline their law-job theory about society as a whole. For societies to survive there are certain basic needs that must be met. It is within this context that the wants and desires of individuals, their "divisive urges," assert themselves. The conflicts produced are unavoidable, but at the same time, essential to group survival. "The law-jobs entail such arrangement and adjustment of people's behaviour that the society (or the group) remains a society (or a group) and gets enough energy unleashed and coordinated to keep on functioning as a society (or as a group)" (1941:291). They consider the law-jobs as universal, applicable, and necessary to all groups and to all societies.

Functionalism is also evident in other writers. For example, in Jerome Frank's (1930) *Law and the Modern Mind,* the entire discussion of the "basic legal myth" and the associated "legal magic" is grounded in terms of an examination of their functional consequences for the legal system. Similarly, Thurman Arnold's (1935) concern with the role of symbolism within legal institutions is consciously functionalist. Felix Cohen (1959) resorts also to functional analysis in his elaboration of "functional jurisprudence." More recently, the writing of Lon Fuller (1969) on law morality, Julius Stone's *Law and the Social Sciences* (1966), and Philippe Nonet's (1976) ideas on jurisprudential sociology are illustrative of the functionalist approach to the study of law and society.

Almost from the beginning, however, the functionalist approach was attacked for both alleged theoretical shortcomings and on ideological grounds. Criticisms included complaints that the whole notion of function is oversimplified. Questions such as: "Functional for whom?" were raised, and not without grounds, for the interests and needs of different groups in a society are often in conflict. What may be functional for one group may be dysfunctional for another. Others argue that functional analysis is a static, anti-historical mode of analysis with a bias toward conservatism. Some sociologists even suggest that there is an implicit teleology in functional analysis, in that this mode of analysis inappropriately attributes purposes to social institutions as if they were conscious beings. As expected, a sizable amount of literature in the field has been devoted to both formulating and refuting these charges (see, for example, Turner and Maryanski, 1979). In spite of these criticisms, Rich points out: "It can be concluded that most sociology of law theorists are adherents to structural-functionalist theory" (1978:153).

Conflict and Marxist Approaches   Conflict and Marxist approaches are based on the assumption that social behavior can best be understood in terms of tension and conflict between groups and individuals. Proponents of these approaches suggest that society is an arena in which struggles over scarce commodities take place. Closely intertwined with the idea of conflict in society is the Marxian notion of *economic determinism.* Economic organization, especially the ownership of property, determines the organization of the rest of society. The class structure and institutional arrangements, as well as cultural values, beliefs, religious dogmas, are ultimately a reflection of the economic organization of a society.

According to Marx, law and the legal system are designed to regulate and preserve capitalist relations. For the Marxists, law is a method of domination and social control used by the ruling classes. Law protects the interests of those in power and serves to maintain distinctions between the dominated and domineering classes. Consequently, law is seen as a set of rules which arise as a result of the struggle between the ruling class and those who are ruled. The state, which is the organized reflection of the interests of the ruling class, passes laws which serve the interests of this class.

This breakdown of society into two classes—a ruling class that owns the means of production and a subservient class that works for wages—*inevitably* leads to conflict. Once conflict becomes manifest in the form of riots or rebellions, the state, acting in the interest of the ruling class, will develop laws aimed at controlling acts which threaten the interests of the status quo. As capitalism develops and conflict between social classes becomes more frequent, more acts will be defined as criminal.

It is not surprising, therefore, that many sociologists interested in law, and in particular, criminal law, have espoused this perspective. The conflict view of criminal law is most noticeable in the recent writings of Marxist criminologists. Quinney (1974a), for example, argues that law in capitalist society gives political recognition to powerful social and economic interests. The legal system provides the mechanism for the forceful control of the majority in society. The state and the legal system reflect and serve the needs of the ruling class. In *The Critique of Legal Order,* Quinney (1974b:16) argues that as capitalist society is further threatened, criminal law is increasingly used in the attempt to maintain domestic order. The underclass will continue to be the object of criminal law as the dominant class seeks to perpetuate itself. To remove the oppression, to eliminate the need for further reward, would necessarily mean the end of that class and its capitalist economy.

Similarly, William Chambliss and Robert Seidman take a conflict approach in their analysis of law. While emphasizing conflicting interests in society, they argue that "The state becomes a weapon of a particular class. Law emanates from the state. Law in a society of classes must therefore represent and advance the interests of one class or the other" (1982:72–73). For them, law is an instrument sought after and employed by powerful interest groups in society. Chambliss (1978:149) further reinforces the notion of law as an instrument of the powerful in society by specifically pointing out that "Acts are defined as criminal because it is in the interests of the ruling class to so define them." Austin Turk (1978) also sees law as "a weapon in social conflict," an instrument of social order that serves those who are in power. The control of legal order represents the ability to use the state's coercive authority to protect one's interests. The control of the legal process further means the control of the organization of governmental decisions and the workings of the law which diverts attention from more deeply rooted problems of power distribution and interest maintenance. Reasons (1974:103–104) considers crime as a phenomenon created by special interests who, with their definition of rectitude, create the laws of society.

Conflict theorists point out that most of the American criminal law comes directly from English common law. C. Ray Jeffery (1957) contends that acts such as murder, theft, trespassing, and robbery, problems that were once resolved in the kinship group, became crimes against the state when Henry II, King of England, centralized political power and declared them wrongs against the crown. Jerome Hall (1952) traces the growth of property and theft laws to the emergence of commerce and industrialization. With the advent of commerce and trade, a new economic class of traders and industrialists emerged, and the need to protect their business interests grew. New laws were established, as a result, to protect the interests and economic well-being of the emergent class. These laws included the creation of embezzlement laws and laws governing stolen property and obtaining goods under false pretense. According to conflict theorists, notions of crime have their origins less in general ideas about right or wrong than in perceived threats to groups with the power to protect their interests through law.

Critics have not been kind to this type of argumentation, holding that it involves enormous simplification, reification, and absence of sensitivity to the complexity of social interaction (Manning, 1975:12). There are many who concede the validity of conflict and interest-group arguments, but who, at the same time, contend that bold assertions about the "ruling class" conceal more than they reveal. Surely, lawmaking phenomena are more complex than implied in these statements that hint at a monolithic ruling class which determines legislative behavior and the creation of rules. In spite of these and other criticisms, Marxism exists in contemporary sociological theorizing and "must exist—because alienation exists. Alienation refers to the way in which human beings under capitalism do not control their work, but instead are dominated by their work and by the requirements of the profit-system" (Aggar, 1979:1). Elements of the Marxist approach enter into a number of sociological studies on law and society and are influential on epistemological, methodological, and theoretical approaches, as evidenced, for example, in the works of Charles E. Reasons and Robert M. Rich (1978) who present the major paradigms in the sociology of law with a particular emphasis on conflict and Marxist approaches.

Another significant current trend in the study of law and society is the critical legal studies movement (Unger, 1983). It is widely considered, by critics and followers alike, to comprise some of the most exciting socio-legal scholarship around and one sociologist of law described it as being "where the action is" (Trubek, 1984). The movement began with a group of junior faculty members and law students at Yale in the late 1960s who have since moved to other places. In 1977, the group organized itself into the Conference of Critical Legal Studies, which has over 400 members, and holds an annual conference which draws more than a thousand participants.

The movement has been greatly influenced by Marxist inspired European theorists and its roots can be traced back to American legal realism (Tomasic, 1985:18). Legal realists in the 1920s and 1930s argued against the nineteenth century belief that the rule of law was supreme. They contended, since a good lawyer could argue convincingly either side of a given case, there was actually nothing about the law that made any judicial decision inevitable. Rather, they pointed out, the outcome of a case depended largely, if not entirely, on the predilections of the judge who happened to be deciding it. Thus, far from being a science, the realists argued, law was virtually inseparable from politics, economics, and culture. They rejected the idea that law is above politics and economics.

Proponents of the movement reject the idea that there is anything distinctly legal about legal reasoning. As with any other kind of analysis, legal reasoning, they maintain, cannot operate independently of the personal biases of lawyers or judges, or of the social context in which they are acting. Furthermore, law is so contradictory that it allows the context of a case to determine the outcome. That attribute of law—its inability to cover all situations—is called *indeterminacy* (Trubek, 1984:578). Critical scholars also reject law as being value-free and above political, economic, and social considerations. Laws only *seem* neutral and independent, even those that reflect the dominant values in society. Moreover, laws legitimize those values that predominate in society. Therefore, laws legitimate the status quo. They maintain that law is actually part of the system of power in society rather than a protection against it.

Although proponents of the movement insist that their ideas are still tentative and evolving, their attacks on law and legal training have created a good deal of criticism. The movement has been called Marxist, utopian, hostile to rules, and incoherent. Critical legal scholars have been accused of favoring violence over bargaining, that they advocate the inculcation of leftist values in legal education, and that they are preoccupied with "illegitimate hierarchies" such as the bar (Schwartz, 1984); their approach to law is "nihilistic," they teach cynicism to their students which may result in "the learning of the skills of corruption." Nihilist law teachers with a proclivity for revolution are likely to train crooks, and they have, therefore "an ethical duty to depart from law school" (Carrington, 1984:227). It is unlikely that the controversy between proponents of the movement and their critics will be settled in the foreseeable future.

SUMMARY

In this chapter an attempt has been made to trace the development of legal systems and to examine the major theorists of law and society in order to perceive the theoretical starting point and evolution of the field, and to consider the theoretical convergence and divergence of classical and contemporary theorists.

In an historical context, legal development, industrialization, urbanization, and modernization are closely intertwined. Legal development is conditioned by a series of integrative demands, stemming from society's economic, political, educational, and religious institutions. From a developmental perspective, the primitive, transitional, and modern legal systems were discussed. These three types are still present in the world's societies. Although one should be careful not to emphasize unilinear evolution, it can be inferred from the discussion that, to the extent legal change takes place in a society, it will follow more or less the pattern outlined. What distinguishes these legal systems from each other is the comparative degree of differentiation between basic legal elements. In the process of development, the once blurred elements of law, courts, legislation, and enforcement become increasingly separated from one another. Accompanying the emergence of laws, court systems, police force, and legislation, is a trend toward increasing size, complexity, differentiation, and bureaucratization.

Among the theorists discussed, there seems to be more or less a general consensus that societal and legal complexities have gone hand in hand. Beyond that, there is little agreement. Many of the European pioneers discussed reacted in various ways to the influence of natural law and attempted to account for it from an evolutionary perspective. The influential sociological theorists have recognized the essential role of legal institution in the social order and have made important explorations of the interplay involved between law and society. The socio-legal theorists were guided by social science principles in the development of their diverse perspectives on law and society. Making sense of the idea of law remains an ongoing enterprise, as evidenced by the efforts of the contemporary theorists discussed.

These efforts at explaining the interplay between law and society should be seen in the context of intellectual, political, and social climates of the particular theorists. In each historical epoch, every interpretation of social reality posits certain questions and provides certain answers. According to S. N. Eisenstadt (1972), tension is inherent in intellectual life due to the tendency to challenge the intellectual construction of social reality. If a theory of law and society is developed by one group of intellectuals, this will provide an incentive for others to view the matter in another way. Eisenstadt's insights account, in part, for the diverse explanations of the relationship between law and society and the nature, province, and function of law in society.

There are two currently widely accepted approaches to the study of law and society. Sociologists embracing the functionalist approach attempt, in various ways, to account for law in society within the overall framework of the theory that society consists of interrelated parts that work together for the purpose of maintaining internal balance. Sociologists advocating conflict and Marxist approaches to the study of law in society consider conflict inevitable and ubiquitous in societies, as a result of inescapable competition for scarce resources. They are preoccupied with debunking myths about society and advocating changes in what they regard as harmful social relations, structures, and processes that exist in today's social order. Finally, proponents of the critical legal studies movement argue that there is nothing inherently rational, scientific, or neutral about the law—nothing that would dictate the outcome of a particular case. They maintain that the law is riddled with contradiction and prejudice, and it is heavily in favor of the wealthy and powerful.

SUGGESTED FURTHER READINGS

EDGAR BODENHEIMER, *Jurisprudence, The Philosophy and Method of the Law*, rev. ed. Cambridge, MA: Harvard University Press, 1974. A review of the historical materials dealing with the development of jurisprudential thought with an emphasis on philosophical, sociological, historical, and analytical components of legal theory.

WILLIAM J. CHAMBLISS and MILTON MANKOFF (eds), *Whose Law, What Order? A Conflict Approach to Criminology*. New York: John Wiley, 1976. A good illustration of the perspectives of conflict criminologists.

WILLIAM M. EVAN, ed., *The Sociology of Law, A Social-Structural Perspective*. New York: Free Press, 1980. A handy reference for alternative theoretical approaches to the study of law in society.

LAWRENCE M. FRIEDMAN, *A History of American Law*, 2nd ed. New York: Simon & Schuster/Touchstone, 1986. A seminal work on the history and development of American law and legal system.

ALAN HUNT, *The Sociological Movement in Law*. Philadelphia: Temple University Press, 1978. A comprehensive examination of the intellectual precursors of modern sociology of law with an emphasis on Roscoe Pound, American legal realism, Emile Durkheim, and Max Weber.

ERVIN H. POLLACK, *Jurisprudence, Principles and Applications*. Columbus: Ohio State University Press, 1979. A lengthy examination of diverse legal theories and their applications. A very useful book for prelaw students and essential for law students.

CHARLES E. REASONS and ROBERT M. RICH (eds.), *The Sociology of Law: A Conflict Perspective*. Toronto: Butterworths, 1978. A compendium designed to present the major paradigms in the sociology of law with particular emphasis on conflict and Marxist approaches.

ROBERT M. RICH, *The Sociology of Law: An Introduction to Its Theorists and Theories*. Washington: University Press of America, 1978. A handy review of principal theorists under the headings of sociology of law, sociology of criminal law, sociological jurisprudence, and anthropology of law.

ROMAN TOMASIC, *The Sociology of Law*. London: Sage Publications, 1985. A compact overview of the various theoretical approaches to law and society with a bibliography of close to a thousand references.

MAX WEBER, *Law in Economy and Society*. Ed. Max Rheinstein, and (trans.) Edward Shils and Max Rheinstein, Cambridge, MA: Harvard University Press, 1954. Weber's major writings on law, rich in historical material and major theoretical formulations.

REFERENCES

AGGER, BEN. 1979. *Western Marxism: An Introduction*, Santa Monica, CA: Goodyear.

ANTALFFY, GYORGY. 1974. *Basic Problems of State and Society*. Budapest: Akademiai Kiado.

ARNOLD, THURMAN. 1935. *The Symbols of Government*. New Haven: Yale University Press.

BARBER, BERNARD. 1971. "Function, Variability, and Change in Ideological Systems." Pp. 244–262 in Bernard Barber and Alex Inkeles, eds., Stability and Social Change. Boston: Little, Brown.

BENNIS, WARREN G. 1966. *Changing Organizations*. New York: McGraw-Hill.

BLACK, DONALD. 1976. *The Behavior of Law.* New York: Academic Press.

BODENHEIMER, EDGAR. 1974. *Jurisprudence, The Philosophy and Method of the Law,* rev. ed. Cambridge, MA: Harvard University Press.

CARRINGTON, PAUL D. 1984. "Of Law and the River," Journal of Legal Education 34 (2) (June):222–236.

CHAMBLISS, WILLIAM J. 1978. "Toward a Political Economy of Crime," pp. 191–211. In Charles E. Reasons and Robert M. Rich (eds.), The Sociology of Law, A Conflict Perspective. Toronto: Butterworths.

CHAMBLISS, WILLIAM, AND ROBERT SEIDMAN. 1982. *Law, Order, and Power.* 2nd ed. Reading, MA: Addison-Wesley Publishing Company.

COHEN, FELIX. 1959. *Ethical Systems and Legal Ideals.* New York: Cornell University Press.

DIAMOND, ARTHUR S. 1971. *Primitive Law, Past and Present.* London: Methuen and Company, Ltd.

DICEY, ALBERT VENN. 1905. *Lectures on the Relation Between the Law and Public Opinion in England During the Nineteenth Century.* London: Macmillan.

DURKHEIM, EMILE. 1964. *The Division of Labor in Society.* Trans. George Simpson. New York: Free Press. Originally published in 1893.

EDER, KLAUS. 1977. "Rationalist and Normative Approaches to the Sociological Study of Law," Law and Society Review 12 (1)(Fall):133–144.

EHRLICH, EUGEN. 1975. *Fundamental Principles of the Sociology of Law.* Trans. Walter L. Moll. New York: Arno. Originally published in 1936.

EISENSTADT, S. N. 1972. "Intellectuals and Tradition," 101 (2) Daedelus:1–19.

FRANK, JEROME. 1930. *Law and the Modern Mind.* New York: Coward-McCann.

FRIEDMAN, LAWRENCE M. 1975. *The Legal System, A Social Science Perspective.* New York: Russell Sage Foundation; 1984. *American Law: An Introduction.* New York: W. W. Norton and Company.

FULLER, LON. 1969. *The Morality of Law,* rev. ed. New Haven: Yale University Press.

GALANTER, MARC. 1977. "The Modernization of Law." Pp. 1046–1060 in Lawrence M. Friedman and Stewart Macaulay, eds., Law and the Behavioral Sciences, 2nd ed. Indianapolis: Bobbs-Merrill.

GOTTFREDSON, MICHAEL R., and MICHAEL J. HINDELANG. 1979. "A Study of *The Behavior of Law,*" American Sociological Review 44 (I)(February):3–18.

GROSS, HYMAN. 1979. *A Theory of Criminal Justice.* New York: Oxford University Press.

GURVITCH, GEORGES. 1942. *Sociology of Law.* New York: Philo. Liby.

HALL, JEROME. 1952. *Theft, Law and Society.* 2nd ed. Indianapolis: The Bobbs-Merrill Company.

HERBERS, JOHN. 1979. "Changes in Society Holding Back Youth in Jobless Web," The New York Times (March 11):1 and 44.

HOEBEL, E. ADAMSON. 1954. *The Law of Primitive Man, A Study in Comparative Legal Dynamics.* Cambridge, MA: Harvard University Press.

HOLMES, OLIVER WENDELL. 1897. "The Path of Law," Harvard Law Review (10)(March):457–478.

HUNT, ALAN. 1978. *The Sociological Movement in Law.* Philadelphia: Temple University Press.

JEFFERY, C. RAY. 1957. "The Development of Crime in Early English Society." Journal of Criminal Law, Criminology and Police Science 47:647–66.

KERIMOV, D. A. 1964. "Liberty, Law, and the Legal Order," 58 Northwestern Law Review, 643–662.

LLEWELLYN, KARL N. 1949. "Law and the Social Sciences—Especially Sociology," American Sociological Review 14 (4)(August):451–462; 1962. Jurisprudence. Chicago: University of Chicago Press.

LLEWELLYN, KARL N., and E. ADAMSON HOEBEL. 1941. *The Cheyenne Way: Conflict and Case Law in Primitive Jurisprudence.* Norman: University of Oklahoma Press.

MAINE, SIR HENRY SUMNER. 1861. *Ancient Law.* London: J. Murray.

MANNING, PETER K. 1975. "Deviance and Dogma," British Journal of Criminology 15(1) (January):1–20.

MARSKE, CHARLES E., CHARLES P. KOFRON, and STEVEN VAGO. 1978. "The Significance of Natural Law in Contemporary Legal Thought," The Catholic Lawyer 24 (1)(Winter):62–76.

MARX, KARL. 1959. "A Contribution to the Critique of Political Economy." Pp. 42–46 in L. S. Feuer, ed., Marx and Engels: Basic Writing on Politics and Philosophy. Garden City, New York: Doubleday.

MARX, KARL, and FRIEDRICH ENGELS. 1955. *The Communist Manifesto.* New York: Appleton-Century-Crofts. Originally published in 1848.

MERTON, ROBERT K. 1957. *Social Theory and Social Structure.* New York: Free Press.

MICHAELS, PRISCILLA. 1978. "Review of Black's *The Behavior of Law,*" Contemporary Sociology 7 (1)(January):10–11.

MONTESQUIEU, BARON DE. 1886. *The Spirit of Laws,* Thomas Nugent, trans. Cincinnati: Robert Clarke and Co. Originally published 1748.

NISBET, ROBERT A. 1969. *Social Change and History.* New York: Oxford University Press.

NONET, PHILIPPE. 1976. "For Jurisprudential Sociology," Law and Society Review 10 (4)(Summer):525–545.

NONET, PHILIPPE, and PHILIP SELZNICK. 1978. *Law and Society in Transition, Toward Responsive Law.* New York: Octagon Books.

PARSONS, TALCOTT. 1964. "Evolutionary Universals in Society," American Sociological Review 29 (3)(June):339–357.

PEPINSKY, HAROLD E. 1976. *Crime and Conflict, A Study of Law and Society.* New York: Academic Press.

PIAGET, JEAN. 1965. *The Moral Judgment of the Child.* New York: Free Press. Originally published in 1932.

PODGORECKI, ADAM. 1974. *Law and Society.* London: Routledge and Kegan Paul.

POLLACK, ERVIN H. 1979. *Jurisprudence, Principles, and Applications.* Columbus: Ohio State University Press.

POSPISIL, LEOPOLD. 1971. *Anthropology of Law, A Comparative Theory.* New York: Harper and Row, Pub.

POUND, ROSCOE. 1942. *Social Control Through Law.* New Haven: Yale University Press; 1943. "A Survey of Social Interests," Harvard Law Review (57):1–39; 1959. *Jurisprudence.* St. Paul, MN: West Publishing Company, vol. 1 and 2.

QUINNEY, RICHARD. 1974a. *Criminal Justice in America.* Boston: Little, Brown; 1974b. *The Critique of Legal Order.* Boston: Little, Brown.

REASONS, CHARLES E. 1974. *The Criminologist: Crime and the Criminal.* Pacific Palisades, CA: Goodyear.

REASONS, CHARLES E., and ROBERT M. RICH, eds. 1978. *The Sociology of Law, A Conflict Perspective.* Toronto: Butterworths.

RICH, ROBERT M. 1978. *The Sociology of Law: An Introduction to Theorists and Theories.* Washington, DC: University Press of America.

ROSTOW, WALT W. 1952. *The Dynamics of Soviet Society.* New York: W. W. Norton & Co., Inc.; 1961. *Stages of Economic Growth, A Noncommunist Manifesto.* London: Cambridge University Press.

SAVIGNY, FRIEDRICH KARL. 1975. "Of the Vocation of Our Age for Legislation and Jurisprudence." Trans. A. Haward. New York: Arno. Originally published in 1831.

SCHWARTZ, BERNARD. 1974. *The Law in America, A History.* New York: McGraw-Hill.

SCHWARTZ, LOUIS B. 1984. "With Gun and Camera Through Darkest CLS-Land." Stanford Law Review 36 (1 & 2)(January):413–464.

SCHWARTZ, RICHARD D., and JAMES C. MILLER. 1975. "Legal Evolution and Societal Complexity." Pp. 52–62 in Ronald L. Akers and Richard Hawkins, eds., Law and Control in Society. Englewood Cliffs, NJ: Prentice-Hall.

SELZNICK, PHILIP. 1961. "Sociology and Narural Law," 6 Natural Law Forum:84–108.

SHERMAN, LAWRENCE W. 1978. "Review of *The Behavior of Law,*" Contemporary Sociology 7 (1)(January):10–15.

SPENCER, HERBERT. 1899. *The Principles of Sociology* (II). New York: D. Appleton and Company.

STONE, JULIUS. 1966. *Social Dimensions of Law and Justice.* Stanford, CA: Stanford University Press.

SUMNER, WILLIAM GRAHAM. 1940. "The Challenge of Facts." Pp. 67–93 in Maurice R. Davie, ed., Sumner Today. New Haven: Yale University Press. Originally published in 1886.

TANGLEY, LORD. 1965. *New Law for a New World.* London: Stephens and Sons.

TOMASIC, ROMAN. 1985. *The Sociology of Law.* London: Sage Publications.

TRUBEK, DAVID M. 1984. "Where the Action Is: CLS and Empiricism," Stanford Law Review 36 (1 & 2)(January):575–622.

TURK, AUSTIN T. 1978. "Law as a Weapon in Social Conflict." Pp. 213–232 in Charles E. Reasons and Robert M. Rich, eds., The Sociology of Law: A Conflict Perspective. Toronto: Butterworths.

TURNER, JONATHAN H. 1972. *Patterns of Social Organization, a Survey of Social Institutions.* New York: McGraw-Hill; 1974. "A Cibernetic Model of Legal Development," Western Sociological Review (5):3–16.

TURNER, JONATHAN H., and ALEXANDRA MARYANSKI. 1979. *Functionalism.* Menlo Park, CA: The Benjamin/Cummings Publishing Company.

UNGER, ROBERTO MANGABEIRA. 1976. *Law in Modern Society, Toward a Criticism of Social Theory.* New York: Free Press; 1983. "The Critical Legal Studies Movement," Harvard Law Review 96 (3)(January):561–675.

VAN DEN BERGHE, PIERRE L. 1967. "Dialectic and Functionalism: Toward a Synthesis." Pp. 294–310 in N. Demerath and R. A. Peterson, eds., System Changer and Conflict: A Reader on Contemporary Sociological Theory and the Debate Over Functionalism. New York: Free Press.

WEBER, MAX. 1954. *Law in Economy and Society,* ed. Max Rheinstein and trans. Edward Shils, and Max Rheinstein. Cambridge, MA: Harvard University Press; 1968. *Economy and Society.* Trans. Guenther Roth, and Claus Wittich. New York: Bedminster Press.

WORMSER, RENE. 1962. *The Story of Law,* rev. ed. New York: Simon and Schuster.

ZIEGERT, KLAUS A. 1977. "Adam Podgorecki's Sociology of Law: The Invisible Factors of the Functioning of Law Made Visible," Law and Society Review 12 (1)(Fall):151–180.

3

The Organization
of Law in Society

Modern societies require law and legal systems capable of establishing and maintaining order, settling disputes and conflict, granting legitimacy to policies, and adopting existing rules of society to new social conditions. In one way or another, law touches everybody in society. The contact may be pleasant or unpleasant, tangible or intangible, direct or indirect, but is nonetheless a constant force in our lives. For a sociological understanding of law in society, we need to know about the social organization of law, the types of social arrangements and relations involved in the legal process, and the social characteristics of people who interpret and administer the law. Thus, the purpose of this chapter is to examine the social organization of legal systems in terms of the judicial, legislative, administrative, and enforcement agencies that carry out the official (and at times the unofficial) business of law.

COURTS

A primary function of courts is to process disputes. By definition, a dispute is a conflict of claims or rights—an assertion of right, claim, or demand on one side, met by contrary claims on the other. When courts hear disputes, they attempt to decide (adjudicate) between or among those who have some disagreement, misunderstanding, or competing claims. Such disputes may arise between individuals, between organizations (private or governmental), or between an individual and an organization. Jones may sue Smith to recover damages caused by a traffic accident; acting under the provisions of a civil rights statute, the federal government may sue the state of Mississippi to force its officials to stop discriminating against blacks in the electoral process; the state of Missouri may charge Doe with burglary and bring him to court to answer the charge. When a judge renders the official judgment of the trial court in a civil or criminal case as to the defendant's guilt or innocence, the process is called *adjudication.*

Unlike legislative and administrative bodies, courts do not place issues on their own agendas. Judges generally do not decide to make rulings about voting rights, racial discrimination, or abortion, and then announce their "decisions." Rather, courts are passive; they must wait until matters are brought to them for resolution. The passivity of courts places the burden on citizens or organizations to recognize and define their own needs and problems and to determine which require legal judgments. As Donald Black (1973:138) notes, this method of acquiring cases " . . . assumes that each individual will voluntarily and rationally pursue his own interests. . . . " Obviously the courts are indifferent to those issues or disputes that individuals or organizations fail to notice or wish to ignore. This reactive nature of courts insures that they consider disputes only after the injuries have taken place or the problems have developed.

In theory, courts differ from other kinds of dispute regulation methods in that they are available to all members of society. In principle, everyone who has a dispute for which there is a legal redress ought to be able to use the courts. Unlike other dispute settlement methods that are available only to specific groups in society (for example, college grievance committees or religious tribunals), courts are truly public. Judicial resolution of disputes entails both the application of legal knowledge and the interpretation of events. The role of courts is to interpret and to apply law. Such judicial interpretation of law is expected to be impartial. Judges are expected to be governed by legal principles, not by personal preferences or by political pragmatism.

Dispute Categories

The dispute processing function of American courts, which will be discussed in detail in Chapter Six, is on the increase. To understand what courts do it is necessary to examine the kinds of disputes they process. Sheldon Goldman and Austin Sarat (1978:6) suggest that there are three important categories of disputes that provide the bulk of work of American courts. The first is called the *private-initiated dispute.* This kind of dispute is characterized by the absence of any initial participation by public authorities. For example, when a husband and wife quarrel, when two businesspersons debate the terms of a contract, when two automobiles collide, these events are likely to give rise to private disputes. Although they may occur in public places and may involve competing interpretations of law, they remain private as long as the government is not a party. Since these disputes arise more or less spontaneously in the course of normal social life, they are usually processed and managed without the intervention of government. Many of these private disputes can be dealt with in the general context of ongoing relationships, or through some kind of bargaining and

negotiation. For example, the husband and wife may seek marriage counseling, the businessperson may arrive at a compromise through negotiation, and a settlement may be reached for the car accident through an insurance company. At times, however, nonlegal intervention is insufficient
for the disputing parties, and the courts may be asked to settle disputes in
a large variety of civil cases where a party seeks legal redress in a private
interest, such as for a breach of contract or the use of a copyrighted story
without permission.

The second category of disputes is called the *public-initiated dispute*. It
occurs when the government seeks to enforce norms of conduct or to punish individuals who breach such norms. These kinds of public disputes
emerge when society attempts to control and channel social behavior
through the promulgation of binding legal norms. A good illustration of
the public-initiated dispute is the ordinary criminal case in which the state,
or some official acting on its behalf, seeks to use the courts to determine
whether a particular breach of law has occurred and whether sanctions
should be applied. It is unique because it always involves and is governed
by the law of the entire community. In the case of criminal law violation,
dispute processing must occur in a public forum, for no society could allow
the development of private mechanisms for the enforcement of breaches
of public norms, since it could easily lead to anarchy. It should be noted,
however, that not all public-initiated disputes are resolved or processed by
means of judicial action. A variety of informal mechanisms ranging from
the warnings that a police officer may give to a traffic violator, to the prosecutor's choice not to go ahead with a criminal case, to the practice of plea
bargaining, may be used to deal with breaches of public norms (Eisenstein
and Jacob, 1977). Furthermore, disputes involving the breach of public
norms are, at times, not called to the attention of public authorities. For
instance, the husband who beats his wife may have committed a violation
of public norms, but until a complaint is lodged with law enforcement agencies, their dispute remains private.

The third kind of dispute is referred to as the *public defendant dispute*.
In this kind of dispute, the government participates as a defendant. Disputes of this nature involve challenges to the authority of some government agency, or questions about the propriety of some government action
which may be initiated by an individual or by an organization. In such
cases, the courts are called upon to review the action of other branches of
government. They involve claims that the government has not abided by
its own rules or followed procedures that it has prescribed. For instance,
parents of children in racially segregated public schools might claim that
school officials violated the constitution's guarantee of equal protection of
the laws. In general, such disputes come to court only after the aggrieved
party has failed to remedy his or her grievance either through the political
process or through procedures provided by the offending government
agency.

These three types of disputes—private-initiated, public-initiated, and
public defendant—represent, for the most part, the work load of American
courts. It should be noted that, contrary to widespread beliefs, courts, in

general, process rather than solve disputes. A court decision is seldom the last word in a dispute. For example, after a divorce decree, the aggrieving parties may continue to argue, not about settlements but about, for instance, visiting rights. Similarly, in some northern cities, court-ordered desegregation did not resolve the issue of where children should go to school, not to mention the more enduring racial issues. Thus, it should be remembered that whether the disputes involve only two individuals who bring the case to court or whether cases have broader ramifications, court decisions are seldom the final word in a dispute. Let us now consider the structure of courts where decisions are rendered.

The Organization of Courts

The American court system is characterized by dual hierarchies. There are both state and federal courts operating side by side (see Figure 3-1). The structure is decentralized. Throughout American history, courts have been considered the third branch of government. Since they do not have an independent constitutional or political base, courts depend on the same political processes that sustain legislative and executive institutions. Each of the fifty states of the United States has its own court system, and, in addition, there is the federal court system. No two state court systems are alike; indeed, the differences both in the functions and the labels given to American courts are many and bewildering, and no generalization is absolutely reliable for all states. Court systems have rarely been the product of long range planning. Nearly all represent a series of patchwork accommodations to changing needs.

Although the organization and the structure of state courts systems vary widely, in most states there are: (1) trial courts (commonly called district courts), where most civil and criminal cases are originally heard, often before a jury; (2) intermediate courts of appeals which primarily review cases decided at the trial court level; and (3) a court of last resort (commonly called a state supreme court), whose major function is reviewing cases decided by the lower appeals courts.

The basis structure of the federal court system follows the same general format. There are federal district or trial courts, federal courts of appeal, and a single U.S. Supreme Court. In addition, there are special federal courts, such as territorial courts, the Court of Customs and Patent Appeals, and the Court of Military Appeals, all of whose decisions are subject to possible reversal by the U.S. Supreme Court.

Federal and state court systems are separate from each other. Most of the nation's legal business is settled in state courts under the provision of state law. However, state court decisions which involve a "federal question," that is, which present a question involving the Constitution (such as free speech), or federal laws (such as racial or sexual discrimination), may be appealed to the U.S. Supreme Court.

The federal district courts carry most of the work load of the federal courts. At least one court of this type exists in every state. A single judge usually presides over trials in the district courts. Juries are used in about

Federal Judicial System

State Judicial System

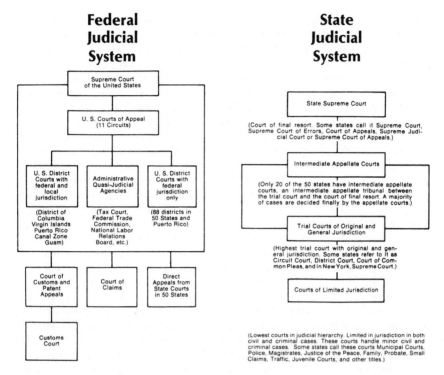

FIGURE 3-1   Court systems. *Source:* The Supreme Court: Justice and the Law (Washington, DC., Congressional Quarterly, 2nd ed., 1977), p. 18.

half of the approximately 600,000 criminal and civil cases decided each year by these courts.

In the hierarchy of the federal judiciary, the several courts of appeals are immediately above the district courts. The nation is divided into eleven geographically defined jurisdictions, called "circuits." There is a court of appeals with a panel of three judges in each circuit. The chief function of these courts is to review decisions made by the district courts within their jurisdictions. They are also empowered to review the decisions of federal regulatory agencies, such as the Federal Trade Commission.

Thus, the typical court case begins in a trial court in the state or federal court system. Most cases go no further than the trial court. For example, the criminal defendant is convicted (by a trial or by a guilty plea) and sentenced by the court, and his or her case ends. The personal injury suit ends in a judgment by a trial court (or an out-of-court settlement by the parties while the court suit is pending), and the disputants leave the court system. Some litigants, however, who are not fully satisfied with the decision of a trial court may, by right, file an appeal. An appeal may take one of two forms: a trial *de novo* (a new trial), or a more limited review of specific aspects of a trial proceeding. For example, a criminal defendant believes that his or her conviction was based on errors by the trial judge (such as the admission of evidence that ought to have been excluded) and seeks a new trial. In other instances, a litigant may seek a review of certain aspects of the trial based on procedural grounds. Most states have only one appellate court, usually known as the supreme court. This court hears appeals from all trial court decisions, criminal and civil, except those of minor courts. In a few states, however, the volume of appeals is so great that one or more intermediate appellate courts have been established to hear appeals in less important cases. Otherwise, the single appellate court has been subdivided into several "divisions" which hear appeals as if they were separate courts. If the case began in the federal district court, the appeal goes to the circuit court of appeals for that geographic area. Supreme courts make the final decision in court cases. State supreme courts render the final decision for all cases involving state law. The U.S. Supreme Court renders the final verdict on all matters involving federal law or the federal constitution.

In general, as disputes move from the trial to the appellate level, they are typically transformed. They become almost exclusively disputes about law or about procedures; issues of law, or questions concerning the way the trial was conducted are argued in appellate courts. Usually, the facts produced by the trial proceedings are not disputed at the appellate level. Time allotted for oral arguments before appellate courts is limited. Disputes are primarily conducted through briefs, motions, and memoranda. In a sense, what all this means is that disputes in appellate courts are a "lawyers' game." While in trial courts decisions are rendered by a single judge or shared by a judge and jury, in appellate courts the decision-making process involves only judges. Some appellate courts have only a single judge, while most have several judges. Disputing in appellate courts is far removed in time and substance from the events that gave rise to the original disagreement. The original parties, their dispute, and its specific resolution become less important than the legal context into which they are placed.

Participants in Court Processes

Courts, as dispute processing institutions, are composed of four distinct groups of participants—litigants, lawyers, judges, and juries. These participants in turn bring to the judicial process diverse interests, values, and perspectives that influence the ways in which disputes are processed. I shall discuss these different types of participants separately.

Litigants   Since the principal function of courts is to process disputes, the most obvious participants must be the disputants. This group includes individuals, organizations, and government officials who are trying to settle disagreements and to regulate their own behavior and the behavior of others. Clearly, not all individuals, groups, or organizations can resort or are willing to resort to courts in their attempts to settle disputes. Questions of cost, efficiency, availability, the fulfillment of the legal requirements of a suit, and the nature of the dispute affect differently the potential users of courts. Consequently, two distinct types of litigants emerge.

Marc Galanter (1974) designates the two types of litigants as "one-shotters" and "repeat players." They are distinguished by the relative frequency with which they resort to court services. As will be shown in Chapter Six, those who use the courts only occasionally are called one-shotters. Illustrations of one-shotters would include an author suing his publisher for breach of contract, or a female professor filing charges against her university for alleged sexual discrimination in promotion. Repeat players are those who engage in many similar litigations over a period of time. While one-shotters are usually individuals, repeat players are organizations, such as finance companies, the Internal Revenue Service, or insurance companies. Their investment and interest in a particular case is moderately small. Because of their high frequency of participation in litigation, repeat-players are more concerned with the ways a decision may affect the disposition of other similar cases in the future than with the outcome of a single case (Ross, 1970). Repeat-players can also invest greater resources in litigation than one-shotters, and their frequent appearances in court enable them to develop expertise. Such expertise is reflected in the way in which they select cases for litigation and in the manner in which they carry on disputes that have been transformed into lawsuits.

By contrast, participants who have only a one-time interest in litigation are generally more concerned with the substantive result of their case than the way in which the outcome may in the future affect the disposition of other cases. For example, the author in the above illustration is more concerned with winning his case against the publisher than with setting a precedent for similar cases. The IRS, on the other hand, is more interested in maintaining specific rules (such as those governing charitable deductions) than with winning one particular case. Organizations in general participate in litigation as plaintiffs, and individuals participate as defendants. Both governmental and nongovernmental organizations have greater access to resources, and they are the most frequent initiators of court cases to process disputes between themselves and private individuals with whom they are dealing.

Lawyers   The operation of courts is based on special standards and rules established by law. The process of identifying and applying rules requires special training and expertise, which is provided by members of the legal profession. Lawyers occupy an intermediary position between disputants and courts and transform litigants' complaints into legal disputes. Disputants generally need to retain the services of qualified lawyers to receive advice about legal rules and how they apply to specific issues in dispute. By being familiar with both court operations and legal rules, lawyers are instrumental in determining whether or not a particular dispute warrants judicial intervention.

Lawyers are repeat players in the adjudication process. Only a small proportion of lawyers are involved in actual litigation. Most are concerned with specific nontrial activities, such as writing wills or carrying out routine transactions. As will be discussed in Chapter Eight, some of the trial attorneys specialize in particular areas of the law (such as divorce or criminal law), while others represent only particular kinds of clients (such as corporations or universities), or limit themselves to particular clients within specifical areas of law (such as taxes). Jonathan Casper (1972) distinguishes among types of trial lawyers by the manner in which they perceive their clientele. He argues that a small number of attorneys view themselves principally as representatives of public interests. These attorneys are concerned, for example, with consumer interests or with the protection of the environment. For them, individual cases are simply vehicles for achieving broad public objectives that generally necessitate major changes in the law. They prefer to take only cases they believe involve major issues. The second type of lawyer represents particular interests or organizations. For example, some companies have their in-house lawyers whose principal role is to represent members of the organization.

The third type of lawyer, typically criminal defense lawyers, are most often involved in actual court work and, therefore, will be considered in greater detail. They are legal specialists who most closely approximate the public's preconception of lawyers. These lawyers handle a broad range of felonies and misdemeanors with only a rare petty offense, traffic, or personal injury case (Wice, 1978:29–30). While the role of defense lawyers is most often couched in the general term of "defending a client," they perform a number of specific roles. These include the roles of advocate, intermediary, and counselor (Cohn, 1976:261). In the primary role of *advocate*, defense lawyers take all possible steps within legal and ethical bounds to achieve a victory for the client, while protecting the rights of the client at each step of the criminal justice process. Often, this can best be accomplished by acting as an *intermediary* between the client and law, working through negotiation and compromise to secure the best possible benefits from the system. The third role is that of *counselor*. It is the responsibility of defense to give advice to the client as to what to expect and what appears to be in the client's best interest. Although most people would agree that defense attorneys should perform the above functions, it is often suggested that they fail to do so. For example, Abraham S. Blumberg echoes some of the prevailing criticisms of defense lawyers. He argues that:

> The real key to understanding the role of defense counsel in a criminal case is the fixing and collection of his fee. It is a problem which influences to a significant degree the criminal court process itself, not just the relationship of the lawyer and his client. In essence, a lawyer-client "confidence game" is played (Blumberg, 1979:242).

Blumberg charges that defense lawyers make sure that the clients know that there is an important connection between fee payment and the zealous exercise of professional expertise, secret knowledge, and organizational "connections" in their behalf. He contends that defense lawyers manipulate their clients and stage-manage cases to at least offer the appearance of services. He calls the criminal lawyer a "double agent" because the main concern is to maintain good relations with members of the court organization. The defense lawyer may give the impression of being an impartial professional who will do everything possible for the client; however, he or she is, in reality, dependent on the goodwill of the prosecutor and the court.

The fourth type of trial lawyers perceive their role primarily as serving individuals who retain them. They are often referred to as "hired guns" (Blumberg, 1979:238). These lawyers are interested only in the case in which they are involved, and they will do everything within legal and ethical limits to insure favorable outcomes for their clients. In their view, they serve a case, not a cause. These different types of lawyers behave differently in advising clients whether to litigate and in preparing strategies of litigation.

Judges   Although a variety of officials work around courtrooms, none has the prestige of the judge, who is responsible for the administration of the court and its reputation for honesty and impartiality. The courtroom is designed so that attention is focused on the judge, who sits on a pedestal above the other participants. Any visitor to a courtroom will notice that the visitor's gallery never rises above the judge and that those who work in the courtroom are not allowed to sit or stand at the judge's level. The judge is the only official in the courtroom who wears special attire—a robe. When the judge enters the courtroom, everyone rises, and all attention is directed at him or her. The judge is addressed as "Your Honor," regardless of individual predilections (Jacob, 1984:10). The judge alone interprets the rules that govern the proceeding, although this power may be shared with a jury of laypersons.

In addition to the basic adjudication functions and the control of the flow of litigation in the courtroom, the judge is also responsible for administering his or her own court. This entails a variety of "housekeeping" tasks, such as appointing clerical assistants, drawing up a budget, and making certain that the physical facilities are adequate for the court's operation. The judge is also instrumental in pretrial conferences and, by law, has a great deal of discretionary power (such as jury instruction on admission of evidence), which has important implications on the outcome of cases. Because of this prestigious role, the judge also performs a variety of nonjudicial functions, such as appointing officials to public agencies (such as the Board of Education, district attorneys in some states, and at times lucrative patronage positions).

Judges come from the middle or upper classes and have a history of party identification, if not activism (Schmidhauser, 1979:49–55). Federal court judges are nominated by the President and confirmed by a majority vote in the U.S. Senate. These federal judges hold office for life, subject only to removal by impeachment and conviction of a major crime. State and local judges are chosen by a variety of methods: some are elected, some are appointed, and some are chosen by a method that combines both election and appointment. In the combined election and appointment system, judges are appointed by an executive (such as a governor), and after completing a term in office, they must secure voter support to serve further terms. This type of system also has a selection procedure in which the executive's choice for a judgeship is screened through a commission or limited to nominees made by a commission. When elected, the majority of judges at the state level serve for a limited period, such as a six-year term.

Almost all judges are lawyers in the United States, but only a small fraction of lawyers are, or ever become, judges (Friedman, 1984:64). By contrast, in civil law countries such as France or Italy, judges are civil servants and have different training and experience than practicing lawyers. Those who aspire to become judge take a competitive examination after law school. The ones who pass will become judges with a career of their own. Previous practice of law is not required. It is also unlikely that they will ever practice law. Their roles and functions are also different from their American counterparts of the adversarial system. Unlike in common-law countries, judges rely on the inquisitorial method which has its roots in ecclesiastical courts. The French criminal trial is a good example of this method. The main figures at the trial are the investigating magistrate and the presiding judge. The magistrate is responsible for the investigation. He sends the material to the trial where the judge dominates the proceedings, interrogates the defendant and witnesses who are the same for both the defense and prosecution. Obviously, there is no "coaching" of witnesses. The interrogation of the judge resembles more of a conversation than a cross-examination (Loh, 1984:497–498). The judges are much more active than in the United States, they play a greater role in building and deciding a case, they put the evidence together, and go far beyond the "refereeing" role characteristic of common-law judges.

Juries   The modern jury has its roots in both civil and criminal inquiries conducted under old Anglo-Saxon law (Hans and Vidmar, 1986:23). Before the twelfth century, criminal and civil disputes were resolved by ordeal. It took many forms. There was ordeal by water. The accused person was bound by rope and dropped in a body of water. If the person floated, it was a sign of guilt, if sunk, of innocence. There were also ordeal by fire— carrying heated stones or iron, and if the subsequent burn did not get infected in three days, the accused was declared innocent—and ordeal of the morsel that did or did not choke the accused. Civil disputes were often resolved by oaths on the assumption that a false oath would expose someone to the judgment of God.

The jury system came to American shores with the British settlers in 1607 (Simon, 1980:5). One of the important symbols during the struggle for independence, it is prominently referred to in three of the first ten amendments of the Constitution. As noted earlier, juries are used in about half of the criminal and civil cases in federal district courts. Although the Constitution provides the right to a jury trial for both criminal and civil cases involving more than twenty dollars, in the state trial courts juries render verdicts in less than 10 percent of all cases. Still, some 300,000 cases a year do come before a jury. But one-quarter to one-half of all the cases that go before a jury are settled out of court. Many of them involve liability claims, in which the impaneling of a jury may be another strategy in the insurance companies' bargaining process. Of the 3 million people called to jury duty annually, for an average of 10 days each, only 60 percent will serve on a jury (Time, 1981:45). At the state and federal levels, generally "only criminal trials make extensive use of juries" (Jacob, 1984:165). Though the right to a jury trial is often waived, juries are essential to the operation of American courts. Juries are used predominantly in common-law countries (Friedman, 1984:69), and it is estimated that 80 percent of all jury trials worldwide take place in the United States (Hans and Vidmar, 1986:31).

Juries are used exclusively in trial courts. Dispute processing in trial courts involves two basic types of issues: issues of law and issues of fact. Issues of law emerge as participants in the dispute seek to identify and interpret norms that will legitimize their behavior. In a sense, a trial is a contest of interpretation and legal reasoning. The judge has the authority to determine which interpretations of law are proper and acceptable, but a trial is more than a question of legal reasoning. It also provides the opportunity for a reconstruction, description, and interpretation of events (that is, issues of fact). The purpose of a trial is to answer the question of who did what to whom and whether such conduct is legal. The function of the jury is to listen to and decide among competing and conflicting interpretations of events. The jury acts as a referee in an adversary contest dealing with the presentation of differing versions of the same event. By a crude division of labor, the jury is the authority on facts; the judge is the authority on law.

The selection of a jury is one of the most important functions of a trial lawyer. Some attorneys maintain that by the time the jury has been chosen, the case has been decided. During the process of *voir dire* (literally, "to see, to tell"), prospective jurors are questioned first by the judge, then the attorneys representing defense and prosecution. The purpose of the *voir dire* is threefold. First, it is used to obtain information to assist in the selection of jurors. Second, it enables the attorneys to develop rapport with potential jury members. Finally, there is an attempt by both sides to try to change the attitudes, values, and perspectives of jurors (Klein, 1984:154). If a juror admits to a racial, religious, political, or other bias that would influence his or her decision, the lawyers whose client would be harmed can ask the judge to excuse the juror for cause.

But lawyers know, and many studies have indicated, that when people are questioned before an authority figure (the judge) and a number of strangers in crowded seating conditions and under stress, they tend to give socially acceptable answers and to conceal or deny their prejudices about litigants (Andrews, 1982:68). For example, national polls have shown that a third or more of Americans consider a criminal defendant probably guilty ("The person wouldn't be on trial if there wasn't something to it"), but few would admit this in the courtroom (Hunt, 1982:82).

The hypothesis that the composition of the jury is the most important determinant of the trial's outcome is implicit in the practice of law (Saks and Hastie, 1978:48). Lawyers rely on their private judgments about how jurors are likely to be biased, and by using their peremptory challenges, they eliminate those who most worry them. Decisions whether to exclude or include a juror are based on a variety of considerations: gut reactions to the juror's looks and manner, advice passed down by other lawyers, and various maxims of rules of thumb. Examples of this legal folklore include admonitions that clergymen, school teachers, and wives of lawyers do not make desirable jurors because they are often sought out for advice and tend to be opinionated. Or cabinetmakers should be avoided because they want everything to fit neatly together, Germans or Scandinavians because those people are too exacting (Saks and Hastie, 1978:49).

Many lawyers assume that Catholics will favor a Catholic litigant and Jews a Jewish one; that union members will be anticorporation; that women, especially mothers of daughters, will be quicker to convict an alleged rapist than men. Some jurors are avoided because they are wearing a loud sport jacket, white socks, or a hairpiece. In damage suits, some people are eliminated because they are fat, on the assumption that fat persons tend to dish out overly generous portions. In criminal cases, legal cookbooks on jury selection would recommend men, Republicans, upper-income groups, bankers, engineers, and certified public accountants for the prosecution and women, Democrats, middle- and lower-income groups, social scientists, and members of racial and ethnic groups such as Latins or Jews for the defense (Simon, 1980:35).

For centuries, folklore, intuition, and unsystematic past experience provided the bases for jury selection. Scientific jury selection enabled this process to move to a more sophisticated level. Since the early 1970s, lawyers have made increasing use of social scientists in jury selection. Scientific jury selection was first used in the winter of 1971–1972 in the conspiracy trial of the Berrigan brothers and other antiwar activists in Harrisburg, Pennsylvania (Saks and Hastie, 1978:55). They were accused of plotting to blow up the heating pipes of the Pentagon and kidnapping the Secretary of State. Scientific jury selection has been used in the Angela Davis trial, the conspiracy trial of John Mitchell and Maurice Stans for allegedly impeding a Securities and Exchange Commission investigation of a fugitive financier, and in a score of other cases (Hunt, 1982).

Reduced to its fundamentals, scientific jury selection consists of three steps. First, a random sample is drawn from the population and the demographic profile of this sample is compared with that of the prospective jurors. If the jurors were randomly selected, the profile should match. If there is substantial over- or underrepresentation of particular characteristics (ethnic groups, age, occupation, and so forth), the jury pool can be challenged. Second, after establishing that the prospective jurors represent the population at large, a random sample is drawn from the former to determine the demographic, personal, and attitudinal characteristics considered to be favorable to one's own side. Third, after establishing the psychological and demographic profile of a "favorable" juror, the social scientist can make recommendations for selection of individual jurors (Loh, 1984:400). This basic procedure is often supplemented with additional information. For example, in the Angela Davis trial, investigators for the defense questioned prospective jurors' neighbors and friends to learn about their attitudes. In another case, a research firm representing a corporate defendant called all potential jurors and questioned them, pretending to be conducting a random telephone survey.

An expansion of the technique is the use of shadow jury. Some social scientists feel that since the opposing attorneys present conflicting views of the facts, jurors tend to make decisions based more on empathy than evidence. Thus techniques of effective communication and persuasion need to be called to the attention of lawyers. To this end, simulated or "shadow" juries are used to gain feedback for lawyers on how to try their cases. The pioneering work with shadow juries took place during the antitrust case brought by California Computer Products of Anaheim against IBM. The IBM attorneys hired the consulting firm, Litigation Sciences, to help in IBM's defense. The researchers recruited six people with backgrounds and attitudes similar to the real jury. The six shadow jurors sat in the courtroom each day during the course of the trial and each evening they telephoned the researchers to report on their impressions of the day's proceedings. Because the plaintiffs presented their case first, the researchers learned how shadow jurors reacted to the arguments and what issues they considered important. Although the judge ruled in favor of IBM after the plaintiffs presented their side, IBM attorneys would have used the knowledge gained from the shadow jury in presenting their side of the case (Hans and Vidmar, 1986:89).

In addition to using shadow juries, some attorneys practice their arguments in front of simulated juries, with social scientists making suggestions about their persuasiveness. In 1980, the law firm representing MCI Communications in an antitrust suit against AT&T hired consultants to develop a profile of potentially favorable jurors. The consultants arranged mock juries made up of such people, in front of whom the MCI attorneys practiced their arguments. The researchers also videotaped MCI's witnesses and then advised them on how their testimony could be presented more succinctly and persuasively. MCI won the case and was awarded $600 million. Of course, with amounts like this at stake, the fees paid to social science consultants—ranging from $50,000 to $500,000—may be a bargain, if they actually help (Hunt, 1982:72).

There are serious reservations about the appropriateness of the use of scientific jury selection. Lawyers, when they are being candid, admit that their goal is not fairness, but the selection of biases that benefit them. In the words of an attorney, "I don't want an impartial jury. I want one that's going to find in my client's favor" (Hunt, 1982:85). But critics of the method contend that it tends to undermine our adversarial system of justice. The techniques for surveying the community and assessing juror values during the voir dire are clearly designed to achieve juror partiality. It leads to an imbalance in the composition of the jury. Thus, it is an advantage only to rich defendants in criminal cases and the richer side in civil suits. One with greater resources will have more lawyers, better lawyers, a larger staff. Jury research is one more such advantage. The viability of the adversary system to guarantee a fair and impartial jury and trial is obviously tested when the adversaries possess unequal resources (Hans and Vidmar, 1986:94)

There is also the danger that prosecutors may start relying on scientific jury selection if they lose too many cases due to the defendants' use of experts. In that case, as Amitai Etzioni wrote, "Could any but the most affluent Americans compete with the state, once it began to apply these procedures to the prosecution?" (quoted in Andrews, 1982:73). Finally, there is the question of the public perception of the trial. There is a possibility that the legitimacy of the trial and subsequent verdict are undermined by the use of scientific methods in jury selection. The entire system of peremptory challenges may come under attack if these issues are not confronted by those who carry out jury research and by those who benefit from the results. If the judges released the list of prospective jurors to lawyers only one day before the trial, and not several days which is the current practice, many of the dangers and ethical problems inherent in scientific jury selection could be minimized. This would drastically reduce the time available for experts to conduct thorough background investigations of prospective jurors and the subsequent advantages for one party in the litigation.

In addition to problems of jury selection, there are other important issues concerning the involvement of jurors in dispute processing in courts. The first is whether juries are effective checks on judicial power. There is really no way of determining whether juries insure that judges will be more restrained in using their power than they would be otherwise. In a study by Harry Kalven and Hans Zeisel (1966), an attempt was made to determine the effectiveness of the jury in checking the judge's power by examining the percentage of cases in which the judges and juries involved in the same case agreed as to the appropriate verdict. The researchers found a high degree of agreement between judge and jury—approximately 75 percent. They also noted that in almost all criminal cases in which judge and jury disagreed, the jury tended to be more lenient. Whether the leniency of the jury can be construed as limiting the exercise of judicial power is open to question: It does, however, show that the participation of laypersons in the decision-making process does make a difference in the outcomes of court decisions.

Another issue deals with the question of representativeness of the jury. Three steps are involved in the selection of jurors: (1) the placement of names on a master list of prospective jurors; (2) the selection of names from this list and the summoning of these persons to the court to constitute a jury panel; and (3) the selection from the panel of persons to serve on juries. Ideally, a jury that is representative of the community it serves is one that provides judgment by peers. Studies show, however, that American juries are not always representative, mainly because the sources from which potential jurors are drawn—typically voter registration lists—are not representative of the various ethnic, social, and economic groups in the community (Alker et al., 1976). Obviously, the representativeness of juries is important, not only because of the need to insure legitimacy of the jury, but also because different kinds of people bring different attitudes and values to the jury.

The representativeness of the jury is further jeopardized by the courts' generally lenient policy toward excuses and deferments. While anyone can theoretically get a temporary postponement for "undue hardship or extreme inconvenience," certain groups may be excused permanently, if they wish. In most jurisdictions, for example, these include people who are over 70 years of age; active ministers and members of religious orders; men and women with the daily care of a child under 12 years of age; and active lawyers, law students, physicians, dentists, and registered nurses. Also excused are people who are engaged in teaching, supervisory, or administrative positions in schools and colleges, and those who are sole proprietors of business. Members of the armed forces and of fire and police departments and elected public officials are also exempted and so are those who can convincingly demonstrate that their presence is required in a particular business or occupation. As a result, jury panels are more likely to be composed of people who have the time or can (or want) to take time off from the place of employment. In many occupations and professions, the prospect of being absent for a prolonged period (average jury duty is 10 days) is not welcomed. Thus, it is not surprising that juries draw disproportionately from the lower-middle and middle classes.

Finally, there are also questions about the competence of jurors in civil cases. Some observers argue that many disputes are so complex that an average person is incapable of understanding either the nature of the dispute or the complicated issues involved. For example, to decide whether IBM had monopolized various markets claimed in Memorex's $900 million antitrust suit, jurors needed a detailed understanding of things like "reverse engineering," "cross elasticity of supply," and "subordinated debentures." The trial lasted ninety-six days. The jury heard eighty-seven witnesses and examined some 3000 exhibits. As a result of the inability to comprehend such a multitude of complex issues, some jurors may become susceptible to appeals to their emotions. These observers would limit the role of jurors and even eliminate juries in civil cases. Others, however, assert that, to the contrary, juries generally do grasp the facts (Corboy, 1975:186–187) and data show from hundreds of jury trials and jury simulations that actual incompetence is a rare phenomenon (Hans and Vidmar, 1986:129).

The Flow of Litigation

Several characteristics of the flow of litigation are significant. The processes by which cases are decided differ widely according to the type of dispute, the participants involved, and the stage of the judicial process at which the dispute is settled. In many instances, civil and criminal cases are quite different, and I shall review them separately.

Criminal Cases   A high degree of discretion is characteristic of every phase of criminal prosecution. The process begins with an alleged crime and the arrest of the suspect (see Figure 3–2). At this point, the police may exercise the option of whether or not to arrest the lawbreaker, as, for example, in cases of a traffic violation, prostitution, public drunkenness, or gambling. Once an arrest is made, however, the next step is to file charges against the prisoner and to set the amount of bail. Most defendants do not plead guilty at the time of arrest. Bail is simply a method to assure the court that the defendant will appear for later proceedings. Again, at this stage judges can exercise a great deal of discretion in setting the amount of bail,

Police   Prosecution   Courts

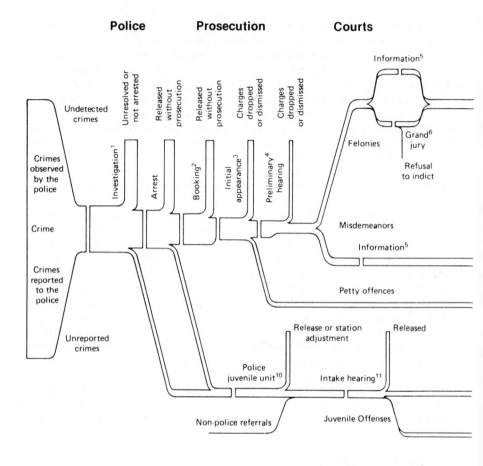

1 May continue until trial.

2 Administrative record of arrest first stage at which temporary release on bail may be available.

3 Before magistrate, commissioner, or justice of peace, formal notice of charge, advice of rights, Budget Summary trials for party offenses usually conducted here without further processing.

4 Preliminary testing of evidence against defendent. Charge may be reduced. No separate preliminary hearing for misdemeanors in some systems.

5 Charge filed by prosecutor on basis of information submitted by police or citizens. Alternative to grand jury indictment often used in felonies, almost always in misdemeanors.

6 Reviews whether government evidence sufficient to justify trial. Some states have no grand jury system, others seldom use it.

FIGURE 3-2 A general view of the criminal justice system: This chart seeks to present a simple yet comprehensive view of the movement of cases through the criminal justice system. Procedures in individual jurisdictions may vary from the pattern shown here. The differing weights of line indicate the relative volumes of cases disposed of at various points in the system, but this is only suggestive since no nationwide data of this sort exists. *Source:* President's Commission on Law Enforcement and Administration of Justice. The Challenge of Crime in a Free Society (Washington, D.C.: U.S. Government Printing Office, 1967), pp. 58–59.

Corrections

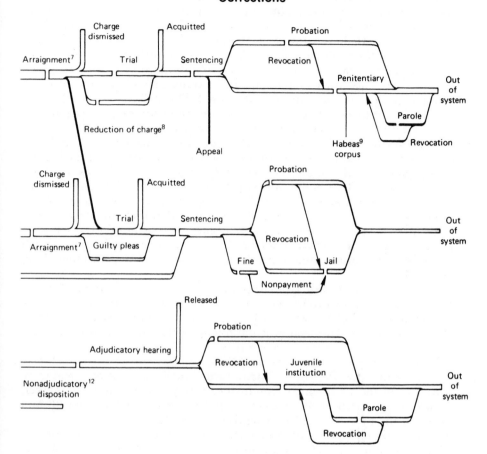

7 Appearance for plea. Defendent elects trial by judge or jury. If available counsel for indigent usually appointed here in felonies. Often not at all in other cases.

8 Charge may be reduced at any time prior to trial in return for plea of guilty or for other reasons.

9 Challenge on constitutional grounds to legality of detention. May be sought at any point in process.

10 Police often hold informal hearings, dismiss or adjust many cases without further processing.

11 Probation officer decides desirability of further court action.

12 Welfare agency, social services, counseling, medical care, etc., for cases where judicatory handling not needed.

FIGURE 3-2 *(cont.).*

which frequently results in many defendants having to wait in prison for trial. Individuals who are unable to pay their bail suffer such consequences as being treated like convicted prisoners, spending a long time in jail before the case is decided, and losing their jobs while in prison, thus forfeiting their chances for probation, all of which makes it difficult for them to prepare a defense. The poor are very much at a disadvantage in this respect. In New York City, for example, a study showed that 25 percent of those arrested could not come up with the twenty-five dollars that would have enabled them to be set free on bail before trial (President's Commission on Law Enforcement and Administration of Justice, 1967:131).

Following bail, the next step depends on the prosecutor, the defendant, and at times, the judge. Although a date is set for a trial during the arraignment or preliminary hearing, only 10 percent of the cases nationwide go to trial. This is due, in part, to the inability of law enforcement agents to establish accurately the identity of the perpetrator on the basis of eyewitness testimony. The use of eyewitness identification is most prevalent in robberies. In other property crimes such as burglaries and auto theft, the proof of identity is seldom by eyewitness. Personal crimes such as rapes and assaults, usually involve parties who know each other (Loh, 1984:551).

There are four basic types of police identification practices. The first is a showup which involves a confrontation between a suspect and a witness. It may take place either at the crime scene if the police are around or at the police station. The second is the lineup at the police station which is basically a "multiple choice recognition test" where a witness is presented with several suspects. The third is a photographic identification which may take place in either showup or lineup form. Finally, there is informal identification in the field which may involve riding around in an unmarked police car in search of the suspect or an "accidental" encounter with him or her at the time of a bail hearing (Loh, 1984:552).

In addition to the initial identification of a suspect, the issue of eyewitness accuracy also comes up on the witness stand during a trial. The unreliability of eyewitness identification and fallibility of testimony on the witness stand are brought about by three general problems of human memory (Woocher, 1977). To start with, the perception of an event is not merely a passive recording. People can perceive only a limited number of events at the same time, and the number remembered is even smaller. Even trained observers find it difficult to describe accurately such basic physical characteristics as height, weight, and age. Humans also find it difficult to judge time, and because of the amount and variety of activities that occur during an action-packed event such as a crime, there is a tendency to overestimate the length of time. Often, crimes take place under poor observation conditions making subsequent recall difficult. The presence of stress and anxiety decrease perceptual abilities. As a result, witnesses often compensate for perceptual selectivity by reconstructing what has occurred from what they assume must have occurred. In essence, they state what they think should have taken place rather than what actually transpired. Finally, eyewitness accuracy is further reduced in situations of cross-racial identifications. People are poorer at identifying members of another race than of their own. For example, whites have greater difficulties recognizing black or oriental faces than vice versa.

The second problem is that memory decays over time. People forget quickly and easily. When it comes to recall at the police station or at the witness stand, people have a tendency to fill gaps in memory by adding extraneous details so "things make sense." For example, a witness may recall an individual accurately but is completely wrong in remembering the circumstances under which he or she encountered that person. A salesperson may identify the defendant as having been in the store with the murder victim when, in reality, the defendant had been in that store on a few earlier occasions but was out of town at the time of the crime.

Finally, the way in which information is recalled from memory invariably reduces the accuracy of eyewitness testimony. The recall of witnesses is influenced by the subtle suggestions they receive under questioning by a police officer or lawyer. Many people also feel compelled to answer questions completely in spite of incomplete knowledge in an attempt to please their interrogators. So they rely on their imagination to supplement factual information.

Even after positive identification of defendants, the majority of cases are settled by negotiations between the prosecutor and the defendant's lawyer. In these cases, the prosecutor is placed in a bargaining situation and may "trade" with the defendant for an admission of a lesser crime. The process is called *plea bargaining*. Thus, in many cases the prosecutor acts as a *de facto* judge and makes most of the decisions regarding the disposition of a case. If the defendant, on the advice of his or her lawyer, does not plead guilty, the person goes to trial. Contrary to popular belief, the ones who plead guilty, do not, on the average, receive a lighter sentence than those who do not. It is really the criminal justice system that benefits by saving time and expense of conducting a trial (Klein, 1984:77).

Plea bargaining, as a form of negotiated justice, is a baffling and controversial topic in the sociological literature (see, for example, Feeley, 1979). There are many objections to plea bargaining, the most common being that criminals are allowed to obtain "cheap" convictions (that is, ones in which they do not pay for the real crimes they committed), that it is moving criminal justice into an administrative process rather than an adversary one, and that it is generating cynicism about criminal justice among the accused, the system's participants, and the public at large.

In explaining the widespread use of plea bargaining, Arthur Rosett and Donald R. Cressey (1976:85–97) assert that court personnel, including prosecutors, "develop a group sense of justice," which differs from attitudes generally held in the community, and which is generally more humane and pragmatic than that of the public. They maintain that prosecutors use case loads as their public excuse for bargaining, but rarely consider case loads in deciding whether to deal with specific cases before them (such as, to prosecute on the basis of initial charges or to negotiate). The real reasons for plea bargaining, they argue, are the weaknesses in cases that could result in acquittals; the desire to adjust the charges to more reasonable levels in terms of the facts and the character of the defendant; and the desire to comply with the courthouse consensus on concepts of fairness and justice. For a typical defendant, it is often his or her own defense lawyer who initiates negotiations and urges a settlement by plea bargaining. In one study, for example, Abraham S. Blumberg (1979:223) found that over half of the 724 defendants entering guilty pleas indicated that their defense counsel first suggested the guilty plea, usually during the first or second meeting between lawyer and client.

The final step in most criminal proceedings is sentencing the defendants who have been found guilty. Although sentencing decisions are made within a specific legal framework, most jurisdictions permit the exercise of considerable discretion. The extent of judicial discretion allowed by legislation varies from state to state. As a result, the decisions handed down by judges vary within and across jurisdictions. In some states, virtually no sentencing discretion is allowed in felony cases, while in others, judges may effectively determine not only the nature of punishment (probation, fine, or imprisonment), but also the extent of punishment (the length of a prison term).

Donald J. Newman points out that there are five common structures for prison sentences, each illustrating a different combination of legislative provisions and judicial discretion. They are:

> 1) both maximum and minimum terms of imprisonment are set by the judge at any point within legislative outer limits; 2) maximum terms are fixed by statute, but the judge may set a minimum at any point up to the maximum; 3) maximum and minimum terms are set by the judge, but the minimum cannot exceed some fraction, usually one-third, of the maximum; 4) the maximum term is set by the judge, but the minimum is fixed by statute; and 5) both maximum and minimum terms are fixed by statutory law allowing the judge no discretion (Newman, 1975:238).

Thus, judges do have some choice between different sentencing options for most crimes, and they tend to exercise it. Generally, the judge's decision is influenced by the recommendations of the prosecutor and probation officers. Other factors that might influence a judge's decision would include the race, sex, age, socioeconomic and criminal background of the defendant, and the type of lawyer involved (for example, privately retained or court appointed). The decision to plea bargain is also a factor (Partridge and Eldridge, 1978).

A high degree of discretion is characteristic of criminal litigation. Although legal norms set the framework for the process, they do not control whether violators will be actually subjected to these legal norms. Instead of the judge or the defense attorney, the prosecutor plays the key role in administering criminal justice. Negotiation, bargaining, and compromise play an important part in the litigation process. Consequently, in many instances, offenders consider trials dangerous because they incite the judge and prosecutor to "throw the book" at the defendant.

Civil Proceedings   In civil cases, a dispute reaches the court when it is filed by the plaintiff's attorney. The attorney generally has the option to choose a court based on a number of considerations, such as the quality and known biases of judges, the delay that may be expected in hearing a case, and the relative convenience of the court for the litigant (Jacob, 1984:213-215). Generally, the litigant has little voice in the selection of courts. It is left to the attorney who handles the case.

Just as in the case of criminal proceedings, bargaining governs negotiating settlements in civil courts. For example, in personal injury cases, plaintiffs who are represented by lawyers usually win a greater settlement than those who attempt to handle their own negotiations (Ross, 1970). Courts are often instrumental in expediting the settlement of cases through pretrial conferences. At times, the judge may even suggest a particular amount that seems reasonable, based on his or her experience with similar cases.

If a satisfactory settlement cannot be reached, the case goes to trial. Only a small proportion of cases that are filed end up in trial. In some types of cases, such as automobile accidents, the plaintiffs generally prefer a jury trial in anticipation of a larger settlement.

At times, disputes are settled prior to civil cases that go to trial, and in such instances the trial is used to legitimize the outcome. This is particularly true in divorce suits. In such cases, a separation agreement has been reached by husband and wife, and then the wife generally takes action in court to formalize and legitimize the agreement.

LEGISLATURES

To begin the study of the organization of legislatures, we first need to look at what they do. A legislature is defined as a collection of individuals who are elected as members of the formal parliamentary bodies prescribed by national and state constitutions. The functions of the legislature, both at the federal and state levels, are numerous. Of course, the hallmark of legislative bodies is their lawmaking function, and part of the next chapter will be concerned with how this function is carried out. Yet, lawmaking takes up only a portion of the legislature's time. Legislative bodies are also engaged in conflict and integrative functions.

Conflict Management Functions   Although conflict management is part of both the administrative and judicial subsystems, the legislature may be distinguished by the extent to which compromise, as a mode of conflict management, is institutionalized in the system. The emphasis is on conflict management rather than on conflict resolution for, in a sense, few political decisions are final (Boulding, 1956:103).

The conflict management functions of legislative bodies can be seen in the context of their deliberative, decisional, adjudicative, and cathartic activities (Jewell and Patterson, 1973:7). Frequently, legislative bodies deliberate without arriving at a decision or taking action. However, the deliberation process itself and the rules under which it takes place contribute to the reconciliation of divergent interests. As David B. Truman (1951:394) notes: "The chief function of debates is as a part of the process of adjustment . . . formal debates facilitate acceptance of the final decisions, not necessarily by the immediate participants but by those on the periphery." In addition to formal debates, deliberation is carried on in the hearing rooms, the offices of legislators, or in the lobbies or cloakrooms surrounding the chambers. At times, these informal deliberations are more important, for they provide an opportunity to incorporate a variety of viewpoints and interests.

Some adjudicative activities are routinely undertaken by legislative bodies. For example, the work of some legislative committees has been adjudicative, as when hearings before investigating committees have been, in effect, trials during the course of which sanctions have been applied. A most celebrated illustration of the application of sanctions by the Senate for the violation of its norms, is that of the late Senator Joseph McCarthy. He, as chairperson of the Permanent Subcommittee on Investigations of the Committee on Government Operations, engaged in a communist witch-hunt during 1953 and 1954, which focused mainly on the Department of State and the U.S. Army. In December 1954, the Senate voted to censure McCarthy for his conduct—not for indiscriminately accusing people of being communists and abusing the investigatory powers of Congress—but for attacking the integrity of the Senate itself.

The cathartic or safety valve mechanism for conflict management can be found in a variety of legislative structures. For example, the public hearing can be a cathartic mechanism, and has been considered as "a quasi-ritualistic means of adjusting group conflicts and relieving disturbances through a safety-valve" (Truman, 1951:372). In a public hearing, representatives of conflicting interests have an opportunity to let off steam by arguing their respective complaints and claims.

Integrative Functions   Legislative bodies contribute to the integration of the polity by providing support for the judicial and executive systems. They provide this support through authorization, legitimation, and representation (Jewell and Patterson, 1973:10). A characteristic of any constitution is the specific delegation of authority to different components of government. In the United States, the legislative branch is given various kinds of authority over the executive branch. Perhaps the most important of these is the budgetary process through which legislative bodies authorize an executive to collect taxes and disperse funds. Legislative bodies also authorize the courts to establish jurisdiction, to create their organizational machinery, and to qualify their members. Moreover, legislatures oversee bureaucratic activities and attempt to balance them against prevailing special interests in a community.

The integrative functions are also promoted through legitimation of activities. Legislative actions are considered by most people as legitimate. For example, when Congress gives the IRS permission to collect more taxes, their exercise of authority is legitimized in the process, and it has the right as well as the power to collect more taxes.

The Organization of Legislatures

Because of the similarities in organizational patterns, I shall consider the federal and state legislative bodies together. Congress consists of two separate bodies—the Senate and the House of Representatives. These two bodies differ in several respects and are eager to protect their privileges and power. The House members are apportioned among the states on the basis of population. After each census, the apportionment of representatives among the states normally changes: States with the fastest growing populations gain representation, and those with little or no population growth or with declining populations lose representation. U.S. Senators are not affected by apportionment or districting. Each state is entitled to two senators. Unlike the situation in the House, where members come up for election at the same time, Senate terms are staggered, so that only one-third of the Senate is up for election every two years, which ensures a greater continuity of both formal and informal organizational arrangements.

Herbert Asher (1973) points out that behavior in both the Senate and House is influenced by a set of informal rules and norms: (1) newcomers to the legislative body serve a period of apprenticeship in which they accept their assignments, do their homework, and stay in the background while learning their jobs; (2) members become specialists in the work of the committees to which they are assigned; (3) members avoid personal attacks on each other; (4) members are willing to reciprocate by compromising and trading votes (supporting each other's proposals) when possible; and (5) legislators do nothing which will adversely reflect upon the integrity of the legislative body and Congress as a whole. The same informal norms and rules operate in state legislatures.

Avoidance of personal disputes, restriction of full participation in the legislative process to senior members, and the norm of reciprocity all function to minimize conflict within legislative bodies. The emphasis on specialization provides Congress with the opportunity to deal with the increasingly complex issues it must consider, though specialization may also create some organizational problems. In general, House members are more likely than Senators to specialize in the work of the committees on which they serve. Senators, on the other hand, are more apt to draw the attention of the media and have presidential ambitions. The norm of protecting the integrity of the legislative body may, and often has, led to controversy between the Senate and the House, and between Congress as a whole and the presidency.

The desirability of these norms has been generally recognized by legislators. An exception of recent origin is that new members are less inclined to play the role of apprentice. Newcomers, especially in the Senate, are more likely now than in the past to become actively involved in the legislative process and to claim their share of the spotlight. One of the reasons for this is that the Senate has created a variety of subcommittees in recent years which provide new members with the opportunity to perform an important role in the work of that body.

Committees represent perhaps the most important element in the organization of legislative bodies. The various types of committees include the standing, joint, and special investigative committees. Standing committees are permanent bodies where the bulk of the legislative work is done. Joint committees are comprised of members of both Houses. Special investigative committees, such as the Senate Select Committee on Presidential Campaign Activities headed by Senate Sam Ervin that exposed the Watergate scandals, have played an important role in American politics.

Participants in the Legislative Process

The legislative process encompasses a variety of participants. In this section, I have chosen to give attention to three sets of participants who are particularly relevant to legislative activity: legislators, executives, and lobbyists. These three sets of participants in the legislative process are examined separately.

Legislators   Who are the legislators who make laws? Are legislatures composed of men and women who represent a cross-section of the population? What groups are "overrepresented" and "underrepresented" in the legislature? Social scientists have carried out a number of investigations on the social origins and occupational backgrounds of political decision makers. A few of these studies have focused on legislators. In spite of substantial gaps in factual knowledge about legislative personnel, certain generalizations about the individuals who serve as legislators can be made.

Most legislators come from a middle- or upper-class background. Contrary to popular beliefs, legislators are not representative of the population at large, and obviously not all citizens have an equal chance to be elected to legislative office. For example, Donald R. Matthews (1960:20), in his study of postwar senators (covering the years 1947 to 1957), found that 24 percent of the senators' fathers were professional men, 35 percent were proprietors and officials, and 32 percent were farmers. Only 2 percent of the senators were the sons of low-salaried workers, 5 percent were the sons of industrial wage earners, and for 2 percent, the relevant facts were unknown. Other studies of the membership of the lower house of Congress show a similar distribution (Matthews, 1954:23).

As a group, legislators have a much higher educational attainment than the general population. In part, this high educational level can be accounted for by their relatively high social class origins (Jewell and Patterson, 1973:79). Protestant Anglo-Saxon males are substantially overrepresented among legislators. Women, blacks, and foreign-born Americans are significantly underrepresented. The religious composition of most state legislatures and both Houses of the Congress is predominantly Protestant (Jewell and Patterson, 1973:78).

The recruitment of legislators is very selective in terms of occupational status. By and large, those in the professional and business occupations dominate the legislative halls in the United States at both state and national levels. The conspicuous fact about the occupations of legislators is that lawyers are predominant. Over half of the members of Congress are lawyers, and overrepresentation is also found at the state level, where they account for 20 percent of legislators. While lawyers remain the largest single occupational group among legislators, the profession's "share" of state legislative seats decreased by 6 percent since 1966. The President of the American Bar Association considers this decline a "bad sign" and, in his words, "I don't think it's good for the country, and I don't think it's good for the profession" (Slonim, 1980:30). Those who echo this highly debatable view believe that the absence of a large number of lawyers "bodes ill for the quality of legislation," because lawmaking by lay people lends itself to ambiguity.

In addition to lawyers, it is common to find state legislatures in which over one-third of the members are businesspersons. Those engaged in the insurance business, real estate, and banking and investment are particularly numerous. In the less urbanized states of the midwest and south, legislators engaged in farming are likely to be about as numerous as those engaged in either business or law. Farmers, however, are not often elected to Congress. Educators account for a small fraction of state legislators, and women are significantly underrepresented at both the federal and state levels.

From the above discussion, it is evident that no legislature comes close to representing a cross-section of the population it serves. The political system inevitably has built-in biases, numerous devices for the containment of minority-group aspirations for office and for the advancement of dominant segments of the population. Some groups win often, others lose often.

The Executive   There are three main functions for the President and governors in the legislative process. First, they serve as a source of ideas for the programs which legislative bodies consider; second, they function as catalytic agents; and third, they implement the law.

Although the extent of executives initiating ideas for legislative programs varies among the states, and certainly between the state and national levels, in most instances executive recommendations are the principal items on the legislators' agenda. Legislative recommendations emerge from individual cabinet departments or from agencies and are sent to the President far in advance of presentation to Congress (Ripley, 1978:293–323). The presidential initiative is a permanent feature of the legislative process.

The President and governors also function as catalytic agents in the legislative process. They not only offer programs but also strive to structure support, both directly within legislative bodies and indirectly through interest groups, party leaders, and other political activists. They are also greatly concerned with the manipulation of public opinion.

The implementation of law constitutes a third executive contribution to the legislative process. The legislative process seldom ends when the executive has signed a bill into law. In many instances, the enactment of a law is not the most important step in making public policy. Much legislation is phrased in general terms to apply to a diversity of concrete situations. Law is interpreted and given new dimensions as it is applied under the direction of the executive. An awareness of the relationships between law implementation and lawmaking is reflected in legislative eagerness to oversee administrative behavior.

Lobbyists   Associations that seek to be influential in the legislative decision-making processes are called interest groups. Whom do interest groups represent? At the most general level, the interest group system in the United States has a distinct bias favoring upper-class and predominantly business interests. Interest groups are usually regarded as selfish— with some justification. The very word "interest" suggests that the ends sought will primarily benefit only a segment of society. Still, not all of the groups that attempt to influence legislative bodies are obviously selfish in nature such as large corporations or industry associations. There are quite a number of groups that claim to represent the public such as the Sierra Club and the League of Women Voters. Other groups represent foreign governments, small or medium size political groups, or public and private universities.

The legislative bodies are the natural habitat of political interest groups. These interest groups enter the legislative process through their lobbying activities. Lobbyists are individuals who get paid to try to influence the passage or defeat of a legislation. Lobbying is considered as a professional undertaking, and full-time experienced lobbyists are considered essential by most interest groups. In Washington alone, it is estimated that as many as 4500 groups are represented by lobbyists covering a wide range of activities such as labor, education, business, welfare, banking, farming, and so on. There are over 15,000 registered lobbyists, or about 30 for each member of Congress, who collectively spend over $2 billion a year in an effort to influence lawmakers (Coleman, 1985:104). This is in addition to the Political Action Committees' (groups that are not affiliated directly with a candidate or political party) expenditures which were in excess of $104 million in 1984. To influence legislative outcomes, PACs such as the National Education Association spent over $2.1 million, National Rifle Association $3.7 million, and the Associated Milk Producers $2 million (Barone and Ujifusa, 1985:1510–1515).

The lobbyist plays a variety of roles in the legislative process. As a contact person, the lobbyist's time and energies are devoted to walking the legislative halls, visiting legislators, establishing relationships with administrative assistants and others of the legislator's staff, cultivating key legislators on a friendship basis, and developing contacts on the staffs of critical legislative committees. As a campaign organizer, the lobbyist gathers popular support for his or her organization's legislative program. As an informant, the lobbyist conveys information to legislators without necessarily advocating a particular position. Finally, as a watchdog, the lobbyist scrutinizes the legislative calendars and watches legislative activity carefully. This way, the lobbyist can be alert to developments in the legislative bodies that might affect client groups (Jewell and Patterson, 1973:341–343).

At both the state and federal levels, there are large-scale lobbying efforts directed toward the enactment or defeat of certain legislations. In all probability, a professional lobbyist will be employed who may be a former government employee who once occupied a high position in the administration, an ex-congressperson, an ex-senator, or an ex-governor. Lobbying groups are willing to pay dearly, for example, for the services of an experienced ex-senator or House member, particularly a former chairman or senior member of a top committee. What these groups are buying, by and large, are prestige and access to the inner sanctum of government. In Washington especially, an ex-lawmaker has privileges that set him or her apart from other lobbyists—including access to the House and Senate chambers, members' private dining rooms, gymnasiums, and swimming pools. But there are some restrictions. A former senator who is a registered lobbyist must wait a year before visiting the Senate for the purpose of influencing his former colleagues. The House has no such rule but forbids a former member to enter the chamber if he or she has an interest in an issue that is being debated. Still, there is nothing to prevent a lawmaker-turned-lobbyist from making his pitch elsewhere.

Supplementing his or her personal efforts, the lobbyist often turns to public relations firms to stir up grass roots sentiment. As a result, a stream of phone calls, letters, and cables will deluge the offices of legislators. The efforts of the National Rifle Association are illustrative of these practices—the gun lobby devoted seven years and $100 million to wipe out federal handgun regulations (*St. Louis Post-Dispatch,* 1986:2B). Contributions in conjunction with these efforts can also be discreetly used among certain legislators to muster support when needed.

At times, however, a "discreet contribution" may turn out to be outright bribery in an attempt to buy political favors in the form of special bills, the right vote on a particular piece of legislation, or assistance in winning government contracts. But bribery can lead to criminal prosecution of political figures, and 42 percent of the criminal indictments against congressional office holders since 1940 involved some sort of bribery charges. A most notorious example of this was the FBI's sting operation known as ABSCAM. Agents posed as representatives of an alleged Arab sheik who wanted some Washington favors. Eight officials were convinced to sponsor special bills or use their influence in the government in return for cash or other rewards. One senator was given stock certificates in a bogus titanium mine for his assistance in obtaining government contracts. Another representative was videotaped stuffing $20,000 in his pocket. Those involved in ABSCAM were convicted of various crimes and given fines and prison terms (Coleman, 1985:105). Fortunately, most lobbyists do not resort to such extreme and illegal measure as outright bribery nor do they wish to test the temptation toleration limits of politicians. But lobbyists often give small personal presents, free samples of company products such as perfume, and free meals at expensive restaurants to create a receptive climate for their efforts.

There are several types of lobbying efforts and techniques that are deployed with varying degrees of efficiency, depending on the cause. First, there are activities directed at influencing legislation during the electoral process by supporting the election of a person to the legislative body whose program one favors. Second, there are activities directed at influencing legislation by "educational work." If one happens to oppose a particular legislative action one can substitute the phrase "educational work" for "propaganda work." The educational propaganda may be specifically directed toward a particular bill, or it may be directed only at the establishment of a political or economic philosophy which will condition subsequent legislation (Ripley, 1978:272–273).

In an attempt to control lobbying activities, in 1946 Congress passed the Federal Regulation of Lobbying Act. This Act requires that persons who are paid to influence legislation be registered and disclose the source and the use of any funds in excess of $500 to the clerk of the House of Representatives and to the secretary of the Senate. The theory is that the legislators and the public will thereby be informed as to the interests of some of the "advice" they receive from lobbyists. Accordingly, there exist regular lists of lobbyists and the amount of money they are willing to admit they are spending on lobbying activities. Similarly, in a number of states, there are laws aimed at increasing the visibility of groups by disclosing the identity of lobbyists and by gathering information on their activities. Typically, these laws relate only to direct communications with the legislature. As with the federal lobbying laws, state lobbying laws prove better in theory than in practice. With but an occasional exception, a general malaise has settled over their administration and enforcement. It remains a difficult task to control lobbyists and their influence over legislators.

ADMINISTRATIVE AGENCIES

Like the study of legislation, the investigation of regulatory and administrative agencies has been neglected by legal sociologists who tend to focus their attention primarily upon courts and litigations. As a result, there is a paucity of research and theorizing on administrative and regulatory bodies in the sociological literature (Tomasic, 1985:111). These agencies deal with an important sociological process, *social control*, which is a major concern in the study of law and society. This section will describe the context within which that control is exercised. In the United States government in the twentieth century, the most striking development has been the multiplication of administrative agencies and the extension of their power and activities. Today, numerous local, state, and federal administrative agencies have a tremendous impact on our lives. They are often called "the fourth branch of government." On the federal level, there are some fifty agencies in Washington alone (Weidenbaum, 1979:15). The average state probably has more than 100 administrative agencies with powers of adjudication or rule making or both (Davis 1975a:8). Individuals are much more directly and much more frequently affected by the administrative process than by the judicial process. The pervasiveness of the effects of just the federal administrative process can quickly be appreciated by considering the following hypothetical scenario.

Our typical couple is awakened by the buzz of an electric clock or perhaps by a clock radio. This marks the beginning of a highly regulated existence. The clock or radio that wakes them up is run by electricity provided by a utility company, regulated by the Federal Energy Regulatory Commission and by state utility agencies. When they go to the bathroom, they use products, such as mouthwash and toothpaste, made by companies regulated by the Food and Drug Administration (FDA). The husband might lose his temper trying to open a bottle of aspirin which has the child-proof cap required by the Consumer Product Safety Commission (CPSC). In the kitchen, his wife reaches for a box of cereal containing food processed by a firm subject to the regulations of the United States Department of Agriculture (USDA) and required to label its products under regulations of the Federal Trade Commission (FTC). The husband, who is conscious of his weight, uses an artificial sweetener in his coffee. Since the banning of cyclamates by the FDA, he has switched to saccharine, but he is worried because that, too, is on the FDA's proposed ban list. Obviously, it does not help his ulcer.

As they get in their car to go to work, they are reminded by a buzzer to fasten the seat belts, compliments of the National Highway Traffic Safety Administration. They paid slightly more for the car than they wanted to, because it contains a catalytic converter and other devices stipulated by the Environmental Protection Agency (EPA). They also pay more for gas because the car can only use unleaded gasoline, another government requirement. On the way to work, they drive at speeds regulated by state and municipal ordinances and subject to the federally mandated sixty-five miles per hour speed limit. They listen to the car radio which is regulated by the Federal Communications Commission (FCC), as is the telephone that they use at home or at their place of work. Our typical wife works in an office, and during the course of the day she provides information about the financial activities of her company to the Securities and Exchange Commission (SEC), and she is also likely to fill out a variety of statistical forms for the Bureau of Census. She finds out in the office that she has lost her retirement benefits; the small company where she works recently terminated its pension plan because of the onerous requirements imposed by the Internal Revenue Service (IRS) and the Department of Labor under the Employee Retirement Income Security Act (ERISA).

In the meantime, the husband begins his work in the factory under conditions negotiated by his union, which was chosen after a lengthy strike in an election supervised by the National Labor Relations Board (NLRB). The equipment he uses in his job and in the lavatory must meet the requirements of the Occupational Safety and Health Administration (OSHA). The material he uses at work was shipped to his company under the guidelines of the Interstate Commerce Commission (ICC for rail and truck), the Civil Aeronautics Board (CAB for air), and the Federal Maritime Commission (for sea).

They take off time from work to negotiate a mortgage on the house they are buying with financing from a savings and loan association regulated by a Federal Home Loan Board (FHLB) with a guarantee by the Federal Housing Administration of the Department of Housing and Urban Development. They also plan to go to a commercial bank (regulated by the Federal Reserve System) to get a loan for the furniture they will need. On the way home, they stop for a hamburger, which is the subject of 41,000 federal and state regulations, many of those stemming from 200 laws and 111,000 precedent-setting court cases (*U.S. News & World Report*, 1980:64).

At home, they decide to watch commercial television, the programming and advertising of which are regulated by the Federal Communications Commission. They light up a cigarette with a package label mandated by the Surgeon General in the Department of Health, Education and Welfare. But they have to cut their television watching short because of a letter they have received from the Internal Revenue Service questioning their tax return for the previous year. After a while, the husband decides to clean his shotgun, regulated by the Alcohol, Tobacco, and Firearms Bureau of the Treasury Department. And he has yet to find out that these regulations cost every consumer five hundred dollars yearly (*St. Louis Post-Dispatch*, 1979:4B). (See Figure 3–3 for a partial list of regulatory agencies.)

The Organization of Administrative Agencies

Administrative agencies are authorities of the government other than the executive, legislative, or judicial branches, created for the purpose of administering particular legislation. They are sometimes called commissions, bureaus, boards, authorities, offices, departments, administrations, and divisions. They may be created by legislative acts, by executive orders authorized by statutes, or by Constitutional provisions. The powers and functions of an agency are generally contained in the legislation that created it (Breyer and Stewart, 1979:6–7).

At the federal level, all the agencies derive their power from Congress, which created them under its constitutional authority to regulate interstate commerce. Congress long ago began delegating this authority when it became clear that the job was too complex and technical to be handled entirely by legislation in the amount of time available, and with the limited expertise of the lawmakers. As economic activity became more complex, legislative bodies were unable or unwilling to prescribe detailed guidelines for regulation. Traditional agencies of government could no longer regulate big business (Friedman, 1986:441). Agencies were established and given considerable discretion in determining the applicability of often vaguely written legislation to specific situations such as mass transport and communication. These agencies were expected to provide certain advantages over the courts in the implementation of public policy. These advantages included speed, informality, flexibility, expertise in technical areas, and continuous surveillance of an industry or an economic problem.

In general, administrative agencies were created to deal with a crisis or with emerging problems requiring supervision and flexible treatment. For example, when Congress decided in the nineteenth century not to permit railroads to operate without close public control, it established, in 1887, the Interstate Commerce Commission—the first federal independent regulatory agency. Its assignment was to supervise the railroads in order to guarantee cheap, safe service and rates that would be fair to small towns

Interstate Commerce Commission, ICC, founded in 1887. Eleven Commissioners set rates, routes, and practices for interstate railroads, truckers, bus companies, and pipelines.

Federal Reserve Board, FRB, founded in 1913. Seven-member Board of Governors sets monetary and credit policy and regulates commercial banks belonging to the Federal Reserve System.

Federal Trade Commission, FTC, founded in 1914. Five Commissioners enforce some antitrust laws, protect businesses from unfair competition and enforce truth-in-lending and truth-in-labeling laws.

Food and Drug Administration, FDA, founded in 1931. A Commissioner in the Department of Health, Education, and Welfare sets standards for certain foods and drugs and issues licenses for the manufacturing and distribution of drugs.

Federal Power Commission, FPC, founded in 1920. Five Commissioners set wholesale rates for the interstate transportation and sale of natural gas and for interstate transmission of electricity.

Federal Communications Commission, FCC, founded in 1934. Seven Commissioners license radio and television stations and oversee interstate and international telephone operations.

Securities and Exchange Commission, SEC, founded in 1934. Five Commissioners regulate securities issues, supervise stock exchanges, and regulate holding and investment companies.

Civil Aeronautics Board, CAB, founded in 1938. Five Commissioners determine interstate airline routes, passenger fares, and freight rates.

Federal Aviation Administration, FAA, founded in 1948. An Administrator in the Department of Transportation certifies airworthiness of aircraft, licenses pilots, and sets safety standards for airports.

Equal Employment Opportunity Commission, EEOC, founded in 1964. Five Commissioners investigate and rule on charges of racial and other discrimination by employers and labor unions.

Environmental Protection Agency, EPA, founded in 1970. An Administrator develops and enforces environmental-quality standards for air, water, and noise pollution and for toxic substances and pesticides.

Consumer Product Safety Commission, CPSC, founded in 1972. Five Commissioners set product-safety standards and initiate recall notices for defective products.

Federal Energy Administration, FEA, founded in 1974. An Administrator regulates price and allocation controls of petroleum products.

Nuclear Regulatory Commission, NRC, founded in 1975. Five Commissioners issue licenses for the design, construction, and operation of nuclear power plants.

FIGURE 3-3 The major federal regulators (in chronological order).

all across the country. The phenomenal development of radio with its con-comitant crowding of airwaves brought about the creation of the Federal Radio Commission–the forerunner of today's Federal Communications Commission. This agency was charged with allocating licenses to stations to be operated "in the public interest." More recently, when environmental issues became a serious national concern, two agencies–the Council on Environmental Quality, and the Environmental Protection Agency–were established.

There is considerable variation in the responsibilities, functions, and operations of the various agencies. Some, such as the Environmental Protection Agency and the Federal Trade Commission, are concerned with only a few activities of a large number of firms, while others, like the Interstate Commerce Commission, oversee a great many matters involving a relatively small number of firms (in this case, transportation). Many agencies in the first category have the official mission of protecting the interests of the general public in regard to health, safety, and activities in the marketplace. Most of the agencies in the second category are not only expected to perform public protection functions but also to safeguard and promote the health of specific occupations, industries, or segments of the economy subject to their jurisdiction.

Administrative agencies are just as subject to pressures of interest groups as are all other policy-makers. Although many of the agencies were originally established in response to protests by various consumer groups against dangerous practices by various industries, their orientation has changed over the years. The agencies gradually shifted their orientation and became the "captive" of the groups they were supposed to regulate. Often appointees were (and still are) selected from the very industries that the agencies were created to regulate. Agency heads frequently take high-level jobs in such industries after finishing their governmental service. There have also been frequent revelations of agency heads fraternizing with representatives of regulated industries and of their willingness to accept favors, such as industry-paid vacations. For these reasons, critics have often pointed out that some high-level agency members seem more interested in protecting the interests of airlines, drug companies, trucking firms, stock-brokers, and other industries that they are supposed to regulate than in directing their energies towards the protection of the interests of the public (Schwartz, 1959).

The activities of the Interstate Commerce Commission illustrate this tendency. Originally, it was set up to protect consumers against predatory practices by the railroad monopolies. By 1920, the agency was almost solely responsive to the railroads, against the interests of consumers, and against other forms of interstate transportation. In case after case, the ICC's rulings benefited the railroads. More recently, the ICC has struck a balance between the interests of railroads and trucking companies, but the interests of consumers are still virtually ignored. Witness, for example, the progressive discontinuation of passenger train services.

Administrative agencies have also been criticized by conservatives as being uncontrollable monsters that threaten the civil liberties of business people and the proper functioning of the economic system (Weidenbaum, 1979). In a somewhat contradictory fashion, conservatives have also depicted regulatory agencies as inefficient, bungling bureaucracies that do little more than waste the taxpayers' money. Liberals have often been able to muster enthusiasm over the creation of new agencies, but have become disappointed with their performance. Agencies are often seen by liberals as becoming the captive of the regulated, and thus unwilling to pursue their public interest obligations.

On an ideological level, governmental regulation has also been controversial because it raises questions regarding the proper role of government in the economy. The conservative of the "free enterprise" position has generally called for a hands-off policy by government in regulating economic activity. According to this view, the same protections against regulation are to be given to corporations. The pursuit of business profits, moreover, is seen by economic conservatives as being in the best interests of the general public. We are all familiar with the cliché, "What is good for General Motors is good for the country." Liberals, by contrast, are more likely to seek restrictions on the rights of businesspersons or corporations to protect what they consider to be the important rights of workers, consumers, and the general public.

A Ford Foundation report (1978:10) notes that administrative agencies are increasingly considered as a problem rather than as a solution to questions requiring fair and efficient action in the public interest. The various forms of economic regulations for consumer protection are under attack from many quarters, and it is argued that attempts to solve problems through the regulatory mode serve to create conflict rather than reduce it. Concern is expressed also over the agencies' failure to develop coherent policies and programs and over the vast amount of discretion vested in some agency administrators.

The Administrative Process

Administrative agencies affect the rights of individuals and businesses by exercising powers of investigation, rule-making, enforcement, and adjudication. This combination of functions does not conflict with the doctrine of the separation of powers, the Constitutional principle that the legislative, executive, and judicial functions of government should not exist in the same person or groups of persons. Notes Freedman: "Administrative agencies were deliberately created as instruments of blended powers. In many instances they were expressly created to combine legislative, executive, and judicial powers" (1978:17). Although a wide range of powers are delegated to an agency by the Enabling Act, there are checks on its activities. The creator of an agency, which is generally the legislature, retains the power to destroy it or alter the rules governing it. The judiciary retains the power of final review of the determinations of administrative agencies, but this right is, as a practical matter, rather limited. The principal administrative processes include investigation, rule-making, and adjudication. I shall consider these separately.

Investigation   The authority to investigate is given to practically all administrative agencies. Without information, administrative agencies would not be in the position to regulate industry, protect the environment, prosecute fraud, collect taxes, or issue grants. Most administrative actions in both formal and informal proceedings are conditioned by the information obtained through the agency's prior investigation. As regulation has expanded and intensified, the agency's quest for facts has gained momentum. Some agencies are created primarily to perform the fact-finding or investigative function. The authority to investigate is one of the functions that distinguishes agencies from courts. This authority is usually exercised in order to perform properly another primary function, that of rule-making.

Statutes usually grant an agency the authority to use several methods to carry out its information-gathering function. Requiring reports from regulated businesses and conducting inspections are methods of accomplishing this information-gathering task. Necessary information is often available from the staff, the agencies' accumulated records, and from private sources. If these resources prove inadequate, the agency may seek further information by calling in witnesses or documents for examination, or by conducting searches. The authority of an agency to investigate is intertwined with the objectives of administrative investigation. The purposes of investigations vary, ranging over the entire spectrum of agency activity. For example, if an agency is responsible for enforcing a statute, its investigations may set the groundwork for detecting violations and punishing wrongdoers. To illustrate, the labor department may seek to inspect employers' payroll records when checking for compliance with minimum wage laws.

Most administrative activity, however, does not focus directly on prosecutorial law enforcement. The authority to investigate is a principal device of administrative supervision. For example, the banks are supervised by the Federal Reserve Board and the Federal Deposit Insurance Corporation through visits by their inspectors for examination of the bank's records, and not through prosecution. Similarly, the Securities and Exchange Commission relies primarily upon compulsory disclosure to regulate security fraud. Agencies regulating transportation, pipelines, and communications have employed investigation for the development of information for the formulation of rules. Their investigations of youth fares for airlines, electricity shortages, and television commercials aimed at children are recent illustrations. In the same vein, before it recommended Congressional legislation for regulation of cigarette packaging and advertising, the Federal Trade Commission held several public hearings to permit concerned parties to present their views and submit information (Gellhorn, 1972:77–78).

Congress has traditionally conferred broad investigative powers upon the agencies. Important and typical are the provisions of the Federal Trade Commission Act, empowering the Commission to: (1) instruct corporations to file annual or special reports and answer specific questions in writing (this may account, in part, for the fact that the federal government is using

4987 different kinds of information-gathering forms [Time, 1978:26]); (2) obtain access to corporate files for examination and reproduction of their contents; and (3) subpoena the attendance of witnesses and the production of documentary evidence (Gellhorn, 1972:79). It would be difficult to devise a broader authorization for fact gathering.

Rule-Making   Rule-making essentially involves the formulation of a policy or interpretation which the agency will apply in the future to all persons engaged in the regulated activity. As a quasi-legislative body, administrative agencies issue three types of rules: procedural, interpretive, and legislative. Procedural rules identify an agency's organization, describe its methods of operation, and list the requirements of its practice for rule-making and adjudicative hearings. Interpretive rules are issued by an agency to guide both its staff and regulated parties as to how the agency will interpret its statutory mandate. These rules range from informally developed policy statements announced through press releases to authoritative rulings binding upon the agency and issued usually after a notice and hearing. Legislative rules are, in effect, administrative statutes. In issuing a legislative rule, the agency exercises lawmaking power delegated to it by the legislature.

Kenneth Culp Davis considers rule-making as one of the greatest inventions of modern government and argues that the United States is entering the age of rule-making (Davis, 1977:241). Rule-making is any agency process for formulating, amending, or repealing a rule, and most rule-making falls into the "notice and comment" category. The Administrative Procedure Act requires simply that the proposed rule be announced in advance and that interested parties should be afforded an opportunity to present their views. Rule-making generally involves policy issues (value judgments), which depend upon the agency's knowledge about current practices, the impact of the proposed rule, the need for public protection against inadequate safeguards, and the possible burden (cost) of government regulation on private or public interests.

The rule-making process, more often than not, is lengthy and complicated. Usually a lawyer's expertise is needed to master the procedural maze and technical requirements imposed by administrative agencies. But even so, an average person may initiate and participate in the process. Unlike legislatures and courts, access to administrative agencies is often direct. No middlemen stand between agencies and their clients (Jacob, 1986:249). Let us consider an illustration of the process in the jurisdiction of the Consumer Product Safety Commission.

Anyone may petition the Commission to issue, change, or withdraw a consumer product safety rule. After the petition is filed, it goes to the general counsel's office, where it is studied to see if it is complete and if the Commission has jurisdiction over the request. If it passes, it is routed to the technical staff which collects data—pro and con—pertinent to the petition. Based on this information, the staff makes a series of recommendations to the Commission, which considers the recommendations and the data and decides whether the petition should be granted. If it is granted, the staff, with public participation, proposes a rule for approval by the Commission. This is published in the Federal Register to allow for public comments, usually due within thirty to sixty days. The technical staff evaluates the comments and decides if any changes in the proposed rule are needed. The Commission reviews that evaluation and makes a final decision. The rule is then published in the Federal Register with the date on which it will become effective.

Adjudication   Administrative agencies of all kinds and at all levels must settle disputes or mediate among conflicting claims. Adjudication is the administrative equivalent to a judicial trial. It applies policy to a set of past actions and results in an order against (or in favor of) the named party.

Independent regulatory agencies bear the main burden of making judicial decisions when disputes arise between two or more private interests, or between private interests and the government. Congress has delegated power to regulatory agencies to make such decisions, a power that transforms them into courts and the administrators into judges. They receive complaints, hold hearings, listen to witnesses and lawyers, study briefs, and make decisions much like any other court. Gellhorn notes: "Although comparative figures are inexact, the conclusion is indisputable that administrative trials far exceed the number of judicial trials" (1972:132).

Much of this adjudication is handled informally through the voluntary settlement of cases at lower levels in an agency. At these levels, agencies dispose of disputes relatively quickly and inexpensively, and they take an immense burden off the courts. Moreover, they are handled by individuals who are experts in technical areas. But this practice is not without criticism. Many individuals—in particular, lawyers pleading cases before the agencies—have expressed concern over the extent of judicial power vested in agencies. They complain that administrators violate due process of law by holding private and informal sessions, by failing to give interested parties an adequate hearing, and by basing their decisions on insufficient evidence.

These complaints stem, in part, from the institutional differences between agency and court trials. Agency hearings, unlike court hearings, tend to produce evidence of general conditions, as distinguished from facts relating specifically to the respondent. This distinction is due to one of the original justifications for administrative agencies—the development of policy. Another difference is that in an administrative hearing, a case is tried by a trial examiner and never by a jury. As a result, the rules of evidence applied in jury trials, presided over by a judge, are frequently inapplicable in an administrative trial. The trial examiner decides both the facts and the law to be applied. Finally, the courts accept whatever cases the disputants present. As a result, their familiarity with the subject matter is accidental. By contrast, agencies usually select and prosecute their cases. Trial examiners and agency chiefs are either experts or at least have a substantial familiarity with the subject matter, since their jurisdictions tend to be restricted.

Partly in response to these complaints and differences, the Administrative Procedure Act of 1946 was passed, providing for broader judicial review of administrative decisions. The courts have always had the power to overturn the agencies' judgments on points of law, as in cases where an agency has exceeded its authority or misinterpreted the law, or simply been unfair. Under the 1946 Act, however, the courts acquired more authority to examine questions of *fact*—that is, to go over the mass of technical evidence examined by the agencies. Though this tendency has not gone far, it sheds light on the problem of maintaining the balance between judicial control and administrative expertise. Judicial review of agency activities also deals with procedural safeguards, such as more formalized hearings and proper notice of action. But the role of courts is limited to procedural matters—advising agencies, sometimes repeatedly, to go about their business in a fairer manner and to pay serious attention to all affected interests. In technical, complex disputes, courts cannot decide major issues. They will not set tariffs, allocate airline routes, or control the development of satellite communications (Breyer and Stewart, 1979:Chapter 4).

Those who are concerned with the concentration of judicial power in agencies generally express the fear that administrators will do too much prosecuting and not enough impartial judging. Yet the opposite tendency may prevail. In some instances, agencies become so occupied with umpiring disputes that they pay insufficient attention to prosecuting offenders. They tend to sit back and wait for complaints to be filed instead of taking the initiative in ferreting out violations of the law. Such a course may seem to be the safe thing to do; to some extent, the regular courts have forced agencies to organize themselves mainly as judicial bodies. But the result of this tendency may be inadequate protection of the very groups these agencies were set up to safeguard.

LAW ENFORCEMENT AGENCIES

The primary functions of the police are law enforcement, maintenance of order, and community service. Like other components of the American legal system, the origins of the American police can be traced to early English history. In the ninth century, Alfred the Great started paying private citizens for arresting offenders. The population was broken down into units of ten families or "tithings," and each person was responsible for watching over the others. Subsequently, the unit was expanded tenfold to the "hundred" and one person, designated as the constable, was in charge of maintaining order. In time, the hundred was increased to include the countywide "shire," under the control of an appointed "shire-reeve," who later on became known as the "sheriff." The first citywide police force was created by Sir Robert Peel in London in 1829. Police officers were uniformed, organized along military lines, and called "Bobbies" after their founder. The American colonists adopted the English system of law enforcement, and the first metropolitan police force was created in Philadelphia in 1833 (Loh, 1984:276).

In 1985, there were 619,634 police personnel in the United States— 470,678 officers and 148,956 civilians. On the average, there were 2.1 full-time officers for every 1,000 inhabitants. City law enforcement averages ranged from 2 per 1,000 residents in those with populations from 25,000 to 49,999 to 3.4 for those with populations of 250,000 or more. Rural and suburban counties averaged 3.3 and 2.9 per 1,000 population, respectively (Federal Bureau of Investigation, 1986:242). Police expenditures are in excess of $20 billion annually. Over 10 million formal arrests were made by police officers in 1985.

In the United States there is no unified system of law enforcement. As Thomas F. Adams observes:

> A police system—if one were to exist—in the United States would be a rank ordering of all the local police agencies in sequence, according to their relative importance; then higher up the scale would be placed the many state agencies, and finally a rank ordering up through all of the federal agencies to a single head or committee. Such a system does not exist in the United States (1973:69).

Bruce Smith (1960) identifies five types of public law enforcement systems in the United States conforming roughly to the major levels of government: (1) the police agencies of the federal government; (2) the state police forces and criminal investigation agencies of the fifty states; (3) the sheriffs in more than 3,000 counties, plus a few county police forces that either duplicate the sheriff's police jurisdiction or displace it; (4) the police of 1,000 cities and more than 20,000 townships or New England towns, to which must be added an unknown number of magisterial districts and county districts in the south and west; and (5) the police of 15,000 villages, boroughs, and incorporated towns, together with a small number of special-purpose forces serving public quasi-corporations and ad hoc districts. If we add to these the law enforcement activities of private police agencies, we end up with a number of systems of law enforcement, related in their functions and at times overlapping in their jurisdictions.

In addition, within these systems are specific police agencies. Some federal agencies have law enforcement powers, such as the Federal Bureau of Investigation, the Secret Service, the Bureau of Narcotics, Post Office Inspectors, the Bureau of Internal Revenue, the Bureau of Customs, the Immigration Border Patrol, and the Alcohol Tax Unit of the Department of Treasury (Adams, 1973:86–93). The federal government also maintains the U.S. Marshal as a law enforcement agent, appointed by the President to a four-year term, whose duties are to preserve order in the courtrooms, handle subpoenas and summons, seize goods, transport prisoners, and serve as a disbursing officer (Souryal, 1977:97).

With some exceptions, law enforcement at the state level was established in the United States at the beginning of the twentieth century. Although their jurisdictions vary from state to state, police agencies perform such varied functions as enforcing traffic laws, investigating fires, inspecting liquor laws, arresting juvenile offenders, and inspecting property. They also assist local police agencies in criminal identification and laboratory and communication services (Adams, 1973:78–86).

Another type of police agency that should be included in a discussion of law enforcement agencies is the private police department. Special needs of private sectors of the community require the services of private police patrols and investigation agencies. An example of a well-organized and efficient police force is the railroad police of the United States and Canada, the largest privately supported police agency in the world. Other businesses, industries, and institutions use private agencies, such as Pinkerton's Incorporated, to guard property, apprehend thieves, investigate offenses, and to detect fraud and embezzlement. These organizations spend more than $1 billion annually on these services. Pinkerton's Incorporated alone has a staff of more than 30,000 (Kakalik and Wildhorn, 1972). Finally, many large corporations have their own private police. As an example, General Motors in 1978 had more than 4200 plant guards, a police force larger than the police departments in all but the five biggest cities in the country (Friedman, 1984:21). The rest of this section will be devoted to the structural features of municipal police departments.

The Organization of Law Enforcement Agencies

Municipal and other police organizations are structured along the lines of complex bureaucratic organizations (see Figure 3-4). A variety of specific organizational tables or patterns describe how the police divide up tasks. In every case a formal and highly complex division of labor characterizes these systems (see, for example, Wilson and McLaren, 1972). In addition to its bureaucratic characteristics, law enforcement agencies are structured like quasi-military institutions which give these agencies their special character. Bittner notes: "Both institutions are instruments of force and for both institutions the occasions for using force are unpredictably distributed. Thus, the personnel in each must be kept in a highly disciplined state of alert preparedness. The formalism that characterizes military organization, the insistence on rules and regulations, on spit and polish, on obedience to superiors, and so on, constitute a permanent rehearsal for "the real thing" (1970:53).

This system of law enforcement is built on a subordinating chain of command (Bordua and Reiss, 1966). Although all units of a particular department may be related to a central command, the overall chain of command is divided into units so that different precincts or squads are immediately responsible to a localized authority. The functional divisions of police departments follow the kinds of activities they handle, such as traffic patrol, investigative work, undercover work (for example, in vice and narcotics), crowd control, and uniformed patrol, whose officers are popularly referred to as "cops"—which is the abbreviation of the British designation of "constable on patrol."

Police departments do not require special education. Most officers entering the force have no more than a high school education although lately some college education without any specialized training is becoming the norm. Police training is pragmatic and brief and usually takes place in a police academy. Most officers come from lower-middle class or working

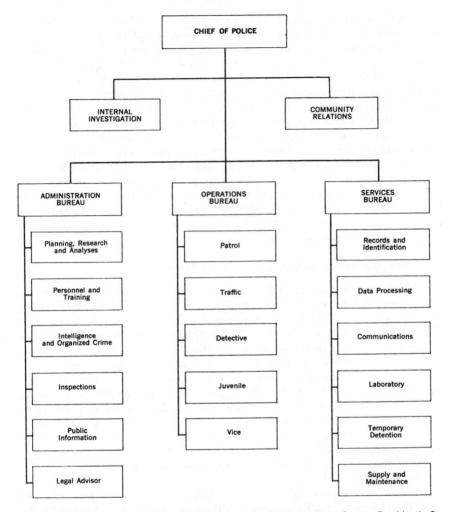

FIGURE 3-4   One form of a well-organized municipal police department. *Source:* President's Commission on Law Enforcement and Administration of Justice, Task Force Report: The Police (Washington, D.C.: U.S. Government Printing Office, 1967), p. 47.

class backgrounds (Jacob, 1986: 156–157). For many, becoming a police officer is an opportunity for upward social mobility, and in some ethnic groups such as the Irish there is a high proportion of family members in law enforcement.

Among police officers, there is a high degree of cohesion and solidarity, much more so than in other occupational groups (Brown, 1981). They are by virtue of occupational expectations suspicious, tend to be skeptical toward outsiders, and much of their outlook and conduct have an authoritarian character (Bartol, 1983). Their subculture includes a code of silence, and fellow officers rarely incriminate each other. They socialize and make friends within the department, and some even conceal their police identity (Skolnick, 1975).

Much of policing consists of routine patrol and maintaining order such as attending to domestic disputes, handling drunks, assisting motorists, escorting dignitaries, processing juveniles, and the like. Contrary to popular image, police officers, with the exception of detectives, spend about 20 percent of their time in criminal investigations (Brown, 1981:322).

The effectiveness of law enforcement agencies (as determined usually by arrest and clearance rates) depends on the way in which the departments are organized. In a study of a nonprofessionalized police department in an east-coast city and a professionalized police department in a west-coast city, James Q. Wilson (1968a) found that the nonprofessionalized department's members had no strong sense of urgency about police work and produced low rates of official actions on offenders. In the professionalized department, however, violations of the law were more likely to be detected, and offenders were more likely to be arrested, producing a higher crime rate.

In another study, James Q. Wilson (1968b) identified three styles of police work: the *watchman* style, the *legalistic* style, and the *service* style. Although elements of all three can be found in any law enforcement agency, different agencies tend to emphasize one style more than the others and as a result practice different law enforcement policies.

The *watchman* style emphasizes the responsibility for maintaining public order, as contrasted to law enforcement. The police officer in such an agency is viewed as a peace officer, ignoring or handling informally many violations of the law and paying much greater attention to local variations in the demand for law enforcement and order maintenance. The role of peace officer is characterized by a great amount of discretion, since peacekeeping is poorly structured by law or by agency regulation. Underenforcement, corruption, and low arrest rates characterize watchman style departments.

The *legalistic* style is just the opposite of the watchman style. Agencies characterized by this style tend to treat all situations, even commonplace problems of maintaining order, as if they were matters of serious law infraction. Members of such agencies issue a high rate of traffic tickets, arrest a high proportion of juvenile offenders, and crack down on illicit enterprises. The police typically act as if there were a single standard of conduct rather than different standards for different groups. As a result, some groups, especially juveniles, blacks, and migrants, are more likely to be affected by law enforcement than others considered "respectable" by the police. Although this style of law enforcement is characterized by technical efficiency and high arrest rates, it also results in inequality in law enforcement with complaints of harassment and police brutality by groups who are most often subjected to police scrutiny.

The *service* style combines law enforcement and order maintenance. An emphasis is placed on community relations, the police on patrol work out of specialized units, and command is decentralized. The pace of work is more leisurely, and more promotional opportunities are available. This style differs from the watchman style in that the police respond to all groups and apply informal sanctions in the case of minor offenses. It differs from the legalistic style in that fewer arrests are made for minor infractions, and the police are more responsive to public sentiments and desires. In this sense, the service style is less arbitrary than the watchman style and more atuned to the practical considerations of public service than the legalistic style. There is little corruption, and complaints against police in service style departments tend to be low.

Police Discretion

The characteristic feature of law enforcement—indeed of the entire judicial process—is that legal officials have wide discretion (the opportunity and freedom to make decisions on an individual basis) as to how and when they are to fulfill the occupational requirements of their office. Albert J. Reiss and David J. Bordua (1967) point out that police discretion and disparity stem in a large part from the general organization of modern police work. As a largely reactive force, primarily dependent on citizen mobilization, the police officer functions in criminal law much like a private attorney functions in civil law—determining when the victim's complaint warrants formal action and encouraging private settlement of disputes whenever possible. Among such private arrangements protected by the police are those of their own relationships with various categories of citizens, so that the degree to which formal legality is extended by police to different categories of individuals varies substantially. In view of the highly decentralized police operation, with minimal direct supervision, it is difficult to control such disparate treatment. Many of the decisions of police officers on the beat do not lend themselves to either command or review. As a result, police exercise a considerable amount of discretionary power, as reflected in disparities in the volume of arrests, parking tickets, and pedestrian stops. For example, James Q. Wilson's (1968:95) investigation of eight separate police agencies showed that, among other things, the arrest rates for moving traffic violations ranged from 11.4 to 247.7 per 1000 population in the cities he studied.

Because of their discretionary power, "the police are among our most important policymaking administrative agencies. One may wonder whether any other agencies—federal, state, or local—make so much policy that so directly and vitally affects so many people" (Davis, 1975a:263). The police need to make policy with regard to nearly all their activities, such as deciding what types of private disputes to mediate and how to do it, breaking up sidewalk gatherings, helping drunks, deciding what to do with runaways, breaking up fights and matrimonial disputes, entering and searching premises, controlling juveniles, and managing race relations. They exercise discretion in both reactive and proactive policing.

Reactive police work is a response to citizen mobilization. But even before a citizen can reach a police officer, discretionary power is exercised by police dispatchers at the communication center. A member of the dispatch crew answers the telephone call made to the police emergency number, interviews the caller to identify the nature and location of the reported problem, and decides whether to dispatch a patrol car. In a study of tele-phone calls to three departments, T. E. Bercal (1970) found that 20 to 40 percent of the calls are handled without dispatching a car. If the dispatcher decides to send a patrol car, the nature of the assignment (for example, burglary or robbery), and which car to assign must be determined. When a car is dispatched, the officer may informally turn down the assignment, or may procrastinate on the way, or even lie about having investigated the call (Rubinstein, 1973:87–123). If the officer follows up on the call, he or she often has to decide whether a crime has been committed. Albert J. Reiss (1971:73) found that in Chicago, while citizens considered 58 percent of their complaints as criminal matters, officers responding to these dis-patches officially processed only 17 percent as criminal matters. Harold E. Pepinsky (1976:21–22) suggests that police officers' decisions are mainly determined by the dispatcher's characterization of the incident.

A great deal of police work is undertaken on the initiative of the po-lice themselves without citizen mobilization (Reiss, 1971:88–114). The ac-tivities of traffic and tactical divisions are primarily proactive policing, as are the various nondispatched activities of detectives and vice divisions. In proactive policing, discretionary power is exercised in the context of whether or not to stop a suspicious pedestrian or automobile for investi-gation.

In both reactive and proactive policing, the use of discretion can take a number of forms: investigation, confrontation, disposition, and decisions about the use of force. Police officials have the option (although limited) of investigating some acts and not others. The police, for example, may elect to ignore or to actively pursue a citizen's complaint. In some cases, the police arrest a suspect while in others—even though the act and cir-cumstances may be similar—the individual is released. And some people are "roughed up" by the police while others are handled with respect. All along the line decisions are made by the police.

Kenneth Culp Davis (1975a:264) notes that the power of the police not to enforce the law in any particular circumstances is enormous. It can even be turned into an affirmative weapon. Jerome H. Skolnick, in *Justice Without Trial* (1975), discusses an Oakland ordinance which permits holding every woman arrested for prostitution for eight days for a venereal check. The ordinance conferred no discretionary power on the police, but officers assumed a discretionary power not to enforce the ordinance against women who cooperated: They detained for testing only 38 percent of the women who were arrested. As one officer explained: "If a girl gives us a hard time ... we'll put a hold on her. I guess we're actually supposed to put a hold on everybody, so there's nothing wrong in putting a hold on her ... but you know how it is, you get to know some of the girls, and you don't want to give them extra trouble" (Skolnick, 1975:108). In this context, Davis (1975a:264) contends that since the ordinance requires holding every woman arrested, assumption of discretion not to enforce against 62 percent of those arrested was contrary to the terms of the ordinance. Here, discre-tion not to enforce was converted into an affirmative weapon: "If a girl gives us a hard time ... we'll put a hold on her." This policy of enforcement discriminates against the innocent woman, because she is more likely to resist, and the experienced woman is more likely to cooperate. The discrimination appears clearly unjust.

There is indeed, a thin line between discretion and discrimination in discretionary law enforcement. If the likelihood that an individual will be considered a criminal is dependent on the discretionary power of the police to respond or to ignore a citizen's complaint, to arrest or to release a suspect, and the like, then the probability that any one person will be labeled a criminal increases or decreases depending on that person's correspondence to police conceptions of the criminal. Some individuals are more likely than others to have their behavior treated as crime by the police, and consequently, are more likely to be labeled as criminal. For example, Nathan Goldman (1963:35–47) found that 65 percent of the black offenders arrested by the police were referred to the juvenile court, as contrasted to 34 percent of the white youths apprehended. Similarly, Donald J. Black and Albert J. Reiss (1970:68) found that 21 percent of black teenagers, but only 8 percent of the white youths encountered by the police were arrested. Although evidence is sketchy, there is reason to assume that young adults, poor citizens, minority members, migrants, and individuals who look disreputable by police standards are more likely to experience one or another form of police brutality and to be arrested than are more "respectable" citizens. They also tend to be less deferential toward officers, and in general, the police are likely to sanction suspects who fail to defer to police authority, whether legal grounds exist or not (Black, 1980:77).

Police discretion not to enforce the law is attributed to a number of conditions. These include the police belief that: (1) the legislative body does not desire enforcement; (2) the community wants nonenforcement or lax enforcement; (3) other immediate duties are more urgent; (4) the offenders promise not to commit the act again; (5) there is a lack of adequate police manpower; (6) there is sympathy with the violator; (7) a particular criminal act is common within a subculture; (8) the victim is likely to get restitution without arrest; (9) the police trade nonenforcement for information; (10) the police feel that the probable penalty is likely to be too severe; and (11) the arrest would unduly harm the offender's status (Davis, 1975a:264–265).

But as Kenneth Culp Davis (1975b:140) emphatically argues: "Police discretion is absolutely essential. It cannot be eliminated. Any effort to eliminate it would be ridiculous. Discretion is the essence of police work, both in law enforcement and in service activities. Police work without discretion would be something like a human torso without legs, arms, or head." Selective enforcement represents low-visibility interaction between individual officers and various citizens. The exercise of discretion is not guided by clear policy directives, nor is it subject to administrative scrutiny. For such reasons, selective enforcement can easily deteriorate into police abuse and discriminatory conduct. Although it cannot be eliminated, Joseph Goldstein (1960) proposes that an impartial civilian body should scrutinize the decisions as to which laws should be enforced. In that way, discretionary conduct would become more visible and might result in selective law enforcement that would then become a subject for open public dialogue. Discretionary law enforcement can also become an area in police-community relations (Clark, 1979:213-218).

SUMMARY

This chapter has been concerned with the organization of law in society in the context of judicial, legislative, administrative, and enforcement agencies.

Court cases generally begin with a dispute. Private-initiated, public-initiated, and public defendant disputes constitute for the most part the work load of American courts. There are fifty-one court systems in the United States, one federal court, and fifty separate state court organizations. This dual hierarchy operates side by side. When disputes move from the trial to the appellate level, they are typically transformed and become almost exclusively disputes about law or about procedures.

Courts as dispute processing institutions are composed of four distinct groups of participants—litigants, lawyers, judges, and juries. Litigants can be distinguished by the relative frequency with which they resort to court services. There are two types: the "one-shotters" and the "repeat players." The most important distinction that can be made among types of litigating lawyers is the manner in which they perceive their clientele. These types include: public-interest, private-interest, criminal defense lawyers, and client-oriented attorneys. The judges are the most prestigious participants in court processes. In addition to basic adjudication functions, and the control of the flow of litigation in the courtrooms, judges are also responsible for administering their courts. Judges' personal backgrounds and values affect their decisions, which in turn are bases for their recruitment to the higher bench. Juries are used exclusively in trial courts. The major issues surrounding the participation of jurors in the processing of disputes include their effectiveness on checking the power of judges; the use of the scientific method in jury selection; the degree of their representativeness of the community; and their competence. Although the flow of litigation is different in criminal and civil cases, a high degree of discretion at every level is characteristic of both.

Although the principal function of legislative bodies is lawmaking, they also engage in conflict-management and integrative functions. At both the federal and the state levels, legislatures are comprised of two separate bodies—the House and the Senate—which differ in several respects. Differences exist between the House and Senate in organization, procedure, and in the regular activities of their members. The House operates under more formal rules than does the Senate. Behavior in both Houses is influenced by a set of informal rules and norms. Much of the important work is done by standing committees and subcommittees.

The participants in the legislative process are legislators, executives, and lobbyists. The majority of legislators come from a middle- or upper-class background. The recruitment of legislators is selective in terms of education, religion, and occupational status. Protestant Anglo-Saxon males are substantially overrepresented among legislators. Executives perform three main functions in the legislative process: They serve as a source of ideas; they function as catalytic agents; and they implement the law. The lobbyist plays a variety of key roles in the legislative process, such as contact person, campaign organizer, and watchdog.

Administrative agencies, often called "the fourth branch of government," reach into virtually every corner of American life. Administrative rules affect the food we eat, the cars we drive, the fuel we use, the clothes we wear, the houses we live in, the investments we make, the water we drink, and even the air we breathe. These agencies are authorities of the government other than the executive, legislative, and judicial branches, created for the purpose of administering particular legislations. Administrative agencies are just as subject to pressures of interest groups as are all other lawmakers. Administrative agencies have powers of investigation, rulemaking, and adjudication. Information is essential for administrative agencies to carry out their functions. Rule-making is administrative lawmaking, and it consists of the power to make or alter rules and regulations. Adjudication is the administrative's equivalent of a judicial trial. Much of it is handled informally through the voluntary settlement of cases at lower levels in an agency. In case of disagreement, administrative decisions can be subjected to judicial review, and the courts have the power to overturn an agency's judgment, both on points of law and on questions of fact.

The police are expected and empowered to enforce the law. In the United States, there is no unified system of law enforcement. An important characteristic of law enforcement is the strongly bureaucratic and militaristic organization of the police. The effectiveness of law enforcement agencies depends on the way in which departments are organized. In professionalized departments, there is a greater tendency to detect violators and a higher arrest rate than in nonprofessionalized departments. Law enforcement is characterized by a high amount of discretion. Both in reactive and proactive policing, the use of police discretion can take a number of forms: investigation, confrontation, disposition, and the decision to use force. There is a thin line between discretion and discrimination in discretionary law enforcement.

SUGGESTED FURTHER READINGS

HENRY J. ABRAHAM, *The Judicial Process, An Introductory Analysis of the Courts of the United States, England, and France,* 4th ed. New York: Oxford University Press, 1980. An up-to-date cross-cultural overview of court organizations, processes, and participants.

DONALD BLACK, *The Manners and Customs of the Police.* New York: Academic Press. 1980. An outstanding collection of essays on police behavior.

ABRAHAM S. BLUMBERG, *Criminal Justice, Issues & Ironies,* 2nd ed. New York: New Viewpoints, 1979. An influential critical overview of the criminal justice system and its participants.

KENNETH CULP DAVIS, *Police Discretion.* St. Paul, MN: West Publishing Company, 1975. A brief and readable study of police discretion in selective enforcement written by a lawyer.

JAMES O. FREEDMAN, *Crises and Legitimacy, The Administrative Process and American Government.* Cambridge: Cambridge University Press, 1978. A discussion of issues confronting administrative agencies.

SHELDON GOLDMAN AND AUSTIN SARAT (eds.), *American Court Systems, Readings in Judicial Process and Behavior.* San Francisco: W. H. Freeman & Company Publishers, 1978. A compendium of some of the best materials available to illuminate the various facets of American courts.

HERBERT JACOB, *Justice in America, Courts, Lawyers, and the Judicial Process.* 4th ed. Boston: Little, Brown, 1984. A good analysis of how justice is organized and administered in American courts.

RANDALL B. RIPLEY, *Congress, Process and Policy,* 2nd ed. New York: W. W. Norton & Co., Inc., 1978. A comprehensive examination of the organization and functions of Congress from the perspective of a political scientist.

JOHN R. SCHMIDHAUSER, *Judges and Justices.* Boston: Little, Brown, 1979. A documentation and analysis of the court systems and their components in Max Weber's theoretical framework.

JEROME H. SKOLNICK, *Justice Without Trial: Law Enforcement in Democratic Society,* 2nd ed. New York: John Wiley, 1975. An influential sociological study of the various facets of law enforcement.

JAMES Q. WILSON, *The Politics of Regulation.* New York: Basic Books, 1980. An insightful analysis of regulatory activities in the economic sphere with plenty of illustrative material.

SEYMOUR WISHMAN, *Anatomy of A Jury.* New York: Times Books, 1986. An informative nontechnical book on the function of the jury in our criminal justice system written by a former criminal lawyer.

REFERENCES

ADAMS, THOMAS F. 1973. *Law Enforcement, An Introduction to the Police Role in the Criminal Justice System,* 2nd ed. Englewood Cliffs, NJ: Prentice-Hall.

ALKER, HAYWARD R. Jr., CARL HOSTICKA and MICHAEL MITCHELL. 1976. "Jury Selection as a Biased Social Process," Law and Society Review 11 (1)(Fall):9–41.

ANDREWS, LORI B. 1982. "Mind Control in the Courtroom," Psychology Today (March):66–73.

ASHER, HERBERT. 1973. "The Learning of Legislative Norms," American Political Science Review (67)(June):499–513.

BARONE, MICHAEL, and GRANT UJIFUSA. 1985. *The Almanac of American Politics 1986.* Washington, DC: National Journal, Inc.

BARTOL, C. R. 1983. *Psychology and American Law.* Belmont, CA: Wadsworth.

BERCAL, T.E. 1970. "Calls for Police Assistance: Consumer Demands for Governmental Service," American Behavioral Scientist 13 (5–6)(May–August):681–691.

BITTNER, EGON. 1970. *The Functions of the Police in Modern Society.* Chevy Chase, MD: National Institute of Mental Health.

BLACK, DONALD. 1973. "The Mobilization of Law," Journal of Legal Studies 2(1)(January):125–149.

BLACK, DONALD. 1980. *The Manners and Customs of the Police.* New York: Academic Press.

BLACK, DONALD J., and ALBERT J. REISS, Jr. 1970. "Police Control of Juveniles," American Sociological Review 35(1)(February):63–77.

BLUMBERG, ABRAHAM S. 1979. *Criminal Justice, Issues & Ironies,* 2nd ed. New York: New Viewpoints.

BORDUA, DAVID J., and ALBERT J. REISS, Jr. 1966. "Command, Control, and Charisma: Reflections on Police Bureaucracy," American Journal of Sociology 72 (1)(July):68–76.

BOULDING, KENNETH E. 1956. *The Image.* Ann Arbor: University of Michigan Press.

BREYER, STEPHEN G., and RICHARD B. STEWART. 1979. *Administrative Law and Regulatory Policy.* Boston: Little, Brown.

BROWN, MICHAEL K. 1981. *Working the Street: Police Discretion and the Dilemmas of Reform.* New York: Russell Sage Foundation.

CASPER, JONATHAN. 1972. *Lawyers Before the Warren Court.* Urbana, IL: University of Illinois Press.

CLARK, ROBERT S. 1979. *Police and the Community, An Analytic Perspective.* New York: New Viewpoints.

COHN, ALVIN W. 1976. *Crime and Justice Administration.* Philadelphia: Lippincott.

COLEMAN, JAMES W. 1985. *The Criminal Elite: The Sociology of White Collar Crime.* New York: St. Martin's Press.
CORBOY, PHILIP H. 1975. "From the Bar." Pp. 179–195 in Rita James Simon (ed.), The Jury System in America. A Critical Overview. Beverly Hills, CA: Sage Publications.
DAVIS, KENNETH CULP. 1975a. *Administrative Law and Government,* 2nd ed. St. Paul, MN: West Publishing Company; 1975b. *Police Discretion.* St. Paul, MN: West Publishing Company; 1977. *Administrative Law, Cases—Text—Problems,* 6th ed. St. Paul, MN: West Publishing Company.
EISENSTEIN, JAMES, and HERBERT JACOB. 1977. *Felony Justice.* Boston: Little, Brown.
FEDERAL BUREAU OF INVESTIGATION. 1986. *Uniform Crime Reports for the United States.* Washington, DC: U.S. Department of Justice.
FEELEY, MALCOLM M. 1979. "Perspectives on Plea Bargaining," Law and Society Review (Special Issue on Plea Bargaining) 13 (2)(Winter):199–209.
FORD FOUNDATION. 1978. *New Approaches to Conflict Resolution.* New York: The Ford Foundation.
FREEDMAN, JAMES O. 1978. *Crisis and Legitimacy, The Administrative Process and American Government.* Cambridge: Cambridge University Press.
FRIEDMAN, LAWRENCE M. 1984. *American Law: An Introduction.* New York: W. W. Norton & Company; 1986. *A History of American Law.* 2nd ed. New York: Simon & Schuster, Inc./Touchstone Book.
GALANTER, MARC. 1974. "Why the 'Haves' Come Out Ahead: Speculations on the Limits of Legal Change," Law and Society Review 9 (1)(Fall):95–160.
GELLHORN, ERNEST. 1972. *Administrative Law and Process.* St. Paul, MN: West Publishing Company.
GOLDMAN, NATHAN. 1963. *The Differential Selection of Juvenile Offenders for Court Appearance.* New York: National Council on Crime and Delinquency.
GOLDMAN, SHELDON, and AUSTIN SARAT, eds. 1978. *American Court Systems, Readings in Judicial Process and Behavior.* San Francisco: W. H. Freeman and Company.
GOLDSTEIN, JOSEPH. 1960. "Police Discretion Not to Invoke the Criminal Process: Low Visibility Decisions in the Administration of Criminal Justice," Yale Law Journal (69)(March):543–594.
HANS, VALERIE P., and NEIL VIDMAR. 1986. *Judging the Jury.* New York: Plenum Press.
HUNT, MORTON. 1982. "Putting Juries on the Couch," The New York Times Magazine (November 28):70–87.
JACOB, HERBERT. 1984. *Justice in America: Courts, Lawyers, and the Judicial Process,* 4th ed. Boston: Little, Brown; 1986. *Law and Politics in the United States.* Boston: Little, Brown.
JEWELL, MALCOLM E., and SAMUEL C. PATTERSON. 1973. *The Legislative Process in the United States,* 2nd ed. New York: Random House.
KAKALIK, JAMES S., and SORREL WILDHORN. 1972. *The Private Police Industry: Its Nature and Extent,* vol. II. Washington, DC: Law Enforcement Assistance Administration.
KALVEN, HARRY JR., and HANZ ZEISEL. 1966. *The American Jury.* Boston: Little, Brown.
KLEIN, MITCHELL S. G. 1984. *Law, Courts, and Policy.* Englewood Cliffs, NJ: Prentice-Hall.
LOH, WALLACE D. 1984. *Social Research in the Judicial Process: Cases, Readings, and Text.* New York: Russell Sage Foundation.
MATTHEWS, DONALD R. 1954. *The Social Background of Political Decision-Makers.* New York: Random House; 1960. *U.S. Senators and Their World.* Chapel Hill: University of North Carolina Press.
NEWMAN, DONALD J. 1975. *Introduction to Criminal Justice.* Philadelphia: Lippincott.
PATRIDGE, ANTHONY, and WILLIAM B. ELDRIDGE. 1978. "The Second Circuit Sentencing Study." Pp. 317–329 in Sheldon Goldman and Austin Farat (eds.), American Court Systems, Readings in Judicial Process and Behavior. San Francisco: W. H. Freeman & Company Publishers.
PEPINSKY, HAROLD E. 1976. *Crime and Conflict, A Study of Law and Society.* New York: Academic Press.
President's Commission on Law Enforcement and Administration of Justice. 1967. *The Challenge of Crime in a Free Society.* Washington, DC: U.S. Government Printing Office.
REISS, ALBERT J., JR. 1971. *The Police and the Public.* New Haven: Yale University Press.
REISS, ALBERT J., JR., and DAVID J. BORDUA. 1967. "Environment and Organization: A Perspective on the Police." Pp. 25–55 in David J. Bordua, ed., The Police: Six Sociological Essays. New York: John Wiley.

RIPLEY, RANDALL B. 1978. *Congress, Process and Policy,* 2nd ed. New York: W. W. Norton & Co. Inc.

ROSETT, ARTHUR, and DONALD R. CRESSEY. 1976. *Justice by Consent: Plea Bargains in the American Courthouse.* Philadelphia: Lippincott.

ROSS, H. LAURENCE. 1970. *Settled Out of Court.* Chicago: Aldine.

RUBINSTEIN, JONATHAN. 1973. *City Police.* New York: Farrar, Straus & Giroux.

St. Louis Post-Dispatch. 1979. "Regulations Cost Every Consumer $500 Yearly." (July 30):4B; 1986. "Police Win Battle Against The NRA." (July 28):2B.

SAKS, MICHAEL J., and REID MASTIE. 1978. *Social Psychology in Court.* New York: Van Nostrand Reinhold Company.

SCHMIDHAUSER, JOHN R. 1979. *Judges and Justices.* Boston: Little Brown.

SCHWARTZ, BERNARD. 1959. *The Professor and the Commissions.* New York: Knopf.

SIMON, RITA J. 1980. *The Jury: Its Role in American Society.* Lexington, MA: Lexington Books, D.C. Heath and Company.

SKOLNICK, JEROME H. 1975. *Justice Without Trial: Law Enforcement in Democratic Society,* 2nd ed. New York: John Wiley.

SLONIM, SCOTT. 1980. "Survey Finds Fewer Lawyer-Legislators," American Bar Association Journal 66 (January):30.

SMITH, BRUCE. 1960. *Police Systems in the United States,* 2nd ed. New York: Harper & Row. Pub.

SOURYAL, SAM S. 1977. *Police Administration and Management.* St. Paul, MN: West Publishing Company.

Time. 1978. "Paper Chase, The Battle Against Red Tape." (July 10):26; 1981. "We, the Jury, Find the . . . " (September 28):44–56.

TOMASIC, ROMAN. 1985. *The Sociology of Law.* London: Sage Publications.

TRUMAN, DAVID B. 1951. *The Governmental Process.* New York: Knopf.

U.S. News & World Report. 1980. "Your Hamburger: 41,000 Regulations," (February 1):64.

WEIDENBAUM, MURRAY L. 1979. *The Future of Business Regulation, Private Action and Public Demand.* New York: AMACOM, A Division of American Management Associations.

WICE, PAUL B. 1978. *Criminal Lawyers, An Endangered Species.* Beverly Hills, CA: Sage Publications, Inc.

WILSON, JAMES Q. 1968a. "The Police and the Delinquent in Two Cities." Pp. 9–30 in Stanton Wheeler, ed., Controlling Delinquents. New York: John Wiley; 1968b. *Varieties of Police Behavior.* Cambridge, MA: Harvard University Press.

WILSON, O. W., and ROY C. MCLAREN. 1972. *Police Administration,* 2nd ed. New York: McGraw-Hill.

WOOCHER, FREDERIC D. 1977. "Did Your Eyes Deceive You?: Expert Psychological Testimony on the Unreliability of Eyewitness Identification," 29 Stanford Law Review:969–1030.

4

The Making of the Law

Legislative, administrative, and judicial bodies create thousands of new laws every year. Each law is unique in its specific social objective. Each has its own distinct set of precipitating factors, special history, and *raison d'être*. Still, some generalizations are possible about how laws are created in society, the sociological factors that enter into the decision to create new laws, and about the social forces that provide an impetus for making or changing laws. This chapter draws attention to the sociological theories of law creation; the ways in which legislatures, administrative agencies, and courts make laws; the roles of vested interests, public opinion, and social science in the decision-making process; and the sources of impetus for laws.

THEORIES OF LAW CREATION

There are several theoretical perspectives on law creation in the sociological literature (Chambliss, 1984:16–17; Hagan, 1980; Tomasic, 1985:101–106). Students of lawmaking have often adopted a number of theories in an effort to account for the processes by which laws are created or defeated. I will consider briefly four such theories to illustrate the diversity of perspectives—the rationalistic model, the functional view, conflict theory, and a "moral entrepreneur" thesis.

According to the *rationalistic* model, laws, in particular criminal laws, are created as rational means of protecting the members of society from social harm. In this perspective, crimes are considered socially injurious. This is the most widely accepted theory on lawmaking (Goode, 1978:143). One of the difficulties with this perspective is that it is the lawmakers who

define what activities may be harmful to the public welfare. Value judgments, preferences, and other considerations obviously enter into the process of definition (for example, why are certain types of behaviors, like prostitution or gambling—which will be discussed in the following chapter—
labeled as criminal?).

The *functionalist* view of lawmaking, as formulated by Paul Bohannan
(1973), is mainly concerned with how laws emerge. Bohannan argues that
laws are a special kind of "reinstitutionalized custom." Customs are norms
or rules about the ways in which people must behave if social institutions
are to perform their functions and society is to endure. Lawmaking is the
restatement of some customs (for example, those dealing with economic
transactions, property, or deviant behavior) so that they can be enforced
by legal institutions.

Basically, this view proposes that failure in other institutional norms
encourages the reinstitutionalization of the norms by the legal institution.
As noted earlier, this perspective implies a consensual model of lawmaking
in a society. From the functionalist perspective, laws are passed because
they represent the voice of the people. Laws are essentially a crystalization
of custom, of the existing normative order. Although there are conflicts in
society, they are relatively marginal, and they do not involve basic values.
In this view, conflict and competition between groups in a society actually
serve to contribute to its cohesion.

The *conflict* perspective, as I discussed it in the preceding chapters,
cites structural cleavages of a society as the basic determinant of laws. More
specifically, the origin of law is traced to the emergence of an elite class.
These elites, it is suggested, use social control mechanisms such as laws to
perpetuate their own positions in society. In the event of conflict over the
prescription of a norm, conflict theorists would argue that the interest
group(s) more closely tied to the interests of the elite group would probably
win the conflict. In order to define who the elites or the powerful groups
of the society are, conflict theorists often employ structural indices of power.
For example, William J. Chambliss (1964), as I noted in Chapter One, claims
that the groups in England having the most power to create the vagrancy
laws were those representing the dominant economic interests at the time.

The *"moral entrepreneur"* theory attributes the precipitation of key
events to the "presence of an enterprising individual or group. Their activities can properly be called *moral enterprise,* for what they are enterprising
about is the creation of a new fragment of the moral constitution of society,
its code of right and wrong" (Becker, 1963:146). The role of moral entrepreneurs in lawmaking is splendidly illustrated by Howard S. Becker's study
(1963:121–146) of the development of criminal law designed to repress the
use of marijuana. He notes that the Marijuana Tax Act of 1937 had its fore-
runners in earlier criminal statutes such as the Volstead Act (alcohol) and
the Harrison Act (opium and derivatives). The Narcotics Bureau of the
Treasury Department was unconcerned with marijuana in its earlier years.
It argued, instead, that the regulation of opiates was the real problem. However, shortly before 1937, the Narcotics Bureau redefined the matter of marijuana use as a serious problem. As a consequence, this agency acted in the

role of moral entrepreneur, in which it attempted to create a new definition of marijuana use as a social danger. For example, the Bureau provided information to the mass media on the dangers of marijuana, including "atrocity stories" which detailed gruesome features of marijuana smoking. Finally, in 1937 the Marijuana Tax Act was passed, ostensibly as a taxation measure but with the real purpose of preventing persons from smoking marijuana.

In addition, it should be noted that the passing of a law may also symbolize the supremacy of the groups that support it. The creation of a law is a statement that the illegal behavior is disreputable. Where groups differ significantly in prestige and status, or where two groups are competing for status, each sees the law as a stamp of legitimacy. They will seek to use it to affirm the respectability of their own way of life. According to Gusfield:

> The fact of affirmation through acts of law and government, expresses the public worth of one set of norms, or one subculture vis-à-vis those of others. It demonstrates which cultures have legitimacy and public domination, and which do not. Accordingly it enhances the social status of groups carrying the affirmed culture and degrades groups carrying that which is condemned as deviant (1967:178).

These are the prominent theories on lawmaking in the law and society literature. None of these theories can account for the creation of all laws. On the basis of research evidence, however, some models come closer to providing a general explanation than do others. But how much closer they come depends on one's theoretical perspective. Some would argue that "the paradigm that is most compatible with the facts is one that recognizes the critical role played by social conflict in the generation of . . . law" (Chambliss, 1976:67). Others in a similar vein would argue for the explanatory power of *their* respective theoretical stances. Since a large number of laws are made by the legislative, administrative, and judicial bodies each day, it is always possible to select a few examples that illustrate almost any conceivable theoretical position. At best, the theories I have discussed explain in part how laws are made. Probably all of these theories are at least partially correct, but it is doubtful that any single theory fully explains the creation of law, although one or another may account for the formation of any particular law or kind of law. With these considerations in mind, let us now turn to an examination of the processes of legislative, administrative, and judicial lawmaking.

LEGISLATION

The main legal task of legislative bodies is to make law. The term "legislation" describes the deliberate creation of legal precepts by a body of government which gives articulate expression to such legal precepts in a formalized legal document. Legislation, as such, must be distinguished from normative pronouncements made by the courts. The verbal expression of a legal rule or principle by a judge does not have the same degree of finality as the authoritative formulation of a legal proposition by a legislative body. Furthermore, although both adjudication and legislation involve the deliberate creation of laws by a body of government, it should be remembered that the judiciary is not a body set up primarily for the purpose of lawmaking. As noted earlier, its main function is to decide disputes under a preexisting law, and the law-creating function of the judges should be considered incidental to their primary function of adjudication.

There are a number of other differences that should be kept in mind between legislative and judicial lawmaking. Judge-made law stems from the decision of actual controversies. It provides no rules in advance for the decision of cases but waits for disputes to be brought before the court for decision. Legislators, by contrast, formulate rules in anticipation of cases. A judicial decision is based on a justification for applying a particular rule, while a statute usually does not contain an argumentative or justificatory statement; it simply states: This is forbidden, this is required, this is authorized. An opinion supporting a court decision is normally signed by the judge who wrote it. By contrast, a statute carries no signature (Fuller, 1968:89–93). In general, legislators have much more freedom to make major changes and innovations in the law than do the courts. The accumulation of precedents and the growth of an evermore complex body of principles have inevitably narrowed the scope of most judicial innovations. Legislators are also more responsive to public and private pressures than judges. While judges deal with particular cases, legislators consider general problem areas with whole classes of related situations. At times, the attention of legislative bodies is drawn to a problem by a particular incident, but the law it eventually passes is designed for general applicability. For example, when Congress passed the Federal Kidnapping Law of 1932, the kidnapping and death of the Lindbergh baby were fresh in their minds, but the law that was enacted was designed to deal with a whole class of such possible occurrences. Thus, it may be concluded that legislators are solely responsible for formulating broad new rules and for creating and revising the institutions necessary to put them into effect.

Legislative lawmaking at times represents a response to some kind of problem, one acute enough to intrude on the well-being of a large number of individuals and their organizations or on the well-being of the government itself, one conspicuous enough to attract the attention of at least some legislators. But legislation can also be generated, among other ways, by apprehension, social unrest, conflict, and technological innovation.

Federal pure food and drug laws resulted from an exposure of the practices of food and drug manufacturers and processors (Friedman and Macaulay, 1977:610–613). More recently, internal security laws were the outgrowth of apprehension over the activities of American communists; manpower retraining and area redevelopment legislation to provide for more rigorous control over the testing of drugs was passed in the wake of disclosures concerning the effects of thalidomide, a drug that caused numerous babies to be born malformed; and legislation to establish a system of communication satellites was passed shortly after the successful experiment with Telstar. The list of legislation passed in response to the emergence of new problems or to the successful dramatization of old ones could be extended infinitely.

But neither the recognition of a social problem by legislators not their recognition of a group's particular claims for action is certain to lead to legislation. The probability of some form of legislative response increases when: (1) influential interest groups mobilize their members to seek legislative action; (2) the unorganized public becomes intensely concerned with an issue, as in the controversy over thalidomide, or conversely, is indifferent to the particular measures advocated by an interest group; and (3) there is no pressure to maintain the status quo or opposition to the proposed legislation.

Typically, the introduction of a legislative proposal is preceded by a series of prelawmaking "stages" of activity. The first stage is the *instigation and publicizing* of a particular problem (such as nuclear waste disposal). Typical instigators include the mass media (such as special TV programs such as *60 Minutes*), a representative who highlights an issue through investigative hearings, or an author (as we shall see later in this chapter) who documents and dramatizes a social problem. The second stage is *information-gathering*. It entails collecting data on the nature, magnitude, and consequences of a problem; alternative schemes for solving the problem and their costs, benefits, and inherent difficulties; the likely political impact of each scheme; and the feasibility of various compromises. The third stage is *formulation*, or devising and advocating a specific legislative remedy for the problem. The fourth stage is *interests-aggregation*, or obtaining support for the proposed measure from other lawmakers through trade-offs (that is, if you support my proposal, I will support yours); the championing of one interest group over others; or mediating among conflicting groups. The fifth stage is *mobilization*, the exertion of pressures, persuasion, or control on behalf of a measure by one who is able, often by virtue of his or her institutional position, to take effective and relatively direct action to secure enactment. Whether an issue goes beyond the first three stages usually depends on the support it receives from individuals, groups, or governmental units that possess authority and legitimacy in the policy area, and on the support that the proponents of a proposal are able to muster up from key figures in the legislature. The last stage is *modification*, the marginal alteration of a proposal, sometimes strengthening it, and sometimes granting certain concessions to its opponents in order to facilitate its introduction (Price, 1972:4–5).

These six stages, although they show a certain sequential character and complementarity, do not simply represent the components the legislative process must "necessarily" include. They also illustrate, for example, the norms which govern the legislative process (for example, the airing of an issue and the attempt to accommodate diverse interests). They further illustrate the thoroughly political character of the legislative lawmaking process.

ADMINISTRATIVE LAWMAKING

As I noted in the previous chapter, administrative agencies engage in law-making through rule-making and the adjudication of cases and controversies arising under their jurisdiction. Administrative lawmaking plays an increasingly important role in modern society and its consequences are felt in all walks of life. The intent of this section is to examine the fundamental processes involved in that kind of lawmaking in the context of administrative rule-making and adjudication.

Administrative Rule-Making

Administrative rule-making is the establishment of prospective rules. *A rule is a law made by an administrative agency.* Through the process of rule-making, an agency legislates policy. Under the requirements of the Federal Administrative Procedure Act, general notice of proposed rule-making must be published in the *Federal Register.* (The *Federal Register* is the daily compendium of new, revised, and proposed rules. The fact that it has grown from 9,500 pages in 1950 to more than 82,000 in 1986 is indicative of a substantial increase in administrative rule-making). The notice must specify the location of the proceedings, the legal authority under which the rules are being proposed, and the substance of the proposed rules. After such a notice is given, interested parties are to be provided with the opportunity to participate in the rule-making proceedings through the presentation of written data. At the discretion of the agency, oral presentation may be presented. Unless notice or hearing is required by the statutes governing the agency's operation, notice of rule-making can be withheld if the agency considers it to be impractical, unnecessary, or contrary to the public interest. This provision potentially excludes a number of administrative rule-making proceedings from any possibility of public participation (Davis, 1977:241–269).

The flexibility of agencies in rule-making procedures is much greater than in administrative adjudication. Formal hearings are not held unless required by statute. Administrators are free to consult informally with interested parties and are not bound by the more rigid requirements of adjudicative hearings. The number of parties that may participate is also potentially far greater than in adjudicative proceedings, where only those directly affected by an administrative order have standing (that is, directly involved in litigation) (Davis, 1977:99–119).

Much of the immense code of federal regulations is composed of the substantive rules of administrative agencies. The Internal Revenue Code, for example, is part of this compendium of regulations, which consists of a seemingly endless number of rules interpreting its statutes which have been passed by Congress. At this point, it should be noted that administrative agencies issue a variety of pronouncements less formal and binding than their "legislative" regulations which are designed to clarify the laws they are administering. Some of these are described as "interpretative regulations" (for example, the IRS regularly issues interpretations of the Internal Revenue Code, such as under what circumstances a college professor may deduct his or her office at home as a business expense). Moreover, in response to inquiries, agencies sometimes issue "advisory rulings" which interpret the law with reference to particular types of situations. In addition, some agencies also publish instructions, guides, explanatory pamphlets, and so forth.

Regulatory agencies state many of their regulatory policies through rule-making. For example, the Civil Aeronautics Board announces its airline fare policy through rule-making proceedings. The Food and Drug administration similarly determines policies governing the labeling, availability, and safety of drugs by rule-making. Rate-setting proceedings of regulatory bodies are also considered to be rule-making. Outside of the regulatory realm, departments such as Commerce and Defense are constantly stating their general policies through the issuance of rules.

Administrative Adjudication

The second way in which agencies create rules is through their adjudicative powers given to them by congressional grants of authority. *Administrative adjudication is the process by which an administrative agency issues an order.* Adjudication is the administrative equivalent of a judicial trial. As I pointed out in Chapter Three, adjudication differs from rule-making in that it applies only to a specific, limited number of parties involved in an individual case before the agency. Administrative orders have retroactive effect, as contrasted with the prospective effect of rule-making. In rule-making the agency is apprising in advance those under its jurisdiction of what the law is. When an agency opens proceedings with the intention of issuing an order, it must eventually interpret existing policy or define new policy to apply to the case at hand. The parties involved do not know how the policy is going to be applied until after the order is issued, giving the agency decision retroactive effect. Adjudicative lawmaking tends to produce inconsistencies because cases are decided on an individual basis. The rule of *stare decisis* (requiring precedent to be followed, which will be discussed in the context of judicial lawmaking) need not prevail (Davis, 1977:535–556), and the high turnover of top level administrators often results in a lack of continuity.

Since many agencies have both the power to issue regulations and the power to adjudicate cases, they can choose between the two methods of lawmaking. When an agency believes that the time has come to formulate a policy decision in an official text, it can draft and issue a regulation (for example, when the Securities and Exchange Commission (SEC) formulates law by writing rules which describe what disclosures must be made in a prospectus). But when an agency prefers to wait until the contours of a problem become clearer, it can continue to deal with the problem on a case by case basis, formulating a series of decisional rules couched in terms that ensure continuing flexibility (for example, as in individual workers' compensation claims). Furthermore, an agency, unlike a court, does not have to wait passively for cases to be brought before it. Its enforcement official can go out looking for cases that will raise the issues its adjudicating officials want to rule on. And since the agency can decide for itself what enforcement proceedings to initiate, it can choose cases that present the issues in such a way that the court will be likely to uphold the agency's ruling if an appeal is taken.

JUDICIAL LAWMAKING

Judicial lawmaking is an accelerating trend in the United States (Glazer, 1975). In many instances, legislators and administrators are willing to let judges take the heat for such controversial actions as allowing abortions or ordering busing to desegregate schools. Similarly, it is often politically expedient to let courts handle such touchy jobs as reapportioning legislatures, regulating employment practices, supervising land use or urban planning, or managing school systems (Stone, 1979:76). In addition, "an increasing number of judges hold the belief that law and the courts are the most appropriate and effective means of redressing the perceived ills of our society" (Rusthoven, 1976:1340). As a result, the judiciary in recent years has assumed a powerful role in our society. Notes Abraham: "It is simply a fact of life that in the United States all social and political issues sooner or later seem to become judicial!" (1973:21).

Although traditional cases still occupy most of the court's time, the scope of judicial business has broadened. Courts have tended "to move from the byways onto the highways of policy making" (Horowitz, 1977:9). In fact, Nathan Glazer argues that we have developed an "Imperial Judiciary"—that is, the courts now have so much power, play such a great role in lawmaking, that they pose a threat to the vitality of the political system. Glazer contends that too much power has moved from the elected, representative branches of government to the largely nonelective judiciary, and the courts "are now seen as forces of nature, difficult to predict and impossible to control" (1975:110). Judicial activity is now extended, for example, to welfare, prison, and mental hospital administration, to education and employment policy, to road and bridge building, to automotive safety standards, and to natural resource management.

In the past few years, courts altered laws requiring a period of instate residence as a condition of eligibility for welfare, laid down elaborate standards for food handling, hospital operations, inmate employment and education, and ordered some prisons closed. Courts have established comprehensive programs of care and treatment for the mentally ill confined in hospitals. They have ordered the equalization of school expenditures on teachers' salaries, decided that bilingual education must be provided for Mexican-American children, and eliminated a high school diploma as a requirement for a firefighter's job. Courts have enjoined the construction of roads and bridges on environmental grounds and suspended performance requirements for automobile tires and air bags (Horowitz, 1977:4–5).

In *Brown v. Board of Education* (347 U.S. 483 [1954]), the judiciary set a precedent in establishing new policies in interracial relations with its decisions forbidding official segregation in public schools. The judiciary also established a new set of laws for processing criminal cases requiring that indigents be given attorneys at public expense in all but minor cases (*Gideon* v. *Wainwright*, 372 U.S. 335 [1963]); defendants must be warned that whatever they say to the police may be used against them, and that they will be permitted attorneys during police interrogation if they request them (*Miranda* v. *Arizona*, 348 U.S. 436 [1966]); and juveniles must be given some of the same rights as adult offenders in hearings which may lead to their imprisonment (*In re Gault*, 387 U.S. 1 [1967]). Reapportionment of national, state, and local legislative bodies has followed the decisions in *Baker* v. *Carr* (369 U.S. 186 [1962]) and *Reynolds* v. *Sems* (377 U.S. 533 [1964]), which required that all legislative districts be approximately the same size. The courts have been, "to put it mildy, very busy, laboring in unfamiliar territory" (Horowitz, 1977:5).

Before discussing when and how judges make law, it is important to review the salient features of the adjudicative process. Adjudication is focused. The typical question before the judge is simply: Does one party have a right? Does another party have a duty? This should be contrasted with the question before legislators and administrators: What are the alternatives? Adjudication is also piecemeal, and the lawsuit is a good illustration of incremental decision-making. Furthermore, courts must act when litigants present their cases before them. In the end, a judgment cannot be escaped. Moreover, fact-finding in adjudication is poorly adapted to the ascertainment of social facts. The unrepresentative character of the litigants makes it difficult to generalize from their situation to a wider context. Finally, adjudication makes no provision for policy review. Judges base their decisions on behavior that antedates the litigation. Consequential facts—those that relate to the impact of a decision on behavior—are equally important but much neglected. This results in an emphasis on rights and duties rather than on alternatives (Horowitz, 1977:33–56).

All these statements suggest that judicial lawmaking is different from legislative or administrative lawmaking. There are three types of judicial lawmaking: by precedents, by interpretation of statutes, and by interpretation of the Constitution. I shall examine these three types separately.

Lawmaking by Precedents

Judicial formulation of rules is frequently based on the principle that judges should build on the precedents established by past decisions, known as the doctrine of *stare decisis*, which is both expeditious and a deeply rooted common-law tradition. By contrast, civil law countries such as France and Germany have a codified legal system where the basic law is stated in *codes*. These are statutes enacted by the national parliament which arrange whole fields of law (family law, housing law, and so forth) in an orderly, logical, and comprehensive way. The judges follow the basic principles of law found in acts of parliament. In common-law countries such as England and the United States, judges base their decisions on *case law*, a body of opinion developed by judges over time in the course of deciding particular cases. The doctrine of precedent, the notion that the judge is bound by what has already been decided, is a strictly common-law doctrine (Friedman, 1984:16).

In the common-law system, following precedents is often much easier and less time-consuming than working out all over again solutions to problems that have already been faced. It enables the judge to take advantage of the accumulated wisdom of preceding generations. It minimizes arbitrariness and compensates for weakness and inexperience. It conforms to the belief that "like wrongs deserve like remedies" and to the desire for "equal justice under the law." More importantly, the practice of following precedents enables individuals (with the assistance of attorneys) to plan their conduct in the expectation that past decisions will be honored in the future. Although certainty, predictability, and continuity are not the only objectives of law, they are certainly important ones. Many disputes are avoided and others are settled without litigation simply because individuals are familiar with how the courts will respond to certain types of behavior.

But judicial formulations of rules are frequently revised and restated by the courts in cases presenting the same or similar problems. A judge may also be confronted with a case for which there are simply no precedents. For example, consider a problem that judges first had to face during the 1920s when farmers began to complain that airplanes were disturbing the peace and frightening their livestock. Obviously, there were no precedents dealing with the rights and duties of landowners and of individuals who flew aircraft over their land. To make a decision, judges searched through property law cases for any analogies that seemed suggestive. Through the selection of appropriate and desirable analogies (which is, indeed, a value judgment), judges make law in instances when they are not guided by precedents. In general, in view of the manner that courts use in dealing with legal rules laid down in earlier decisions (by rephrasing, qualifying, broadening, narrowing, or changing such rules, or by analogies), a precedent must be considered as a weaker and less authoritative source of law than a statute.

The Interpretation of Statutes

In interpreting statutes, judges determine the effects of legislative decisions. For many, a legislative decree is not a law until enforced and interpreted by the courts (Jacob, 1984:37). In the vast majority of cases involving the application of statutes, the courts have no trouble determining how to apply the statute. Most cases fall squarely inside or outside the law's provisions.

In some cases, however, the intent of a legislature is ambiguous. Some statutes contain unintentional errors and ambiguities because of bad drafting of the law. Other statutes are unclear because those who pushed them through the legislature sought to avoid opposition by being vague or silent on potentially controversial matters. An important reason for the lack of clarity in many instances is that the proponents have not been able to foresee and provide for all possible future situations. This provides the courts with an opportunity to engage in lawmaking. For example, antitrust statutes permit much judicial lawmaking for Congress has set up only the most general guidelines. Exactly what constitutes a restraint of trade or monopolization are questions that the court determines. In doing so, courts not only make law, but also set explicit policy to guide other businesses and government agencies.

On rare occasions, judges find that all their efforts to discover the legislative intent of a statute are in vain. It is simply not clear how the statute applies to the case before them. In those cases, the judges must do just what they do when faced with a case for which there are no precedents. They must perform a creative act of lawmaking. In all probability, this is exactly what the legislature, unwilling to prescribe details for an unknown future, counted on them to do. It is the duty of judges to infer a purpose that is applicable to a particular case from what they know of the legislature's broader purposes and of the shared purposes and aims of the community.

The Interpretation of Constitutions

The courts are often called upon to interpret the Constitution. Every controversial statute and a variety of controversial executive actions are challenged in the courts on grounds of unconstitutionality (Jacob, 1984:38). For example, in an attempt to avert a threatened strike, the President orders federal officials to seize and operate the nation's steel mills. The steel companies challenge his power to do so under Article II of the Constitution, which deals with the powers and duties of the President. Or an overzealous sheriff in a small town breaks into the offices of a business firm and searches for evidence of illegal sales without a search warrant. When the firm's owners are brought to trial for unlawful operations, they challenge the admission of the evidence offered against them on the grounds that it has been illegally obtained, and that admitting it would violate the "due process" clause of the Fourteenth Amendment, which is supposed to protect individuals against irregular official procedures.

The opportunities to interpret constitutional provisions arise more often in federal than in state courts, because the national Constitution is considered more ambiguous in many of its key provisions. State constitutions, by contrast, are much more detailed documents and leave much less room for judicial interpretations. Usually both state and federal courts ratify the decision of the governmental officials by finding the challenged legislation or executive action constitutional. At times, however, they declare the law or action unconstitutional. When deciding on the constitutionality of a government action, the courts have to decide what meaning they wish to give to the Constitution and which social objectives to pursue. For example, the Supreme Court "has given quite different interpretations to the 'due process of law' clauses of the Fifth and Fourteenth Amendments, ranging from a guarantee of property against governmental intervention to a guarantee of civil rights against official abuse" (Jacob, 1984:38).

Judicial lawmaking is usually directed at other government agencies rather than at private individuals. Courts interpret statutes and constitutional provisions, and in so doing they permit or prohibit the action of other government agencies. For example, courts have prohibited racial discrimination by government agencies in schools, parks, and elections, but they have not prohibited racial discrimination (on constitutional grounds) by private individuals (for example, obtaining professional services such as dental, medical, or legal). Most judicial lawmaking efforts are concerned with the regulatory activities of agencies (Shapiro, 1968). There are, however, some issues that are rarely decided in courts. Foreign affairs (because they are considered political and not judicial issues) are generally beyond the scope of court action. For example, when the American participation in the Vietnam conflict was challenged, the Supreme Court, by a six to three vote, refused to rule on its constitutionality. Moreover, courts are seldom involved in matters such as the appropriation of funds or the levying of taxes.

INFLUENCES ON THE LAWMAKING PROCESSES

Lawmaking is a complex and continuous process, and it exists as a response to a number of social influences that operate in society. The forces that influence lawmaking cannot always be precisely determined, measured, or evaluated. At times, a multitude of forces are in operation simultaneously. Although a variety of forces can exert influence on the lawmaking process, in this section I shall consider only the roles of vested interests, public opinion, and the social sciences.

Interest Groups

The interest-group argument holds that laws grow out of special interests of particular groups in the population. The image of society that is contained in this perspective stresses cultural differences, value clashes, and social conflict. Examples of interest-group influence in lawmaking abound. Laws governing the use of alcohol, regulations concerning sexual conduct, abortion bills, pure food and drug legislation, antitrust laws, and the like are all documented instances of interest group activity (Quinney, 1970:49–94). Even alterations in existing statutes are not immune from influence by those who see some threat or advantage in the proposed changes. For example, Pamela A. Roby (1969) demonstrated, in a study of the New York State Penal Code regarding prostitution, that the changes originally proposed in this law were drastically altered by the time the new statute took effect. Throughout the legislative process, various groups (for example, the police, the New York Hotel Association, the Civil Liberties Union, and the Mayor's Office) were all involved in shaping the legislation to fit their interests or views.

The nature of the interaction between interest groups and lawmakers varies to an extent based on the branch of the government. Judges, although they are not immune to interest group pressures, are generally not lobbied in the same way as legislators or administrators. To reach the courts, a lawyer must be hired, formal proceedings must be followed, and grievances must be expressed in legal terminology. Minorities and the poor find the courts attractive because they are more readily available. To influence legislators, a group must be economically powerful or able to mobilize a large number of voters (Jacob, 1984:150). No such prerequisites are needed in the courts. If a group has enough money to hire an attorney, it can seek court action to further its interests. As a result, minority groups are often among the most active lobbies in courts. The NAACP, for example, has in-stituted and won numerous cases in its efforts to improve the legal protec-tion of blacks. The technique is not new, of course, but in recent decades, urban interests, feeling underrepresented in state and national legislatures, have turned increasingly to the lawsuit.

The techniques used by interest groups to influence courts are dif-ferent from those used to influence legislative or administrative bodies. Notes Jacob: "The principle techniques are: to bring conflicts to a court's attention by initiating test cases, to bring added information to the courts through *amicus curiae* (friend of the court) briefs, and to communicate with judges indirectly by placing information favorable to the group's cause in legal and general periodicals" (1984:151). By instituting test cases, interest groups provide judges with opportunities to make policies by which they overcome the otherwise passive nature of the judicial process. By providing information through *amicus curiae* briefs, interest groups expand the con-fines of the judicial process. For example, the American Civil Liberties Union files many such briefs with the Supreme Court in cases that raise questions of constitutional liberty. The final technique is to publish deci-sions in legal periodicals. Judges generally read these journals to keep abreast of legal scholarship and sometimes even cite them as authority for their ruling. Publication in these journals gets one's views before the courts and before their attentive public.

Interactions between interest groups and legislative and administra-tive lawmakers are more overtly political in nature. Many interest groups maintain Washington and state capital offices staffed with people who keep track of developments in the legislative and administrative branches and attempt to influence their activities. Some groups pay for the services of law firms in dealing with legislators or administrators. These firms provide expertise in such areas as antitrust and tax regulations and use their per-sonal contacts with important lawmakers on behalf of their clients.

A number of specific conditions can be identified that enhance the potential influence of interest groups on lawmakers (Ripley, 1978:274-275). In many instances, there may not be two competing groups on an issue. When only one point of view is presented, the group is likely to get much of what it wants. For example, when banking interests push for a higher ceiling for usury laws in a state, without organized opposition, they are more likely to succeed. Similarly, if the groups on one side of a controversy are unified and coordinated on the principal issues they want to push, or they can minimize their disagreements, they will enhance their chances of success. For instance, the walnut growers are represented by a single highly organized group and are thus likely to get what they want. By contrast, chicken farmers are dispersed and have no effective single group to speak for them. Consequently, they have difficulty in achieving their legislative ends (Ripley, 1978:274). If certain key members of legislative bodies (such as a subcommittee chairperson) believe in the interest group's position, the probability of success is greatly enhanced. The visibility of an issue is another consideration in influencing lawmakers. When the issue is not too visible, or when interest groups seek single discreet amendments to bills (such as to alter soybean export quotas in addition to others proposed by farming interests), as contrasted to large legislative packages, the chances for success increase. Conversely, as the visibility of issues increases and public attention grows (such as draft registration or wage-price controls), the influence of interest groups tends to diminish. Interest groups are likely to have greater influence on issues that coincide with the interests of the groups they purport to represent. For example, the AFL-CIO may be very influential in matters concerning working conditions, but they are likely to receive less attention from lawmakers when they advocate higher tariffs for imported goods or when they make attempts to guide foreign policy. Finally, interest groups are likely to have greater influence on amendments than on entire pieces of legislation. This is because of the fact that amendments are generally technical and less understood by the public.

In general, the effectiveness of interest groups in influencing lawmakers is related to such considerations as their financial and information resources, their offensive or defensive positions, and the status of the group in the eyes of lawmakers. Financial resources determine the ability of an interest group to support court suits, lobbying, public relations, and other activities. Interest groups that support the status quo have an advantage over groups trying to bring change, because while the latter must overcome several obstacles in the lawmaking process, the former may frustrate change at any of several points in the process. But the influence of an interest group depends mainly on its status as perceived by lawmakers. An interest group is particularly influential in situations where a lawmaker shares the same group affiliation (for example, when farm groups talk to legislators who are farmers), where the group is considered important to the legislator's constituency, and where the group is recognized as a legitimate and reliable source of information. In addition, a group's competence to influence lawmaking is enhanced by its ability to bring about social or economic disruptions. Threats of disorder, disruption, and violence have been, at times, effective bargaining weapons of relatively powerless groups. Similarly, the threat of a decline in the supply of such products as food, medical services, or energy have been used to influence lawmakers. For example, energy supply problems have been employed to justify the removal of price controls on oil and natural gas. There is little doubt that the ability of an interest group to create a crisis, whether a social disorder, an economic slowdown, or the reduction of supply of a needed product or service, gives it considerable clout in the lawmaking process.

Public Opinion

When the relationship between law and popular will was refined in the nineteenth century, theorists of law and society were concerned with the origins of law and the development of legal institutions (see Chapter

Two). Legal development was viewed as a sequence of events. First, practices and sentiments occur in a group of people, without their awareness that they are the "right" ones or the "only" ones. Eventually, particularly on occasions of deviance from prior practice, *a* way of acting or believing becomes *the* way of acting or believing. Custom becomes law.

It is easier to substantiate the association between popular sentiments and law in so-called primitive societies (Llewellyn and Hoebel, 1941:10–15). As a society becomes more complex, there is a less direct correspondence between public opinion and the law. In a primitive society, one comes to know intimately the law of one's tribe. It is highly unlikely that today one can know, let along tinker with, much of the law that could affect one's life. As a result of such limited awareness, there is a fair amount of selectivity involved in the expression of opinions toward the law. Some questions, therefore, arise in the discussion on the influence of public opinion on lawmaking. One concerns the timing of the relationship between public opinion and lawmaking. At what point does the accumulation of practice and belief make the reflection of those practices and beliefs in law an inevitability? For example, how many marijuana violations cause the law relating to marijuana to be changed?

A related question is concerned with the identification of those individuals whose opinion is expressed in lawmaking and with the means of translating those opinions into legal outcomes. The *people* may mean a numerical majority, an influential elite, blacks, women, the poor, the middle class, the young, the aged, migrant workers, students, college professors, and so forth. Popular views may be similar throughout all segments of the population, but on many important issues opinions will differ.

A more meaningful way of looking at the influence of public opinion on lawmaking would be to consider the diverse opinions of many "publics" (that is, segments of society) bearing on specific concerns. These opinions are expressed through a multitude of channels such as the media, political parties, and the various types of interest groups. Care should be exercised, however, in not overestimating the catalytic part played by public opinion in lawmaking which is conditioned by economic forces. As Friedman states:

> The "public opinion" that affects the law is like the economic power which makes the market. This is so in two essential regards: Some people, but only some, take enough interest in any particular commodity to make their weight felt; second, there are some people who have more power and wealth than others. At one end of the spectrum stand such figures as the president of the United States and General Motors; at the other, migrant laborers, babies, and prisoners at San Quentin (1975:163).

The differential influence of public opinion on lawmaking processes is a well-known phenomenon and is recognized by lawmakers. Lawmakers are aware that some people are more equal than others because of money, talent, or choice. Notes Friedman:

> They know that 100 wealthy, powerful constituents passionately opposed to socialized medicine, outweigh thousands of poor, weak constituents, mildly

in favor of it. Most people do not shout, threaten, or write letters. They remain quiet and obscure, unless a head count reveals they are there. This is the "silent majority"; paradoxically, this group matters only when it breaks its silence—when it mobilizes or is mobilized by others (1975:164).

Lawmakers also know that most people have no clear opinions on most issues with which judicial, administrative, and legislative bodies must deal. This means that they have a wide latitude within which to operate. Thus, for example, when a legislator claims to be representing the opinion of his or her district he or she is, on most issues, representing the opinion of only a minority of the constituents, because most do not know or care about the issue at hand and do not communicate their views on it (Ripley, 1978:38).

In spite of these considerations, public opinion does exert an influence on the lawmaking process. Dennis S. Ippolito and his associates (1976) identify three types of influences that press lawmakers into formulating certain decisions. These three types are direct, group, and indirect influences.

Direct influences refer to constituent pressures that offer rewards or sanctions to lawmakers. Rewards for compliance and sanctions for noncompliance may be votes in an election or reelection campaign, financial assistance, and other forms of pressure that could possibly range from the representative's standing in lawmaking bodies to prestige in his or her own particular community. But this kind of influence is not confined to legislators. Members of the judiciary are also pressured by partisan publications to make certain decisions consistent with opinions and interests that run throughout the jurisdiction of a particular court.

The second type of influence is distinctly that of organized interest groups representing a special constituency. Political parties, interest groups, and citizen action groups are continually influencing the lawmaking process. In the area of administrative law, for example, special interest groups press regulatory agencies for rules and regulations that are in keeping with their own immediate interests. Public opinion in these and other areas is represented by organization leaders. The motivation behind joining such groups is the perceived need for expressing a point of view in a manner that will influence lawmakers. In this context, public opinion becomes organized around a specific issue or an immediate objective (for example, pros and cons of gun control or abortion). Through the process of organizing, interests are made specific, and public opinion backing is sought in the attempt to gain an advantage in pressing for change or redress through the legal machinery.

The third type of public opinion model is that which influences the lawmaking process indirectly. Here a lawmaker acts in the capacity of an "instructed delegate." The decisions made are on behalf of the desires of a particular constituency, for example, residents living around an airport who oppose expansion of facilities. Ippolito (1976:3) and his colleagues state that indirect influence occurs when legislators act in accordance with constituent preferences because they either share such preferences or they believe such preferences should prevail over their own judgment. This type of influence is indicative of the importance attached to public opinion polls.

Public opinion polls seek to determine the aggregate view people hold in a community on current important issues. Polling is flourishing in the United States. Today there are more than half a dozen well-established commercial firms that take public opinion polls. Among the most respected are the Gallup, Harris, Yankelovich, Sindlinger, The Opinion Research Corporation, and the Roper and Cambridge Research Reports. In addition, there are a variety of smaller specialized public and private and university polling organizations. Scores of surveys have been commissioned by federal agencies and by various state bodies. A typical sample size for national polls is 1500 respondents. Pollsters claim that with a sample of that size, there is a 95 percent probability that the results obtained are no more than three percentage points off the figure that would be obtained if every adult in the country were interviewed.

Opinion polls have the power to affect what lawmakers do (Lipset, 1976). On a variety of domestic issues, for example, public opinion led or prompted lawmakers toward passage of a program that might have otherwise been delayed for months or years. Legislation concerning minimum wages, social security, and medical programs are examples of issues on which public opinion has preceded and prompted legislative action. However, in other instances, such as civil liberties and civil rights, public opinion has either lagged behind government policy ot tended to support measures that are repressive of constitutional rights. For example, since the mid-1950s the Supreme Court has played a leading role in interpreting and formulating policies on civil rights that were more progressive than the views reflected in public opinion polls (Simon, 1974).

Generally, the use of polls in lawmaking is encouraged. For example, Irving Crespi suggests that lawmakers could be more effective if they learned to draw upon the full fruits of survey research. Direct evidence—unfiltered by the interpretations of special interests or lobby groups—of the wants, needs, aspiration, and concerns of the general public needs to be accounted for in lawmaking activities. In lawmaking processes, Crespi argues that there should be first an attempt to determine the views of both the general public and that segment of the public that would be directly affected by a particular law. It could then make public opinion part of the formative stages of the lawmaking process, and not simply a force to be coped with after the fact. Says Crespi: "The difference between treating public attitudes and opinions as a relatively minor variable instead of an influence that should be authoritative is ultimately the difference between technocratic and democratic government" (1979:18).

Lawmaking and Social Science

Lawmakers have long been aware of the contribution that social scientists can make to the lawmaking process. For example, the Brandeis brief of 1908, defending the constitutionality of limited working hours for women, is considered an early landmark for the use of social science in lawmaking (Zeisel, 1962:142). The ideas of the economist John R. Commons (1934) influenced the way most states in the United States deal with compensation for industrial accidents and unemployment. In the major U.S. Supreme Court decision of *Brown* v. *Board of Education of Topeka* (347 U.S. 483 [1954]), the court drew upon a spectrum of the social sciences—ranging from discreet psychological experiments to broad-ranging economic and social inquiry—in reversing an earlier ruling which had established the separate but equal standards in racial matters. The Court ruled that racial segregation in elementary schools is psychologically harmful. In a footnote—the famous footnote eleven—the Court also cited a number of social science studies summarizing evidence showing that segregation retards black children's educational development.

In an era increasingly dominated by scientific and technical specialists, it is not surprising that lawmakers reflect the quest for specialization and expertise. There is a growing reliance on the use of social science research results in a variety of areas ranging from school desegregation studies (Wolf, 1976) to consumer surveys in trademark suits. With the aid of social scientists, ad hoc committees of legislative bodies have, at times, also produced important studies on matters such as insurance, investment banking, and public utilities (Zeisel, 1962).

Efforts to bring social science to bear on lawmaking processes involve the use of quantitative social science data and the reliance on the social scientist as an expert witness in specific legal cases. Social science data may be collected and analyzed for academic purposes and later utilized by one or more sides of a dispute as it was, for example, used in *Brown* v. *Board of Education*. Social science research may also be reactive in the sense that it is initially requested by parties in a dispute. In such instances, the materials may address facts in the case (for example, research on sex discrimination in the jury selection for the Attica trial) or initiate an intervention in a lawmaking process (for example, the disparate effects of wage garnishment on blacks). Social science research may also be undertaken in a proactive fashion. In such a situation, a social scientist may undertake an investigation (such as, the social impact of mandatory day-care for companies with more than 500 employees) with the anticipation of subsequent use of the results by lawmakers (Berk and Oppenheim, 1979:125).

Social scientists can also participate in the lawmaking process as expert witnesses who testify typically for one of the litigants or appear before a legislative body. At times, social scientists are asked to directly assist either the court or the legislator in the preparation of background documents pertinent to a particular issue or to serve on Presidential Commissions intended for policy recommendations.

Although social science influences what lawmakers do, there are controversies surrounding the role of social scientists in lawmaking. Consider, for example, the controversy which broke out in the later 1960s over reinterpretations of the Equal Educational Opportunity Report, commonly known as the Coleman Report, after its principal author, James S. Coleman (1966, 1967). In the late 1960s, Coleman's data on pupil achievement were the basis for a number of major court decisions calling for school busing.

With the use of massive busing to achieve "racial balance" in public schools, social science findings about the effects of integration on black children have been hotly debated (Howard, 1979:104). In reviewing the studies on busing, David J. Armor (1972) has questioned the assumption that school integration enhances blacks' educational achievement, aspirations, self-esteem, or opportunities for higher education. He contends that it is possible that desegregation actually retards race relations. Other scholars, such as Thomas F. Pettigrew and Robert L. Green (1976), have accused Armor of presenting a distorted and incomplete review of a politically charged topic. Incidentally, the entire controversy could have been avoided, for Coleman had not found any race effect as such in his analysis of student body characteristics and educational achievement. Instead, he had found a social class effect. At the time of his testimony, this fact was not made clear to the court.

Daniel Patrick Moynihan proposes two general reasons why social scientists have been criticized for their involvement in lawmaking processes. First, he points out that social science is basically concerned with the prediction of future events, whereas the purpose of the law is to order them. Notes Moynihan: "But where social science seeks to establish a fixity of *relationships* such that the consequences of behavior can be known in advance—or, rather, narrowed to a manageable range of possibilities—law seeks to dictate future performance on the basis of past *agreements*" (1979:16). For example, it is the function of the law to order alimony payments; it is the function of social science to attempt to estimate the likelihood of their being paid, of their effect on work behavior and remarriage in male and female parties, or similar probabilities. The second reason he suggests is that "social science is rarely dispassionate, and social scientists are frequently caught up in the politics which their work necessarily involves" (1979:19). Social scientists are, to a great extent, involved with problem-solving, and the identification of a "problem" usually entails a political statement that implies a solution. Moynihan states: "Social scientists are never more revealing of themselves than when challenging the objectivity of one another's work. In some fields almost *any* study is assumed to have a more-or-less-discoverable political purpose" (1979:19). Furthermore, there is a distinct social and political bias among social scientists. As a result, the social sciences attract many people who are more interested in shaping the future than preserving the past. Moynihan feels that this orientation coupled with "liberal" tendencies and the limited explanatory power of social sciences results in a weakening of influence on lawmakers. He points out, for example, that after examining a number of recent studies concerning the effects of rehabilitation programs on criminals, no consistent effects could be shown one way or the other. Moynihan notes: "Seemingly, all that could be established for certain about the future behavior of criminals is that when they are in jail they do not commit street crimes" (1979:20). Similarly, there are still controversies concerning the deterrent effects of the death penalty. Obviously, when social science data yield uncertain results, the root causes of major problems remain illusive. When well-intentioned social scientists dispute about alternatives, it is not surprising that lawmakers are, at times, skeptical about social science and social scientists.

SOURCES OF IMPETUS FOR LAW

An impetus is a basic prerequisite for setting the mechanism of lawmaking in motion. Demands for new laws or changes in existing ones come from a variety of sources. In the following pages, several sources of impetus for law creation are considered. These sources, which are not mutually exclusive, include detached scholarly diagnosis, a voice from the wilderness, protest activities, social movements, public interest groups, and the mass media.

Detached Scholarly Diagnosis

The impetus for law may come from a detached, scholarly undertaking. From time to time, academicians may consider a given practice or condition as detrimental in the context of existing values and norms. They may communicate their diagnoses to their colleagues or to the general public through either scholarly or popular forums. In some cases, they may even carry the perceived injustice to the legislature in search of legal redress. Perhaps the best way to illustrate how an impetus for law can be provided by a member of an academic community is to refer to my study on wage garnishment (a legal process which enables a creditor upon a debtor's default to seize his or her wages in the hands of the employer prior to being paid to the debtor), carried out some years ago.

In the mid-1960s, I had undertaken an investigation on the impact of wage garnishment on low-income families. The findings indicated that existing wage garnishment laws at that time in Missouri were more counterproductive than functional as a collection device. Approximately 20 percent of the debtors were dismissed by their employers upon the receipt of the first garnishment suit. Such an action was detrimental not only to the debtor, but to his or her family, creditor, employer, and society at large.

As a result of the deleterious and unintended consequences of garnishment (broken homes), I proposed a simple procedure in the study to provide the debtor whose wages were subject to garnishment with legal safeguards so he or she will not be dismissed from a job or be forced into bankruptcy. At the same time, a provision was made also to enable creditors to maintain an effective collection method.

On the basis of my data and recommendations, House Bill 279 was designed and introduced in the 74th General Assembly of the State of Missouri. Under the proposed bill, the service of the writ would be made upon the defendant only, and the employer of the defendant would not be involved in the litigation process. Upon entry of the judgment, the court may order the debtor to make payments to the clerk of the court, which would be dispersed in turn by the clerk. In settling the amount of these payments, the court would take into consideration the circumstances of the defendant, including his or her income and other obligations or considerations bearing on the issue. If the debtor fails to obey the order of the court, *then, and only then,* may the creditor summon the employer as a garnishee. The primary intention of the bill was to prohibit employers from discharging employees upon the receipt of the first garnishment suit, thus saving thousands of jobs for low-income individuals annually in Missouri. It was estimated that on the national level, approximately 500,000 individuals are fired each year as a direct result of the practice of wage garnishment. The societal implications of the proposed changes were obvious (Vago, 1968:7–20). Today wage garnishment is regulated nationally. This is the result of the Consumer Credit Protection Act (PL 90–321), passed in 1968. The Act protects consumers from being driven into bankruptcy by excessive garnishment of wages by limiting the amount of wages subject to garnishment to 25 percent of the employee's weekly disposable income. It also forbids the firing of an employee because of wage garnishment.

There have been a number of attempts by university professors in a variety of disciplines to provide an impetus for lawmaking as an outgrowth of their investigations. For example, publications by David Caplovitz, such as *The Poor Pay More* (1963) and *Consumers in Trouble: A Study of Debtors in Default* (1974), resulted in proposals for much needed reform of the consumer credit laws. In *Genetic Fix* (1973), Amitai Etzioni examines the implications of "human engineering" and suggests that the Mondale Bill (the establishment of a scientific review committee in the form of a Health-Ethics Commission) should be used as a model for safeguarding such activities. Marc F. Plattner's influential article, "Campaign Financing: The Dilemmas of Reform" (1974), stimulated further reexamination of existing procedures in this domain. Martin S. Feldstein (1975, a and b) is concerned with changes in unemployment insurance and social security laws, as the titles of his articles indicate: "Unemployment Insurance: Time for Reform," and "Toward a Reform of Social Security." Anthony Downs, in *Urban Problems and Prospects* (1976), calls a series of specific solutions on housing, community schools, and transportation dilemmas to the attention of lawmakers. The list could go on *ad infinitum.* But the point has been argued and illustrated that detached scholarly diagnoses can, indeed, stimulate lawmaking. The source of impetus, however, is not limited to ivory towers. It can have other origins, as the following sections will demonstrate.

A Voice from the Wilderness

Many persons outside of academe through their writings succeed, or even excel, in calling public attention to a particular problem or social condition. There is a long list of those whose literary efforts stimulated changes in the law. For our purposes, it will suffice to call attention to a few better-known such ventures.

Around the turn of the century, there was a fair amount of concern in the United States about the quality of food products. In particular, numerous scandals had arisen over the quality of meat products. It was alleged that during the Spanish American War, American soldiers were forced to eat cans of "embalmed beef." A number of horrible practices of manufacturers were revealed in the mass media, but a federal food and drug law had still not passed when, in 1906, Upton Sinclair published *The Jungle,* a novel about life in Chicago, centering around the stockyards.

The first half of the book deals with a vivid description of conditions in the Chicago meatpacking plants. To illustrate:

> Tubercular pork was sold for human consumption. Old sausage, rejected in Europe and shipped back "mouldy and white," would be "dosed with borax and glycerine, and dumped into the hoppers, and made over again for home consumption." Meat was stored in rooms where "water from leaky roofs would drip over it, and thousands of rats would race about on it." The packers would put out poisoned bread to kill the rats; then the rats would die, and "rats, bread and meat would go into the hoppers together." Most horrifying of all was the description of the men in the "cooking-rooms." They "worked in tank-rooms full of steam," in some of which there were "open vats near the level of the floor." Sometimes they fell into the vats "and when they were fished out, there was never enough of them left to be worth exhibiting—sometimes they would be overlooked for days, till all but the bones of them had gone out to the world as Durham's Pure Leaf Lard" (Quoted by Friedman and Macaulay, 1977:611–612).

When it was published, the book created a furor. A copy was sent to President Roosevelt, who, in turn, appointed two investigators whose report confirmed Sinclair's findings. It is hard to say to what extent Sinclair's book provided an impetus for the passage of the Pure Food and Meat Inspection Law in 1906, but it is undisputable that it played an important role in it.

In the domain of environmental protection laws, it would be difficult not to consider the book *Silent Spring,* by Rachel Carson (1962). It was the first time that the environmental threat posed by pesticides was announced to a wide audience. Others in the same vein included Richard Falk's *This Endangered Planet* (1971), Fairfield Osborn's *Our Plundered Planet* (1948), and the *Moment in the Sun,* by R. and L. T. Reinow (1967).

Even a short list of influential authors would be incomplete without a reference to Ralph Nader. He was an unknown young lawyer at the time he published his book, *Unsafe at Any Speed* (1965), which alerted the public to the automobile industry's unconcern for safety in the design and construction of American cars. This book is a model of the kind of muckraking journalism which, at times, initiates the rise of public concern over a given issue. As a result of his book, and General Motors' reaction to it, Nader became front-page news, and his charges took on new weight. More than anyone else, he has singlehandedly contributed to and provided the impetus for the passing of a substantial number of auto safety provisions. Since 1966, Nader "has been responsible almost entirely through his efforts for the passage of seven major consumer-related laws—the Traffic and Motor Vehicle Safety Act (1966), Natural Gas Pipeline Safety Act (1968), Wholesale Meat Act (1967), Radiation Control Act (1968), Wholesale Poultry Products Act (1967), Coal Mine Health and Safety Act (1969), and the Occupational Health and Safety Act (1970)" (Buckhorn, 1972:226).

There are other ways of transforming "private troubles into public issues" (Spector and Kitsuse, 1973:148). For example, we are all familiar with Rosa Parks, a black seamstress who, on December 1, 1955, sat down in the back of a city bus in Montgomery, Alabama, then refused to relinquish her seat to a white man when the "noncolored" section became over-crowded. Her action launched the famous black boycott of the buses that created a new era in the civil rights struggle and provided considerable impetus for civil rights legislation. And let's not forget Carrie Nation's efforts to demonstrate the advantages of Prohibition by chopping up saloons with her celebrated hatchet.

Protest Activity

Protest activity involves marches, sit-ins, strikes, and boycotts which dramatically illustrate, with the media's help, a group's problems or objectives. Generally, such activities, along with rioting, have been viewed as tools of people who are unable or unwilling to engage in the more conventional law-initiating techniques or who regard these techniques as useless. It should be noted at the onset that "the relationship among law, protest, and social change is neither unidirectional nor symmetrical—nor always predictable. One major function of protest may be to secure changes in the law as a means of inducing change in social conditions. Another may be to bring about change directly without the intervention of the law. Still a third may be to bring about legal change which ratifies or legitimizes social change accomplished by other means. These functions are not mutually exclusive" (Grossman and Grossman, 1971:357). But the impact of protest activities on law creation is clearly evident, for "The law in general, and the Court in particular, lacks a self-starter or capacity for initiating change on its own" (Grossman and Grossman, 1971:358).

Racial minorities, poverty organizations, antiwar groups, and opponents of nuclear power have been among those who have employed protest techniques in recent years in attempts to create laws in favor of their objectives. Much of this activity is designed to generate favorable media coverage and through this, the support of organizations and persons important in the eyes of lawmakers. But the young, the poor, and minority groups have not been the only ones to use protest techniques such as strikes and boycotts. Strike action has long been a central tactic of organized labor, including the unions of public employers in pursuing political and economic goals. In the mid-1970s, physicians used the strike weapon as a method of seeking governmental relief from medical malpractice insurance costs. Boycotts have been used by consumers protesting high prices. The national meat boycott of 1973 is an important example of such consumer action. It helped to generate enough pressure to force then President Nixon to place a ceiling on meat prices. The controls, however, caused a meat shortage as farmers cut back on their supply.

To what extent protest activities provide an impetus for lawmaking is difficult to say. But, "few major social movements or great changes have occurred without the unrest and disorder which, if one approves is called protest or civil disobedience, and if one disapproves, it is called breaking the law, violence, or worse. Violence in particular is as much a part of enforcing the law as it is of seeking changes in the law" (Grossman and Grossman, 1971:358).

Social Movements

Social movements can also stimulate lawmaking. By definition, a social movement is a type of collective behavior in which a group of individuals organize to promote certain changes or alterations in certain types of behavior or procedures. Invariably, the movement has specified stated objectives, a hierarchical organizational structure, and a well-conceptualized and precise change-oriented ideology. The movement consciously and purposefully articulates the changes it desires through political, educational or legal channels.

A good example is the movement to legalize abortion. People had for some time regarded illegal abortion as dangerous, but efforts to prevent it (and thus end the death or serious injury of women) were unsuccessful. Then, a combination of women's rights and medical groups began to demand the legalization of abortion. Medical spokespersons argued that abortion is rightfully a medical decision to be made by a physician and his or her patient. Women's leaders argued that a woman has an unassailable right over her own body and ought to be able to choose whether or not to terminate the pregnancy. At the same time, no significant groups in society had a stake either in a high birthrate or in providing expensive illegal abortions. On the contrary, the general consensus was that the economic interests of the nation were concerned with the issues of overpopulation. Furthermore, with modern medical techniques, a legal abortion is classified as minor surgery, both cheap and safe.

With relative speed, in the 1960s states began to repeal or greatly liberalize laws against abortion. Within this climate of opinion, the Supreme Court completed the process in 1973 by declaring state laws against abortion unconstitutional except in the case of the last three months of pregnancy, and in the licensing of those permitted to perform the operation. Today there is no illegal abortion problem of any magnitude, and maternal mortality resulting from illegal abortion has been reduced by a significant amount. This is just one illustration of a social movement. Clearly, there are many others including ecology, civil rights, feminism, "crime without victims," "law and order movements," and so forth. It should be pointed out that not all social movements are successful in bringing about changes through laws. As a matter of fact, at any given moment, hundreds of groups with hundreds of messages are trying to get public attention. Most fail. In the United States, winning public attention, thus public support, is becoming a highly professional activity. Groups that can afford to hire or that can recruit public relations and advertising experts have a considerable advantage over other groups in getting a public hearing for their grievances. It is interesting to note that, regardless of the expertise available to them, all groups share the problem of developing an effective strategy to attract attention in a way that will not at the same time provoke outrage and opposition.

Public Interest Groups

Among lawmakers, it is a well-known and acknowledged fact that private interests are more adequately represented than public interests (Lazarus: 1974:122). There are literally hundreds of organizations and individuals in Washington and in state capitals who represent one or more private interests on a full- or part-time basis. They range from extremely well-financed organizations, such as the American Petroleum Institute involved in worldwide affairs and supported by thousands of engineers, lawyers, and public relations experts, to small, single-issue groups, such as the Sportsman's Paradise Homeowners Association. Some, such as oil companies, regulate refinery output to maintain prices, and they lobby government representatives for favorable tax policies. Others, such as United States Shipbuilders and the National Maritime Union, win direct and indirect subsidies from Congress in the guise of national defense requirements. Power utilities are legal monopolies whose rate structures are decided by utility commissions which are, in turn, the focus of tremendous pressures to allow expansion and higher rates for the benefit of managers and investors. There are over 17,000 entries in the *Encyclopedia of Associations*. Most of them represent specific, private interests.

By contrast, the number of groups that claim to represent public interests is quite small. The most notable among these include: John Gardner's Common Cause, the Sierra Club, and the Public Interest Research Groups (PIRGs). These groups have been instrumental in the initiation of a series of changes in the law aimed at benefiting and protecting the public.

The Common Cause organization, founded in 1970, now has an annual budget of over $6 million and dues-paying membership of 300,000. It "has fought pitched battles on issues of the deepest concern to the American people—the Vietnam war, environmental pollution, racial injustice, poverty, unemployment, and women's rights" (Gardner, 1973:18). The organization is dedicated to "opening up the system" through the reform of campaign financing, open meeting laws and disclosure laws. For example, in 1973, it initiated proposals for legislations which included making highway trust funds available for mass transit use, an unequivocal press-shield law, and "tax equity" (Wieck, 1973:21).

Spurred by the belief that the world faces an ultimate ecocatastrophe unless immediate and successful efforts are made to halt the abuse and deterioration of the environment, Sierra Club members "are no longer the outdoor recreationists of yesterday, but rather today's environmental politicos, in the vanguard of society's newest social movement" (Faich and Gale, 1971:282). The Sierra Club and similar organizations have been active in recent years in providing the impetus for a series of laws dealing with the protection of the environment. Some of these include the Air Pollution

Control Act of 1967, the Clear Air Act of 1970, the Clean Water Act of 1972, in addition to the formation of a number of new federal agencies to both monitor compliance with the numerous existing pollution and environmental protection laws and to help establish new policies.

Modeled after Nader's Center for Responsive Law, but independent of it, are the various public interest research groups that now, after only a few years of organizing, include close to 400,000 student members at over 150 schools in twenty-four states. These groups are student-funded and -directed organizations, composed of a small professional staff of lawyers, scientists, and organizers, aided by hundreds of volunteer student researchers. For example, the Missouri Public Interest Research Group (MOPIRG) drafted a new consumer code to protect poor people in St. Louis and have distributed a handbook on tenants' rights in Missouri. MOPIRG also participated in a study of the Educational Testing Service and is working with St. Louis unions to secure better enforcement of the occupational safety and health laws. Just recently they have been instrumental in setting up a small claims court in Missouri. In other states as well, the Public Interest Research Groups are active in pointing out deficiencies in the system and proposing legal solutions for their improvement through research, public information, and law reform.

Impetus for law may also come from the various quasi-public specialized interest groups. They may be representing certain economic interests, such as consumer groups, organized labor, or the National Welfare Rights organization. Or they can represent certain occupational interests such as the American Medical Association, which not only exercises considerable control over the practice of medicine in this country, but actively takes stands, raises money, and lobbies in favor of specific positions on such issues as abortion, euthanasia, drugs, and alcohol. The same can be said for the American Association of University Professors (though not on the same issues). Still others include groups representing what may be called moral interests, such as temperance, various types of antidrug concerns, various forms of "child saving" (for example, delinquency control), sexual deviance, the "work ethic," and antipornography. The important point to remember is that all these organizations can agitate for changes in the law and can provide the needed impetus for it.

In order for a group to effectively promote its interests and to provide an impetus for lawmaking, it naturally must have access to lawmakers. But access to lawmakers depends, at least in part, on the socioeconomic status of the group. Groups with the most financial resources, the most prestigious membership, and the best organization are likely to have the greatest access to legislators. It takes a substantial amount of money to maintain lobbyists in Washington and throughout the state capitals. Moreover, lawmakers, too, on the local as well as the higher levels, may be more sympathetic to groups that represent interests of the middle and upper classes than to groups representing poor people, welfare recipients, and the like. Generally, groups with "mainstream" views, seeking only small changes in the status quo, may be given more sympathetic hearing than those advocating large scale radical changes.

The Mass Media

The mass media (newspapers, magazines, radio, and television stations) function in part as an interest group. Each component of the mass
media is a business, and like other businesses, it has a direct interest in
various areas of public policy. For example, the media have had a general
objective of securing legislation, such as freedom of information and open
meeting laws, which facilitate their access to the news, and legislation or
court decisions which allow them to protect the confidentiality of news
sources. Associations like the National Association of Broadcasters are regularly concerned with the activities of the Federal Communications Commission which controls their licensing of television and radio stations.

The mass media also function as conduits, although not altogether
impartial ones, for others who would shape policy. Wealthier groups, for
example, purchase media time or space in an effort to align public opinion
behind their causes. Through the media, these groups may reach the ear
of legislators and administrators by publicly exposing problems and proposals about which they might not otherwise hear, or in some instances,
about which they might not want to hear.

The mass media, especially the news media, are able to generate widespread awareness and concern about events and conditions—to bring matters before the public so that they become problematic issues. For example,
columnist Jack Anderson, the irreverent muckraker, repeatedly sniffs out
malodorous secrets that vested interests—oil companies, the Pentagon,
the junta in Chile, the distributors of chemical defoliants—do not want
aired.

The Watergate case aptly demonstrates a number of ways in which the
mass media influence current events. Without dogged investigations by the
mass media, the scandal probably would have remained buried. Without
the blitz of mass media coverage, the issues probably would not have
achieved as rapid, widespread, or as deep an impact on the public. Many
of the most scandalous incidents of the Watergate affair have involved the
improper solicitation and employment of campaign funds. Outraged segments of public opinion demanded the prevention of future Watergates.
The legislative response to this outcry was the passage of a bill in April
1974 that would drastically alter the way in which Presidential and Congressional campaigns are funded. This is illustrative of situations in which, as
a result of investigative reporting, the mass media provide a direct impetus
for legislation. A more recent example of the role of mass media in influencing current events is seen in the context of the Iran-Contra scandal.
Special congressional committees have been impaneled to look into the
precipitating events leading to the scandal, and the Attorney General has
opened a criminal investigation into the possibility that millions of dollars
raised through secret U.S. arms sales to Iran had been diverted to the Con-
tra supply effort in an attempt to topple Nicaragua's government, which is
controlled by the leftist Sandanista Party. It is likely that these events will
result in a series of laws dealing with the discretionary power of government agencies and officials (St. Louis Post-Dispatch, 1987:1B).

Since public opinion is an important precursor of change, the mass media can set the stage by making undesirable conditions visible to a sizeable segment of the public with unparalleled rapidity. Through the exposure of perceived injustices, the mass media play a crucial role in the formation of public opinion. Ralph Turner and Lewis M. Killian (1972:215–216) discuss six processes considered essential in understanding how the mass media can influence public opinion. First, the mass media *authenticate* the factual nature of events, which is decisive in the formation of public opinion. Second, the mass media *validate* opinions, sentiments, and preferences. It is reassuring to hear one's views confirmed by a well-known commentator. It also enables a person to express his or her views more effectively by borrowing the commentator's words. A third effect of the mass media is to *legitimize* certain behaviors and tabooed viewpoints. Issues that were only discussed in private can now be expressed publicly since they have already been discussed on television (for example, legal rights of homosexuals). Fourth, the mass media often *symbolize* the diffuse anxieties, preferences, discontents, and prejudices that individuals experience. By giving an acceptable identification for these perplexing feelings, the mass media often aid their translation into specific opinions and actions. By providing symbols—the "me" generation, Yuppies, law and order, the new morality—the mass media create a number of objects toward which specific sentiments can be directed. Fifth, the mass media *focus* the preferences, discontents, and prejudices into lines of action. Finally, the mass media *hierarchize* persons, objects, activities, and issues. As a result of the amount of consideration, preferential programming, and placement of items, they indicate relative importance and prestige.

The generalization that the views of individuals whose prestige and influence are established carry more weight than the views of others applies to public opinion. As a result, the "influences stemming from the mass media first reach 'opinion leaders' who in turn, pass on what they read or hear to those of their everyday associates for whom they are influential" (Katz, 1957:61). Opinion leaders are usually leaders in only one sphere of activity. They tend to be different from the rest of the public in that they are more highly educated and are engaged in more prestigious occupations. They are also more powerful, active, and influential in specific community, interest-group, or political affairs. Consequently, their opinions are considered much more influential and, therefore, targeted by much of the media efforts.

In addition to investigative reporting and the shaping of public opinion, the mass media can pressure or challenge lawmakers into taking action on an issue or into changing their stand on a question. Influential newspapers such as *The New York Times* or the *Washington Post* can make or break legislators by the use of the editorial pages. Endorsement by a major newspaper can greatly facilitate a candidate's chances for being elected. Conversely, opposition to a candidate on the editorial page can influence the outcome of an election. Legislators are quite aware of the power of the press, and as a result, editorial recommendations are given serious consideration. Similarly, articles in various influential weekly or monthly publications such as *Commentary, Daedalus, Encounter, Monthly Review, New Leader, New Republic, Public Interest, Progressive, Social Policy,* and the diverse specialized professional and legal journals can agitate for change.

Finally, an indirect way by which the mass media can furnish an impetus for lawmaking is through the provision of a forum for citizens' concerns. For example, the "letters to the editor" page in newspapers is a traditional outlet for publicizing undesirable conditions. Such letters can accomplish several objectives. First, the letter can alert the community that an issue is before a lawmaking body; second, it can persuade the reader to take a position; third, it can make clear that there are responsible and articulate people in the community who are concerned with the issue; and fourth, it can enlist the active support of others. Similarly, many radio and television stations have local talk shows and public-affairs programs which can be used to air grievances and to seek redress.

SUMMARY

This chapter has been concerned with the complex and continuous process of lawmaking in society. A number of theoretical perspectives to account for lawmaking have been reviewed. They include the rationalistic model, the functional view, conflict theory, and the "moral entrepreneur" thesis. None of these theories can account for the creation of all laws. At best, they explain in part how laws are made.

Three general types of lawmaking processes—legislative, administrative, and judicial—were analyzed. Legislators are solely responsible for formulating broad new roles and for creating and revising the institutions necessary to put them into effect. Legislative lawmaking basically consists of finding major and minor compromises to ideas advanced for legislation by the executive, administrative agencies, interest groups, and various party agencies and spokespersons. Administrative lawmaking consists of rulemaking and adjudication. Rule-making is essentially legislation by administrative agencies. Adjudication differs from rule-making in that it applies only to a specific, limited number of parties involved in an individual case and controversy before the agency. Judicial lawmaking is an accelerating trend in the United States. Three types of judicial lawmaking were examined—by precedent, by interpretation of statutes, and by interpretation of Constitution. Judicial lawmaking is generally directed at other government agencies rather than at private individuals.

Interest groups, public opinion, and social science all exert an influence on the lawmaking process. Interest groups influence judicial lawmaking by initiating test cases, providing additional information to the courts through *amicus curiae* briefs, and by communicating indirectly with judges by placing information in legal and general periodicals. Interactions between interest groups and legislative and administrative lawmakers are more overtly political in nature. The notion that laws reflect public opinion can be misleading. Some groups are more influential than others, and the differential influence of public opinion on lawmaking processes is a well-known phenomenon. Still, public opinion does exert an influence on law-makers through rewards and sanctions (for example, voting for or against a particular legislator); through interest groups; and through the use of public opinion polls. Lawmakers are aware of the contributions social scientists can make to the lawmaking process. These contributions are based on social science research and expressed to lawmakers either directly in the form of expert testimony, or indirectly through the use of research findings as they bear upon a particular piece of legislation or judicial and administrative decision. But the participation of social scientists in the lawmaking processes is not without controversies. There are questions about the use of research results, their validity and reliability, and the political bias of social scientists. In spite of the controversies, it was noted that social science evidence cannot be kept out of the lawmaking process.

Demands for lawmaking come from a multitude of sources. Ideas for change are born in the minds of a few people who are ready and willing to articulate their dissatisfaction. They represent diverse interests and causes and channel their discontent through different means. Once in a while, a scholarly investigation generates concern over a social condition or practice and points to a legal solution. At times, a novel can detect or warn about a deleterious situation which affects the public. The impetus for lawmaking can also come from institutionalized forces, such as lobbying activities and public interest groups. Occasionally, the creation of laws has been stimulated by organized protest activities or social movements. Finally, the mass media can set the stage for lawmaking by calling attention to an issue.

SUGGESTED FURTHER READINGS

RAYMOND A. BAUER and KENNETH J. GERGEN (eds.), *The Study of Policy Formation.* New York: Free Press, 1968. A compendium on the various facets of lawmaking and decision-making theories.

DANIEL M. BERMAN, *A Bill Becomes a Law, Congress Enacts Civil Rights Legislation,* 2nd ed. New York: Macmillan, 1966. An effective attempt to explain the functioning of Congress by describing the way in which a particular bill became a law.

LON L. FULLER, *Anatomy of the Law.* New York: Frederick A. Praeger, Publishers, 1968. See in particular Part Two, "The Sources of Law."

JOHN W. GARDNER, *In Common Cause,* rev. ed. New York: W. W. Norton & Co., Inc., 1973. An interesting and provocative account of a group serving the public interest.

NATHAN GLAZER, "Towards an Imperial Judiciary?" *The Public Interest* (41)(Fall) 1975:104–123. An intriguing and controversial article on the increase in judicial lawmaking.

JOHN HAGAN, "The Legislation of Crime and Delinquency: A Review of Theory, Method, and Research," *Law & Society Review* 14 (3)(Spring), 1980:603–628. A review of over 40 studies drawn from the crime and delinquency legislation literature.

SEYMOUR MARTIN LIPSET, "The Wavering Polls," *The Public Interest* (43)(Spring) 1976:70–89. An essay on the advantages and limitations of public opinion polls and their implications on lawmaking.

DANIEL PATRICK MOYNIHAN, "Social Science and the Courts," *The Public Interest* (54)(Winter) 1979:12–31. A highly provocative article on the role of the social sciences in judicial lawmaking.

NELSON W. POLSBY, *Congress and the Presidency,* 3rd ed. Englewood Cliffs, NJ: Prentice-Hall. 1976. See Chapter Five, "National Policy-Making I: The Legislative Labyrinth," for a clear and detailed account of congressional lawmaking.

ERIC REDMAN, *The Dance of Legislation*. New York: Simon & Schuster, 1973. A firsthand account of the drafting and passing of a piece of legislation—the National Health Service Bill—and the various maneuvers, plots, frustrations, and sheer work involved.

GLENDON A. SCHUBERT, *Human Jurisprudence, Public Law as Political Science*. Honolulu: The University Press of Hawaii, 1975. A somewhat technical but fascinating account of the processes by which judges make law.

ROMAN A. TOMASIC (ed.), *Legislation and Society in Australia*. Sydney: George Allen and Unwin, 1980. A series of case studies and theoretical articles on the making and implementation of law in Australia.

REFERENCES

ABRAHAM, HENRY J. 1973. *The Judiciary, The Supreme Court in the Governmental Process*, 3rd ed. Boston: Allyn and Bacon, Inc.

ARMOR, DAVID J. 1972. "The Evidence on Busing." The Public Interest (25)(Summer):90–126.

BECKER, HOWARD S. 1963. *Outsiders*. New York: Free Press.

BERK, RICHARD A., and JERROLD OPPENHEIM. 1979. "Doing Good Well: The Use of Quantitative Social Science Data in Adversary Proceedings," Law and Policy Quarterly 1 (2)(April):123–146.

BOHANNAN, PAUL. 1973. "The Differing Realms of the Law." Pp. 306–317 in Donald Black and Maureen Mileski, eds., The Social Organization of the Law. New York: Seminar Press.

BUCKHORN, ROBERT F. 1972. *Nader, The People's Lawyer*. Englewood Cliffs, NJ: Prentice-Hall.

CAPLOVITZ, DAVID. 1963. *The Poor Pay More*. New York: Free Press; 1974. *Consumers in Trouble, A Study of Debtors in Default*. New York: Free Press.

CARSON, RACHEL L. 1962. *Silent Spring*. Boston: Houghton-Mifflin.

CHAMBLISS, WILLIAM J. 1964. "A Sociological Analysis of the Law of Vagrancy," Social Problems 12 (1)(Summer):67–77; 1976. "The State and Criminal Law." Pp. 66–106 in William J. Chambliss and Milton Mankoff, eds., Whose Law, What Order? A Conflict Approach to Criminology. New York: John Wiley.

CHAMBLISS, WILLIAM J., ed. 1984. *Criminal Law in Action*. 2nd ed. New York: John Wiley.

COLEMAN, JAMES S. 1966. "Equality Schools or Equal Students," The Public Interest (7) (Summer):70–75; 1967. "Toward Open Schools," The Public Interest (9)(Fall):20–27.

COMMONS, JOHN R. 1934. *Institutional Economics*. New York: Macmillan.

CRESPI, IRVING. 1979. "Modern Marketing Techniques: They Could Work in Washington, Too," Public Opinion 2 (3)(June–July):16–19, 58–59.

DAVIS, KENNETH CULP. 1977. *Administrative Law, Cases-Text-Problems*. St. Paul, MN: West Publishing Company.

DOWNS, ANTHONY. 1976. *Urban Problems and Prospects*, 2nd ed. Chicago: Markham Publishing Company.

ETZIONI, AMITAI. 1973. *The Genetic Fix*. New York: Macmillan.

FAICH, RONALD G., and RICHARD P. GALE. 1971. "The Environmental Movement from Recreation to Politics," Pacific Sociological Review (14)(July):270–287.

FALK, RICHARD. 1971. *This Endangered Planet*. New York: Random House.

FELDSTEIN, MARTIN S. 1975a. "Toward a Reform of Social Security," The Public Interest (40)(Summer):75–95; 1975b. "Unemployment Insurance: Time for Reform," Harvard Business Review (53)(March–April):51–61.

FRIEDMAN, LAWRENCE M. 1975. *The Legal System, A Social Science Perspective*. New York: Russell Sage Foundation; 1984. *American Law: An Introduction*. New York: W. W. Norton.

FRIEDMAN, LAWRENCE M., and STEWART MACAULAY. 1977. *Law and the Behavioral Sciences*, 2nd ed. Indianapolis: Bobbs-Merrill.

FULLER, LON. 1968. *Anatomy of the Law*. New York: Frederick A. Praeger, Publishers.

GARDNER, JOHN W. 1973. *In Common Cause*, rev. ed. New York: W. W. Norton & Co., Inc.

GLAZER, NATHAN. 1975. "Towards an Imperial Judiciary?" The Public Interest (41)(Fall):104–123.

GOODE, ERICH. 1978. *Deviant Behavior, An Interactionist Approach*. Englewood Cliffs, NJ: Prentice-Hall.

GROSSMAN, JOEL B., and MARY H. GROSSMAN, eds. 1971. *Law and Social Change in Modern America.* Pacific Palisades, CA: Goodyear.

GUSFIELD, JOSEPH R. 1967. "Moral Passage: The Symbolic Process in Public Designations of Deviance," Social Problems 15 (2)(Fall):175–188.

HAGAN, JOHN. 1980. "The Legislation of Crime and Delinquency: A Review of Theory, Method, and Research," Law & Society Review 14 (3)(Spring):603–628.

HOROWITZ, DONALD L. 1977. *The Courts and Social Policy.* Washington, DC: Brookings Institution.

HOWARD, A. E. DICK. 1979. "The Road From 'Brown'," The Wilson Quarterly 3 (2)(Spring):96–107.

IPPOLITO, DENNIS S., THOMAS G. WALKER, and KENNETH L. KOLSON. 1976. *Public Opinion and Responsible Democracy.* Englewood Cliffs, NJ: Prentice-Hall.

JACOB, HERBERT. 1984. *Justice in America, Courts, Lawyers, and the Judicial Process.* 4th ed. Boston: Little, Brown.

KATZ, ELIHU. 1957. "The Two-Step Flow of Communication: An Up-to-Date Report on an Hypothesis," Public Opinion Quarterly 21 (1)(Spring):61–78.

LAZARUS, SIMON. 1974. *The Gentile Populists.* New York: Holt, Rinehart and Winston.

LIPSET, SEYMOUR MARTIN. 1976. "The Wavering Polls," The Public Interest (43)(Spring):70–89.

LLEWELLYN, KARL N., and E. ADAMSON HOEBEL. 1941. *The Cheyenne Way: Conflict and Case Law in Primitive Jurisprudence.* Norman: University of Oklahoma Press.

MOYNIHAN, DANIEL PATRICK. 1979. "Social Science and the Courts," The Public Interest (54)(Winter):12–31.

NADER, RALPH. 1965. *Unsafe at Any Speed: The Designed-in Dangers of the American Automobile.* New York: Grossman.

OSBORN, FAIRFIELD. 1948. *Our Plundered Planet.* Boston: Little, Brown.

PETTIGREW, THOMAS F., and ROBERT L. GREEN. 1976. "School Desegregation in Large Cities," Harvard Educational Review (46)(February):1–53.

PLATTNER, MARC F. 1974. "Campaign Financing: The Dilemmas of Reform," The Public Interest (37)(Fall):112–130.

PRICE, DAVID E. 1972. *Who Makes the Law? Creativity and Power in Senate Committees.* Cambridge, MA: Schenkman.

QUINNEY, RICHARD. 1970. *The Social Reality of Crime.* Boston: Little, Brown.

REINOW, R., and L. T. REINOW. 1967. *Moment in the Sun.* New York: Dial Press.

RIPLEY, RANDALL B. 1978. *Congress, Process and Policy,* 2nd ed. New York: W. W. Norton & Co., Inc.

ROBY, PAMELA. 1969. "Politics and Criminal Law: Revision of the New York State Penal Law on Prostitution," Social Problems 17 (1)(Summer):83–109.

RUSTHOVEN, PETER J. 1976. "The Courts as Sociologists," National Review (December 10):1339–1341.

St. Louis Post-Dispatch. 1987. "Warning on Contras." (January 26):1B.

SHAPIRO, MARTIN. 1968. *The Supreme Court and Administrative Agencies.* New York: Free Press.

SIMON, RITA JAMES. 1974. *Public Opinion in America: 1936–1970.* Skokie, IL: Rand McNally.

SPECTOR, MALCOLM, and JOHN I. KITSUSE. 1973. "Social Problems: A Reformulation," Social Problems 21 (2)(Fall):145–159.

STONE, MARVIN. 1979. "Should Judges Make Law?" U.S. News & World Report (June 4):76.

TOMASIC, ROMAN. 1985. *The Sociology of Law.* London: Sage Publications.

TURNER, RALPH, and LEWIS M. KILLAN. 1972. *Collective Behavior,* rev. ed. Englewood Cliffs, NJ: Prentice-Hall.

VAGO, STEVEN. 1968. "Wage Garnishment: An Exercise in Futility Under Present Law," The Journal of Consumer Affairs 2 (1)(Summer):7–20.

WIECK, PAUL R. 1973. "The John Gardner Brigade," New Republic (168):21–22.

WOLF, ELEANOR P. 1976. "Social Science and the Courts: The Detroit Schools Case," The Public Interest (42)(Winter):102–120.

ZEISEL, HANS. 1962. "Social Research on the Law, The Ideal and the Practical." Pp. 124–143 in William M. Evan, ed., Law and Sociology, Exploratory Essays. New York: Free Press.

5

Law and Social Control

Social control refers to the ways members of a society or a group promote predictability of behavior and social order. The forms of social control are varied so that law comprises only one kind of social control. The focus of this chapter is on social control through laws which come into play when other forms of social control mechanisms are ineffective or unavailable. The chapter examines the processes of informal and formal social control, the use of criminal sanctions, the effectiveness of the death penalty, and civil commitment to control deviant behavior. Part of the chapter is concerned with crimes without victims (drug addiction, prostitution, and gambling), white-collar crime, and the control of dissent. Finally, administrative law is considered as a means of control in the context of licensing, inspection, and the threat of publicity.

There are two basic processes of social control: the internalization of group norms and social control through external pressures (Clinard and Meier, 1985:13–14). In the first one, social control is the consequence of socialization, the process of learning the rules of behavior for a given social group. Individuals develop self-control by being taught early what is appropriate, expected, or desirable in specific situations. People acquire a motivation to conform to the norms, regardless of external pressures. Most students do not cheat because of the fear of being caught, and most people pay their taxes, most of the time. There is conformity to norms because individuals have been socialized to believe that they should conform, regardless of and independent of any anticipated reactions of other persons.

Mechanisms of social control through external pressures include both negative and positive sanctions. Negative sanctions are penalties imposed on those who violate norms. Positive sanctions, such as a promotion, bonus, or encouragement, are intended to reward conformity. These positive and negative sanctions are forms of social control. Some types of social control are formal or official while others are informal or unofficial in character. Typical reactions to deviance and rule-breaking may generate informal or formal sanctions. Although there is a considerable amount of overlapping between informal and formal mechanisms of social control, for analytical purposes they will be treated separately.

INFORMAL SOCIAL CONTROLS

Informal social controls are exemplified in the functions of folkways (established norms of common practices such as those that specify modes of dress, etiquette, and language use) and mores (societal norms associated with intense feelings of right or wrong and definite rules of conduct that are simply not to be violated, for example, incest). These informal controls consist of techniques whereby individuals who know each other on a personal basis accord praise to those who comply with their expectations and show displeasure to those who do not (Shibutani, 1961:426). These techniques may be observed in specific behaviors such as ridicule, gossip, praise, reprimands, criticisms, ostracism, or verbal rationalizations and expressions of opinion. Gossip, or the fear of gossip, is one of the more effective devices employed by members of a society for bringing individuals into conformity with norms. Unlike formal social controls, these informal controls are not exercised through official group mechanisms, and there are no specially designated persons in charge of enforcement.

Informal mechanisms of social control tend to be more effective in groups and societies where relations are face-to-face and intimate and where the division of labor is relatively simple. For example, Emile Durkheim argues that in simple societies, such as tribal villages or small towns, legal norms more closely accord with social norms than in larger and more complex societies. Moral disapproval of deviance is nearly unanimous in such communities; as Daniel Glaser (1971:32) notes, "Tolerance of behavioral diversity varies directly with the division of labor in a society." In simple societies laws are often unwritten, necessitating the direct teaching of social norms to children. Socialization in such simple societies does not present children with contradictory norms that create confusion or inner conflict. Intense face-to-face interaction in such societies produces a moral consensus that is well-known to all members; it also brings deviant acts to everyone's attention quickly.

There is evidence in the sociological literature to support the contention that informal social control is stronger in smaller, more homogeneous communities than in larger, more heterogeneous communities. In his influential study of deviance in the seventeenth-century Massachusetts Bay Colony, Kai T. Erikson found that the small size and the cultural homogeneity of the community helped control behavior, since everyone in the community pressured potential deviants to conform to dominant norms. There was a substantial amount of surveillance by neighbors in the community watching for acts of deviance. Moral censure immediately followed any observed act of deviance (Erikson, 1966:169–170). Even today, reaction to certain crimes (for example, rape or murder) in a small, homogeneous, and close-knit community may be so intense and immediate that justice for a defendant in a criminal case may be difficult, since public pressure on the legal system to exact harsh and immediate punishment may make the provision of due process rights doubtful. In such instances, it may be necessary to change the location of the trial to minimize public pressure. Such a change of venue order is more likely to take place in small communities than in larger ones where the court would not assume that the defendant can receive a fair trial because of prejudice (Friendly and Goldfarb, 1967:96–101).

Undoubtedly, informal social controls operate more effectively in smaller communities where people know each other and regularly interact. In such communities law enforcement agents can probably expect better cooperation. As the President's Commission on Law Enforcement and Administration of Justice (1967a:6) points out: "A man who lives in the country or in a small town is likely to be conspicuous, under surveillance by his community so to speak, and therefore under its control. A city man is often almost invisible, socially isolated from his neighborhood and therefore incapable of being controlled by it. He has more opportunities for crime."

The notion of the greater effectiveness of informal social control mechanisms in small communities is supported by Sarah L. Boggs' study of formal and informal social controls in central cities, suburbs, and small towns in Missouri. Boggs found that residents of large cities were more apt than suburban or small-town residents to feel that crime was likely to occur in their community. City residents were also more likely to think that their neighbors would not report a burglary that they observed, and more urban residents knew of a crime or a suspicious incident in their community within the previous year. Most people in all areas felt that their own neighborhood was safe, but fewer felt that way in the cities. When they were asked *what* it was that made their neighborhood safe, 83 percent of those in rural areas and small towns said that it was informal controls; 70 percent in suburbs and 68 percent of those in the cities attributed safety to informal controls. When they said that their neighborhood was kept safe by informal social controls, the people meant that they felt secure because of the character of the community and its residents—"good, decent, law-abiding, middle-class citizens" (Boggs, 1971:323). Safety in a neighborhood was also attributed to the social network in the community which might lead to bystander intervention in a crime. Respondents who lived in suburbs and large cities were more likely than those who lived in rural areas and small towns to attribute safety to such formal control agents as the police (Boggs, 1971:234). Boggs concluded that people in cities were most inclined to expect crime, but least likely to feel that they could rely on their neighbors rather than the police to protect their community. As a result, they were more likely to take precautions, such as purchasing weapons or a watchdog than their counterparts who lived in suburbs, small towns, and rural areas.

In another study on the use of formal and informal social control mechanisms, Richard D. Schwartz (1977) examined two Israeli agricultural settlements. The communities were originally similar to each other, to the extent that there were no major differences in ideas of legal control. One settlement was a collective or *kvutza,* with no formal mechanism to resolve disputes of a legal nature, and the other was a semiprivate settlement or *moshav,* which had a judicial committee to handle legal disputes. The collective had no legal committee because the intense and frequent face-to-face interaction provided an effective means of social control by group pressure. By contrast, in the semiprivate settlement, there was less interaction and less consensus: behavior was less visible to members of the community than it was in the collective. Schwartz found that informal social control was less effective in the semiprivate settlement than in the collective where the flow of information soon made any deviant action known to all members of the community.

Similar conclusions about the role of informal social control mechanisms can be drawn from studies dealing with developing nations. For example, in comparing a low crime-rate community and a high crime-rate community in Kampala, Uganda, Marshall B. Clinard and Daniel J. Abbott found that the areas with less crime showed greater social solidarity, more social interaction among neighbors, more participation in local organizations, less geographical mobility, and more stability in family relationships. There was also greater cultural homogeneity and more emphasis on tribal and kinship ties in the low-crime community, helping to counteract the anonymity of recent migrants to the city. The stronger primary group ties among residents of the low-crime area made it more difficult for strangers in the community to escape public notice. To prevent theft, residents of an area must feel that it is wrong; share some responsibility for protecting their neighbors' property; be able to identify strangers in the area; and be willing to take action if they observe a theft (Clinard and Abbott, 1973:149).

On the basis of these studies, it can be posited that if there is intense social interaction on an intimate face-to-face basis, normative consensus, and surveillance of the behavior of members of the community, informal social control will be strong to the extent that legal or formal controls may be unnecessary. This contention is reinforced by Roberto Mangabeira Unger's (1976) argument which was discussed in Chapter Two. To reiterate, Unger contends that bureaucratic law emerges when state and society become differentiated, and there is a felt need for an institution standing above conflicting groups. This occurs when the community disintegrates, that is, when individuals may no longer be counted on to act in set ways without overt guidance. Such a disintegration comes about as the division of labor creates new opportunities for power and wealth, which, in turn, undercut old hierarchies determined by birth. This process is accompanied by an increased reliance on formal social controls.

FORMAL SOCIAL CONTROLS

Although there is no precise dividing line, formal social controls are usually characteristic of more complex societies with a greater division of labor, heterogeneity of population, and subgroups with competing values and different sets of mores and ideologies. Formal controls arise when informal controls are insufficient to maintain conformity to certain norms and are characterized by systems of specialized agencies and standard techniques. The two main types are those instituted by the state and authorized to use force, and those imposed by agencies other than the state, such as the church, business and labor groups, universities, and clubs.

Formal social controls are incorporated in the institutions in society and are characterized by the explicit establishment of procedures and the delegation of specific bodies to enforce them (laws, decrees, regulations, codes). Since they are incorporated in the institutions of society, they are administered by individuals who occupy positions in those institutions. Generally, anyone who tries to manipulate the behavior of others through the use of formal sanctions may be considered an agent of social control (Clinard and Meier, 1985:15–16).

Social institutions are organized for securing conformity to established modes of behavior and consist of established procedures for satisfying human needs. These procedures carry a certain degree of compulsion. They involve mechanisms of imposing conformity. Nonpolitical institutions may resort to a variety of penalties and rewards to insure compliance. For example, an organization may fire an employee; a church may withhold religious services at a wedding or burial, or even excommunicate a member; a league owner may fine or suspend a professional athlete for infractions of rules. These same organizations may also use formal rewards to insure conformity. To illustrate, through bonuses and promotion, an organization often rewards those who make an outstanding contribution. Dedicated church members may be commended for exemplary service, and professional athletes are often enticed by financial rewards.

The state, through its legal institutions, exercises another type of social control through the use or the threat of force and coercion:

> Such control resolves itself into such forms as the restraints of all social parasites, exploiters (usually defined by law), criminals, and all other imperfectly socialized and antisocial persons whose behavior threatens the well-being of society as a whole; and the establishment and preservation of that degree of social adjustment, equilibrium, and social solidarity—"law and order"— among the various parts that will make possible effective joint action or common needs and objectives and ensure the efficient operation, stability, and continuity of the society (Roucek, 1978:13).

It should be noted at the outset that control through law is seldom exercised by the use of positive sanctions or rewards. A person who, throughout his or her life, obeys the law and meets its requirements seldom receives rewards or commendations. State control is exercised primarily, but not exclusively, through the use or threat of punishment to regulate the behavior of citizens. The next two sections focus on the use of criminal sanctions with particular emphasis on the death penalty debate and civil commitment to control certain types of behavior.

Formal Social Control of Deviance: Criminal Sanctions

The social control of criminal and delinquent behavior exemplifies the most highly structured formal system (the criminal justice system) used by society. The laws, enacted by legislators and modified by court decisions, define criminal and delinquent behavior and specify the sanctions imposed for violations. Over time, there has been an increasing reliance on law to regulate the activities and thus the lives of people. As the law has proliferated to incorporate more types of behavior, many changes in penalties for certain crimes have also occurred (Packer, 1968). These increases inevitably result in more social control and in further changes in the control methods. As more behaviors are defined as criminal, more acts become the interest of the police, the courts and the prison system.

In the sociological literature, the term "legalization" is used to describe the process by which norms are moved from the social to the legal level. Not all social norms become laws; in fact, only certain norms are translated into legal norms. Why is it that the violation of certain norms, but not others, is chosen to be incorporated into the criminal code? Austin T. Turk (1972) suggests that there are certain social forces involved in the legalization and creation of legal norms: moral indignation, a high value on order, response to threat, and political tactics.

As I discussed in the preceding chapter, laws may be created by the actions of "moral entrepreneurs" who become outraged over some practice they regard as reprehensible, for example, smoking marijuana. Others prefer order and insist on provisions to regulate life and to make society as orderly as possible. They promulgate laws to insure order and uniformity, as in the case of traffic regulation. Some people react to real or imaginary threats and advocate legal control measures. For instance, some people may assume that the availability of pornographic material is not only morally wrong, but directly contributes to the increase in sex crimes. In this instance, it would appear certain that these people would attempt to legally prohibit the sale of pornographic material. The final source of legalization of norms is political, where criminal laws are created in the interest of powerful groups in society. This source is identified with the conflict perspective which I have considered in the preceding chapters.

The process of legalization of social norms also entails the incorporation of specific punishments for specific kinds of criminal law violators. Rusche and Kirchheimer note: "Every system of production tends to discover punishments which correspond to its productive relationships"

(1968:5). Michel Foucault (1977) tells us that prior to the industrial revolution, life was considered cheap and individuals had neither the utility nor the commercial value that is conferred on them in an industrial economy. Under these circumstances, punishment was severe and often unrelated to the nature of the crime (for example, death for stealing a chicken). When more and more factories appeared, the value of individual lives, even criminal ones, began to be stressed. Beginning in the last years of the eighteenth century and the early years of the nineteenth century, efforts were made to connect the nature of a given punishment to the nature of the crime.

Fitting the punishment to the crime is a difficult and at times controversial task. The definition of crime and the penalty for it varies over time and from one society to another. In a democracy, the power to define crime and punishment rests with the citizenry. This power is largely delegated to elected representatives. Their statutes are often broad and subject to various interpretations. As Chapter Three demonstrated, legislative enactments allow judges, prosecutors, and juries considerable flexibility and discretion in assessing guilt and imposing punishment.

But what does it mean to punish an individual who violates a criminal law? Edwin H. Sutherland and Donald R. Cressey (1974:298) provide the following definition of the ingredients of punishment as a form of social control: "Two essential ideas are contained in the concept of punishment as an instrument of public justice. (a) It is inflicted by the group in its corporate capacity upon one who is regarded as a member of the same group . . . (b) Punishment involves pain or suffering produced by design and justified by some value that the suffering is assumed to have."

Punishment of lawbreakers is considered to have several purposes. Paul W. Tappan (1960:241–261) offers a summary of the objectives of punishment. He suggests that punishment is designed to achieve the goal of *retribution* or *social retaliation* against the offender. This means punishment of the offender for the crime that has been committed and to an extent that (in principle) matches the impact of the crime upon its victim (for instance, a person, organization). The state is expected to be the agent of vengeance on behalf of the victim. Punishment also involves *incapacitation*, (for example, a prison term), which prevents a violator from misbehaving during the time he or she is being punished. Moreover, punishment is supposed to have a *deterrent* effect, both on the lawbreaker and on potential deviants. *Individual* or *specific deterrence* may be achieved by intimidation of the person, frightening him or her against further deviance, or it may be effected through reformation, in which the lawbreaker changes his or her deviant behavior. *General deterrence* results from the warning offered to potential criminals by the example of punishment directed at a specific wrongdoer. It aims to discourage others from criminal behavior by making an example of the offender being punished.

The concept of deterrence is often used to designate punishment in the form of threats directed at offenders or potential offenders so as to frighten them into law-abiding conduct. The effectiveness of these threats is conditioned by the operation of three variables: (1) the severity of the punishment for an offense; (2) the certainty that it would be applied; and

(3) the speed with which it would be applied. Research generally supports the view that certainty of punishment is more important than severity for achieving deterrence, but there is little research data as yet on the swiftness of punishment. For example, in a study of a series of criminal offenses, Charles R. Tittle (1969) found strong and consistent negative relationships between certainty of punishment and crime rates for different states, as measured in terms of the ratio between felony admissions to state prisons and the total crimes known to the police in different states. Those states with the lowest crime rates had a proportionately larger number of incarcerated persons. On the other hand, severity of punishment bore no marked relationship to crime rates. Tittle's findings left him to conclude that measures to improve the efficiency of police work probably would have significant effects on crime rates, but that increasing the severity of punishment would be of limited effectiveness.

However, sociologists have recognized that punishment may deter only some crimes and some offenders. For example, William J. Chambliss (1975) makes a distinction between crimes that are instrumental acts and those that are expressive. Illustrations of *instrumental* offenses include burglary, tax evasion, embezzlement, and other illegal activities directed toward some material end. Examples of *expressive* acts are murder, assault, and sex offenses, where the behavior is an end in itself. Chambliss hypothesizes that the deterrent impact of severe and certain punishment may be greater on instrumental crimes because they generally involve some planning and weighing of risks. Expressive crimes, by contrast, are often impulsive and emotional acts. Perpetrators of such crimes are unlikely to be concerned with the future consequences of their actions.

Chambliss further contends that an important distinction can be made between individuals who have a relatively high commitment to crime as a way of life and those with a relatively low commitment. The former would include individuals who engage in crime on a professional or regular basis. They often receive group support for their activities, and crime for them is an important aspect of their way of life (such as, for prostitutes or participants in organized crime). For them, the likelihood of punishment is a constant feature of their life, something they have learned to live with, and the threat of punishment may be offset by the supportive role played by their peers. On the other hand, a tax evader, embezzler, or an occasional shoplifter does not view this behavior as criminal and receives little, if any, group support for these acts. Fear of punishment may well be a deterrent for such low-commitment persons, particularly if they have already experienced punishment (for example, a tax evader who has been audited and then subjected to legal sanctions).

On the basis of these two types of distinctions—instrumental and expressive acts, and high and low commitment offenders—Chambliss contends that the greatest deterrent effect of punishment will be in situations which involve low-commitment individuals who engage in instrumental crimes. Deterrence is least likely in cases involving high commitment persons who engage in expressive crimes. The role of deterrence remains questionable in situations that involve low commitment individuals who commit

expressive crimes (such as murder), which can be illustrated by the arguments used for or against the death penalty.

THE DEBATE OVER THE DEATH PENALTY

As the most severe form of punishment, the death penalty is the most obvious, controversial, and emotional issue in the concept of deterrence. Historically, property offenses rather than violent crimes accounted for the
majority of executions. In the eighteenth century, the death penalty was
imposed in England for more than two hundred offenses, including poach-
ing and smuggling. Executions were performed in public. They were a popular spectacle. The public applauded a skillful execution of a criminal much
as afficionados today cheer the matador who skillfully slays a bull (Foucault,
1977). The standard methods of execution included hanging, beheading,
disemboweling, and quartering. The increased severity and frequency of
executions during this period were associated with the growth of urbanization and wealth. Notes Loh: "Capital statutes 'served the interests of private property and commerce' against those who might seek to undermine
them" (1984:194). Although the colonies inherited many of the capital punishments from England, by the middle of the nineteenth century most of
them were repealed and the death sentence was imposed primarily for murder and, to a lesser extent, rape.

In the 1972 decision *Furman* v. *Georgia,* capital punishment was declared unconstitutional by the U.S. Supreme Court. The Court held that
the discretionary application of the death penalty to only a fraction of those
eligible to be executed was capricious and arbitrary and hence unconstitutional. However, a number of states since responded to the Court ruling
by legislating modifications in state laws which make the death penalty
mandatory for certain offenses such as multiple killings; killing in connection with a robbery, rape, kidnapping, or hostage situation; murder for hire;
killing a police officer or prison guard; and treason. Some of these revised
statutes were held to be constitutional by the Supreme Court in 1976.

According to the U.S. Department of Justice (1985:1), since 1930, when
national reporting began, 3891 executions were carried out in the United
States. In 1984, 37 states and the Federal government had laws authorizing
the death penalty. All persons under death sentence in 1984 were convicted
of murder. Of the 1405 death row inmates, 1388 were male and 17 were
female; 804 were white, 585 were black, and 16 were classified as other races
(for racial differences in sentencing see, for example, Miethe and Moore,
1986 and Radelet and Pierce, 1985). Nearly 63 percent of those under death
sentence were in Southern states. Florida had the largest number (215),
followed by Texas (178), and California (172). There were 21 executions in
1984, all in Southern states. During the same year, there were 18,690 victims
of murder or nonnegligent manslaughter and there were 17,770 arrests for
these crimes. For a ten-year period between 1975 and 1984, 204,000 Americans were murdered, there were 198,000 arrests, 2,384 persons were sentenced to death, and 32 offenders were executed.

The dilemma of whether to kill the killers comes up only in a small fraction of homicides. The criteria for capital murder vary from state to state and from case to case. In general, there must be "aggravating circumstances." These can be as specific as the murder of a police officer or prison guard; as common as homicide committed along with a lesser felony such as burglary; or as vague as Florida's law citing "especially heinous, atrocious or cruel" killing. Some 10 percent of homicides qualify, representing about 2000 murders in 1986. Those killings are the ones the threat of capital punishment is meant to prevent.

What are the preventive effects of capital punishment? The arguments for the death penalty are mostly anecdotal but at times can become visceral. Proponents of the death penalty contend that it is a deterrent to others and that it protects society. It constitutes retribution for society and the victim's family and serves to protect police officers and prison guards. It also removes the possibility that the offenders will repeat the act. There is not much empirical evidence in support of the death penalty as a deterrent. Were it not for the work of Isaac Ehrlich, the deterrence debate would be very much one-sided. Using econometric modeling techniques to construct a "supply-and-demand" theory of murder, Ehrlich (1975) in an article subtitled "A Question of Life and Death" argued that the death penalty prevents more murders than do prison sentences. He speculates that because of the 3,411 executions carried out from 1933 to 1967, enough murderers were discouraged so that some 27,000 victims' lives were saved. As might be expected, his conclusions drew immediate criticisms.

A variety of concerns were raised. Among others, Ehrlich did not compare the effectiveness of capital punishment with that of particular prison terms. When data from 1965–1969 are omitted, the relationship between murder rates and executions is not statistically significant (Loh, 1984:258). While considering the increases in homicides in the 1960s, he failed to account for the possible influences of rising racial tensions, the Vietnam War, and increased ownership of handguns. Moreover, for deterrence to be effective, murderers need to take into consideration the probable costs of their action. Emotions and passions at play can make a cost-benefit analysis unlikely. Most murderers, in Chambliss' words, are low-commitment individuals, often under the influence of drugs or alcohol, who are unlikely to assess rationally the consequences of their action. For them, the death penalty remains a highly questionable deterrent.

Aside from ethical and moral considerations, there are many arguments against the death penalty. Almost every study of capital punishment has shown that there is no material difference in the rate of homicides in states which have capital punishment and states which do not (Sellin, 1959:28). The homicide rate per 100,000 in Michigan, which did not have the death penalty in the 1950s, was 3.49. In Indiana, which did have the death penalty, the homicide rate for the same period was 3.50. Similarly, Minnesota and Rhode Island, states with no death penalty, had proportionately as many killings as their respective neighbors which had capital punishment, Iowa and Massachusetts. Studies in Canada, England, and other countries also found nothing to suggest that the death penalty is a more effective deterrent than long prison sentences. Although a cause-and-effect relationship cannot be inferred between capital punishment and murder rates, Lawrence M. Friedman (1984:214) speculates that capital punishment may work efficiently in some societies "which use it quickly, mercilessly, and frequently. It cannot work well in the United States, where it is bound to be rare, slow, and controversial."

Opponents of the death penalty argue that prison terms without parole would deter as many potential murderers as capital punishment. Data indicate that the certainty of being punished is negated by the fact that the death penalty is seldom imposed and that juries are less willing to convict when the penalty is death. Trials of capital cases are also more costly and time-consuming than trials for other cases, and maintenance costs for inmates in death row are higher than for inmates in the rest of the prison. An exhaustive system of judicial review is required in capital cases. Today no death-row inmate will be executed until his or her case has been brought to the attention of the state's highest court, a federal district court of appeals, and the U.S. Supreme Court. The total trials and appeals costs can exceed $1.5 million. But imprisoning one inmate for fifty years would require less than $1 million in Missouri. This negates the argument that prison is too costly and there are good fiscal reasons for executing murderers. There is also the possibility that an innocent person will be executed. A recent study shows that 343 cases of people convicted of a capital offense between 1900 and 1985 turned out to be innocent; they had nothing to do with the crime or the crime never happened. The findings also indicate that one innocent person has been convicted for every twenty executions carried out since the turn of the century (*St. Louis Post-Dispatch,* 1985:6B).

The death penalty is also more likely to affect the poor and minority group members than more affluent whites. This has to do in part with the quality of legal help available to murder defendants. Those with court-appointed lawyers are more likely to be sentenced to death than those represented by private attorneys. Court-appointed lawyers in most states are not required to stay on a homicide case after a conviction. Issues for appeal are likely to be raised by different court-appointed attorneys if at all for the poor.

Nevertheless, the debate on the penological effectiveness of capital punishment continues despite the paucity of empirical evidence in support of its alleged deterrent effect. Aside from the moral need for eliminating the death penalty, the evidence shows that capital punishment does not deter murder. Yet, there is a growing advocacy of the death penalty in the United States. Public opinion surveys show that those who are in favor of capital punishment for persons convicted of murder increased from 53 percent in 1972 to 74 percent in 1982 (Sourcebook, 1985:242–243). At this point, it should be noted that the majority of murders are committed by family members or acquaintances of the victim, and in more than half of all homicides handguns are used. A former attorney general of the United States correlated homicide rates with the prevalence of guns, and reported the highest rate of homicide in states where gun controls are lax and gun ownership is common (Clark, 1971:82–84). Some startling figures to support his conclusion: In 1984 "Handguns killed 48 people in Japan, 8 in Great Britain, 34 in Switzerland, 52 in Canada, 58 in Israel, 21 in Sweden, 42 in West Germany, 10,728 in the United States" (*Forbes,* 1985:28). Controlling handguns might be a more effective method of reducing homicide rates than capital punishment.

Formal Social Control of Deviance: Civil Commitment

The formal control of deviant behavior is not limited to criminal sanctions. There is another form of social control through laws that operate extensively in American society—the civil commitment (Forst, 1978:1). Civil commitment is a noncriminal process, which commits disabled or otherwise dependent individuals, without their consent, to an institution for care, treatment, or custody, rather than punishment. It is based on two legal principles: (1) the right and responsibility of the state to assume guardianship over individuals suffering from some disability; and (2) police power within constitutional limitations to take the necessary steps to protect society. Procedurally, the civil commitment is different from criminal commitment. In civil commitment certain procedural safeguards are not available, such as a right to a trial by jury, which involves confronting witnesses against the defendant, or to avoid testifying against oneself. Moreover, the formal moral condemnation of the community is not an issue in civil commitment. Forst notes: "This situation may arise if the behavior is intentional but not morally blameworthy, as in a civil suit for damages, or if the behavior would have been morally blameworthy, but because of mental impairment, criminal culpability is either mitigated or negated. In the latter instance, the civil issue is not the person's *behavior* but his *status*" (1978:3). In this view, a heroin addict, a mentally defective, or a sex offender is not held morally responsible for these actions. The general consensus is that the individual deserves treatment, not punishment, even though the treatment may entail the deprivation of his or her liberty in a mental institution without due process.

In the United States, about one in twelve persons will spend some part of his or her life in a mental institution. On any given day of the year, nearly half a million Americans are in confinement in mental wards; in fact, nearly half of all hospital beds in the United States are occupied by people suffering from mental disorders. But civil commitment for mental illness and incompetence is only one of the many types of civil commitments used to control deviant behavior. Other types include the incarceration of juveniles in training schools or detention homes; the commitment of chronic alcoholics and alcohol-related offenders; the commitment of drug addicts; and the institutionalization, through the civil law, of sex offenders (variously known as sexual psychopaths, sexually dangerous persons, or mentally disordered sex offenders). Martin L. Forst (1978:7) contends that the various types of civil commitments "constitute one of the primary forms of social control through law in American society." He further notes that this form of social control is more extensive than the social control exercised by the traditional criminal commitment.

Mental health professionals, in particular psychiatrists, exercise considerable power by placing individuals in institutions without the guarantee of a trial. For example, Thomas S. Szasz (1965:85–143) describes the case of a Syracuse, New York gas station operator who had been pressed by real estate developers to sell his property so that a shopping center could be built on the site. When the developers attempted to erect a sign on the property, the enraged gas station operator fired warning shots from a rifle into the air. He was arrested but was never brought to trial. On the recommendation of the prosecuting attorney, the operator was ordered to undergo a psychiatric examination to determine his fitness to stand trial. He was held incompetent and was committed to a state mental hospital. Still in the hospital after ten years, he had already served more time than he would have spent in prison had he been tried and convicted.

In the legal arena, the causes of criminal behavior and the responsibility for such behavior lies within the individual. But in a legal system that posits individual causation, complications arise in attempts to control individuals who are threatening yet have broken no law. One way to control such individuals is to define their conduct as a mental disorder. Greenaway and Brickey state: "This definition has the combined effect of imputing irrationality to the behavior and providing for the control of the individual through ostensibly benign, but coercive psychiatric intervention" (1978:139). Thus, it is not surprising to find that many state mental hospitals include people who have committed trivial misdemeanors or who have not been convicted of any crime at all, but have been sent there for "observation." The police and courts may refer individuals whose behavior appears odd for psychiatric examination, and if they are found to be "insane," they can be confined in a mental hospital against their will for long periods, in some cases, for life.

The use of civil commitment as a form of social control is not limited to the United States. In the Soviet Union, for example, many dissenters in recent years have been sent not to concentration camps in Siberia but to insane asylums. The list of poets, writers, and intellectuals who have been defined as "mentally ill" rather than criminal by the Soviet authorities is a lengthy one. The psychiatrists in the Soviet Union may not be as cynical as we might think. Given that their "reality" is a Marxist-Leninist one, it may seem obvious to many of them that people who have not adapted to that reality are psychologically impaired and should be placed in protective confinement. But whether or not they are aware of the political implication of their diagnosis, psychiatrists in the Soviet Union are clearly using the label of mental illness as a method of social control.

There are diverse explanations for the increased use of civil commitment as a mechanism of social control. Forst states:

> There are those (the positive criminologists) who view the increase as a beneficial shift from the traditional emphasis on punishing people to rehabilitating them ... Another explanation for the increased use of civil commitments (the divestment of the criminal law) is that the civil commitment serves as a substitute for, or a supplement to, the criminal law in order to socially control undesirable forms of behavior (1978:9–10).

The use of civil commitment is not without criticisms. Some critics advocate the abolition of all civil commitment laws because the constitutional rights of the individuals subjected to them are violated, in spite of the number of recent laws designed to protect the rights of the mentally ill. Others oppose it because it allows people to avoid the punishment they deserve. While the issue remains controversial, the use of civil commitment as a form of social control is on the increase both in the United States and elsewhere.

CRIMES WITHOUT VICTIMS

The United States invests enormous resources in controlling victimless crimes where harm occurs primarily to the participating individuals themselves (Schur, 1965:170). There are some 12 million arrests recorded in the FBI Uniform Crime Report for 1985. Many of these arrests involved crimes without victims. For example, more than 113,000 arrests were made for prostitution; 1.5 million for drunkenness and violation of liquor laws (driving under the influence of alcohol is excluded); 811,000 for drug abuse violations, of which 451,000 were for possession of marijuana; and 32,000 for gambling (Federal Bureau of Investigation, 1986:163–164).

The criminalization of some acts that have no victims stems from the fact that society regards these acts as morally repugnant and wishes to restrain individuals from engaging in them. Many of those arrested for victimless crimes are never prosecuted: Arrest and overnight lockup are used simply as a means of exerting social control over the drunk or prostitute without going through the bothersome lengths of creating a convincing prosecution case. For example, habitual drunks may build up formidable "criminal" records by being repeatedly arrested, even though they may never have harmed anyone except possibly themselves (La Fave, 1965:439). One study found that two-thirds of repeatedly arrested alcoholics have been charged with nothing more than public intoxication and related offenses, such as vagrancy, throughout their long "criminal" careers (Pittman, quoted by Landsman, 1973:288).

Much of the victimless crime literature deals with drug addiction, prostitution, gambling, abortion, homosexuality, pornography and obscenity, suicide, alcoholism, and heterosexual deviance. These are crimes *mala prohibita* (that is, behaviors made criminal by statute, but there is no consensus as to whether these acts are criminal of themselves). They are acts against public interest or morality and appear in criminal codes as crimes against public decency, order, or justice. Crimes like rape or murder are *mala in se* (that is, evils in themselves with public agreement on the dangers they pose) (Rich, 1978:27).

Victimless crimes are also differentiated from other crimes by the element of consensual transaction or exchange. These crimes are also differentiated from other kinds of crimes by the lack of apparent harm to others and by the difficulty in enforcing the laws against them as a result of low visibility and the absence of complainants. In other words, they are plaintiffless crimes—that is, those who are involved are willing participants who, as a rule, do not complain to the police that a crime has been committed. Although many people do not consider these activities "criminal," the police and the courts continue to apply laws against such groups as drug users, prostitutes, gamblers, homosexuals, and pornography distributors—laws that large sections of the community do not recognize as legitimate and simply refuse to obey. The formal controls exerted on these types of behavior are expensive and generally ineffective. Still, they serve certain functions. Robert M. Rich (1978:28) notes that persons who are labeled as criminals serve as an example to community members. When the laws are enforced against lower-class and minority group members, it allows the ones in power (middle- and upper-class people) to feel that the law is serving a useful purpose because it preserves and reinforces the myth that low-status individuals account for most of the deviance in society. Finally, the control of victimless crimes, in the forms of arrests and convictions, strengthens the notion in the community that the police and the criminal justice system are doing a good job in protecting community moral standards. Let us now consider law as a means of social control for certain victimless crimes such as drug addiction, prostitution, and gambling.

Drug Addiction

The nonmedical use of drugs, such as opium and heroin, although an ancient practice, only relatively recently became a criminal act in the United States. Prior to 1914, there had been only sporadic attempts to regulate the use of drugs. Although some states attempted to control drug use by passing laws to provide for civil commitment to institutions for drug addicts and outlawing the use of particular narcotic substances, it was not until 1914 that any systematic attempt was made to regulate drug use in the United States. In 1914, the *Harrison Act* was passed. It was the first attempt to deal comprehensively with the narcotics and dangerous drugs known at that time. It was essentially a tax measure, or more aptly, a series of prohibitive taxes. Drug use was restricted to medical purposes and research by licensed individuals and facilities. But in the Act's interpretation, court rulings in specific cases, and in supplementary laws, criminal sanctions were provided for the unauthorized possession, sale, or transfer of drugs. The states, too, have enacted a variety of antinarcotic laws. In the United States, penalties for violating drug laws have become more severe in recent years with increased and mandatory jail sentences for the sale and possession of many controlled substances, such as heroin or cocaine (Uelmen and Haddox, 1983).

Americans now consume roughly 60 percent of the world's production of illegal drugs. An estimated 20 million are regular users of marijuana, 4–8 million are cocaine abusers, and 500,000 are heroin addicts (*U.S. News & World Report*, 1986:48). Studies by the National Institute of Drug Abuse find that a third of all college students will use cocaine at least once before they graduate (Meyer, 1986:1,30). There is substantial evidence that the best predictor of cocaine use is heavy, early marijuana use (Grabowski,

1984:vii). Up to 80 percent of all Americans will try an illicit drug by their mid-20s. Although the use of narcotics has decreased slightly since 1980, drugs are now far more available at cheaper prices and greater purity. The sheer volume of available drugs in the United States is phenomenal; in 1986 more than 12 tons of heroin, 65 tons of marijuana, and 150 tons of cocaine were consumed. The former head of the Drug Enforcement Administration estimates the United States has a $110 billion-a-year drug habit, but less than $2 billion in federal funds is dedicated to drug-enforcement and prevention (Bensinger, 1986). Although funds for drug-enforcement programs have effectively increased over the past few years, there was a noticeable decrease in expenditures for programs on prevention and treatment of drug abuse to $234 million in 1985 from $332 million in 1980 (*The Wall Street Journal*, 1986b:46).

Legally, psychoactive drugs are classified into three basic categories— legal drugs (alcohol, caffeine, nicotine); prescription drugs (amphetamines, barbiturates, tranquilizers) which must be prescribed by a physician; and illegal drugs (marijuana, heroin, hallucinogens), which may not be sold under any circumstances. Cocaine and morphine make up a subcategory. They have limited medical use and high potential for abuse. The categories are not based on the potential harm or addictive quality of the drugs. Under the Federal Controlled Substance Act of 1970, marijuana and heroin are classed together, although heroin is physically addictive and marijuana is not.

Marijuana has reached a kind of a low-profile stasis, and it is no longer a symbol of rebellion or creativity. Its use on college campuses is down, and prices have leveled off. Unlike most other drugs, 50 percent of the marijuana consumed in the United States is produced domestically, and in some states, such as Hawaii, Oregon, and California, it is the biggest cash crop; and for the country as a whole, it was worth $18.6 billion in 1985 (Glassman, 1986:12). State marijuana laws have also changed radically in recent years. In most states, the possession of a small amount of marijuana is no longer a felony. The huge majority of the some 451,000 annual marijuana arrests (a number that has been fairly constant since 1975) are for possession— with charges regularly dropped. Several states treat possession as they do a traffic violation and a person found with an ounce or less is subject to a small fine.

Although there has been an increase in the arrest rates for the sale, transportation, and possession of illegal drugs, and more severe mandatory prison terms of conviction, the criminal law has not been successful at effectively controlling illicit drug use in the United States. Some of the byproducts of the massive legal efforts to control drugs resulted in the formation of elaborate illegal organizations for the supply of illicit drugs. Many users turn to other criminal activities to support their habit. Drug laws have contributed to a situation in which politicians and police ignore drug traffic—usually because of payoffs. Since drug use is a victimless crime, the lack of complainant makes enforcement difficult. In enforcement, the police frequently use entrapment and illegal search and seizure tactics (Sheley,

1985:122). In short, there is little prospect of effective control of drugs through the criminal law in the United States. An alternative to the legal control of hard drugs might be the consideration of drug addiction and drug use more as a medical than a legal problem, as it is, to an extent, in the case of Great Britain and many Western European countries.

Prostitution

If there is one area in the criminal law which arouses the most anxiety concerning public morals, it is sexual conduct. The range of sexual conduct covered by the law is so great and extensive that the law makes potential criminals of most teenagers and adults. One of the justifications for such a complete control of sexual behavior is to protect the family system. A number of state laws control acts that would otherwise endanger the chastity of women before marriage, such as the variety of laws on rape (statutory and forceable), fornication, incest, and sexual deviance of juveniles. The criminal laws on adultery are also designed to protect the family by preventing sexual relations outside of marriage (Quinney, 1975:83–84). In addition, a complex set of federal and state laws control the advertising, sale, distribution, and availability of contraceptives; the performance of abortion; voluntary sterilization; and artificial insemination (Weinberg, 1979). Because of the complexity and extensiveness of legal controls on sexual conduct and related matters, this section will be limited to a discussion of the legal controls of female prostitution which involves an estimated half a million women in the United States (Clinard and Meier, 1985:210).

It is now recognized that laws against prostitution discriminate against women. Many women's groups maintain that a woman should have the right to engage in sexual relations for pay if she so desires. However, law enforcement authorities do not yet share this position, and there is still a tendency to regard only the women as offenders and not their clients.

State laws vary on prostitution. In many states, solicitation is considered a misdemeanor punished by a fine or a jail sentence of up to one year. Frequent arrests, however, may result in a charge of felony. There are three broad categories of arrests for prostitutes: (1) for accosting and soliciting; (2) on a charge of "common prostitution" which can be subsumed under disorderly conduct or vagrancy; and (3) detention under health regulations (La Fave, 1965:457–463). Law enforcement of prostitution is sporadic and much of the control is limited to containment. There is a fair amount of discretion involved in the control of prostitutes. At times there is practically no enforcement, and at other times police conduct special campaigns directed at streetwalkers in certain neighborhoods. In general, most of the police control of prostitutes is aimed at the individual practitioners and streetwalkers. The high-class call girls are relatively immune to legal control (Rich, 1978:63).

Laws against prostitution are attempts to control private moral behavior through punitive social control measures. The *Wolfenden Report* expresses rather eloquently the rationale for the continued legal control of prostitution.

If it were the law's intention to punish prostitution per se, on the grounds that it is immoral conduct, then it would be right that it should provide for the punishment of the man as well as the woman. But that is not the function of the law. It should confine itself to those activities which offend against public order and decency or expose the ordinary citizen to what is offensive or injurious; and the simple fact that prostitutes do parade themselves more habitually and openly than their prospective customers, and do by their continual presence affront the sense of decency of the ordinary citizen. In so doing they create a nuisance which, in our view, the law is entitled to recognize and deal with (1963:143–144).

The report also recognizes that prostitution has prevailed for many centuries, and it cannot be really controlled by criminal law. As long as there is a demand for the services of prostitutes and there remain women who choose this form of livelihood—even when there is no economic necessity for it—the *Wolfenden Report* concludes that, in view of these conditions, "no amount of legislation directed towards its abolition will abolish it" (1963:132). Still, from time to time, community leaders and law enforcement agents would like to "clean up" some areas of the cities, and through these efforts, they persist to try to control prostitution through the law.

One day, perhaps, they will learn from history and will recognize that in a free-enterprise society such efforts will remain in vain. A growing number of critics argue that the criminal statutes improperly and unwisely extend the concern of criminal law to harmless matters of private morality, such as prostitution acts between consenting adults. In several Western European countries prostitutes ply their trade legally. In West Germany, for example, the law requires cities with populations of 500,000 or more to designate 10 percent of their area as an "amusement" zone, with prostitution included among the amusements (*The Wall Street Journal*, 1986a:16). Critics, such as Gilbert Geis (1979), would revise these prohibitions to narrow the kinds of behavior they proscribe to acts that are clearly harmful to society. Prostitution is not considered as one of them. The decriminalization of prostitution would, in essence, extend the practice of official tolerance already operative in many places (Adler and Adler, 1975:224). It would allow the police to deal with more important matters, and it would probably help lower the number of sex crimes. Opponents of decriminalization argue for increased legal control of prostitution since they believe it leads, for example, to other crimes, such as drug addiction, blackmail, assault, and even murder.

Gambling

Gambling, like drug use or prostitution, is a consensual transaction and a plaintiffless crime. The players are willing participants who generally do not notify the police that a crime has been committed. Enforcement activity therefore must be initiated by the police who then act as the complainant on the behalf of the community. By contrast, enforcement activity for other crimes, such as burglaries or muggings, usually occurs in response to citizen complaints.

Historically, the prohibition and regulation of gambling has largely been a function of the state. Federal involvement with gambling began in the late nineteenth century, when Congress put an end to the operation of corrupt lotteries by denying them mailing privileges and the ability to transact business across state lines. The next major federal action dealing with gambling occurred in 1949, when Congress enacted legislation to eliminate the gambling ships which had been operating off the coast of California. Other actions dealt with the interstate transportation and transmission of wagering information and gambling paraphernalia. The Organized Crime Control Act of 1970 further extended jurisdiction over interstate gambling and made it a federal offense to operate certain illegal gambling businesses. Congress has also affected gambling activities through the exercise of its taxing powers by levying excise and occupational taxes on gambling operations and a stamp tax on gambling devices, and by subjecting gambling winnings to the federal income tax (Commission on the Review of the National Policy Toward Gambling, 1976:5).

Local police departments have the primary responsibility for gambling enforcement, although the role of state level agencies is growing. The Commission on the Review of the National Policy Toward Gambling (1976:44–46) identifies a number of control techniques used by law enforcement agencies. The Commission notes that the most frequent source of gambling arrests is the direct observation of illegal gambling activity. Such arrests are primarily "nonserious," involving individual street players or low-level employees of gambling organizations. Arrests at higher levels, for example, large bookmakers or numbers offices, are rarely, if ever, made in this manner. They require investigation leading to a probable cause for search and arrest warrants. The use of informants in gambling control is widespread. Most police departments rely on this technique, as well as on undercover investigators who can often accumulate evidence against individuals and on operations by placing bets. In recent years, the use of electronic surveillance, authorized by Congress in 1968 under Title III of the Omnibus Crime Control and Safe Streets Act, became particularly widespread in the control of illegal gambling. Electronic surveillance is best-suited for the use of gambling investigation because of the dependence of gambling operations on telephones. One of the devices that is used is the pen register, which records phone numbers dialed from a particular telephone. By attaching a pen register to the telephone line of a gambling location, police can often identify additional locations and individuals involved in illegal gambling operations.

Of the tens of thousands of individuals arrested annually in the United States for gambling offenses, a relatively small proportion are convicted. Of those convicted, a very small percentage receive jail or prison sentences, or substantial fines. For example, during the six-year period from 1969 to 1974, there were 36,207 arrests for gambling in Chicago. Only 6 percent of those arrested were convicted. But there are exceptions to the generally low conviction rates for gambling. For example, approximately 70 percent of persons appearing in Connecticut Circuit Courts on gambling charges between 1970 and 1974 were convicted (Commission on the Review of the National Policy Toward Gambling, 1976:46–47).

The criminal law seems to be ineffective in controlling and preventing persons from engaging in illegal gambling. The parties involved in gambling do not complain about it, and a typical gambling transaction is probably more easily, rapidly, and privately consummated than is any other kind of illegal consensual transaction. It is much easier to place a bet with a bookie than to buy cocaine or have an encounter with a prostitute. Aside from the difficulties of detection, the criminal sanction for illegal gambling exerts little deterrent force. Generally, the penalties for those who are convicted tend to be light. Public opinion does not consider gambling as particularly wrongful, a sentiment both affected by and reflected in the lenience with which gambling offenders are treated (Packer, 1968:348). There seems to be an ambivalence in attitudes toward gambling. It is reflected in a resistance to proposals to reduce or eliminate reliance on criminal sanctions, accompanied by an equivalent resistance to any but the most sporadic attempts at enforcement.

Illegal gambling provides the largest single source of revenue to organized crime. In fact, gambling laws are now justified as necessary to combat organized crime (Sheley, 1985:121). In most urban areas, bookmakers associated with crime syndicates specialize in bets on horse racing, professional football and basketball, boxing, hockey, and baseball. Increasingly, they are also involved in college football and basketball. Syndicates also run "numbers games." It involves placing a bet on the possible occurrence of certain numbers, such as the last three digits of the U.S. treasury balance (Light, 1977). A complicated hierarchical organization is required to distribute the forms and to collect and pay off bets. Organized crime syndicates employ "writers," "runners," or "sellers," terms to indicate the persons who accept numbers bets directly from betters. Bets collected by them are given to a "pickup man" who forwards them to the next level in the hierarchy, the "bank." In larger operations, bets may be carried from the pickup man to another intermediary, the controller. Tickets with winning numbers are redeemed by cashiers or delivered by runners. In addition to bookmaking and numbers games, gambling syndicates also operate illegal casinos, "sponsor" backgammon tournaments, and provide opportunities for wagers to be made on a variety of activities—even election outcomes in the political arena.

Attempts to control illegal gambling consume a large amount of law enforcement time and resources. Ostensibly, control of gambling activities also includes fighting organized crime, maintaining a favorable public image of the police department, keeping undesirable activities or persons out of a city, and maintaining public order. The objective of organized crime control is reflected both in the intent of some gambling searches and in the view of the police that illegal gambling is related to organized crime. The objectives of preserving the department's public image and of maintaining public order are related, in that where open gambling such as street cards and dice are permitted to continue, citizens are likely to conclude that the police are either corrupt or derelict in their duty. In some instances, however, "meeting the quota" has become a major stimulant for illegal gambling control by the police. In such instances, officers produce what may be called "symbolic" gambling arrests, that is, gambling arrests that meet the quota, thus fulfilling the department's stated policy of continuing enforcement activity.

An additional problem with gambling control is that most of the corruption of police and of the courts is associated with these offenses. Few police officers are willing to accept bribes from murderers, burglars, or other criminals whose acts are blatantly harmful and have identifiable victims. However, many police officers tend to feel that gambling is not particularly serious, and that, in any case, it is impossible to eradicate. Hence, organized crime is often readily able to buy police protection for its activities. The Knapp Commission found corruption in the New York Police Department to be "at its most sophisticated among plainclothesmen assigned to enforce gambling laws" (Commission on the Review of the National Policy Toward Gambling, 1976:40). Participation in organized payoffs—a "pad"—netted individual New York plainclothes officers $300 to $1500 a month. In return for protection, gambling establishments paid as much as $3500 a month. Similarly, it was found that in Philadelphia, police throughout the city accept protection money from gamblers. It should be noted, however, that police corruption exists not only in gambling enforcement, but in other areas as well. Investigations have also uncovered misconduct related to the enforcement of narcotics, prostitution, liquor establishments, construction site regulations, and traffic. (See, for example, Chambliss, 1978.) These forms of police corruption are largely an urban problem.

One response to the difficulty and wastefulness in trying to enforce laws against gambling is to remove completely the criminal label. As the Knapp Commission recommended: "The criminal law against gambling should be repealed. To the extent that the legislature deems that some control over gambling is appropriate, such regulation should be by civil rather than criminal process. The police should in any event be relieved from any responsibility for the enforcement of gambling laws or regulations" (Wynn and Goldman, 1974:67). Although a number of similar suggestions have been made, the question of the decriminalization of gambling still remains a hotly debated and controversial issue.

WHITE-COLLAR CRIME

The term "white-collar crime" was first used by Edwin H. Sutherland (1949:9) in an address to the American Sociological Association in 1939. "White-collar crime" he proposed, "may be defined approximately as a crime committed by a person of respectability and high status in the course of his occupation." He documented the existence of this form of crime with a study of the careers of seventy large, reputable corporations, which together had amassed 980 violations of the criminal law, or an average of 14 convictions apiece. Behind the offenses of false advertising, unfair labor practices, restraint of trade, price-fixing agreements, stock manipulation, copyright infringement, and outright swindles were perfectly respectable middle-class and upper-middle-class executives. Gilbert Geis (1978:279) argues that "white-collar crimes constitute a more serious threat to the well-being and integrity of our society than more traditional kinds of crime." Moreover, as the President's Commission on Law Enforcement and Administration of Justice (1967b:104) concludes, "[w]hite-collar crime affects the whole moral climate of our society. Derelictions by corporations and their managers who usually occupy leadership positions in their communities, establish an example which tends to erode the moral base of the law ... " It raises questions about the equity of law and provides justification for other types of law violations.

The case of the $23 million "unauthorized loan" is illustrative of the question of equity of law dealing with white-collar crime. The defendants were charged with setting up a check-kiting operation: the art of repeatedly taking checks written on one account and quickly depositing them into another, and vice versa, staying a step ahead of the clearing system and thus creating a false impression of the balances in the accounts. Once false balances have been created, a kiter can take out money against them, and that is just what perpetrators of this scheme did, leaving Marine Midland Bank holding the bag for a loss in excess of $23 million. The two already wealthy individuals found themselves indicted for the felony of grand larceny and the misdemeanor of scheming to defraud. And because larceny requires an intent to deprive an owner of his or her property *permanently*, the defendants' repayment—as well as their ability to repay—played an important role in defense. Their attorneys argued that it was a *temporary* borrowing, they never intended to deprive the bank permanently of the funds. They insisted that they had no intention of keeping the money—so that what they were doing did not qualify for larceny. The jurors apparently agreed. The defendants were found innocent of the felony charge of grand larceny which carries a possible seven-year prison sentence because they claimed they intended to return the money *and* had the ability to pay. They were convicted only of a misdemeanor count of scheming to defraud, for which the maximum sentence is one year. The defendants intend to appeal the conviction (Cony and Penn, 1986).

The full extent of white-collar crime is difficult to assess. Many illegal corporate activities go undetected, and many wealthy individuals are able to evade taxes for years without being found out. White-collar crimes ("crimes in the suites") are usually regarded as somehow less serious than the crimes of the lower class ("crimes of the streets"), and there is often strong pressure on the police and the courts not to prosecute at all in these cases—to take account of the offenders' "standing in the community" and to settle the matter out of court. For example, a bank that finds its safe burglarized at night will immediately summon the police, but it may be more circumspect if it finds that one of its executives has embezzled a sum of money. To avoid unwelcome publicity, the bank may simply allow the offender to resign after making an arrangement for him or her to pay back whatever possible.

The concept of white-collar crime generally incorporates both occupational and corporate crimes (Coleman, 1985:3–5). Some individuals commit crimes in connection with their occupations. For example, physicians may give out illegal prescriptions for narcotics, make fraudulent reports for medicare payments, and give false testimony in accident cases. Lawyers may engage in some illegalities, such as securing false testimony from witnesses, misappropriating funds in receivership, and various forms of ambulance chasing in order to collect fraudulent damage claims arising from accidents. Corporate crimes are considered those illegal activities that are committed in the furtherance of business operations but which are not, however, the central purpose of business. A convenient distinction between occupational and corporate crimes may be in the context of immediate and direct benefit to the perpetrator. In occupational crimes, generally the benefit is for the individual who commits a particular illegal activity, for example, the physician who receives money for giving out illegal prescriptions. In corporate crime, the benefit is usually for the organization. For example, an executive bribes a public official to secure favors for his or her corporation. In this instance, the benefit would be for the corporation and not directly for the individual. The desire to increase profits is a crucial factor in a wide range of corporate crimes. The remainder of this section will focus on what is strictly called corporate crimes. It is distinguished from ordinary crime in two respects: the nature of the violation and the fact that administrative and civil law are more likely to be used as punishment than the criminal law.

In the United States, corporate crime did not exist until the nineteenth century. The reason for it is simply that there were no laws against dangerous or unethical corporate practices. Prior to the nineteenth century, corporations were free to sell unsafe products, to keep workers in unsafe conditions, to pollute the atmosphere, to engage in monopolistic practices, to overcharge customers, and to make outrageously false advertising claims for their products. By the end of the nineteenth century and the beginning of the twentieth century, increasingly laws were passed that attempted to regulate some of the more flagrant business practices that prevailed at the time. Examples would include the Sherman Anti-Trust Act (1890) and the Pure Food and Drug Act (1906). Since that time, a vast array of laws has been passed to regulate the various facets of potentially harmful corporate activities.

The extensive nature of corporate crime is unquestioned today; it has been revealed by many government investigative committees. In a study of the 582 largest publicly owned corporations in the United States, over 60 percent had at least one enforcement action completed against them in 1975 and 1976 (U.S. Department of Justice, 1979:XIX). The average number of actions initiated against these corporations for illegal activities (such as price fixing, foreign payoffs, illegal political contributions, manufacture of unsafe foods and drugs) was 4.2.

It is estimated that corporate crimes in the form of faulty goods, monopolistic practices, and similar law violations annually cost consumers between $174 and $231 billion (U.S. Department of Justice, 1979:16). The loss to taxpayers from reported and unreported violations of federal regulations by corporations is between $10 and $20 billion. About $1.2 billion goes unreported in corporate tax returns each year. Price fixing among corporations costs the consumer $60 billion a year (Simon and Eitzen, 1986:4–5). The loss alone from the electrical price-fixing conspiracy of the 1960s was nearly $2 billion, far greater than the total burglary losses during any given year. In 1979, nine major oil companies were sued by the Justice Department for illegal overcharges of more than $1 billion. The companies were accused of charging too much for products derived from natural gas liquids and artificially increasing consumer costs. In contrast, the largest robbery in the United States thus far involved the 1978 theft of $5.4 million from the Lufthansa airport warehouse in New York City. Previously, the much-publicized Brinks armored car robbery of about $2 million in Boston had been the largest robbery loss. But these cases are atypical; the typical robbery involves armed theft of about $250, burglary of about $350, and larceny of about $125.

Undoubtedly, corporate crimes impose an enormous financial burden on society. In addition, it has been estimated that each year 200,000 to 500,000 workers are needlessly exposed to toxic agents such as radioactive materials and poisonous chemicals because of corporate failure to obey safety laws. Nearly a half of all deaths among asbestos insulation workers are directly caused by exposure to that substance (Coleman, 1985:35). Many of the 2.5 million temporary and 250,000 permanent worker disabilities from industrial accidents each year are the result of managerial acts that represent culpable failure to adhere to established standards (Geis, 1978:279). Corporate crimes cause injuries to persons on a larger scale than the so-called "street crimes." Far more people are killed annually through corporate criminal activities than by the 20,000 or so individual criminal homicides; even if death is an indirect result, the person still died (U.S. Department of Justice, 1979:16).

Corporate crime is controlled by a variety of regulatory agencies. The control of corporate activities may be *prospective*, as in licensing, when control is exercised before deviant acts occur; *processual*, as in inspection where control is continuous; and *retrospective*, as when a lawsuit is brought for damages after deviance has occurred. These types of controls will be discussed further in the final section of this chapter. In addition, if a business concern defies the law, the government may institute, under civil law, an injunction to "cease and desist" from further violations. If further violations occur, contempt of court proceedings may be instituted. Fines and various forms of assessments are also used in attempts to control deleterious corporate activities, as, for example, in cases of levying fines on water and air polluters. At times, the government can also exercise control through its buying power by rewarding firms that comply and withdrawing from or not granting governmental contracts to those who do not (Nagel, 1975:341–352).

But, as Christopher D. Stone (1978:244–245) points out: "Whether we are threatening the corporation with private civil actions, criminal prosecutions, or the new hybrid 'civil penalties,' we aim to control the corporation through threats to its profits." Corporate offenders are rarely criminally prosecuted and even more rarely imprisoned. A large proportion of these offenders are handled through administrative and civil sanctions and the penalty is monetary. In a sense, the penalty imposed for violating the law amounts to little more than a reasonable licensing fee for engaging in illegal activity. Essentially, it is worth it for a large corporation to violate the laws regulating business. Typically, the fines are microscopic. For example, until 1955 the greatest fine a judge could levy against a company for violating the Sherman Anti-Trust Act was $5,000. In 1955 it was increased to $50,000, and in 1976 it was further increased to $250,000. This is not much of a deterrent to a company like General Electric or General Motors.

Controlling corporations through the law becomes, as Stone (1978:250) puts it, a "misplaced fate on negative reinforcement." The law constitutes only one of the threats that the corporation faces in dealing with the outside world. Often paying a fine is considered part of doing business. For a businessperson, reducing the profits by a lawsuit does not involve the same loss of face as losses attributable to other causes. For example, being sued by the antitrust division, while "a mess," is "understandable." It is not a question of improving such behavior, but a realization by businesspersons that it could happen to anyone. In financial reports, losses through lawsuits are explained in footnotes as non-recurring losses.

The current legal controls on corporate crime are inefficient. The government's response to corporate violations cannot be compared to its response to ordinary crime. Generally, penalties imposed on corporations are quite lenient, particularly in view of the gravity of the offenses committed, as compared to the penalties imposed on ordinary offenders. Few members of corporate management ever go to prison even if convicted; generally they are placed on probation. If they go to prison, it is almost always for a very short time period. For example, a study found that of the 56 federally convicted executives, 62.5 percent received probation, 28.6 percent were incarcerated, and the rest had their sentences suspended. The average prison sentence for all those convicted averaged 2.8 days (U.S. Department of Justice, 1979:xii). Gilbert Geis (1978) points out that it is, indeed, ironic that the penalties for corporate crime are the least severe, while they are given to the very persons who might be the most affected by them, or who might "benefit" the most from them. In other words, if these offenders are potentially the most deterred, an increase in punishment and the intensity of enforcement might result in the greatest benefit to society. As it stands now, however, the penalty for corporate crime is far less than the harm caused.

SOCIAL CONTROL OF DISSENT

"The United States," writes Jethro K. Lieberman (1972:74) "has a long history of welcoming dissent in the abstract and punishing it in the concrete." Law supports the government as the legitimate holder of power in society. The government in turn is legitimately involved in the control of its citizens. The principal objectives of the government are to provide for the welfare of its citizens, to protect their lives and property, and to maintain order within society. To maintain order, the government is mandated to apprehend and punish criminals. In a democratic society, there are questions, however, about the legitimacy of a government that stifles dissent in the interest of preserving order. In principle, in a democratic society, tradition and values affirm that dissent is appropriate. At the same time, for social order to prevail, a society needs to insure that existing power relationships are maintained over time. Furthermore, those in positions of power who benefit from the existing power arrangement use their influence to encourage the repression of challenges to the government. Consequently, governments generally opt for the control and repression of dissent.

An effective way of controlling dissent is through the various selection processes used to place individuals into desirable social positions (Oberschall, 1973:249–250). In most political systems, the leaders have ways of controlling the selection and mobility of persons through patronage systems, the extension of the government bureaucracy, and cooptation in its many forms. Loyalty and conformity are generally the primary criteria for advancement. Another form of control in this context is the dismissal of individuals who do not comply with the stated expectations and voice "unpopular" opinions. In some instances, the leaders can directly control the supply and demand of certain services and skills. For example, "by exercising influence on budgets, examinations, student stipends, and university expansion, a government can within a couple of years reduce the total number of students in higher education for the purpose of quashing a troublesome student movement and floating population of unemployed graduates that it has brought into being and subsidized" (Oberschall, 1973:250).

Control can also be achieved through the manipulation of the structure of material benefits (Janowitz, 1976; Mandel, 1975). For example, Frances Fox Piven and Richard A. Cloward (1971) contend that welfare programs serve as a social control mechanism in periods of mass unemployment by diffusing social unrest and thus reducing dissent. They argue that public assistance programs are used to regulate the political and economic activity of the poor. In periods of severe economic depression, the legitimacy of the political system is likely to be questioned by the poor. The possibility of upsetting the status quo of power and property relationships in society increases. Demands grow for changing the existing social and economic arrangements. Under this threat, public assistance programs are initiated or expanded by the government. They cite case after case from sixteenth-century Europe to mid-twentieth-century America, documenting their thesis that social welfare has, throughout the ages, been used as a mechanism of social control and a way by the government to diffuse social unrest through direct intervention. They note, however, that when economic conditions improve, the relief roles are cut back in response to pressures from those who employ the poor so as to insure an adequate supply of low-wage labor.

Another option for the government to use in the control of dissent is its coercive social control apparatus to deal with crime, enforce the law, and keep social interaction peaceful and orderly. As compared to other mechanisms, "a coercive response to social disturbances is the cheapest and most immediately available means of control to the authorities" (Oberschall, 1973:252). The government is expected by the citizens, and is required by law, to protect life and property, and to arrest the perpetrators of illegal activities. In addition to these coercive responses to dissent, the government has in its arsenal a variety of less overt, though equally effective, control mechanisms. For example, David Wise (1978:399–400) points out that the Central Intelligence Agency, although prohibited by law, has engaged in domestic operations to monitor and control the activities of Americans. For twenty years, the CIA opened 215,000 first-class letters, screened 28 million letters, and photographed the outside of 2.7 million. During the Nixon era, in Operation Chaos, the CIA followed antiwar activists, infiltrated various antiwar groups, undertood illegal break-ins and wire taps, indexed 300,000 names in its "Hydra" computer, and compiled separate files on 7,200 Americans.

From 1955 to 1975, the Federal Bureau of Investigation investigated 740,000 "subversive" targets. The FBI has also engaged in illegal break-ins, installed taps on telephones, falsified the credit ratings of some individuals on the subversive list, obtained their tax returns, staged arrests by local police on narcotic pretexts, made anonymous phone calls to friends or family members of some targets telling them of immoral or radical conduct, provided distorted information to civil rights and antiwar organizations in an attempt to create dissension and disruption within the group, and tried to disrupt marriages of suspected dissidents by sending anonymous letters to husbands, wives, or to newspaper gossip columnists (Newsweek, 1979:45). As late as 1972, the FBI had close to 7,500 "ghetto informants" on its payroll and still maintains a network of 1,500 "domestic intelligence" informants whom it pays $7.4 million a year (Wise, 1978:400).

The Internal Revenue Service, with more than 90,000 employees, 700 offices across the country, and a budget of more than $2 billion, is one of the most powerful and feared of all federal agencies. The average American may never have any dealings with the FBI, the CIA, or similar organizations, but he or she comes in contact at least once a year with the IRS, on April 15. The tax system in the United States essentially rests on voluntary compliance. At the heart of the tax system is the citizens' trust and belief that the government will not use the vast powers of the IRS to punish citizens for their political views. That confidence was rudely shattered by the events of Watergate.

The congressional investigations that followed showed that one harassing tactic of the Nixon administration directed at its "enemies" was to subject them to frequent tax audits. The IRS, under pressure by the Nixon administration, established a secret section that eventually became known as the Special Services Staff (SSS). Operating under what was called "red seal" security, and situated in the basement of IRS headquarters in Washington, the SSS acted like a clandestine intelligence unit, in close liaison with the FBI and compiled files on 8,585 persons and 2,873 organizations (Wise, 1978:326).

The Special Service Staff was "given responsibility for investigating and collecting intelligence on 'ideological, militant, subversive, radical and similar type organizations' and individuals (and) . . . 'non-violent' groups and individuals, including draft-card burners, peace demonstrators and persons who 'organize and attend rock festivals which attract youth and narcotics' " (Wise, 1978:327). The IRS, like the FBI, became an instrument for social control, making its own judgments about what political views and cultural preferences were acceptable.

The Army Intelligence Unit and the highly secret National Security Agency have both been actively involved in the surveillance of dissenters. The National Security Agency for years was reading and listening in on international communications. In the 1960s, for example, Western Union, RCA, and ITT made available copies of international cables to the National Security Agency (NSA) in "Operation Shamrock." Later, when some of the communications companies switched to storing their cables on magnetic tape, NSA transported the tapes daily to its headquarters in Maryland for copying and then back to New York the same day. When these round trips became too burdensome, the CIA, in the guise of a television tape processing company, provided the NSA with office space to copy the tapes in New York.

The government, through these various intelligence agencies has, indeed, created a system of institutionalized social control of dissent. The government has shown a strong tendency to closely watch the activities of persons who threaten it. Obviously, the government has to exert some control over its citizens, but in exerting control, care needs to be exercised to protect individual rights as guaranteed by the Constitution. There is a thin line between governmental control of dissent and the creation of a police state. The control technology is available to the government. To illustrate the potentials of just one aspect of that technology, there are some 100,000 computers in use in the Federal government providing electronic access to more than 3.5 billion records. Social security numbers have become national "identifiers," and the protections of the 1974 Privacy Act are eroded because the information in the data base can be used with little notice or recourse. "Computer matches"—the cross-checking of records by one agency against another—are conducted routinely (Havemann, 1986). This is how the government is withholding the income tax refunds of student loan and other loan defaulters. The technology is available now to create an electronic dossier on every citizen in the United States. Effective checks and controls need to be imposed on the users of this technology so they do not overstep their boundaries as it happened in the Nixon era.

ADMINISTRATIVE LAW AND SOCIAL CONTROL

A widely held misconception about the law is the notion that it consists almost entirely of criminal law with its apparatus of crime, police, prosecutors, judges, juries, sentences and prisons. Another misconception is the notion that all law can be divided into criminal law and civil law. But the resources of legal systems are far richer and more extensive than either of these views implies (Summers and Howard, 1972:198). This section is concerned with how distinctive legal ways can be used to control what Robert S. Summers and George G. Howard (1972:199) call "private primary activity." They use this concept to describe various pursuits, such as production and marketing of electricity and natural gas, provision and operation of rail, air, and other transport facilities, food processing and distribution, construction of buildings, bridges, and other public facilities, and radio and television broadcasting. But these activities are not confined to large-scale affairs such as electrical production or provision of air transport and the like. The list can be expanded to include provision of medical services by physicians, ownership and operation of motor vehicles by ordinary citizens, construction of residences by local carpenters, and the sale and purchase of stocks and bonds by private individuals. Private primary activities are not only in themselves positively desirable, but are essential for the functioning of modern societies. These activities generate legal needs which are met through administrative control mechanisms.

In modern societies, all kinds of services are needed, such as those provided by physicians, transport facilities, and electrical companies. But an incompetent physician might kill rather than cure a patient. An unqualified airline pilot might crash, killing everyone on board. A food processor might poison half a community. In addition to incompetence or carelessness, deliberate abuses are also possible. An individual may lose his or her entire savings through fraudulent stock operations. A utility company might abuse its monopoly position and charge exorbitant rates. An owner of a nuclear waste disposal facility may want to cut corners, thus exposing the public to harmful radiation.

Private primary activities, Summers and Howard (1972:199) note, can cause harm, avoidable harm. At the same time, such activities can have great potential for good. Airplanes can almost be made safe, and stock frauds by fly-by-night operators can be reduced. Legal control of these activities is then justified on two grounds: the prevention of harm and the promotion of good. For example, in the case of radio and television broadcasting, laws can be concerned with both the control of obscenity and the problem of balanced programming, such as covering public affairs, in addition to entertainment and sports. Control is exerted on private primary activity through administrative laws, primarily in the context of licensing, inspection, and the threat of publicity.

Licensing

The power of administrative law goes beyond the setting of standards and the punishing of those who fail to comply. Horack notes: "The belief that law enforcement is better achieved by prevention than by prosecution has contributed to the emergence of administrative regulation as a primary means of government control" (quoted by Summers and Howard, 1972:202). Requiring and granting licenses to perform certain activities is a classic control device. A license may be required to engage in an occupation, to operate a business, to serve specific customers or areas, or to manufacture certain products. Physicians and lawyers must obtain specific training and then demonstrate some competence before they can qualify for licenses to practice. Here, licensing is used to enforce basic qualifying standards. Airplane companies just cannot fly any route they wish and broadcasters are not free to pick a frequency at will. Underlying all regulatory licensing is a denial of a right to engage in the contemplated activity except with a license.

The control of professions and certain activities through licensing is justified as protection for the public against inferior, fraudulent, or dangerous services and products. But under this rubric, control has been extended to occupations that at the most only minimally affect public health and safety. In some states, licenses are required for cosmetologists, auctioneers, weather control practitioners, taxidermists, junkyard operators, and weather vane installers. Hawaii licenses tattoo artists; New Hampshire lightning-rod salespersons. In Delaware, eighty-six occupations are licensed, including circus exhibitors, bowling-alley operators, florists, and billiard parlor owners. Until recently, it was a misdemeanor for someone without a license to repair a watch in North Carolina. The penalty was a six-month jail sentence, the same for practicing medicine without a license (*U.S. News & World Report*, 1979:70). In addition to requiring a license to practice these occupations, control is exerted through the revocation or suspension of the license. For example, under administrative law the state may withdraw the right to practice from a lawyer, physician, or beautician, and it may suspend a bar or restaurant owner from doing business a few days a year or even permanently.

Local, state, and federal administrative controls through licensing are widely used mechanisms of social control. Administrative laws generally specify the conditions under which a license is required, the requirements which must be met by applicants, the duties imposed upon the licensees, the agency authorized to issue such licenses, the procedures in revoking licenses and the grounds which constitute cause for revocation and the penalties for violations.

Inspection

Administrative law grants broad investigatory and inspection powers to regulatory agencies. Periodic inspection is a way of monitoring ongoing activities under the jurisdiction of a particular agency. Such inspections determine whether cars, planes, and trains can move, agricultural products can meet quality standards, newspapers can obtain second class mailing privileges, and so forth. Similar procedures are used to prevent the distribution of unsafe foods and drugs, to prohibit the entry of diseased plants and animals into the country, or to suspend the license of a pilot pending a disciplinary hearing.

In a variety of industries, government inspectors operate on the premises. For example, when a Food and Drug Administration inspector finds botulism in soup, the manufacturer will withdraw the product from grocers' and manufacturers' shelves and destroy all cans—because of the unstated but understood FDA threat to prosecute through the Justice Department (Gellhorn, 1972:102).

Inspections constitute a major tool of administrative supervision and control. For instance, the nation's banks are overseen by the Federal Reserve Board and the Federal Deposit Insurance Corporation through visits by their inspectors for examination of the bank's records. A housing official may inspect buildings to determine compliance with building codes. In some instances, inspection takes place occasionally, such as when insuring compliance with building codes. In other instances, inspection is continuous, as in food inspection. Both forms of inspection, sporadic and continuous, also exert pressure for self-regulation and contribute to the maintenance of internal controls specified by the law. At times, these inspections may also lead to proposals for corrective legislation governing regulatory standards.

Threat of Publicity

In small communities where people tend to know each other, adversely publicizing wrongdoers can have a significant effect on changing their behavior. Such a system of social control normally would not work in an urban industrial society for individual deviance. Large companies selling widely known brand name products might, however, be greatly influenced by the threat of well-circulated adverse publicity (Nagel, 1975:347).

Perhaps the most potent power in any administrator's hands is the power to publicize (Gellhorn, 1972:110). A publicity release detailing the character of a suspected offense and the offender involved can inflict immediate damage. For instance, just before Thanksgiving in 1959, the Secretary of Health, Education and Welfare destroyed practically the entire cranberry market by announcing at a press conference that some cranberries were contaminated by a cancer-producing agent. The effectiveness and power of publicity as a control mechanism was more recently confirmed by the announcement that botulism in a can of soup had killed a man. The publicity led to the bankruptcy of Bonvivant Soup Company (Gellhorn, 1972:110). It should be noted, however, that this power of control is not confined to public officials. For example, the demise of the Corvair is directly attributable to Ralph Nader's book *Unsafe at Any Speed* (1965) and his subsequent efforts.

In many areas, publicity serves a highly useful if not indispensable control function. The 1970 federal air pollution legislation, for example, provides for making known to the public the extent to which each automobile manufacturer is complying with the auto emission standards of the Environmental Protection Agency. Quite often, polluting companies agree to cease and desist orders of administrative agencies out of fear of the consequences of adverse publicity (Nagel, 1975:347). Furthermore, in the enforcement of legislation protecting consumers against the manufacture and sale of impure food and drugs, the ability of administrative agencies to inform the public that a product may contain harmful ingredients can play an important role in preventing consumption of the product under investigation until the accuracy of this suspicion can be determined.

In some cases, however, firms that have a monopoly on their products, such as local gas and electric companies, are not likely to be hurt by adverse publicity. Agencies are, at times, also reluctant to stigmatize firms since adverse publicity is considered a form of informal adjudication, although it is often used and justified by the notion that people have a right to know.

SUMMARY

This chapter has considered law as a mechanism of formal social control. Law comes into play when other forms of social control are weak, ineffective, or unavailable. Individuals and groups are led to behave in acceptable ways through the processes of socialization and external pressures in the form of sanctions from others. Mechanisms of social control through external pressures may be formal and informal, and include both negative and positive sanctions. Informal social controls are exemplified in the functions of folkways and mores. Informal social controls tend to be effective when there is intense social interaction on an intimate face-to-face basis, normative consensus, and surveillance of the behavior of members of the community. Formal social controls are characteristic of more complex societies with a greater division of labor and different sets of mores, values, and ideologies. Formal social controls arise when informal controls are insufficient to maintain conformity to certain norms. Laws are one type of formal social control. Other types of formal social controls rely on both penalties and rewards while control through the law is exercised primarily, but not exclusively, by the use of punishments to regulate behavior.

The social control of criminal and delinquent behavior represents the most highly structured formal system used by society to attempt to control deviant behavior. The concept "legalization" is used to describe the process by which norms are moved from the social to the legal level. It also entails the incorporation of specific punishments for special kinds of criminal law violators. The goals of punishment include retribution or social retaliation, incapacitation and both specific and general deterrence. Punishment is considered as a deterrent in situations which involve low-commitment individuals who engage in instrumental crimes. The death penalty, as the most severe form of punishment, remains controversial, and there is no agreement on its deterrent effect.

Formal control of deviant behavior is not limited to criminal sanctions. The use of civil commitment as a mechanism of legal control is more widespread. In civil commitment there are no procedural safeguards available for the defendant. Civil commitment operates through the process of defining deviant behavior as a mental disorder, and includes the involuntary commitment of alcoholics, drug addicts, and sex offenders. It allows mental health professionals, particularly psychiatrists, to exercise a considerable judicial power by placing individuals in institutions without the guarantee of a trial.

The United States invests enormous resources in controlling victimless crimes. These are crimes *mala prohibita* and are differentiated from other crimes by the element of consensual transaction or exchange. Those who are involved in these crimes are willing participants who, as a rule, do not complain to the police that a crime has been committed. It was shown that the legal control of victimless crimes, such as drug addiction, prostitution, and gambling, tend to be generally expensive, ineffective, and often lead to the corruption of law enforcement agents.

White-collar crimes constitute a greater threat to the welfare of society than more traditional kinds of crime. The notion of white-collar crime incorporates both occupational and corporate crimes. Some persons commit crimes in connection with their occupation, others do it while promoting the interest of a corporation for which they work. Corporate crime is a relatively recent phenomenon in the United States. The three broad types of legal control of corporate activities are prospective, processual, and retrospective. In general, laws dealing with corporate crime are ineffective and the sanctions are insufficient to act as effective deterrents. Corporations tend to consider law violation and the resulting fine as part of their regular business expenses.

The social control of dissent is accomplished through the various selection processes, the manipulation of the structure of material benefits, and the use of coercive control mechanisms. In the past, the American government has relied heavily on the operations of various intelligence agencies to create a system of institutionalized social control of dissent.

Control through administrative law is exercised in the context of licensing, inspection, and the use of publicity as a threat. A license is an official permit to engage in certain types of activities. In addition to requiring a license to practice certain occupations or carrying out certain activities, control can also be exercised through the revocation or suspension of the license in instances of noncompliance. Inspection allows a way of monitoring ongoing activities under the jurisdiction of a particular agency. It may be sporadic or continuous and both forms exert pressure for self-regulation and contribute to the maintenance of internal controls specified by law. The threat of adverse publicity is considered a powerful administrative control mechanism. Since most large companies are sensitive to adverse publicity, administrative agencies can use the threat of such publicity to insure compliance with the law. In the next chapter, the law as a method of conflict resolution will be considered.

SUGGESTED FURTHER READINGS

WILLIAM J. BOWERS, with GLENN L. PIERCE and JOHN F. MCDEVITT, *Legal Homicide: Death as Punishment in America, 1864–1982*. Boston: Northeastern University Press, 1984. A review of the major trends and debates concerning the death penalty in the United States.

JAMES W. COLEMAN, *The Criminal Elite: The Sociology of White Collar Crime*. New York: St. Martin's Press, 1985. A comprehensive study of white collar crime that brings together the growing body of data on the subject and presents it in an integrated theoretical framework.

MARTIN L. FORST, *Civil Commitment and Social Control*. Lexington, MA: Heath, 1978. A lucid and informative discussion of civil commitment as a form of social control through law, based on empirical investigation.

JACK P. GIBBS (ed.), *Social Control: Views from the Social Sciences.* Beverly Hills, CA: Sage Publications, 1982. A collection of papers from scholars of several fields regarding the notion of control—social, psychological, political—in their disciplines. Several conceptual, theoretical and empirical issues are identified and discussed.

WILLIAM K. GREENAWAY and STEPHEN L. BRICKEY (eds.), *Law and Social Control in Canada.* Scarborough, Ontario: Prentice-Hall of Canada, Ltd., 1978. A series of articles from the critical conflict perspective on the role of law in social control in Canada.

ALLAN V. HORWITZ, *The Social Control of Mental Illness.* New York: Academic Press, 1982. A series of case studies on the social control of mental illness in the theoretical framework of Donald Black's *The Behavior of Law.*

MARVIN D. KROHN and RONALD L. AKERS (eds.), *Crime, Law and Sanctions, Theoretical Perspectives.* Beverly Hills, CA: Sage Publications, 1978. A collection of judiciously selected articles dealing with the social origins of law, compliance, and control theories, and the use of criminal sanctions.

HERBERT L. PACKER, *The Limits of Criminal Sanction.* Stanford, CA: Stanford University Press, 1968. A stimulating and provocative discussion on the limits of law in social control.

ROBERT N. RICH, *Crimes Without Victims: Deviance and the Criminal Law.* Washington, DC: University Press of America, Inc., 1978. A comprehensive discussion of the origins of, and problems involved in, dealing with a variety of victimless crimes. A useful reference on victimless crimes.

DAVID R. SIMON and D. STANLEY EITZEN, *Elite Deviance,* 2nd ed. Boston: Allyn and Bacon, 1986. A good discussion of the various forms of immorality, corruption, political and corporate deviance, and occupational crimes.

U.S. Department of Justice, *Illegal Corporate Behavior.* National Institute of Law Enforcement and Criminal Justice. Law Enforcement Assistance Administration. Washington, DC: U.S. Government Printing Office, October 1979. The first large-scale comprehensive investigation of the nature, extent, and control of corporate crime in the United States. Marshall B. Clinard directed the project.

DAVID WISE, *The American Police State, The Government Against the People.* New York: Vintage Books, 1978. A detailed and informative account of the illegal activities of the government to repress dissent.

REFERENCES

ADLER, FREDA, and HERBERT M. ADLER, 1975. *Sisters in Crime, The Rise of the New Female Criminal.* New York: McGraw-Hill.

BENSINGER, PETER B. 1986. "An Inadequate War Against Drugs," Newsweek (July 28):8.

BOGGS, SARAH L. 1971. "Formal and Informal Crime Control: An Exploratory Study of Urban, Suburban, and Rural Orientations," The Sociological Quarterly 12 (1)(Summer):319–327.

CHAMBLISS, WILLIAM J. 1975. "Types of Deviance and the Effectiveness of Legal Sanctions." Pp. 398–407 in William J. Chambliss, ed., Criminal Law in Action. Santa Barbara, CA: Hamilton Publishing Company; 1978. *On the Take, From Petty Crooks to Presidents.* Bloomington, IN: Indiana University Press.

CLARK, RAMSEY. 1971. *Crime in America.* New York: Pocket Books.

CLINARD, MARSHALL B., and DANIEL J. ABBOTT. 1973. *Crime in Developing Countries: A Comparative Perspective.* New York: John Wiley.

CLINARD, MARSHALL B., and ROBERT F. MEIER. 1985. *Sociology of Deviant Behavior,* 6th ed. New York: Holt, Rinehart and Winston.

COLEMAN, JAMES W. 1985. *The Criminal Elite: The Sociology of White Collar Crime.* New York: St. Martin's Press.

Commission on the Review of the National Policy Toward Gambling. 1976. *Gambling in America.* Washington, DC: U.S. Government Printing Office.

CONY, ED, and STANLEY PENN. 1986. "Tale of a Kite," The Wall Street Journal (August 11):1,10.

EHRLICH, ISAAC. 1975. "The Deterrent Effect of Capital Punishment: A Question of Life or Death," American Economic Review 65:397–417.

ERIKSON, KAI T. 1966. *Wayward Puritans: A Study in the Sociology of Deviance.* New York: John Wiley.

Federal Bureau of Investigation. 1986. *Uniform Crime Reports for the United States.* Washington, DC: U.S. Department of Justice.

Forbes, 1985. "Startling Statistics," (November 4):28.

FORST, MARTIN L. 1978. *Civil Commitment and Social Control.* Lexington, MA: Heath.

FRIEDMAN, LAWRENCE N. 1984. *American Law: An Introduction.* New York: W. W. Norton.

FRIENDLY, ALFRED, and RONALD L. GOLDFARB. 1967. *Crime and Publicity: The Impact of News on the Administration of Justice.* New York: The Twentieth Century Fund.

FOUCAULT, MICHEL. 1977. *Discipline and Punish, The Birth of the Prison.* Translated by Alan Sheridan. New York: Pantheon.

GEIS, GILBERT. 1978. "Deterring Corporate Crime." Pp. 278–296 in M. David Ermann and Richard J. Lundman, eds., *Corporate and Governmental Deviance: Problems of Organizational Behavior in Contemporary Society.* New York: Oxford University Press; 1979. *Not the Law's Business, An Examination of Homosexuality, Abortion, Prostitution, Narcotics, and Gambling in the United States.* New York: Schocken Books.

GELLHORN, ERNEST. 1972. *Administrative Law and Process.* St. Paul, MN: West Publishing Co.

GLASER, DANIEL. 1971. "Criminology and Public Policy," The American Sociologist 6 (6) (June):30–37.

GLASSMAN, JAMES K. 1986. "Going to Seed," The New Republic (August 25):11–13.

GRABOWSKI, JOHN, ed. 1984. *Cocaine: Pharmacology, Effects, and Treatment of Abuse.* NIDA Research Monograph 50. National Institute on Drug Abuse. Washington, DC: U.S. Government Printing Office.

GREENAWAY, WILLIAM K., and STEPHAN L. BRICKEY, eds. 1978. *Law and Social Control in Canada.* Scarborough, Ontario: Prentice-Hall of Canada, Ltd.

HAVEMANN, JUDITH. 1986. "Federal Computers Are Putting A Glitch Into Laws On Privacy," St. Louis Post-Dispatch (July 12):B1.

JANOWITZ, MORRIS. 1976. *Social Control of the Welfare State.* New York: Elsevier North-Holland.

LA FAVE, WAYNE R. 1965. *Arrest: The Decision to Take a Suspect into Custody.* Boston: Little, Brown and the American Bar Foundation.

LANDSMAN, STEPHAN. 1973. "Masschusetts' Comprehensive Alcoholism Law—Its History and Future," Massachusetts Law Quarterly 58 (3)(Fall):273–290.

LIEBERMAN, JETHRO K. 1972. *How the Government Breaks the Law.* Baltimore: Penguin.

LIGHT, IVAN. 1977. "Numbers Gambling Among Blacks: A Financial Institution," American Sociological Review 42 (6)(December):892–904.

LOH, WALLACE D. 1984. *Social Research in the Judicial Process: Cases, Readings, and Text.* New York: Russell Sage Foundation.

MANDELL, BETTY REID, ed. 1975. *Welfare in America. Controlling the "Dangerous Classes."* Englewood Cliffs, NJ: Prentice-Hall.

MEYER, THOMAS J. 1986. "1 in 3 College Students Tries Cocaine, Study Finds; Bennett Urges Presidents to Crack Down on Drugs," The Chronicle of Higher Education (July 16): 1,30.

MIETHE, TERANCE D. and CHARLES A. MOORE. 1986. "Racial Differences in Criminal Processing: The Consequences of Model Selection on Conclusions About Differential Treatment," The Sociological Quarterly 27 (2):217–237.

NADER, RALPH. 1965. *Unsafe at Any Speed.* New York: Grossman.

NAGEL, STUART S. 1975. *Improving the Legal Process.* Lexington, MA: Heath.

Newsweek. 1979. "Another Dirty Trick by the FBI," (September 24):45.

OBERSCHALL, ANTHONY. 1973. *Social Conflict and Social Movements.* Englewood Cliffs, NJ: Prentice-Hall.

PACKER, HERBERT L. 1968. *The Limits of Criminal Sanction.* Stanford, CA: Stanford University Press.

PIVEN, FRANCES FOX, and RICHARD A. CLOWARD. 1971. *Regulating the Poor, The Functions of Public Welfare.* New York: Pantheon.

President's Commission on Law Enforcement and Administration of Justice. 1967a. *The Challenge of Crime in a Free Society.* Washington, DC: U.S. Government Printing Office; 1967b. *Crime and Its Impact—An Assessment.* Washington, DC: U.S. Government Printing Office.

QUINNEY, RICHARD A. 1975. *Criminology, Analysis and Critique of Crime in America.* Boston: Little, Brown.

RADELET, MICHAEL L., and GLENN L. PIERCE. 1985. "Race and Prosecutorial Discretion in Homicide Cases," Law and Society Review 19 (4):587–621.

RICH, ROBERT M. 1978. *Crimes Without Victims: Deviance and the Criminal Law.* Washington, DC: University Press of America, Inc.

ROUCEK, JOSEPH S. 1978. "The Concept of Social Control in American Sociology," Pp. 3–19 in Joseph S. Roucek, ed., Social Control For the 1980s, A Handbook for Order in a Democratic Society. Westport, CT: Greenwood Press.

RUSCHE, GEORG, and OTTO KURCHHEIMER. 1968. *Punishment and Social Structure.* New York: Russell and Russell.

St. Louis Post-Dispatch. 1985. "25 Innocent People Executed, ACLU Says," (November 14):6B.

SCHUR, EDWIN M. 1965. *Crimes Without Victims, Deviant Behavior, and Public Policy.* Englewood Cliffs, NJ: Prentice-Hall.

SCHWARTZ, RICHARD D. 1977. "Social Factors in the Development of Legal Controls: A Case Study of Two Israeli Settlements," Pp. 579–590 in Lawrence M. Friedman and Stewart Macaulay, eds., Law and the Behavioral Sciences, 2nd ed. Indianapolis: Bobbs-Merrill.

SELLIN, THORSTEN. 1959. *The Death Penalty: Report for the Model Penal Code Project of the American Law Institute.* Philadelphia: Executive Office of American Law Institute.

SHELEY, JOSEPH F. 1985. *America's "Crime Problems:" An Introduction to Criminology.* Belmont, CA: Wadsworth Publishing Company.

SHIBUTANI, TAMOTSU. 1961. *Society and Personality: An Interactionist Approach to Social Psychology.* Englewood Cliffs, NJ: Prentice-Hall.

SIMON, DAVID R. and D. STANLEY EITZEN. 1986. *Elite Deviance,* 2nd ed. Boston: Allyn and Bacon, Inc.

Sourcebook of Criminal Justice Statistics—1984. 1985. U.S. Department of Justice. Bureau of Justice Statistics.

STONE, CHRISTOPHER D. 1978. "Social Control of Corporate Behavior," Pp. 241–258 in M. David Ermann and Richard J. Lundman, eds., Corporate and Governmental Deviants: Problems of Organizational Behavior in Contemporary Society. New York: Oxford University Press.

SUMMERS, ROBERT S., and GEORGE G. HOWARD. 1972. *Law, Its Nature, Functions and Limits,* 2nd ed. Englewood Cliffs, NJ: Prentice-Hall.

SUTHERLAND, EDWIN H. 1949. *White Collar Crime.* New York: Dryden Press.

SUTHERLAND, EDWIN H., and DONALD C. CRESSEY. 1974. *Criminology.* 9th ed. Philadelphia: Lippincott.

SZASZ, THOMAS S. 1965. *Psychiatric Justice.* New York: Macmillan.

TAPPAN, PAUL W. 1960. *Crime, Justice, and Correction.* New York: McGraw-Hill.

The Wall Street Journal. 1986a. "No Longer Amused, Frankfurt Decides To Relocate Its Red-Light District," (July 28):16; 1986b. "Reagan Starts Drive Against Drug Abuse, May Seek More Tests of U.S. Employees," (July 31):46.

TITTLE, CHARLES R. 1969. "Crime Rates and Legal Sanctions," Social Problems 16 (4) (Spring):409–423.

TURK, AUSTIN T. 1972. *Legal Sanctioning and Social Control.* Rockville, MD: National Institute of Mental Health.

UELMEN, GERALD F. and VICTOR G. HADDOX. 1983. *Drug Abuse and the Law,* 2nd ed. New York: Clark Boardman Company, Ltd.

UNGER, ROBERTO MANGABEIRA. 1976. *Law in Modern Society, Toward a Criticism of Social Theory.* New York: Free Press.

U.S. Department of Justice. 1979. *Illegal Corporate Behavior.* National Institute of Law Enforcement and Criminal Justice. Law Enforcement Assistance Administration. Washington, D.C.: U.S. Government Printing Office (October); 1985. "Capital Punishment 1984." Bureau of Justice Statistics. Bulletin (August).

U.S. News & World Report. 1979. "Red-tape: It's Bad at Grass Roots, Too," (September 24):69–72; 1986. "America on Drugs," (July 28):48–55.

WEINBERG, ROY D. 1979. *Family Planning and the Law,* 2nd ed. New York: Oceana Publications, Inc.

WISE, DAVID. 1978. *The American Police State, The Government Against the People.* New York: Vintage Books.

Wolfenden Report. 1963. *Report of the Committee on Homosexual Offenses and Prostitution.* Briarcliff Manor, NY: Stein and Day.

WYNN, JOAN RANSOHOFF, and CLIFFORD GOLDMAN. 1974. "Gambling in New York City: The Case for Legalization," Pp. 66–75 in Lee Rainwater, ed., Social Problems and Public Policy, Deviance and Liberty. Chicago: Aldine Publishing Co.

6

Law as a Method
of Conflict Resolution

At every level in society conflict is ubiquitous. Sociologists consider social conflict as a relationship between two or more parties who (or whose representatives) believe they have incompatible goals (Kriesberg, 1973:17). This relationship is usually characterized by some overt signs of antagonism (Aubert, 1963:26). The scope of conflict ranges from marital discord to total war. Conflicts may involve individuals, small groups, organizations, social classes, racial groups, or entire nations. Conflicts vary in their intensity, duration, mode of settlement, outcomes, and consequences. One of the functions of law in society is the orderly resolution of conflicts. The intent of this chapter is to examine the questions of why, how, and under what circumstances laws are used to resolve conflicts between individuals, between individuals and organizations, and between organizations.

A NOTE ON TERMINOLOGY

There is no consensus in the sociological and legal literature on the terminology concerning the role of the law in controversies. Terms such as "conflict resolution" (see, for example, Aubert, 1963; 1969; Ford Foundation, 1978), "conflict regulation" (see, for example, Wehr, 1979), "conflict management" (see, for example, Lord and Adelman, 1978), "dispute processing" (see, for example, Felstiner, 1974, 1975), "dispute settlement" (see, for example, Gulliver, 1969), and "dispute resolution" (see, for example, Kavashima, 1969) are often used more or less interchangeably.

Some authors, such as Richard L. Abel (1973), William L. F. Felstiner (1974; 1975), and Paul Wehr (1979) contend that disputes are processed in society, rather than settled, and conflicts are managed or regulated rather than resolved. Third-party intervention, whether through legal or nonlegal means, represents for them only the settlement of the resolution of the public component of the dispute or conflict, rather than the alleviation of the underlying forces or tensions that have created that conflict. Richard L. Abel (1973:228) epitomizes this position and chides anthropologists and sociologists who "have tended to write as though 'settlement' must be the ultimate outcome of disputes, 'resolution' the inevitable fate of conflicts." Then he adds that "it has recently become almost commonplace to observe that the outcome of most conflicts and disputes are other conflicts and disputes, with at most a temporary respite between them" (Abel, 1973:28).

Other authors point out that the actual dispute is preceded by several stages. For example, Laura Nader and Harry F. Todd (1978:14–15) contend that there are three distinct phases or stages in the disputing process, the grievance or preconflict stage, the conflict stage, and finally, the dispute stage. The *grievance* or *preconflict* stage refers to situations which an individual or a group perceive to be unjust and consider grounds for resentment or complaint. The situation may be real or imaginary, depending on the aggrieved parties' perception. This condition may erupt into conflict or it may wane. If it is not resolved in the preconflict or grievance stage, it enters into the *conflict* stage, in which the aggrieved party confronts the offending party and communicates his or her resentment or feelings of injustice to the person or group. The conflict phase is dyadic, that is, it only involves two parties. If it is not deescalated or resolved at this stage, it enters into the final *dispute* stage when the conflict is made public. The dispute stage is characterized by the involvement of a third party in the disagreement. P. H. Gulliver (1969:14) suggests that "no dispute exists unless and until the right-claimant, or someone on his behalf, actively raises the initial disagreement from the level of dyadic argument into the public arena, with the express intention of doing something about the denied claim." Ideally, then, a grievance is monadic, involving one person or a group, a conflict is dyadic, and a dispute is triadic, since it involves the participation of a third party who is called upon as an agent of settlement.

Essentially, the legal approach to conflict resolution entails the transition from a dyad of the conflicting parties to the triad, "where an intermediary who stands outside the original conflict has been added to the dyad" (Aubert, 1963:26). The stages discussed by Nader and Todd are not always clear-cut or sequential. A person may file a lawsuit without ever confronting the offender, or one party may quit or concede at any stage in the disagreement.

When disagreements formally enter into the legal arena (that is, trial), from the perspective of the law, disputes are authoritatively settled rather than processed through the intervention of third parties (that is, judges), and conflicts are resolved rather than simply managed or regulated. The use of the terms "conflict resolution" or "dispute settlement" is thus, in this sense, justified. In this chapter, I shall use these concepts interchangeably, and at the same time, I will repeatedly emphasize, in different contexts, that the law resolves or settles only the legal components of conflicts and disputes, rather than ameliorating the underlying causes. The law, in brief, deals with disagreements that have been translated into legal disputes or conflicts. A legal resolution of conflict does not necessarily lead to a re- duction of tension or antagonism between the aggrieved parties.

METHODS OF CONFLICT RESOLUTION

In every society disputes abound and there is a wide variety of methods for their settlement. While most societies use similar methods, the differences among them consist in the preference given to one method over others. Cultural factors and the availability of institutions for settling disputes will usually determine such preferences. There are two major forms of resolving legal disputes throughout the world. "*Either* the parties to a conflict deter- mine the outcome themselves by negotiations, which does not preclude that a third party acting as a mediator might assist them in their negotiations. *Or*, the conflict is adjudicated, which means that a third, and ideally im- partial, party decides which of the disputants has the superior claim" (Ehr- mann, 1976:82). These forms are used (and are sometimes intertwined) for the settlement of civil, criminal, and administrative suits. For nonlegal dis- putes, there are a variety of other means for settlement.

Simon Roberts (1979:57–59) points out that in some societies, direct interpersonal violence constitutes an approved method of dispute settle- ment. Such interpersonal violence may be a way of retaliation for violence already suffered or as a reaction to some other form of perceived injustice. Occasionally, physical violence may be channeled into a restricted and con- ventionalized form such as dueling. In Germany before the Second World War, for example, dueling was a popular form of dispute settlement among university students, members of the officer corps in the military, and the nobility in general. Duels took place under controlled conditions and ac- cording to specific rules. The participants wore protective clothing, and usually the first sign of bloodletting marked the end of the dispute. It was often a question of honor to challenge the insulting party to a duel who was, by convention, compelled to accept it. In the event of an insult or injustice, all the offended party had to do was to slap the offender. This act was a challenge to a duel, and the parties involved promptly settled on the time and place. Dueling scars on one's face represented symbols of courage and high status.

Another form of physical violence is feuding (Gulliver, 1979:1). It is a state of recurring hostilities between families or groups, instigated by a desire to avenge an offense (insult, injury, death, or deprivation of some sort) against a member of the group. The unique feature of a feud is that responsibility to avenge is carried by all members of the group. The killing of any member of the offender's group is viewed as appropriate revenge, since the group as a whole is considered responsible. Nicholas Gubser (1965) describes a feud which lasted for decades within a Nunamiut Eskimo com- munity caused by a husband's killing of his wife's lover. When a man is killed, in Gubser's words,

The closely related members of his kindred do not rest until complete revenge has been achieved. The immediate relatives of the deceased . . . recruit as much support from other relatives as they can. Their first action, if possible, is to kill the murderer, or maybe one of his closest kin. Then, of course, the members of the murderer's kindred are brought into the feud. These two kindreds may snipe at each other for years (1965:151).

At times, the feud can turn into a full-scale battle when in addition to the families the communities are drawn into a dispute. This happened from time to time in the famous feud between the Hatfields of Virginia and the McCoys of Kentucky which broke out in 1882 and lasted for several years.

Conflict, at times, is channeled into rituals. For example, the parties to the dispute may confront each other before the assembled community and voice their contentions through songs and dances improvised for the occasion. In the form of a song, the accuser states all the abuse he or she can think of; the accused then responds in kind. A number of such exchanges may follow until the contestants are exhausted, and a winner emerges through public acclaim for the greater poetic or vituperative skill.

In some societies, shaming is used as a form of public reprimand in the disapproval of disputing behavior. Ridicule directed at those guilty of antisocial conduct is also used to reduce conflict. At times, the singing of rude and deflating songs to, or about, a troublesome individual is also reported as a means of achieving a similar end. Ridicule, reproach, or public exposure may also take the form of a "public harangue," in which a person's wrongdoings are embarrassingly exposed by being shouted out to the community at large (Roberts, 1979:62).

In attempts to resolve disputes, parties may choose to resort to supernatural agencies. The notion that supernatural beings may intervene to punish wrongdoers is rather widespread. This notion is often accompanied by the belief that harm may be inflicted by witches or through the practice of sorcery. In some societies, witchcraft and sorcery are seen as a possible cause of death and of almost any form of illness or material misfortune. Jane Fishburne Collier (1973:113–120), for example, identifies a variety of witchcraft beliefs among the Zinacantecos in Mexico. They include witches who send sickness, ask that sickness be sent, perform specific actions (such as causing the victim to rot away), control weather, talk to saints, or cause sickness by an evil eye. Notes Collier: "Witchcraft beliefs underlie all of the reasons given for actions during a hearing" (1973:122). Consequently, in such societies the procedures for identifying witches or sorcerers responsible for particular incidences or misfortunes assume great importance in the handling of conflict (Roberts, 1979:64).

Obviously, not all dispute situations can be handled by violence, rituals, shaming, ostracism, and supernatural agencies. Most societies have access to a number of other procedures to deal with disputes. The important considerations are the presence or absence of a third party, the bases for the third party's intervention, and the type of outcome, if any. Additional methods used in attempts to deal with grievances, conflict, or disputes include "lumping it," avoidance, negotiation, mediation, arbitration, and adjudication.

"Lumping it" refers simply to inaction, to not making a claim or complaint. Galanter says: "This is done all the time by 'claimants' who lack information or access or who knowingly decide gain is too low, cost too high (including psychic cost of litigating where such activity is repugnant)" (1974:124–125). In "lumping it," the issue or the difficulty that gave rise to the disagreement is simply ignored and the relationship with the offending party continues. For example, a college professor may not want to press a particular claim (for example for a higher increment) against the administration and continues his or her relationship with the university.

Avoidance refers to limiting the relationship with other disputants sufficiently so that the dispute no longer remains salient (Felstiner, 1974:70). This kind of behavior Albert O. Hirschman (1970) calls "exit" which entails withdrawing from a situation or terminating or curtailing a relationship. For example, a consumer may go to a different store rather than press grievances. In consumer transaction disputes, for example, "the exit option is widely held to be uniquely powerful: by inflicting revenue losses on delinquent management" (Hirschman, 1970:21) it can be considered not only expedient in dispute settlement, but a way of imposing sanctions. Avoidance entails a limitation or a break in the relationship between disputants, while "lumping it" refers to the lack of resolution of a conflict, grievance, or dispute for the reason that one of the parties prefers to ignore the issue in dispute, generally basing the decision on feelings of relative powerlessness or on the social, economic, or psychological costs involved in seeking a solution. Avoidance is not always a viable alternative, especially in situations when the relationship must continue, for example, with certain companies that have monopolies, such as gas or electric companies, or with the Social Security Administration or the Welfare Department. An important aspect of avoidance is the reduction of social interaction or its termination. Lumping behavior entails the ignoring of the issue in dispute while continuing the relationship.

Negotiations in disputes take place when disputants seek to resolve their disagreements without the help of neutral third parties. Negotiation is a two-party arrangement in which disputants try to persuade one another, establish a common ground for discussion, and feel their way by a process of give and take towards a settlement. It involves the use of debate and bargaining (Raiffa, 1982). A basic requirement for successful negotiation is the desire of both parties to settle a dispute without escalation and without resort to neutral third parties. Aubert states: "The advantage of negotiated solutions is that they need not leave any marks on the normative order of society. Since the solution does not become a precedent for later solutions to similar conflicts, the adversaries need not fear the general consequences of the settlement" (1969:284). When interests are contradictory to the extent that gains and losses must cancel each other, negotiations are inadequate in resolving the conflict, and in such situations, parties may bring the case to court for legal settlement. In industrialized countries, such as the United States, lumping behavior, avoidance, and negotiation are the most frequent responses to dispute situations (Best and Andreasen, 1976).

Mediation is a dispute resolution method that interposes a disinterested and noncoercive third party, the mediator, between the disputants. Unlike litigation, where the ultimate decision is imposed by the judge, the mediator does not make the final decision. Rather, the terms of settlement are worked out solely by and between the disputants. Mediation begins with an agreement. It is nonadversarial and the basic tenet is cooperation rather than competition. The role of the mediator in the dispute is that of a guide, facilitator, and catalyst.

A mediator may be chosen by the disputants or appointed by someone in authority. A mediator may be selected because the person has status, position, respect, power, money, or the alleged power to invoke sanctions in behalf of a deity or some other superhuman force. A mediator may have none of these, but simply be a designated agent of an organization set up to handle specific disputes. Bringing disputes to a mediator may be the choice of both parties or of one but not the other party to a conflict, or it may be the result of private norms or expectations of a group which "require" that disputes be settled as much as possible within the group.

Mediation essentially consists of influencing the parties to come to an agreement by appealing to their own interests. The mediator may use a variety of techniques to accomplish this objective.

> He may work on the parties' ideas of what serves them best . . . in such a way that he gets them to consider the common interests as more essential than they did previously, or their competing interests as less essential. He may also look for possibilities of resolution which the parties themselves have not discovered and try to convince them that both will be well served by his suggestion. The very fact that a suggestion is proposed by an impartial third party may also, in certain cases, be sufficient for the parties to accept it (Eckhoff, 1978:36).

Ideally, both parties should have confidence in the mediator, be willing to cooperate, listen to his or her advice, and consider the mediator as impartial. A mediator may also use warnings, promises, or flattery in attempts to reconcile differences between the parties. Eckhoff points out:

> The conditions for mediation are best in cases where both parties are interested in having the conflict resolved. The stronger the common interest is, the greater reason they have for bringing the conflict before a third party, and the more motivated they will be for cooperating actively with him in finding a solution, and for adjusting their demands in such a way that a solution can be reached (1978:36).

The use of mediators is widespread in the more than 300 community dispute resolution centers in the United States. (U.S. Department of Justice, 1986:2). The initial idea for such centers came from Richard Danzig (1973). Using the example of resolving intratribal disputes by conciliation in Liberia, he suggested the establishment of neighborhood community moots. Such moots involve community members with shared values who might be able to resolve more effectively than courts those disputes that affect the disputants and the neighborhood, such as family and housing disputes and minor criminal charges. Although there is a great variation among centers in the types of cases they handle, almost all tend to concentrate on disputes between persons with an ongoing relationship. Participation in mediation is voluntary. The majority of disputants are referred to the centers by judges, police, prosecutors, and court clerks. Mediators include lawyers, law students, undergraduates, and lay persons. Prior to acting as mediators, they receive training in mediation techniques. These neighborhood centers are listed in the ABA's Dispute Resolution Project Directory, which is updated annually (American Bar Association, 1987).

There are many advantages of such neighborhood justice systems (McGillis, 1982). These nonjudicial forums can increase access to justice because of their low cost (or no cost), convenient hours, and location. Mediation provides a better process than other forums for handling disputes because participants are able to explore the underlying problems contributing to the dispute without legal formalities, time limits, and lawyers acting as intermediaries in the discussion. The reliance on informal alternatives also frees the courts to attend to more serious cases.

Related to mediation is the *ombudsman* process which combines mediatory and investigatory functions in dispute resolution. In the classic Scandinavian model, the ombudsman is a public official designated to hear citizen complaints and carry out independent fact-finding investigations to correct abuses of public administration. The system is widely used as an alternative to courts in other countries. In Denmark, for example, courts are very rarely used by the consumer (Blegvad, 1983:207). Instead the ombudsman negotiates with the firms in disputes on behalf of clients. In the United States, some corporations, hospitals, and universities are beginning to rely on the process to correct organizational abuses and resolve internal disputes. Some newspapers and radio stations in the format of "action lines" also perform the role of ombudsman in disputes. A major criticism against the ombudsman process is that the person acting as mediator often represents the vested interest of a particular agency which suggests bias in favor of his or her employer. For example, the hospital ombudsman may be partial to the hospital and biased against the client (Marshall, 1985:108).

Arbitration is another way of involving a third party in a dispute. Unlike in mediation where a third party assists the disputants to reach their own solution, in arbitration a decision is made for them by a third party which is final and binding. Disputants agree beforehand both to the intervention of a neutral third party and to the finality of his or her decision. Unlike in courts, the proceedings in arbitration can remain private and participants can opt for simplicity and informality. Arbitration tends to reduce the cost of dispute resolution, especially when attorneys are not used and because of the lack of opportunity to appeal the arbitrator's decision. It is also faster than adjudication because participants can proceed as soon as they are ready rather than wait for a trial date to be assigned.

Today, almost all of collective bargaining contracts contain a provision for final and binding arbitration. Arbitration clauses are showing up more often in business contracts and even in executive employment letters (*The New York Times*, 1986a:1F). The conduct of commercial arbitrators (such as the American Arbitration Association with offices in major cities) is governed by a code of ethics. Many private organizations, professional groups, and trade associations have their own formal arbitration machinery for the settlement of disputes among members. Similarly, labor-management disputes are often brought before arbiters designated in advance, whose decisions are binding by mutual consent of the disputants and ultimately enforceable by private sanctions and by the courts. It should be noted: "Agreement to submit disputes to private but formal arbitration is characteristic of parties whose relationship involves long-term performance or other aspects of permanence" (Sarat and Grossman, 1978:27).

A Ford Foundation (1978:44–48) report notes that arbitration is increasingly considered as an alternative to judicial and administrative processes. Compulsory arbitration, especially for small claims, can free courts for more substantial disputes, and depending upon the issues involved, it may reduce the cost to litigants and be a more effective way of solving problems. For example, in Philadelphia, a case that is under $10,000 is automatically assigned by the court to arbitration. Three arbitrators are selected by the deputy court administrator from a panel of lawyers. They make their decisions on the pleadings supplemented by oral arguments by the attorneys for the parties. It is estimated that the average arbitrated case costs one-fifth less per day than it would in the Philadelphia court system. Similar systems of compulsory arbitration exist in England, Germany, and in the Scandinavian countries.

A much publicized form of arbitration is known as the *rent-a-judge* system (Goldberg, et al., 1985:280–309). In this process, the disputants in an attempt to avoid the use of a regular court select a retired judge to hear and decide a pending case as an arbitrator would. The same procedure is used as in court, and the decision of the judge is legally binding. Unlike in arbitration, the "referee's" decision can be appealed for errors of law or on the ground that the judgment was against evidence, though such appeals are rare. In California, where this system of private judging is quite prevalent, former judges have decided on hundreds of cases. The system is considered both an alternative to adjudication and a sort of "rich-man's justice" that undermines public methods of dispute resolution and threatens constitutional values.

There are also some hybrid processes of dispute resolution that have been used with considerable success (Goldberg, et al., 1985:7–13). One is *med-arb*, in which the issues which were not solved by mediation are submitted to arbitration, with the same person serving first as mediator, then as arbitrator. Med-arb has been used often in contract negotiation disputes between public employers and their unionized employees. Another is the *minitrial*, which has been repeatedly utilized in a number of major intercorporate disputes. In this method, attorneys for each disputant are given a short time (not more than a day) in which to present the basic elements of their case to senior executives of both parties. After the presentation, the senior executives try to negotiate a settlement of the case, usually with the aid of a neutral advisor. If there is no settlement, the advisor gives the parties his opinion of the likely outcome if the dispute were litigated. This dose of reality at times helps to break the deadlock.

Adjudication is a public and formal method of conflict resolution and is best exemplified by courts. Courts have the authority to intervene in disputes whether or not the parties desire it and to render a decision and to enforce compliance with that decision. In adjudication, the emphasis is on the legal rights and duties of disputants, rather than on compromises or on the mutual satisfaction of the parties. Adjudication is also more oriented toward zero-sum decisions than the other mechanisms I have noted. Courts require disputants to narrow their definitions of issues in the identification of the nature of their problems. Felstiner states: "Adjudication as a consequence tends to focus on 'what facts' and 'which norms' rather than on any need for normative shifts" (1974:70). In other words, courts deal with issues and facts. Consequently, they can only deal with disagreements, grievances, or conflicts that have been transformed into legal disputes. For example, in a divorce case, the court may focus on one incident in what is a complex and often not very clear-cut series of problems. It results in a resolution of a legal dispute but not necessarily of the broader issues that have produced that conflict.

Although courts occasionally seek compromise and flexibility, generally the verdict of the court has an either/or character: the decision is based upon a single definite conception of what has actually taken place and upon a single interpretation of legal norms. When a conflict culminates in litigation, one of the parties must be prepared for a total loss. Aubert says: "One aspect of legal decisions that is closely linked to their either/or character is the marked orientation toward the past" (1969:287). The structure of legal thinking is also oriented toward comparisons between actions and sanctions rather than around utility and effectiveness. Because of this orientation, and because of the use of precedents, there is a fair amount of predictability of how similar cases will be settled by courts. But since the courts are dealing only with the legal issues, they do not take into consideration the possibility that the applicable legal facts and norms may have been influenced by different social conditions, and that, in many instances, courts are only treating the symptoms rather than the underlying causes of a problem. With these limitations, the courts work "to clean up all the little social messes (and the occasional big ones) that recurrently arise between the members of the society from day to day" (Hoebel, 1954:280).

In this section, I have distinguished among a number of procedures used for settling disputes. Some are public, some private. Some are official, some unofficial. Some are formal, some informal. These procedures overlap, and each has its limitations and advantages. They are related in different ways to outcomes and consequences. A number of procedures may also be used for the settlement of a single dispute.

Obviously, no one procedure is applicable for every kind of problem. A number of considerations appear relevant in the selection of a particular method. One is the relationship between the disputants, that is, is there an ongoing relationship between the disputants, such as business partners, or is it the result of a single encounter, such as an automobile accident. When an ongoing relationship is involved, it is more productive for the parties to work out their difficulties through negotiation or mediation, if necessary. An advantage of mediation is that it encourages the restructuring of the underlying relationship so as to eliminate the source of conflict rather than dealing only with the manifestation of conflict. Another consideration is the nature of the dispute. If a precedent is required, such as in civil rights cases, litigation in the form of class action may be appropriate. The amount at stake in a dispute also plays a role in deciding on the type of dispute resolution procedure. Small, simple cases might end up in small claims courts while more complex issues might require court-ordered arbitration, such as in contract negotiation disputes between public employers and unions. Speed and cost are other relevant factors. For example, arbitration may be speedier and less costly than a court trial. Finally, consideration must be given also to the power relationship between the parties. When one party in a dispute has much less bargaining strength than the other, as in the case of a pollution victim faced by a powerful corporation, an adjudicatory forum in which principle not power will determine the outcome may be desirable (Goldberg, 1985:10–11). In the remainder of this chapter, I shall consider why some disputants turn to legal mechanisms of conflict resolution, under what circumstances they choose the law rather than some other procedures, and the limitations of the law in resolving conflicts.

DEMANDS FOR COURT SERVICES
IN CONFLICT RESOLUTION

In the words of former Chief Justice Warren E. Burger, the public "has an almost irrational focus—virtually a mania—on litigation as the way to solve all problems" (Quoted by Lauter, 1986:46). Indeed, litigation is becoming a national pastime, and more and more people are telling their troubles to a judge. In 1984, the latest year for which data are available, 13.6 million civil lawsuits were filed in state courts—one for every seventeen people (*U.S. News & World Report,* 1986:9). Between 1970 and 1984, the number of civil suits filed in district courts increased almost 200 percent, from 87,300 to 261,500 (U.S. Department of Commerce, 1986:179). During the same period, the number of employees of district courts more than doubled from 5,346 to 11,755, the number of judges increased from 507 to 657, and the budget rose from $126 million to $925 million (Posner, 1985:27). The number of lawyers increased 82 percent, from 355,242 to 649,000 (Curran, 1986:20), while the population grew 16 percent, from 203.3 million to 236.1 million.

The increase in district court cases, dramatic as it has been, is dwarfed by the growth of case loads in appeals courts—from 3,765 in 1960 to 29,580 in 1983. This is an increase of 686 percent (Posner, 1985:65). The same conditions prevail in state courts. For example, since 1960, the number of lawsuits has more than tripled in Massachusetts and doubled in Los Angeles County. Although New York City's population has not grown, its civil court case load rose 50 percent from 1978 to 1984 (Lauter, 1986:46). This extraordinary rise in civil litigation coincidentally comes at a time when the courts are already inundated by criminal cases.

There are several explanations for the increase in civil litigations over time. It is possible that there has been an increase in the number of individuals who have, at one time or another, been involved in litigation. An expansion in the volume of litigation may result even from a small increase in the total number of litigants. Such an expansion may be attributed to changes in the social and political conditions that facilitate the translation of conflicts and disputes into lawsuits. Although litigation requires a substantial investment of time and money, in recent years a number of attempts have been made to reduce or redistribute such costs through, for example, the provision of free legal services. Because of the greater availability of inexpensive or free legal services to individuals who were formerly unable to afford to bring disputes to court, the amount of litigation also may have increased (Goldman and Sarat, 1978:54).

Another explanation for the increase in the number of cases reaching the courts may be that the number of litigants has not increased, but rather that the relatively few individuals or organizations (that is, repeat players) who typically use courts to settle disputes have in recent years simply found more occasion to do so (Goldman and Sarat, 1978:55). The increase in litigation is also related to the increase in the range and variety of legally actionable or resolvable problems.

> As the scope of law expands, as more legal rights and remedies are created, the amount of litigation increases as a result of the new opportunities for court action. As new rights are created, litigation may be necessary to clarify the way in which those rights will be defined and understood by the courts. Furthermore, the creation of new rights may direct the attention of organized interest groups to the judiciary. Interest groups may come to perceive litigation as a viable strategy for stimulating group mobilization to achieve the group's political goals (Goldman and Sarat, 1978:55).

At the same time, it is also plausible that litigation is not viewed by the parties as an effort to settle a conflict; "instead it is a tactical engagement in a sustained war" (Barton, 1975:575). In such a situation, the resolution of the legal issue or the conflict becomes secondary to creating publicity for a cause or to obtaining a delay of decision through procedural grounds.

Sheldon Goldman and Austin Sarat (1978:55–57) identify three generic factors that may explain litigation. The first they call *social development.* Variation in the frequency of litigation is a function of changes in the level of complexity, differentiation, and skill of the society in which courts operate. Social development and changes in the structure of society bring about increased reliance on courts to process disputes. In less-developed societies, as a result of stable and enduring contacts among individuals, disputes are easier to resolve informally. Consequently, courts play a less important role in disputes. In more complex societies, on the other hand, relationships are typically more transitory in nature, disputes often take place between strangers, and under such circumstances, informal dispute processing is impractical. Furthermore, in developed societies there is no longer a single dominant ethos or a set of customs due to heterogeneity, secularization, and the closer interaction among different subgroups with specific norms (Barton, 1975:574). For example, corporate executives and environmentalists offer radically different ethical norms for the same activities, such as potentially hazardous waste disposal.

The second generic factor that explains why disputes are translated into demands for court services is subjective cost/benefit calculations on the part of disputants. For some disputants, the decision to use courts is a relatively objective, well-thought-out decision, since they must calculate a "risk" factor and weigh what they may lose against the possible benefits of doing nothing or of using different methods of conflict resolution. For others, however, resorting to courts may be an act "that has value because of its cathartic effect, even though it may not produce tangible, material benefits" (Goldman and Sarat, 1978:56). In such a situation, vindictiveness, spite, or the desire for a "moral" victory outweigh the financial considerations. Moreover, the decision to use the court by the disputant decreases the pressure upon them to resolve disputes in terms of nonlegal resources that they can mobilize. Informal and private settlements seem less likely where the parties have the option for legal recourse (Turk, 1978:224).

The third generic factor in litigation is that legislatures and courts are creating more legally actionable rights and remedies. Goldman and Sarat state: "The greater the reach and scope of the legal system, the higher its litigation rate will be" (1978:56). To some extent, the expanded use of courts is attributable to the expansion of rights and remedies stemming from Supreme Court decisions. The growing scope of law increases litigation implicitly or explicitly by expanding the jurisdiction of the courts. The creation of new rights is likely to stimulate litigation designed to vindicate or protect those rights. For example, the "criminal rights explosion" of the 1960s followed the logic that the creation of new rights would stimulate subsequent litigations which in turn would create new rights which would require further litigation.

Thus, with the creation of new norms, courts actually (although unintentionally) promote disputing, since these new norms may lead to claims that would not have been otherwise asserted. For example, the 1973 Supreme Court decision in *Roe* v. *Wade* invalidating statutes prohibiting abortions led to a series of disputes concerning such issues as whether the federal government had to pay for abortion through its medicaid program, and whether hospitals receiving federal funds had to make facilities for abortions available. Moreover, in clarifying certain norms, courts may make other normative conflicts salient and thus more likely to be disputed. Thus, the abortion decision has also led to disputes over issues of whether parents must consent to a minor's abortion and whether a husband can veto his wife's decision to terminate a pregnancy (Lempert, 1978:97–98).

In addition, since the mid-1950s the courts have discovered a slate of new constitutional rights, protections, and entitlements for whole groups of people—for example, disenfranchised voters, women, Hispanics, prisoners, children, and mental patients. Each of these new rights in turn create potentially conflict-laden situations conducive to further litigation. At the same time, questions are being raised by critics about the "rights industry" running amok and its impact on major institutions (Morgan, 1984).

Variations in Litigation Rates

There are two general ways of measuring judicial involvement in dispute settlement (Lempert, 1978:97). It can be measured in terms of the percentage of disputes that courts play some part in resolving, and in terms of the percentage of the adult population who take disputes to courts. With both measures, there are some difficulties. As Richard Lempert (1978:99) points out, there are several ways in which courts contribute to dispute settlement:

1. Courts establish norms that influence or control the private settlement of disputes. For example, norms established in an appellate opinion resolving one dispute can lead other disputants to resolve their conflict without legal intervention.
2. Courts ratify private settlements and provide guarantees of compliance. For example, in divorce cases where the parties have already reached an agreement, courts ratify that agreement which carries with it the probability of sanctions should it be breached.
3. Courts can escalate the cost of disputing, thereby increasing the likelihood of private settlement.
4. Courts provide opportunities to disputants to learn about each other's cases, thus increasing the probability of private settlement by decreasing mutual uncertainty.
5. Court staff act as mediators to encourage consensual private settlement.
6. Courts resolve certain issues in the case, leading disputants to agree on others.
7. Courts authoritatively resolve disputes.

Thus, at times, it is difficult to determine the extent to which courts contribute to dispute settlement. The clearest case is when disputes are adjudicated and a settlement is imposed after a full trial. But many cases do not end up at trials. A settlement may be reached during a pretrial conference or through informal negotiations where the judge is a participant. Judges also exert informal pressure, even after litigation has commenced, and attorneys usually listen to the recommended solutions. Settlement is also encouraged by the mounting financial costs. Under the uniquely American rule that each side pays his or her own way (the "English rule," for example, forces the loser to pay both sides' fees and court costs), often the plaintiff's lawyers who make big enough nuisances of themselves will usually get an out-of-court settlement. Defendants calculate that it is cheaper to settle than try a case even if there is a good likelihood for them to win. Thus, attempts to explore the dispute settlement functions of courts over time must consider the different roles courts play and the influences they exert. Lempert notes: "Exploration is complicated by difficulties in measuring the various ways that courts contribute to dispute settlement, and these difficulties are compounded if the measures must allow comparisons over time" (1978:100). Complications arise also in attempts to measure longitudinally the percentage of the adult population who use court services in disputes. The figures may be inaccurate to the extent that certain individuals or organizations are "repeat players" (Galanter, 1974). Moreover, many courts do not keep adequate records for long periods of time. Where records are kept, the record-keeping procedures vary. Historically, a number of minor courts, such as Justice of the Peace or Magistrate Courts, did not keep records. Over time, the court systems had changed through reorganization, new courts were established and others eliminated. There were also changes in the jurisdiction of many courts. Consequently, there are some questions of validity and reliability of longitudinal studies that deal with rates of litigation over time. In view of these precautions, let us turn briefly to some studies that have challenged the idea that the dispute-processing function of the courts has increased in recent years as a result of social and economic changes.

In modern industrialized societies such as the United States the use of courts as a forum for conflict resolution is on the increase as a result of societal developments toward increased complexity, heterogeneity, and the prevalence of impersonal and contractual relations. Although data are available to support this contention, some authors contend that social and economic developments do not necessarily lead to higher rates of litigation. For example, Lawrence M. Friedman (1973:338) argues that there is no evidence that nineteenth-century America witnessed proportionately less interpersonal litigation than mid-twentieth-century America, despite more cohesive kin and residential systems. Similarly, over time in Spain, the litigation rate "has remained remarkably constant and at a relatively low rate ... the process of economic change does not seem to have affected the rate of litigation ... " (Jose Toharia, quoted by Grossman and Sarat, 1978:59).

A comparable conclusion was reached by Vilhelm Aubert (1969) in his study of the Norwegian legal system. He notes that the demand for dispute resolution during the last 100 years has remained stable or has even decreased throughout a period characterized by vast social changes and great economic progress, while the demand for most other kinds of services has multiplied at a very rapid rate. Aubert concludes that "the pure legal model plays a modest part in actual instances of conflict resolution in Norway today" (1969:302). Similarly, Joel B. Grossman and Austin Sarat conclude that "industrialization is a useful predictor of levels of legal activity but not litigation rates; legal activity but not litigation rates appears to be greater in more industrialized areas" (1978:67). Their study was based on litigation rates in federal courts in the United States from 1902 to 1972.

In a study of the civil load of two trial courts in California between 1890 and 1970, Lawrence M. Friedman and Robert V. Percival sampled civil case files of the superior courts in two counties. They found that highly developed economic systems do not show growth in their litigation. On the contrary, rates rend to decline in the face of rapid economic growth. Although they are careful about the generalizability of their data, they conclude that "the dispute settlement function in the courts is declining" (1978:77). They attempt to explain the decline in litigation by suggesting that uncertainty—a prime breeder of litigation—has declined in the law and that rules are more "settled" now than in 1890. The routine administrative function has replaced the dispute settlement functions in these courts. It is plausible that the court itself—its style, its mode of operation—discourages its use for dispute settlement. In reanalyzing the data used by Friedman and Percival, Richard Lempert comes to the opposite conclusion: although " . . . the mix of judicial business has changed over the years" and there is "little reason to believe that courts today are functionally less important as dispute settlers than they were in 1890 . . . overall, I do not believe that we can conclude from the Friedman and Percival data that the dispute settlement function of courts . . . has diminished over time" (1978:133). Lempert further comments that the conclusion about the diminution in the dispute settlement activity of trial courts is overstated because Friedman and Percival neglect the mediative activity of trial judges and court personnel (1978:131). This neglect is attributable, in part, to the difficulty, if not the impossibility, of measuring activities of courts over time.

In addition to these studies contending that social and economic developments, with their concomitant increases in the complexity and impersonality in social relations, do not lead to higher rates of litigation, there is also a substantial amount of differentiation in the use of courts in disputes among modern industrialized nations. Henry W. Ehrmann (1976:83–84) points out that litigiousness, the propensity to settle disputes through the judicial process, is a cultural factor of some importance. Studies that have attempted to compare such attitudes cross-culturally have used as a measure the index of civil cases initiated per unit of population. Some of the findings of cross-cultural studies run counter to widely held assumptions about the litigiousness of various nations. In citing a study by Brian Able-Smith and Robert Stevens suggesting that "in England 'the law' plays a less important role than in almost any other western country," Ehrmann (1976:84) provides figures to show an extraordinarily high litigation rate for Great Britain, "higher than that for Western Germany, whose population is frequently described as being addicted to solving conflicts by lawsuits." The litigation rate per hundred thousand population in Great Britain was 3605 in 1969, and 2085 in West Germany during the same year. Enormous differences exist also in the rate of litigation between Denmark and other Scandinavian countries. Resort to the judiciary in disputes is about ten times higher in Denmark than in Norway, Sweden, or Finland. Ehrmann finds it difficult to explain the differences between these countries, especially in view of the fact that Norway has about three times as many attorneys per 100,000 population as Denmark.

It is also difficult to explain the relatively high litigation rates for Japan in view of the contention that the courts are still not a highly valued site for conflict resolution. The litigation rate for Japan was 1257 per hundred thousand population in 1970. Comparable rates for Scandinavian countries for the same year were 683 for Sweden, 493 for Finland, and 307 for Norway. In an often quoted article, "Dispute Resolution in Japan," Takeyoshi Kawashima (1969) discusses specific social attitudes toward disputes that are reflected in the judicial process. Traditionally, the Japanese prefer extrajudicial, informal means of settling a controversy. Litigation in Japan presupposes and admits the existence of a dispute and leads to a decision which makes clear who is right and wrong in accordance with legal standards. This is contrary to the attitude in favor of a compromise which does not assign a moral fault to disputants. This attitude is related to the nature of social groups in Japan, which are hierarchical in the sense that social status is differentiated in terms of deference and authority and the relations among individuals in social groups are intimate and diffuse. Legal intervention in disputes would upset the harmonious social relationships. As a result, Kawashima contends, the Japanese not only hesitate to resort to a lawsuit, but are quite ready to settle a dispute through informal means of dispute resolution, such as mediation and conciliation.

Moreover, in Japan the individual who asserts legal rights and insists on judicial intervention

> is thought to be "inflexible" and selfish. . . . Introduction of a lawyer into a business conference is thought to be an unfriendly act . . . equal to an explicit threat of litigation. . . . When acts such as drafting a contract or the bringing of a suit are unavoidable, the contract is made as short and flexible as possible, or the act of suit is viewed as deplorable, even by the plaintiff. . . . The law . . . goes directly contrary to the Japanese feeling that the relations (even business relations) should be based upon a warm subjective relationship which can solve every practical problem by mutual compromise and accommodation, regardless of formal rights and obligations. The most notable practical result of this attitude is a paucity of litigation in Japan (Strick, 1977:209).

Undoubtedly, it is difficult to reconcile the differences between these arguments and the relatively high rate of litigation in Japan. It is possible that the attitudes toward the law as a means of conflict resolution are changing, and that in urban areas there is a greater reliance on the judiciary to settle disputes. However, I have no data to support these contentions and the puzzle has yet to be solved empirically.

Complete and reliable data are lacking also for the United States. However, the differences that exist between two neighboring states, Massachusetts and New Hampshire, are startling. In the former state, the litigation rate for 1971 per hundred thousand was 1814, and in the latter for the same year 345. The differences point to the likely fact that the socioeconomic characteristics of a state or the particularities of its historic court system will have an effect on people's inclination to take their disputes to the courts (Ehrmann, 1976:84). But why the difference in litigation rates between two neighboring New England states should be that enormous remains unexplained.

Even within a state, differences in litigation rates exist among cities of comparable size and characteristics. In a study of four Wisconsin cities, Herbert Jacob (1969:92) suggests that "political culture may be a significant explanatory device for accounting for the differences in litigation rates." A traditional political culture is characterized by a relatively low level of bureaucratization in government and a reluctance to invoke governmental processes. There is a greater reliance on private dispute-settling processes in a traditional culture, than in a more modern one with a more highly bureaucratized government. In traditional political cultures people make greater efforts to settle disputes between themselves as neighbors and friends, and they have greater opportunities to settle conflicts within the confines of established private relationships. In a modern political culture, personal relationships are more strained, individuals deal with each other more on a contractual basis, and they have, as a result, less confidence in using private dispute-settling procedures. At the same time, they are more willing "to invoke the public processes of government for solving their problems, be they a neighborhood-development program needing a city council decision or a creditor-debtor conflict which requires the services of a court" (Jacob, 1969:92). Jacob provides some evidence for his contention that the use of courts will be greater in more modern political cultures. In his study on debtors, he found that the process of taking a debtor to court in order to collect a loan occurs more frequently in modern political cultures. But beyond this, available data do not permit one to make further generalizations.

Finally, in recent years the term "litigation explosion" has received considerable publicity. Is there really such an "explosion," or is it a myth? Richard A. Posner (1985) talks about the caseload "crisis" of federal courts. He notes that civil cases increased from 48,886 to 210,503, more than 330 percent, from 1960 to 1983 (1985:65). Appeals, as indicated earlier, increased 686 percent for the same time period. Even for a one-year period, from 1984 to 1985, there was a 7.3 percent increase in civil filings in federal courts (Administrative Office of the U.S. Courts, 1986:11). Federal litigation has increased much faster than the population, and this is a significant fact. But there are fifty state court systems in addition to federal courts where some 95 percent of cases are filed. State court cases number in the millions. Is there a similar litigation explosion in state courts as in federal courts? A recent study of court filings in twenty-five states by the National Center for State Courts contends that the litigation explosion is a myth and litigation rates have actually declined between 1981 and 1984, the most recent year with available data (Lauter, 1986:46). The states that have shown an increase are the ones with large population growth such as California, Florida, and Texas. A surprising finding was that even in small claims courts, where simplified legal procedures are supposed to ease barriers to filing suits, filings have been decreasing. But in spite of the decline, there were some 13.6 million suits filed in state courts in 1984.

But filing a case does not necessarily mean that it is judicially resolved. Most cases do not reach the trial stage. This is particularly true in accident and personal injury matters. Insurance companies tend to settle most claims out-of-court. In California, for example, less than 1 percent of filed accident claims go to trial; the rest are settled along the way (Friedman, 1985:18).

Thus, what is important are not the numbers, but the types of cases filed. In recent years, whole new areas of litigation opened up such as malpractice, products liability, and employment discrimination. Social security cases have burgeoned as the government has attempted to restrict benefits, and suits in which the government is seeking to collect money from individuals have grown 6600 percent since 1975 (Lauter, 1986:46). Disputants in traditional cases such as contract disputes, consumer matters, landlord-tenant quarrels, and real estate are slowly discovering alternative mechanisms of dispute resolution. There is a change in the types of cases as courts respond to social and legal developments over the years.

PREREQUISITES FOR THE USE OF COURTS
IN CONFLICT RESOLUTION

Courts provide a forum for the settlement of a variety of private and public disputes. The courts are considered a neutral and impartial place for dispute-processing. Other than criminal cases, legal disputes are processed in civil courts. Individuals and organizations who want to use the courts for dispute-processing must meet certain legal requirements. At the minimum, plaintiffs must be able to demonstrate justiciability and standing (Jacob, 1969:17–19).

Justiciability means that the conflict is viable to trial and courts. The court must be mandated to provide a remedy. In the United States, most disputes are justiciable in one court or another, although the jurisdiction of particular courts vary. For example, federal courts are not permitted to grant divorces, adoptions, or probate wills. Various state courts exist for these and most other cases excluded from the federal judiciary. The potential litigant must turn the grievance into a legal dispute, and must determine with or without the aid of an attorney whether the complaint is justiciable. Essentially, justiciability refers to real and substantial controversy which is appropriate for judicial determination, as differentiated from disputes or differences of a hypothetical or abstract character. Furthermore, in some instances, the courts may not be authorized to intervene in certain types of disputes. For example, the Wagner Act forbade court intervention in most labor disputes.

Standing is a more severe limitation to litigation than justiciability. Only individuals with a stake in the outcome may initiate litigation. For example, a taxpayer may not sue the government to prevent the expenditure of funds for an objectionable purpose because the ordinary taxpayer's stake in the expenditure is minimal (Jacob, 1969:18). Similarly, a mother-in-law cannot sue for a divorce: such proceedings must be initiated by the husband or wife.

Herbert Jacob (1969:18) points out that the limits to justiciability and standing are not social accidents. They are related to political compromises achieved over the distribution of powers and functions between various branches of the government and interest groups who had favorable access to one branch of government or another. The jurisdiction of courts in most cases is determined by legislation. The decision to present one kind of dispute or another in a court is a political one. For example, civil rights groups in the 1960s worked for the passage of laws which, among other things, gave federal courts broadened jurisdiction over disputes affecting civil rights, because they considered federal courts to be more favorably dis- posed to them than state courts or administrative agencies. The use of courts for collection purposes (in creditor-debtor disputes) or the settlement of complex public policy disputes are also the product of legislative compro- mises brought about by interest group pressures.

However, justiciability and standing are not the only limitations to the use of courts in disputes. There is also the old legal axiom *de minimus non curat lex:* The law will not concern itself with trifles. Trivial matters may not be litigated. For example, a court may refuse to hear a suit to recover a $1 overcharge even if the cause appears just (Lempert and Sanders, 1986:137). In addition, untold numbers of disputes arise over which the courts have clear jurisdiction and someone has standing to sue. But using the court is dependent on a number of considerations. These considerations are su- perimposed on the legal barriers to litigation.

Resort to court services in disputes is voluntary for the plaintiffs; for defendants, participation in a legal dispute is involuntary. The plaintiffs approach the courts with different expectations and often through differ- ent circumstances than do defendants. Jacob notes: "Whereas the initiation of court action may promise relief to the plaintiff, it threatens deprivation for the defendant. Since the plaintiff initiates court action he can exert a certain degree of control over it, but the action often descends without warning upon defendants" (1969:19).

Economic resources for both plaintiffs and defendants are important in their decision to pursue a suit through trial and appeal. With the ex- ception of magistrate courts, and individuals who qualify for legal aid ser- vices, plaintiffs are unlikely to use the courts unless they have sufficient funds to hire an attorney and bear the costs of litigation. The litigant must bear court fees for filing cases, for calling witnesses, and for compensating the jury. Disputants must also be able to afford the costs of delay, which occur when disputes are submitted to the courts. For example, automobile accident cases involving large sums of money do not reach the court dock- ets for several years in many large American cities. In the interim, the plain- tiff has expenses. Often the cost of waiting must be calculated against the benefits of a quick settlement for only part of the claim. Obviously, for many people economic resources play an important role in the use of court services and may be decisive in out-of-court settlements.

Before initiating a law suit, individuals must recognize the relevance of court services to their problems. Jacob (1969:20) notes that the use of the judiciary varies with education, for better educated individuals are more likely to differentiate between the courts and other agencies and to be aware of their various services. Perception of the courts also varies with other factors, such as integration into a social group in which court usage has previously occurred or where it is relatively prevalent. Says Jacob: "Thus it may be that certain ethnic groups of communities are more litigious than others. Members of such groups are more likely to perceive court action as relevant to their problems and consequently they become more frequent consumers of court services" (1969:20).

Socioeconomic status is also related to the use of the judiciary in disputes. Those who cannot afford a lawyer and the necessary court fees are less likely to litigate than those who have sufficient funds. Moreover, social status is related to the kind of court services that are used. In general, the poor are more likely to be defendants and recipients of court-ordered sanctions. Middle-class litigants are less likely to be subjected to court sanctions and more likely to benefit from the use of court services in their own behalf from the legitimation of their private agreements or from out of court negotiations.

A TYPOLOGY OF LITIGANTS

As I noted in Chapter Three, the use of courts varies also by the types of litigants. Marc Galanter advances a typology of litigants by the frequency of the utilization of courts. Those who have only occasional recourse to the courts are called one-shotters, and those who are engaged in many similar litigations over time are designated as repeat players. Illustrations for the former would include the wife in a divorce case or the auto injury claimant. The latter is exemplified by insurance or finance companies. Based on this typology, Galanter proposes a taxonomy of litigation by the configuration of parties. He comes up with four types of litigation—one-shotter versus one-shotter, repeat player versus one-shotter, one-shotter versus repeat player, and repeat player versus repeat player.

The largest number of cases involving disputes between one-shotters are divorces and insanity commitments. Disputes between one-shotters are "often between parties who have some intimate tie with one another, fighting over some unsharable good, often with overtones of 'spite' and 'irrationality' " (Galanter, 1974:108). The courts are used when an ongoing relationship is ruptured and the law is invoked ad hoc and instrumentally by the parties. When such disputes take place between neighbors or business partners, there may be a strong interest in vindication, and the court decisions are seldom appealed.

The second type of litigation, repeat players versus one-shotters, is exemplified by suits initiated by finance companies against debtors, landlords against tenants, or the IRS against taxpayers. Except for personal injury cases, insanity hearings, and divorces, the great bulk of litigation is found in disputes between repeat players and one-shotters. Here, the law is used for routine processing of claims by parties for whom the making of such claims is a regular business activity. In many instances, courts authorize repeat players to borrow the government's power for their private purposes. Repeat players may use that power to achieve many objectives, such as to collect debts, oust tenants, or prohibit some harmful activity. In such a case, the plaintiff comes to court with a grievance. If the court considers the complaint a legitimate one, it issues a judgment or an injunction. The judgment authorizes the plaintiff to make use of the government's police power to effectuate it. Thus, a real estate agent may, for example, call on the sheriff to oust a tenant, to reclaim some property, to sell property belonging to a defendant, or to seize the defendant's wages or property. When the court issues an injunction on behalf of the plaintiff, it orders the defendant not to engage in the activity about which the plaintiff complained. If the defendant persists, he or she may be fined or imprisoned.

The third combination of litigants involves one-shotters versus repeat players. Illustrations of this would include tenant versus landlord, injury victim versus insurance company, student versus university, defamed versus publisher, and client versus welfare agency. Outside of the personal injury area, litigation in this combination is not routine. It usually represents the attempt of some one-shotters to invoke outside help to create leverage on an organization with which the individual has a dispute.

The fourth type of litigation is repeat players versus repeat players. Examples of this would include litigation between union and management, purchaser and supplier, regulatory agency and firms of regulated industry, or church/state litigations focusing on value differences (who is right) rather than interest conflicts (who gets what). With these types of litigation in the background, let us now turn to certain types of conflict situations between individuals, between individuals and organizations, and between organizations where one of the disputants resorts to the judiciary in an attempt to resolve the conflict.

DISPUTES BETWEEN INDIVIDUALS

Although most controversies between individuals never come to the attention of courts, the handling of interpersonal differences is a traditional function of courts. Most individual disputes involve one-shotters. For those individuals whose disagreements come before a court, the experience is likely to be the most intimate they will have had with the government, and the manner in which the dispute is handled is likely to have a marked affect on their attitudes toward the government. Judicial resolution of individual disputes also affects the distribution of values. Some people gain, others lose, some individuals are honored, others are stigmatized, and as with all types of disputes, a court decision seldom resolves the underlying conditions for the conflict.

Individual disputes include private litigation as opposed to organizations, criminal defendants, or state agencies. These disputes generally deal with the distribution of economic resources and a variety of noneconomic problems. Economic disputes include various claims associated with contests over wills, trusts, estates, landlord-tenant controversies, and disputes over property, titles, and sales. The major distinction between economic and noneconomic individual disputes is that the former directly involve a conflict over the control of economic resources, whereas the latter, while often involving money, do not necessarily stem from economic conflicts.

Noneconomic conflicts would include allegations of slander and libel, cus-tody cases, divorce proceedings, insanity commitments, and malpractice suits.

Courts often make an effort to encourage disputants to settle their differences by agreement, since this is a less costly way to reestablish an equilibrium which any conflict is likely to disturb. Settlements may even be encouraged after the disputants have brought their complaint to a court. Such efforts may be initiated by the judge in pretrial hearings or in open court. The success of such efforts depends to a great extent on the skills of the judge and on the nature of the disputes. When the parties are unable or unwilling to resolve their disputes by agreement, and when they have decided against letting matters rest, formal adjudication must take over and will normally end in a decision which claims to be binding on the parties (Ehrmann, 1976:83).

In the adjudication of individual disputes, one party wins and the other loses. Robert B. Seidman (1978:213–214) points out that in situations in which parties want to, or must, cooperate after the dispute, both must leave the settlement procedures without too great a sense of grievance. If, however, there are opportunities for avoidance (that is, parties need not live or work together), then the disputants may continue their antagonism. Compromises tend to resolve the disputes in the sense that they reduce any continuing antagonism. Win or lose situations, however, will not ameliorate antagonism.

Therefore, disputants who wish to maintain an ongoing relationship will generally engage in compromise settlements. Businesspersons do not sue customers whose trade they want to keep. Married couples who want to stay together do not sue each other; instead, they consult marriage coun-selors who look for compromises.

The structure of social relationships thus plays a role in the decision as to whether to take a dispute to court. When continuing relations are important to the individuals involved in the dispute, they are generally more predisposed to resolve their differences through nonlegal means. In a now classic paper, Stewart Macaulay describes the avoidance of the law as a way of building and maintaining good business relations. Businesspersons pre-fer not to use contracts in their dealings with other businesspersons. Says Macaulay: "Disputes are frequently settled without reference to the contract or potential or actual legal sanctions. There is a hesitancy to speak of legal rights or to threaten to sue in these negotiations" (1969:200). Similar sen-timents prevail in other countries. For example, "For a Korean, it is not decent or 'nice' to insist on one's legal right. When a person hauls another person into court, he is in fact declaring war on him. . . . He has lined him-self up on the side of the bureaucrats to use the power of the state to op-press his fellow man. Thus, a Korean cannot think of law as anything other than oppressive. . . . This reluctance to maintain one's legal right is partic-ularly pronounced in the area of property" (Hahm, quoted by Friedman and Macauley, 1977:1026).

How the either/or court decision would militate against continuing relations is further illustrated by Jane Fishburne Collier in her work on the Zinacanteco Indians of Southern Mexico. She points out that Indians who wish to preserve a valued relationship will seek a settlement procedure that promotes reconciliation.

> Cases end when an appropriate settlement has been found. In Zinacanteco eyes, an ideal settlement involves reconciliation: both sides agree to forget their differences and drink together, or the guilty person begs pardon and is forgiven through acceptance of a bottle of rum. Settlements often involve agreements to pay money or repair damages, though such agreements are seen as a part of the reconciliation process. A case that ends without reconciliation and drinking is considered less than satisfactory (Collier, 1973:38).

However, continuing relationships are but part of a broader issue of whether to litigate in individual disputes. Nader and Todd point out: "It is not enough to state that because litigants wish to continue their relation they will seek negotiated or mediated settlement with compromise outcomes" (1978:17). In some instances, ties within the family itself may give rise to disputes over inheritance among brothers or sisters, or arguments between males and females over the males' attempts to control the behavior of their unmarried sisters. At the same time, social relations may act not as an impetus to conflict but as a constraint on escalation. For example, Barbara B. Yngvesson (1978:59), in her study of a small Scandinavian fishing village, notes that "disputes are focused less on *acts* than on *people. What was done* is less important than *who did it.* An act considered normal when done by a kinsman or fellow community member may generate an entirely different response when done by an 'outsider.' "

Thus, it is no longer sufficient to generalize that a preference for continuing relations will turn disputants to some kind of compromise or reconciliation mechanism rather than to litigation. In a variety of instances, disputants resort to legal rather than nonlegal ways, with the full awareness of the risks involved in their attempts to settle their disputes.

There is practically an unlimited variety of economic and noneconomic disputes that take place between individuals and end up before a judge for decision. Affluent litigants may want possession of boats, silverware, or family dogs. Married couples want a divorce, and unmarried ones argue over property rights. A client may sue his or her attorney for legal malpractice, and a patient may institute charges against a physician for medical malpractice. For example, a woman in New York sued her physician for an off-centered belly button stemming from an unsuccessful plastic surgery operation. (A jury awarded her $854,000 for damages incurred by having her belly button two inches off center.) A clergyman is charged with clerical malpractice and the plaintiff alleges that his advice to remain married to her husband caused her "severe trauma, insomnia, and a chronic lower-back problem (Saturday Review, 1979:7). (As a result of this suit, an insurance company began to offer malpractice coverage for the clergy; for about $20 a year, $300,000 of protection will be provided. Today, several insurance companies offer such protection, and in 1986, there were some 2000 cases involving the clergy and more than $100 million has been awarded to those suing them (*The New York Times*, 1986b:1F). A Colorado man is suing his parents for $350,000, charging that they gave him inhumane and inadequate care as a child, making it impossible for him to fit into society as an adult. A California man, upset at being stood up on a date, unsuccessfully sued his would-be companion for $38 to compensate him for sprucing up and driving forty miles for nothing. Such cases may strike many people as frivolous and amusing. They may be, but at the same time they are illustrative of the spectrum of individual disputes that end up in court.

Data on patterns of outcomes in individual disputes are scarce. In adjudication, courts are supposed to decide disputes by reference to the facts of who did what to whom, and by identifying, interpreting, and applying appropriate legal norms. Sheldon Goldman and Austin Sarat (1978:526) suggest that this requires that judges remain neutral with regard to both the issues of the case and its result. They use the concept "result impartiality" in referring to the extent to which cases are decided independently of the personal attributes of the parties involved. Impartiality is displayed when both parties in a dispute are given the same opportunities and are shown the same considerations. It requires that the judge should not be influenced by an interest in the outcome or by attitudes toward the disputants and the particular situations in which they are involved.

To study the question of impartiality, it is necessary to examine a number of decisions involving similar situations to discover whether over time different kinds of disputants are equally likely to gain favorable results. For impartial results, the pattern of decision should be random and should not consistently favor one type of litigant over another. For example, if courts in custody cases at times rule for the mother and at other times for the father, it may be concluded that they show equal regard for both sexes. However, if they consistently favor mothers over fathers, regardless of the facts or the applicable law, then the results would not be impartial.

Goldman and Sarat point out, however, that the difficulty with this way of determining result impartiality is that it does not take into account other factors responsible for variation from the standard of randomness that go beyond the attitudes and values of the judges. A most obvious factor is that, even if courts are impartial in their procedures, they may still produce biased results if the laws that they apply favor one type of litigant. This is particularly true in custody cases, since most state divorce laws still favor the mother.

Time and resources also influence result impartiality. Time favors disputants who are better-organized and who have more expendable resources. Goldman and Sarat note:

Delay favors such parties in three ways. First, by complicating the task of challenging ongoing activities, delay advantages parties who derive benefits from the neglect of rules that favor their adversaries. Second, delay tends to protect the 'possessor,' that is, those who have resources that might be endangered in the course of litigation. Third, delay means that courts cannot efficiently protect all of the rights that are formally recognized by law (1978:527).

The outcome of court decisions may also be influenced by the type of attorney that disputants are able to retain. Availability of resources to disputants directly affects the quality of legal talent they can hire. Access to a skillful attorney increases the likelihood of a favorable court decision, since courts assume that in individual disputes both parties can marshal the resources and legal skills needed to present a case effectively.

To an extent, these considerations can be useful in attempts to predict outcomes of individual disputes. In some instances, however, both parties may be able to afford delays and the services of highly trained attorneys, and to have convincing legal arguments on their side. In such instances, the determination of the outcome of the case will have to wait until the judge hands down the verdict.

DISPUTES BETWEEN INDIVIDUALS AND ORGANIZATIONS

In this section I will discuss disputes between individuals and organizations. The first part of the section will consider individuals as plaintiffs and organizations as defendants. The second part will deal with legal disputes initiated by organizations against individuals. I will use the term "organization" to cover a broad range of social groups that have been deliberately and consciously constructed in order to achieve certain specific goals—hospitals, credit agencies, universities, General Motors, regulatory agencies, the American Medical Association, public interest law firms, and so forth.

Disputes between individuals and organizations may take place over a variety of issues, many of which may be included in four general categories: (1) disputes over property and money (economic disputes); (2) claims for damages and restitution; (3) issues of civil rights; and (4) disputes concerning organizational actions, procedures, and policy. These broad categories of disputes are, of course, not mutually exclusive.

Economic disputes are exemplified by the following types of actions: suits for unpaid rent; eviction; claims for unpaid loans and installment purchases; foreclosures and repossessions, and suits on contracts and insurance policies.

Claims of damages and restitution most frequently involve automobile accidents and lawsuits against insurance companies. However, other forms of injury, for example, airplane accidents, faulty appliances, medical and academic malpractices, also give rise to claims. Damage suits may also be initiated to compensate for losses sustained from the failure to honor a contract or to perform a service properly. Slander and libel actions also fall within this category. Although money may change hands as a result of these actions, the actions themselves seek compensation for alleged improper behavior and its consequences. It should be noted that economic disputes and claims for damages and restitution also occur in individual disputes as well as in disputes between individuals and organizations.

Civil rights disputes include claims of discrimination by race, sex, or national origin in matters of employment, hiring, promotion, retention, pay, housing, and admission policies. Other issues that may lead to civil rights disputes would include other discriminatory practices, such as the exclusion of handicapped people and setting arbitrary age or educational limits.

The final category of disputes includes challenges to a variety of actions, procedures, and policies of organizations. Decisions of zoning boards or tax assessors may be challenged as a violation of statutes or of administrative procedures. Plaintiffs may seek a reversal of particular decisions, or a voiding of statutes or injunctions prohibiting the continued application of particular policies. In organizations that distribute benefits, such as the program of Aid to Families with Dependent Children (AFDC), food stamps, aid to the disabled, and Medicaid, there are disputes about the appropriate form of benefits, conflicting and inconsistent eligibility rules on employment and training incentives, and disputes about how administrators should deal with beneficiaries. In business organizations, disputes over policies governing warranties, replacement of defective products, or unethical collection practices also come to courts.

Usually, organizations are plaintiffs in the first category of disputes and defendants in the other three. In general, as Marc Galanter (1978:529) concludes, organizations are more successful as both plaintiffs and defendants than are individuals. They enjoy greater success against individual antagonists than against other organizations: individuals fare less well contending against organizations than against other individuals. Galanter's conclusion is reinforced by Donald Black's (1976:92) proposition that "[l]aw is greater in a direction toward less organization than toward more organization." Black notes that half of the plaintiffs in civil litigation in the United States are organizations, while two-thirds of the defendants are individuals, and "organizations are uniformly more successful than individuals" (Wanner, quoted by Black, 1976:93). In small claims courts as well, more organizations sue individuals than the other way around. In these instances, the plaintiffs nearly always win. For example, David Caplovitz (1974:222) found that legal actions against debtors in his sample of 1331 cases, drawn from four cities, resulted in creditor victories in all but 3 percent of the cases. Moreover, if an organization loses its case against an individual, it is more likely to appeal, and, if it does, it is more likely to win a reversal (Black, 1976:93).

Black also points out that "[a]lthough any group is more likely to bring a lawsuit against an individual than vice versa, then, the likelihood of a lawsuit by a group increases with its organization. On the other hand, the likelihood of a lawsuit by an individual against a group decreases with the organization of the group" (1976:93). In other words, a large organization such as the Internal Revenue Service is more likely to sue an individual than in reverse. Organization, as Black notes, provides an immunity from law and "an offense committed by an organization or its representatives is less serious than an offense by an individual on his own, and the more organized the organization, the less serious it is" (Black, 1976:94).

Although organizations have a greater chance of winning and a higher frequency of initiating lawsuits, it does not mean that individuals do not sue organizations. On the contrary, individuals are taking their disputes with organizations to courts at an unprecedented rate. Workers increasingly seek compensation in courts for health damages, allegedly suffered in hazardous working environments. There is a rapid growth of suits by consumers claiming harm from defective products or harm suffered while on company premises. For the remainder of this section, I shall consider disputes initiated by individuals and organizations separately. For the former, I shall illustrate the use of law as a method of conflict resolution in academe, and for the latter, I shall discuss the use of courts as collection agencies in the field of consumer credit.

Law as a Method of Conflict Resolution in Academe

As William A. Kaplin (1978:1) observes, "With increasing frequency, disputes that arise on campuses across America end not on campus but in court." Both faculty members and students appear more often in court than before as litigants. Faculty- and student-initiated lawsuits against the university may be considered in the context of faculty-administration, student-faculty, and student-administration relations.

The *faculty-administration* relationship in postsecondary institutions is defined by an increasingly complex web of legal principles and authorities. The essence of this relationship is contract law, but "that core is encircled by expanding layers of labor relations law, employment discrimination law, and, in public institutions, constitutional law and public employment statutes and regulations" (Kaplin, 1978:87). The growth in the number and variety of laws and regulations governing faculty-administration relations provides a fertile ground for grievances, and coincides with an increase in the number of lawsuits stemming from that relationship.

Many legal disputes center on the meaning and interpretation of the faculty-institution contract. Depending on the institution, a contract may vary from a basic notice of appointment to a complex collective bargaining agreement negotiated under federal or state labor laws. In some instances, the formal document does not encompass all the terms of the contract, and other terms are included through "incorporation by reference," that is, by referring to other documents such as the faculty handbook or even to past custom and usage at an institution. In the context of contract interpretation, legal disputes arise most often in terms of contract termination and due notice for such termination.

A number of suits instituted by faculty members to redress their grievances against university administrations have focused on faculty-personnel decisions, such as appointment, retention, promotion, and tenure policies, and pecuniary matters affecting women and minority groups. As a result of civil rights legislation, hiring procedures must follow clearly established affirmative action guidelines. Many traditional practices of departments and universities are being questioned, such as the use of "the old boy network" or other selection processes not in compliance with these guidelines. Similarly, termination procedures must also follow specific guidelines and deadlines, and in recent years faculty members have increasingly resorted to lawsuits on the grounds of procedural matters (Vago and Marske, 1980).

Other potentially conflict-laden situations in academe arise from *student-faculty* relations. Students are increasingly considering themselves as buyers of education, treating education like other consumer items and, concomitantly, there is a growing emphasis on the proper return for their educational dollars. Ladd and Lipset note: "In fact, the students are the 'consumers,' the buyers, the patrons of a product sold by the faculty through a middle-man, the university system. In economic class terms, the relationship of student to teacher is that of buyer to seller, or of client to professional. In this context, the buyer or client seeks to get the most for his money at the lowest possible price" (1973:93).

Since students are purchasers of education, they expect "delivery" of a product. In this context, the question of academic malpractice becomes important. Although the legal definition of academic malpractice is yet to be codified, it is generally considered as improper, injurious, or negligent instruction, and/or action that has a "negative effect" on the student's academic standing, professional licensing, or employment (Vago, 1979:39). Although the concept of academic malpractice is rather amorphous, several patterns have emerged. A faculty member may be charged with malpractice by a student who perceives a particular course as "worthless," or by a student who contends that he or she did not obtain any "relevant" information, or that for some reason it did not fit into the student's general educational outlook, requirement, or area of concentration. In such instances, individual professors are charged, and the object of the lawsuit is usually the recovery of tuition monies, and occasionally an intent to seek punitive damages, since the legal doctrine of *respondeat superior* (that is, the sins of the employee are imputed to be those of the employer) is usually invoked.

Several cases have been also litigated in which students have claimed contract damages for an institution's failure to provide bargained-for services. In a most extraordinary case, for example, the defendant-student has alleged in a counterclaim that Columbia University

> ... had represented that it would teach the defendant wisdom, truth, character, enlightenment, understanding, justice, liberty, honesty, courage, beauty, and similar virtues and qualities; that it would develop the whole man, maturity, well-roundedness, objective thinking and the like; and that because it failed to do so it was guilty of misrepresentation, to the defendant's pecuniary damage (Vago, 1979:41).

In this case, the trial court granted the university's motion for summary judgment which was sustained on appeal.

Disputes resulting from a failure of a student to pass an internal examination may also culminate in attempts to involve the courts. In such a situation, a student may question the expertise and competency of professors to evaluate examinations, or a department may be accused of following improper procedures during examinations. Questions of expertise and competency usually arise in the area of alleged academic overspecialization (that is, is someone qualified to evaluate an examination in social psychology when his or her professed specialty is the sociology of law?). Issues of improper procedures often arise in the context of due process involving the department's or the university's failure to list specific guidelines for examination procedures, or not living up to those guidelines, or not providing clearly written guidelines and appeal procedures. But when it comes to strictly academic decisions made by faculty members about a student's academic career, the right of judges to overturn such decisions is limited. According to a 1985 Supreme Court ruling, "When judges are asked to review the substance of a genuinely academic decision . . . they should show great respect for the faculty's professional judgment" and courts are not "suited to evaluate the substance of the multitude of academic decisions that are made daily by faculty members" (Palmer, 1985:33).

The student's failure to pass a professional examination is another ground for lawsuits. Here the charge is usually that a given department "failed" to properly prepare the student to successfully take an external examination, such as a bar examination, and thus provided a "defective product." In a recent case, a court ruled against a graduate of the Southern University Law School who claimed the university was responsible for his failure to pass—on three different occasions—the state bar examination. The court held that it was against Louisiana law to sue a state agency and that the university is such an agency; the court also noted that a properly drafted contract suit may have stated a "remediable" course of action (Vago, 1979:41).

Student-administration relations provide a third area for potential conflict in academe. Increasingly, suspension and dismissal procedures, the rights of students to organize, alleged censorship activities over student publications, and sex discrimination are being challenged by students in courts.

Although institutions of higher learning have the right to dismiss, suspend, or otherwise sanction students for misconduct or academic deficiency, this right is determined by a body of procedural requirements which must be observed in such actions. Under the due process clause, students are entitled to a hearing and notice prior to disciplinary action. In general, recent court rulings indicate a judicial trend toward increased protection of student rights, in both public and private institutions, in suspension and dismissal cases (Kaplin, 1978:250).

First-amendment rights have been increasingly cited in student-administration disputes. Under the first amendment, students have a legal right to organize and to use appropriate campus facilities. In some instances, however, postsecondary institutions retain the authority to revoke or withhold recognition, and to regulate the organizational use of campus facilities. When a mutually acceptable and satisfactory balance between the organization's rights and the institution's authority cannot be attained, the organizing students may turn to the courts to settle their dispute with the administration as has been the case, for example, with various gay rights organizations.

The first-amendment principles also apply to student publications. The chief concern here is censorship and administrative control over publications. In one case, for example, financial support for the campus newspaper was terminated on the grounds that the paper printed prosegregation articles and that it urged the maintenance of an all black university. The court of appeals held that the administration's action violated the student staff's first amendment rights. Other currently controversial issues include questions of obscenity and libel in the context of student publications (Vago and Marske, 1980).

Lawsuits against university administrations on the basis of alleged sex discrimination, particularly in athletics, are also on the increase (Kaplin, 1978:283–290). These involve, for example, the use of university sports facilities and locker rooms, and the ability to participate in university team sports.

The growing frequency and diversity of lawsuits as a method of conflict resolution in academe has important implications for contemporary higher education. Postsecondary institutions are the parties that are most adversely affected by successful litigation. The economic and social costs of such litigations can be enormous. The need for universities to develop and maintain effective mechanisms of internal conflict management is obvious. The following section will consider disputes initiated by organizations against individuals in the domain of consumer credit.

The Courts as Collection Agencies

Disputes between individuals and organizations, where organizations are the plaintiffs, most often are triggered by disagreements over property and money. Such disputes are most prevalent in the creditor-debtor relationship, where the creditor is usually an organization such as a finance and loan company, car dealership, department store, or hospital. In such situations, there is a gross power disparity between the debtor and the organization, a relative debtor ignorance concerning the technical aspects of the product, and the stakes are small in dollars but large in their impact on the debtor (Goldberg, et al., 1985:389).

Kagan comments: "If the extension of credit is the lifeblood of a dynamic commercial society, the forcible collection of unpaid debts is its backbone" (1984:324). When a debtor defaults on his or her contractual obligation to make payments, the standard legal remedy is for the creditor to sue in civil court. The purpose is to establish the legality of the debt and its amount. Of course, creditors "hope to collect the debt by invoking the power of the court, but even if they do not collect, a judgment against the debtor is still of value for income tax purposes. Bad debts are worth 50 cents in deductions on every tax dollar" (Caplovitz, 1974:191).

If the creditor is successful in the suit, he or she obtains a judgment against the debtor. Once obtained, there are a variety of legal remedies available for collecting the judgment, including garnishment, liens, and the forced sale of the debtor's property. As I noted earlier, a garnishment is a court order directing someone who owes or possesses money due to the debtor (such as an employer) to pay all or some of that money to the court, which then turns it over to the creditor (Vago, 1968; 1971). A lien establishes a creditor's claim on property (such as a house or car). A forced sale involves seizure and sale at an auction of the debtor's property. The proceeds then are turned over to the creditor to satisfy the judgment.

Prior to court action, a creditor may resort to a number of social pressures and sanctions of varying severity ranging on a continuum from impersonal routine "reminders" and dunning letters or telephone appeals to get the debtor "in" to make some kind of "arrangement" with him and to remind or threaten him or her, to personal visits to the debtor's home in an attempt to elicit payments or at least promises. At times, creditors resort to unusual extrajudicial methods of collection. For example, a London firm is using a rather unconventional method of extracting money from debtors—smell: "Smelly Tramps, Ltd. is just what it sounds: a motley crew of ragged, foul-smelling tramps, who specialize in dunning particularly evasive debtors. The tramps are really otherwise respectable chaps, dressed in disgusting clothes and treated with a special stomach churning chemical" (The Economist, 1979:104). Their technique is simply to sit around the victim's office or home until he or she signs a check.

When such dunning efforts fail and creditors have exhausted nonlitigation alternatives, they are likely to sue. A characteristic of most civil suits for debt is that the plaintiff usually wins by default. Most defendants are not represented by counsel. In fact, many of them are not present when their cases are heard. Their absence is treated as an admission of the validity of the claim and a default judgment is entered against them. Such judgments are rendered in over 90 percent of consumer cases (Caplovitz, 1974:220–221).

There are a number of reasons why defendants fail to respond to summons and to appear in court. Some recognize the validity of the creditor's claim and see no point in attempting to contest it or cannot afford an attorney to do so (Kagan, 1984). Others may simply find it impossible to leave work (with consequent loss of pay), travel to court, and spend most of the day waiting for their cases to be called. The fact that most courts are open from 9 A.M. to 5 P.M., hours when most debtors are at work, further contributes to default judgments. At times, the wording of summons is so complicated and obtuse that many debtors simply cannot grasp what is at stake, or that they must appear if they are to avoid a default judgment. Others simply do not know that they are being sued. Instead of properly serving the summons, process servers in some areas (because of the inability to locate debtors or the fear of going into certain neighborhoods) destroy it and claim it has been served. Although accurate statistics on the frequency of such "sewer service" do not exist, it is evidently commonplace in many cities (Caplovitz, 1974:193–195). These individuals learn the hard way about suits against them—when a garnishment or eviction notice is served.

Although I have focused on suits for debts, there are a number of other important types of actions initiated by organizations against individuals. Real estate companies regularly initiate legal action in the form of evictions against unknown thousands of tenants. The Internal Revenue Service continuously files suits against individuals (and at times organizations) for back taxes or for tax evasion. Radio and television stations regularly use the courts to settle disputes with former announcers or disc jockeys who have decided to join competing stations, contrary to the desires of their former employers. In the final section, I shall consider disputes between organizations.

DISPUTES BETWEEN ORGANIZATIONS

There are two general types of organizational conflicts: (1) conflict between groups within the organization; and (2) conflict between organizations. For example, intraorganizational conflict within a university would include disputes between the faculty and administration over issues of collective bargaining, unionization, faculty freedom, and staff reduction based on alleged financial exigencies. Interorganizational conflict, for example, would include disputes between the university and the community over matters of zoning, land use, or between the university and the federal government concerning issues of compliance with federal regulations in the context of occupational safety, labor management, antitrust, and civil rights.

Although the emphasis in this section is on interorganizational disputes, the generalizations that will be made are, of course, applicable to intraorganizational disputes. Such disputes may arise between private firms, between private firms and government, between government agencies, and between public interest groups and private firms or government, or both. After a brief consideration of the various types of interorganizational disputes, I will examine in greater depth the activities of public interest law firms in environmental disputes.

Disputes between organizations cover a wide spectrum of participants and controversies. Businesspersons may take their disagreements to court over contract interpretation, trademarks, or alleged patent infringements. The federal government is involved as a plaintiff in suits to acquire land needed for federal projects (highways, dams, parks, buildings) which the acquiring agency is unable to purchase through negotiation, in actions to enforce compliance by private companies with contracts with federal agencies, and in suits brought under the antitrust statutes. Disputes between the government and private firms arise over matters of licensing and regulation, labor relations, Sunday closing laws, and governmental contracts. The government is often the defendant in cases involving zoning and land use, location of public housing projects, and in tax reassessment.

In recent decades, complex public policy disputes and regulatory disputes stemming from the government's regulation of the economic and social systems have become more pronounced. The regulation of economic activities has become pervasive and it involves major decisions about the distribution of goods and services.

Social policy disputes develop in situations when the government pursues broad national objectives that may involve or impinge upon many interests and groups, such as racial equality and economic opportunity, environmental protection, income security, and public health and safety.

Examples of agencies with such objectives are the Occupational Safety and Health Administration, the Equal Employment Opportunity Commission, and the Environmental Protection Agency. In fact, all large-scale social welfare programs—cash transfers, food stamps, housing, health, and education—generate similar complex public policy disputes (Ford Foundation, 1978:3).

Regulatory disputes frequently involve difficult technical questions, while social policy disputes raise difficult political and value questions. In both types of disputes, information about important variables is often incomplete or inaccurate, effects of alternative choices are hard to ascertain, and often there are no easy answers to cost/benefit questions or to questions of trade-offs among various interests. The various regulatory agencies discussed in Chapter Three, in addition to major policy issues, also process large numbers of routine disputes. For example, the Civil Aeronautics Board (CAB), in addition to allocating airlines routes (large complex disputes), in any given year will also handle thousands of passenger and shipper complaints, tariff applications, and referrals. The Securities and Exchange Commission (SEC), in addition to a number of formal hearings annually, also rules on thousands of registration statements. In 1976, the Equal Employment Opportunities Commission (EEOC) received 97,674 complaints, resolved 82,537 and had a backlog of 122,000 cases (Ford Foundation, 1978:4).

In many instances, the formal quasi-adjudicative procedures used by regulatory agencies are often ill suited to resolving large and complex disputes. Delays in settling disputes are frequent, and the situation is further compounded by the fact that some agencies traditionally engaged in economic regulations are now being asked to consider environmental claims as well. The regulatory process, in a sense, encourages conflict, rather than acts to reconcile opposing interests. When agencies grant licenses, set rates, or determine the safety of drugs, they often allow the parties to the proceedings to have a full adversary hearing with impartial decision-makers, formal records, and rights of cross-examination and appeal. This leads the parties to approach the agency as if they were in a lawsuit.

Frequently, agency rulings, instead of settling an issue, result in subsequent disputes. For example, the Federal Trade Commission (FTC) decided that the American Medical Association illegally restrained competition among its physician-members by restricting their advertising and solicitation of patients. The Commission ordered the AMA to stop imposing the restriction. The AMA is likely to appeal this unfavorable ruling, although the FTC permitted the AMA to publish reasonable ethical guidelines to discourage deceptive advertising by physicians (*St. Louis Post-Dispatch*, 1979:1).

Public Interest Law Firms in Environmental Disputes

Since the mid-1960s, the types of activities associated with Ralph Nader and his consumer organizations, with the Sierra Club and its environmental programs, and with a new institutional form embodied in law firms that characterize their activities as partly or wholly "public interest" law have proliferated. *Public interest law* is the term frequently used to describe the activities of the foundation-supported law firms which represent environmentalists, consumer and like groups, as well as test-case litigation in civil rights and poverty controversies. It is generally oriented towards causes and interests of groups, classes, or organizations, rather than individuals (Handler, 1976:99). Although public interest law firms engage in activities such as lobbying, reporting, public relations, counseling, and the like, litigation is by far their most important activity. Education, employment discrimination, and consumer and environmental problems are the four areas that account for the largest proportion of their activities.

Educational controversies include school financing, legal rights of students and parents, bilingual education, special education, and the political activity of teachers. Employment discrimination activities consist of class action suits against private and public discriminators, and the government agencies responsible for enforcing fair employment laws. A typical lawsuit seeks to establish affirmative action plans for minorities or women in hiring and promotion. Consumer matters include attacks on import restrictions to lower costs to the consumer and to improve quality, product safety, and guarantee and warranty practices.

Environmental defense has been a major area for public interest law firms, and several of the largest foundation-supported firms, such as the Natural Resources Defense Council and the Environmental Defense Fund, concentrate exclusively in this area, while other firms, such as the Center for Law and Social Policy, devote substantial resources to this type of work (Trubek, 1978:151). Public interest lawyers have been active in a variety of environmental domains. They have challenged dams and other water resources projects, raised questions about nuclear power plants, attacked the pricing policies of electric utilities, stopped the use of dangerous pesticides, and sought to improve enforcement of such major environmental statutes as the National Environmental Policy Act, the Clear Air Act, and the Federal Water Pollution Control Act. Accounts of environmental policy disputes regularly fill the daily press. Disputes include such questions as: "Shall we expand or contract our programs for flood control and stream channelization? Should we relax or tighten the rules governing air pollution? Should we build a dam on a scenic stream, or allow nuclear energy plants to damage aquatic life in the natural bodies of water they use for cooling?" (Trubek, 1978:152).

Essentially, environmental disputes typically fall into two broad categories—enforcement and permitting cases. Enforcement disputes come about when a public interest group raises questions about a party's compliance with certain state or federal law setting specific environmental standards such as air or water quality. Permitting cases involve disputes over the planned construction of new facilities such as a dam or airport. Environmental disputes are also different from more traditional disputes in several ways: Irreversible ecological damages may be involved; at least one party to the dispute may claim to represent broader public interest—including the interests of inanimate objects, wildlife, or unborn generations; and the implementation of a court decision may pose special problems (what will happen to the community if the major employer is forced to close a factory responsible for water pollution) (Goldberg, et al., 1985:403–404).

The background of the actors in environmental disputes may also be different. Unlike those involved in many other disputes involving racial discrimination in schools, housing, or employment, environmentalists do not come from oppressed groups. In fact, they tend to draw most of their support from the white middle class. More often than not, their commitment is born of ideology rather than of pressing social or economic need. Consequently, environmental disputes seem to lack the immediacy of disputes in other areas. Often, they go on for years. Unlike in other disputes, delay favors the dissidents, and environmentalists prefer to postpone as long as possible decisions involving, for example, permits to construct new facilities (Dembart and Kwartler in Goldberg, 1985:404).

The incidence of environmental disputes is increasing. David M. Trubek (1978) attributes this to the increase in public awareness that our civilization causes substantial and possibly irreparable damage to the natural environment and to the growing significance of public action affecting the environment. Consequently, the recognition of the costs society pays for environmental damage and the failure of companies to internalize environmental costs lead to a proliferation of regulatory law designed to protect the natural environment. Many environmental controversies are about the extent to which the government should regulate private sector decisions that are considered as causes of environmental degradation. At the same time, the government itself is also a potential cause of environmental damages. Public programs of many types from flood control to mineral leasing have a potential for environmental damage.

Environmental disputes are further complicated by the establishment of a number of mission-oriented government agencies, such as the Army Corps of Engineers or the various highway departments. These agencies are set up to carry out programs: build dams, construct highways, or develop nuclear power. Such activities may cause environmental harm, but if an agency recognizes this harm, it will be forced to curtail its own activities and thus undermine, at least in part, the justification for its existence. At the same time, since they are perfectly lawful, they tend to magnify the advantages of those organized groups that favor development and to increase the obstacles facing environmental groups that set out to challenge agency decisions (Trubek, 1978:157). Much environmental advocacy occurs in complex policy disputes. In many such disputes the resources available to environmental advocates may be insufficient to ensure that their concerns receive the degree of attention from decision-makers that they would if the full extent of their demands were reflected in their representational resources.

SUMMARY

Starting with the premise that conflict is inherent in all social relationships, this chapter examined the role of law as a method of conflict resolution. It was shown that there is no consensus in the sociological and legal literature on the terminology concerning the role of law in conflict situations. The concepts of conflict resolution and dispute settlement were used interchangeably to show how the law resolves the legal components of conflict and disputes. It was repeatedly emphasized that the law does not deal with the underlying causes of conflict and does not reduce tension or antagonism between the aggrieved parties.

Nonlegal methods of conflict resolution include violence, rituals, shaming and ostracism, supernatural agencies, "lumping it," avoidance, negotiation, mediation, and arbitration. In industrialized countries such as the United States, lumping behavior, avoidance, and negotiation, are the most frequent responses to dispute situations. Adjudication is a public and formal method of conflict resolution and is best exemplified by courts. Court decisions have an either/or character, and the adversary nature of court proceedings forces disputes into the mold of a two-party conflict.

As a result of social developments, the increased availability of legal mechanisms for conflict resolution, and the creation of legally actionable rights and remedies, there is a growing demand for court services in conflict resolution. Data indicate that litigation rates in the United States have increased substantially during the last two decades. There are some authors, however, who challenge the notion that the dispute-processing function of the courts has increased in recent years as a result of social and economic changes. There are obvious difficulties in measuring litigation rates over time, and similar problems exist in cross-cultural studies of litigation rates.

Courts provide a forum for the settlement of a variety of private and public disputes. To quality for the use of court services, at the minimum planitiffs must be able to demonstrate justiciability and standing. Those who have only occasional recourse to the courts are called one-shotters, and those who are engaged in many similar litigations over time are designated as repeat players. There are four combinations of litigations: one-shotter versus one-shotter, repeat player versus one-shotter, one-shotter versus repeat player, and repeat player versus repeat player.

Most individual disputes involve one-shotters. Such disputes include private litigation as opposed to organizations, criminal defendants, or state agencies. Since litigation is costly and time-consuming, courts often make an effort to encourage disputants to settle their differences by agreement. A preference for continuing relations will not, in general, deter individuals from litigation. Those disputants who are better organized and have more expendable resources fare better in litigations.

Disputes between individuals and organizations may take place over economic issues, claims for damages and restitution, issues of civil rights, and issues concerning organizational actions, procedures, and policy. In general, more organizations are plaintiffs and more individuals are defendants, and organizations tend to be uniformly more successful than individuals.

For disputes initiated by individuals against organizations, law as a method of conflict resolution in academe was used as an illustration. Faculty and student initiated lawsuits against the university were considered in the context of faculty-administration, student-faculty, and student-administration relations.

Disputes between individuals and organizations where organizations are the plaintiffs were analyzed in the context of creditor-debtor relationships. When nonlegal methods of collection fail, creditors are likely to enlist the courts in the collection process. Of the legal devices available for collecting the judgments, garnishment of wages is used most frequently. A characteristic of most civil suits for debts is that the plaintiff usually wins by default.

Disputes between organizations cover a wide spectrum of participants and controversies. In interorganizational disputes, the activities of public interest law firms in environmental disputes were examined. In general, the party which is better organized with greater resources and greater capacity to generate data will have a higher probability to influence the outcome of the dispute.

SUGGESTED FURTHER READINGS

JEROLD A. AUERBACH, *Justice Without Law?* New York: Oxford University Press, 1983. An outstanding review of nonjudicial methods of dispute resolution in an historical context.

MAUREEN CAIN and KALMAN KULCSAR eds., *Disputes and the Law.* Budapest: Akademiai Kiado, 1983. A collection of papers on methods of dispute resolution in different cultures.

RICHARD DANZIG, "Towards the Creation of a Complementary, Decentralized System of Criminal Justice." *Stanford Law Review* 26:1–54, 1974. A seminal article on utilizing tribal methods of dispute processing in modern societies.

STEPHEN B. GOLDBERG, ERIC GREEN and FRANK E. A. SANDER, *Dispute Resolution.* Boston, Little, Brown and Company, 1985. An analysis and application of various conventional and not so conventional techniques of dispute processing.

P. H. GULLIVER, *Disputes and Negotiations: A Cross-Cultural Perspective.* New York: Academic Press, 1979. An important theoretical contribution to the understanding of disputes by a leading anthropologist.

Law & Society Review 15 (3–4) 1980–1981. A special issue on dispute processing and civil litigation.

TONY F. MARSHALL, *Alternatives to Criminal Courts: The Potential for Non-Judicial Dispute Settlement.* Hampshire, England: Gower, 1985. An analysis of alternatives to judicial dispute processing with emphasis on criminal justice agencies.

LAURA NADER and HARRY F. TODD, JR. eds., *The Disputing Process—Law in Ten Societies.* New York: Columbia University Press, 1978. A collection of ten articles dealing with the disputing process from a cross-cultural and comparative perspective.

SIMON ROBERTS, *Order and Dispute, An Introduction to Legal Anthropology.* New York: St. Martin's Press, 1979. An anthropological approach to disputes in less complex societies.

CATHIE J. WITTY, *Mediation and Society, Conflict Management in Lebanon,* New York: Academic Press, Inc.: 1980. An attempt to develop a general theory of mediation based on two comparative case studies—one Lebanese and the other American.

REFERENCES

ABEL, RICHARD L. 1973. "A Comparative Theory of Dispute Institutions in Society," Law and Society Review 8 (2)(Winter):217–347.

Administrative Office of the U.S. Courts. 1986. *Federal Judicial Workload Statistics.* Washington, D.C.: The Administrative Office of the U.S. Courts.

American Bar Association. 1987. *Dispute Resolution Program Directory.* Washington, D.C.: American Bar Association.

AUBERT, VILHELM. 1963. "Competition and Dissensus: Two Types of Conflict and Conflict Resolution," The Journal of Conflict Resolution 7 (1):26–42; 1969. "Law as a Way of Resolving Conflicts: The Case of a Small Industrialized Society," Pp. 282–303 in Laura Nader, ed., Law in Culture and Society. Chicago: Aldine.

BARTON, JOHN H. 1975. "Behind the Legal Explosion," Stanford Law Review 27 (February):567–584.

BEST, ARTHUR and A. ANDREASEN. 1976. *Talking Back to Business: Voiced and Unvoiced Consumer Complaints.* Washington, D.C.: Center for the Study of Responsive Law.

BLACK, DONALD. 1976. *The Behavior of Law.* New York: Academic Press.

BLEGVAD, BRITT-MARI. 1983. "Accessibility and Dispute Treatment: The Case of the Consumer in Denmark," Pp. 203–219 in Maureen Cain and Kalman Kulcsar, eds., Disputes and the Law. Budapest: Akademiai Kiado.

CAPLOVITZ, DAVID. 1974. *Consumers in Trouble, A Study of Debtors in Default.* New York: Free Press.

COLLIER, JANE FISHBURNE. 1973. *Law and Social Change in Zinacantan.* Stanford, CA: Stanford University Press.

CURRAN, BARBARA A. 1986. "American Lawyers In the 1980s: A Profession In Transition," Law & Society Review 20 (1):19–52.

DANZIG, RICHARD. 1973. "Toward the Creation of a Complementary, Decentralized System of Criminal Justice," Stanford Law Review 26 (1):1–54.

ECKHOFF, TORSTEIN. 1978. "The Mediator, The Judge and The Administrator in Conflict-Resolution," Pp. 31–41 in Sheldon Goldman and Austin Sarat, eds., American Court Systems, Readings in Judicial Process and Behavior. San Francisco: W. H. Freeman & Company Publishers.

Economist, The. 1979. "The Odour of Solvency," 273 (October 6–12) (7101):104.

EHRMANN, HENRY W. 1976. *Comparative Legal Cultures.* Englewood Cliffs, NJ: Prentice-Hall.

FELSTINER, WILLIAM L. F. 1974. "Influences of Social Organization on Dispute Processing," Law and Society Review 9 (1)(Fall):63–94; 1975. "Avoidance as Dispute Processing: An Elaboration," Law and Society Review 9 (4)(Summer):695–706.

Ford Foundation. 1978. *New Approaches to Conflict Resolution.* New York: Ford Foundation.

FRIEDMAN, LAWRENCE M. 1973. *A History of American Law.* New York: Simon & Schuster; 1985. *Total Justice.* New York: Russell Sage Foundation.

FRIEDMAN, LAWRENCE M. and STEWART MACAULAY. 1977. *Law and the Behavioral Sciences,* 2nd ed. Indianapolis: Bobbs-Merrill.

FRIEDMAN, LAWRENCE M. and ROBERT V. PERCIVAL. 1978. "A Tale of Two Courts: Litigation in Alameda and San Benito Counties," Pp. 69–79 in Sheldon Goldman and Austin Sarat, eds., American Court Systems, Readings in Judicial Process and Behavior. San Francisco: W. H. Freeman & Company Publishers.

GALANTER, MARC. 1978. "Who Wins?" Pp. 529–534 in Sheldon Goldman and Austin Sarat, eds., American Court Systems, Readings in Judicial Process and Behavior. San Francisco: W. H. Freeman & Company Publishers; 1974. "Why the 'Haves' Come out Ahead: Speculations on the Limits of Legal Change," Law and Society Review 9 (1)(Fall):95–160.

GOLDBERG, STEPHEN B., ERIC D. GREEN, and FRANK E. A. SANDER. 1985. *Dispute Resolution.* Boston: Little, Brown and Company.

GOLDMAN, SHELDON and AUSTIN SARAT, eds. 1978. *American Court Systems, Readings in Judicial Process and Behavior.* San Francisco: W. H. Freeman & Company Publishers.

GROSSMAN, JOEL B. and AUSTIN SARAT. 1978. "Litigation in the Federal Courts: A Comparative Perspective," Pp. 58–68 in Sheldon Goldman and Austin Sarat, eds., American Court Systems, Readings in Judicial Process and Behavior. San Francisco: W. H. Freeman & Company Publishers.

GUBSER, NICHOLAS J. 1965. *The Nunamiut Eskimos: Hunters of Caribou.* New Haven: Yale University Press.

GULLIVER, P. H. 1969. "Introduction to Case Studies of Law in Non-Western Societies," Pp. 11–23 in Laura Nader, ed., Law in Culture and Society. Chicago: Aldine; 1979. *Disputes and Negotiations: A Cross-Cultural Perspective.* New York: Academic Press.

HANDLER, JOEL F. 1976. "Public Interest Law: Problems and Prospects," Pp. 99–115 in Murray L. Schwartz ed., Law and the American Future. Englewood Cliffs, NJ: Prentice-Hall.

HIRSCHMAN, ALBERT O. 1970. *Exit, Voice, and Loyalty: Responses to Decline in Firms, Organizations, and States.* Cambridge, MA: Harvard University Press.

HOEBEL, E. ADAMSON. 1954. *The Law of Primitive Man, A Study in Comparative Legal Dynamics.* Cambridge, MA: Harvard University Press.

JACOB, HERBERT. 1969. *Debtors in Court, The Consumption of Government Services.* Chicago: Rand McNally.

KAGAN, ROBERT A. 1984. "The Routinization of Debt Collection: An Essay on Social Change and Conflict in Courts," Law & Society Review 18 (3):323-371.

KAPLIN, WILLIAM A. 1978. *The Law of Higher Education.* San Francisco: Jossey-Bass.

KAWASHIMA, TAKEYOSHI. 1969. "Dispute Resolution in Japan," Pp. 182-193 in Vilhelm Aubert, ed., Sociology of Law. Harmondsworth, England: Penguin Books, Ltd.

KRIESBERG, LOUIS. 1973. *The Sociology of Social Conflicts.* Englewood Cliffs, NJ: Prentice-Hall.

LADD, EVERETT C. Jr. and SEYMOUR MARTIN LIPSET. 1973. *Professors, Unions and American Higher Education.* Domestic Affairs Study 16. Washington, D.C.: American Enterprise Institute for Public Policy Research.

LAUTER, DAVID. 1986. "Report Says Litigation Explosion Is a 'Myth'," The National Law Journal (April 28):46.

LEMPERT, RICHARD. 1978. "More Tales of Two Courts: Exploring Changes in the 'Dispute Settlement Function' of Trial Courts," Law and Society Review 13 (1)(Fall):91-138.

LEMPERT, RICHARD and JOSEPH SANDERS. 1986. *An Invitation to Law and Social Science.* New York: Longman.

LORD, WILLIAM, LEONARD ADELMAN, PAUL WEHR, ET AL. 1978. *Conflict Management in Federal Water Resource Planning.* Boulder: Institute of Behavioral Science, University of Colorado.

MACAULAY, STEWART. 1969. "Non-Contractual Relations in Business," Pp. 194-209 in Vilhelm Aubert, ed., Sociology of Law. Harmondsworth, England: Penguin Books, Ltd.

MCGILLIS, DANIEL. 1982. "Minor Dispute Processing: A Review of Recent Developments," in Roman Tomasic and Malcolm M. Feeley, eds., Neighborhood Justice: Assessment of an Emerging Idea. New York: Longman.

MARSHALL, TONY F. 1985. *Alternatives to Criminal Courts.* Hampshire, England: Gower.

MORGAN, RICHARD E. 1984. *Disabling America: The "Rights Industry" In Our Time.* New York: Basic Books.

NADER, LAURA and HARRY F. TODD JR., eds. 1978. *The Disputing Process—Law in Ten Societies.* New York: Columbia University Press, "Introduction," Pp. 1-40.

PALMER, STACY E. 1985. "Supreme Court Curbs Judges' Right to Overturn Academic Decisions," The Chronicle of Higher Education (December 18):1,33.

POSNER, RICHARD A. 1985. *The Federal Courts: Crisis and Reform.* Cambridge, MA: Harvard University Press.

RAIFFA, HOWARD. 1982. *The Art and Science of Negotiation.* Cambridge, MA: The Belknap Press of Harvard University.

ROBERTS, SIMON. 1979. *Order and Dispute, An Introduction to Legal Anthropology.* New York: St. Martin's Press.

St. Louis Post-Dispatch. 1979. "AMA Ordered to Lift Ban on Doctors' Ads," (October 24):1.

SARAT, AUSTIN AND JOEL B. GROSSMAN. 1978. "Courts and Conflict Resolution: Problems in the Mobilization of Adjudication," Pp. 22-30 in Sheldon Goldman and Austin Sarat, eds., American Court Systems, Readings in Judicial Process and Behavior. San Francisco: W. H. Freeman & Company Publishers.

Saturday Review. 1979. "Getting Hot Under the Collar," (June 9):7.

SEIDMAN, ROBERT B. 1978. *The State, Law and Development.* New York: St. Martin's Press.

STRICK, ANNE. 1977. *Injustice for All.* New York: Penguin Books.

The New York Times. 1986a. "Staying out of Court," (August 31):1F; 1986b. "Suing the Clergy," (September):1F.

TRUBEK, DAVID M. 1978. "Environmental Defense, I.: Introduction to Interest Group Advocacy in Complex Disputes," Pp. 151-194 in Burton A. Weisbrod, Joel F. Handler and Neil K. Komesar, eds., Public Interest Law, An Economic and Institutional Analysis. Berkeley: University of California Press.

TURK, AUSTIN T. 1978. "Law as a Weapon in Social Conflict," Pp. 213-232 in Charles E. Reasons and Robert M. Rich, eds., The Sociology of Law, A Conflict Perspective. Toronto: Butterworths.

U.S. Deparment of Commerce. 1986. *Statistical Abstract of the United States 1986.* Washington, D.C.: Bureau of the Census.

U.S. Department of Justice. 1986. "Toward the Multi-Door Courthouse—Dispute Resolution Intake and Referral," National Institute of Justice Reports. SNI 198 (July):2-7.

U.S. News & World Report. 1986. "13.6 Million Suits," (August 18):9.

VAGO, STEVEN. 1968. "Wage Garnishment: An Exercise in Futility Under Present Law," The Journal of Consumer Affairs 2 (1)(Summer):7-20; 1971. "The Legal Problems of Low Income Consumers—Some Methodological Considerations," Journal of Legal Education 23 (1):165–170; 1979. "Consumer Rights in Academe," Social Policy 9 (5)(March–April):39–43.

VAGO, STEVEN and CHARLES E. MARSKE. 1980. "Law as a Method of Conflict Resolution in Academe," The Journal of Educational Thought 14 (1)(April):2–16.

WEHR, PAUL. 1979. *Conflict Regulation.* Boulder, CO: Westview Press.

YNGVESSON, BARBARA B. 1978. "The Atlantic Fishermen," Pp. 59–85 in Laura Nader and Harry F. Todd, Jr., eds., The Disputing Process—Law in Ten Societies. New York: Columbia University Press.

7

Law and Social Change

In the review of theoretical perspectives in Chapter Two, I have shown that theorists of law and society have often been preoccupied with efforts to explain the relationship between legal change and social change in the context of the broad historical course of development of legal institutions. These theorists viewed the law both as an independent and dependent variable in society and emphasized the interdependence of the law with other systems in society. In light of the theoretical concerns raised in Chapter Two, this chapter will further examine the interplay between law and social change. The law will again be considered both as a dependent and independent variable, that is, both as an effect and cause of social change. The chapter will also analyze the advantages and limitations of the law as an instrument of social change, and will discuss a series of social, psychological, cultural, and economic factors that have an influence on the efficacy of law as an agent of change.

The first concern in understanding the relationship between law and social change is definitional. What is social change? The term "change," in everyday usage, is often employed loosely to refer to something that exists which did not previously exist, or the demise or absence of something that formerly existed. But not all change is social change. Many changes in life are small enough to be dismissed as trivial, although at times they may add up to something more substantial. In its most concrete sense, social change means that large numbers of persons are engaging in group activities and relationships that are different than those in which they or their parents engaged in previously. Society is a complex network of patterns of relationships in which all the members participate in varying degrees. These relationships change and behavior changes at the same time. Individuals are faced with new situations to which they must respond. These situations reflect such factors as new technologies, new ways of making a living, changes in place of residence, and new innovations, ideas, and social values. Thus, social change means modifications of the way people work, rear a family, educate their children, govern themselves, and seek ultimate meaning in life. It also refers to a restructuring of the basic ways in which people in a society relate to each other with regards to government, economics, education, religion, family life, recreation, language, and other activities (Vago, 1980).

Social change in society is a product of a multitude of factors, and in many cases, the interrelationships among them. In addition to law, there are many other mechanisms of change, such as technology, ideology, competition, conflict, political and economic factors, and structural strains. All the mechanisms are in many ways interrelated. One should be very careful not to assign undue weight to any one of these "causes" in isolation. Admittedly, it is always tempting and convenient to single out one "prime mover," one factor, one cause, one explanation, and use it for a number of situations. This is also the case with legal change: it is extremely difficult, perhaps impossible, to set forth a cause-and-effect relationship in the creation of new laws, administrative rulings, or judicial decisions. Although there are exceptions, as it will be alluded to in this chapter, one should be somewhat skeptical and cautious concerning one-factor causal explanations in general, and in particular for large-scale social changes.

RECIPROCAL RELATIONS BETWEEN LAW
AND SOCIAL CHANGE

The question of whether law can and should lead, or whether it should never do more than cautiously follow changes in society, has been and remains controversial. The conflicting approaches of the British social reformer Jeremy Bentham and the German legal scholar Friedrich Karl Von Savigny have provided contrasting paradigms for these propositions. At the beginning of industrialization and urbanization in Europe, Bentham expected legal reforms to respond quickly to new social needs and to restructure society. He freely gave advice to the leaders of the French Revolution, since he believed that countries at a similar stage of economic development needed similar remedies for their common problems. In fact, it was Bentham's philosophy, and that of his disciples, which turned the British Parliament—and similar institutions in other countries—into active legislative instruments bringing about social reforms partly in response to and partly in stimulation of felt social needs. Writing at about the same period, Savigny, as I noted in Chapter Two, condemned the sweeping legal reforms brought about by the French Revolution that were threatening to invade Western Europe. He believed that only fully developed popular customs could form the basis of legal change. Since customs grow out of the habits and beliefs of specific people, rather than expressing those of an abstract humanity, legal changes are codifications of customs and they can only be national, never universal.

Well over a century later, the relationship between law and social change remains controversial. Still, "[t]here exists two contrasting views on the relationship between legal precepts and public attitudes and behavior. According to the one, law is determined by the sense of justice and the moral sentiments of the population, and legislation can only achieve results by staying relatively close to prevailing social norms. According to the other view, law, and especially legislation, is a vehicle through which a programmed social evolution can be brought about" (Aubert, 1969:69). At one extreme, then, is the view that law is a dependent variable, determined and shaped by current mores and opinions of society. According to this position, legal changes would be impossible unless preceded by social change; law reform could do nothing except codify custom. This is clearly not so, and ignores the fact that throughout history legal institutions have been found to "have a definite role, rather poorly understood, as instruments that set off, monitor, or otherwise regulate the fact or pace of social change" (Friedman, 1969:29). The other extreme is exemplified by Soviet jurists, such as P. P. Gureyev and P. I. Sedugin (1977), who see the law as an instrument for social engineering. Accordingly, "[d]uring the period of the transition from capitalism to socialism, the Soviet state made extensive use of legislation to guide society, establish and develop social economic forms, abolish each and every form of exploitation, and regulate the measure of labour and the measure of the consumption of the products of social labour. It used legislation to create and improve the institutions of socialist democracy, to establish firm law and order, safeguard the social system and state security, and build socialism" (Gureyev and Sedugin, 1977:12).

These views represent the two extremes of a continuum dealing with the relationship between law and social change. The problem of the interplay between law and social change is obviously not a simple one. Essentially, the question is not: Does law change society? or Does social change alter law? Both contentions are likely to be correct. Instead, it is more appropriate to ask under what specific circumstances can law bring about social change, at what level, and to what extent? Similarly, the conditions under which social change alters law need to be specified.

In general, in a highly urbanized and industrialized society like the United States, law does play a large part in social change, and vice versa, at least much more so than is the case in traditional societies or in traditional sociological thinking (Nagel, 1970:10). There are several ways of illustrating this reciprocal relationship. For example, in the domain of intrafamily relations, urbanization, with its small apartments, has lessened the desirability of three-generation families in a single household. This social change helped to establish social security laws which in turn helped generate changes in the labor force and in social institutions for the aged. Changes in landlord-tenant relations brought about changes in housing codes, resulting in changes in tenancy relations. As a result of technological change, the relation of personal property owners to other individuals has become more impersonal and frequently more likely to lead to injury, and as a result, there have been alterations in the legal definition of fault, which in turn has changed the American insurance system. Finally, in the context of employer-employee relations, much of American labor history prior to

the 1930s pointed toward the enactment of precedents and statutes guaranteeing the right to unionize, and once the Wagner Act was passed, the
percentage of the labor force in unions did drastically increase, although
it has since reached a plateau (Nagel, 1970:11).

Although there is a demonstrable reciprocal relationship between law
and social change, for analytical purposes, I will briefly consider this relationship as unilateral. To this end, in the next section I will examine the
conditions under which social change induces legal change; then, in the
following section, I will discuss law as an instrument of social change.

SOCIAL CHANGES AS CAUSES
OF LEGAL CHANGES

Historically, social change has been slow enough to make custom the principle source of law. Law could respond to social change over decades or
even centuries. Even during the early stages of the industrial revolution,
changes induced by the invention of the steam engine or the advent of
electricity were gradual enough to make legal responses valid for a generation. Notes Friedmann: "But today the tempo of social change acceler-
ated to a point where today's assumptions may not be valid even in a few
years from now" (1972:513). In the words of Alvin Toffler (1970:11),
"[c]hange sweeps through the highly industrialized countries with waves of
ever accelerating speed and unprecedented impact." In a sense, people in
modern society are caught in a maelstrom of social change, living through
a series of contrary and interacting revolutions in demography, urbanization, bureaucratization, industrialization, science, transportation, agriculture, communication, biomedical research, education, and civil rights. Each
of these revolutions has brought spectacular changes in a string of tumul-
tuous consequences, and transformed people's values, attitudes, behavior,
and institutions.

These changes further transformed the social and economic order of
society. Contemporary society is characterized by a great division of labor
and specialization in function. In modern society

> interpersonal relations have changed; social institutions, including the family,
> have become greatly modified; social control previously largely informal has
> become formalized; bureaucracy, that is, large-scale formal organizations, has
> proliferated both in the private and public sectors; and new risks to the in-
> dividual have emerged including the risk of disrupted income flow through
> unemployment, of industrial accidents, and of consumer exploitation; and
> increased chronic illness and physical impairments have accompanied the
> extension of life (Hauser, 1976:23–24).

The emergence of new risks to the individual as a result of the atten-
uation of the various family functions, including the protective function,
has led to the creation of legal innovations to protect the individual in
modern society. Illustrations of such innovations include provisions for
worker's compensation, unemployment insurance, old age pensions, med-

icare, and various forms of categoric and general provisions for "welfare" (Hauser, 1976:24).

Many sociologists and legal scholars contend that technology is one of the great moving forces for change in law (Miller, 1979:4-14). Law is influenced by technology in at least three ways:

> The most obvious ... is technology's contribution to the refinement of legal technique by providing instruments to be used in applying law (e.g., fingerprinting or the use of a lie detector). A second, no less significant, is technology's effect on the process of formulating and applying law as a result of the changes technology fosters in the social and intellectual climate in which the legal process is executed (e.g., televised hearings). Finally, technology affects the substance of law by presenting new problems and new conditions with which law must deal (Stover, quoted by Miller, 1979:14).

Illustrations of technological changes leading to legal changes abound (Loth and Ernst, 1972). The advent of the automobile and air travel brought along new regulations. The automobile, for example, has been responsible for an immense amount of law: traffic rules, rules about drunk driving, rules about auto safety, drivers' license laws, rules about pollution control, registration, and so on. New devices in crime detection (fingerprinting and electronic snooping, among a host of others) resulted in changes in the law, such as the kinds of evidence admissible in court. The computer makes possible our present systems of credit, merchandising, manufacturing, transportation, research, education, dissemination of information, government, and politics. The computer also has inspired legislation on both the federal and state levels to safeguard privacy, to protect abuse of credit information, and to require an employer to tell a job applicant who is rejected the source and nature of any adverse report on his or her credit or past record or opinions that caused the rejection.

Change in law may be induced by a voluntary and gradual shift in community values and attitudes. People may come to think that poverty is bad and laws should be created to reduce it in some way. People may come to condemn the use of laws to further racially discriminatory practices in voting, housing, employment, education, and the like, and may support changes that forbid the use of laws for these purposes. People may come to think that businesspersons should not be free to put just any kind of foodstuff on the market without proper governmental inspection, or fly any plane without having to meet governmental safety standards, or to show anything on television that they wish. So laws may be enacted as appropriate, and regulatory bodies may be brought into being as necessary. And people may come to think that the practice of abortion is not evil, or that the practice of contraception is desirable, or that divorce is not immoral. Hence laws on these topics may undergo repeal or revision.

Changes in social conditions, technology, knowledge, values, and attitudes, then, may induce legal change. In such instances, the law is reactive and follows social change. It should be noted, however, that changes in law are one of many responses to social change. But the legal response in some respects is important, since it represents the authority of the state and its sanctioning power. A new law in response to a new social or technological problem may aggravate that problem—or alleviate and help to solve it. Often, the legal response to social change, which inevitably comes after a time lag, induces new social changes. For example, laws created in response to air and water pollution brought about by technological changes may result in unemployment in some areas, where polluting firms are unwilling or unable to install the required pollution abatement controls. Unemployment, in turn, may result in relocation, may affect crime rate in the community, or may bring about coercive pressures from the disaffected. These correlations and chain reactions can be extended practically indefinitely. Thus, law can be considered as both reactive and proactive in social change. In the next section, the proactive aspect of law as an initiator of social change will be considered.

LAW AS AN INSTRUMENT OF SOCIAL CHANGE

There are numerous historical illustrations in which the enactment and implementation of laws have been used deliberately to induce broad social changes in society. With the advent of Roman jurists, the notion of law as an instrument of social change became clearly conceptualized. Says Nisbet: "The conversion of Rome from republic to empire could not have been accomplished except by means of explicit legal decree buttressed by the doctrine of imperial sovereignty" (1975:173). Since Roman times, major ages of social change and mobility almost always involved great use of law and of litigation. There are several illustrations of the idea that law, far from being simply a reflection of social reality, is a powerful means of *accomplishing* reality, that is, of fashioning it or making it. It is generally acknowledged that, in spite of the ideas of Marx, Engels, and Lenin that law is an epiphenomenon of bourgeois class society doomed to vanish with the advent of the Revolution, the Soviet Union succeeded in making enormous changes in society by the use of laws (Dror, 1968). More recently, the attempts by Nazi Germany and later on by Eastern European countries to make wholesale social changes through the use of laws—such as nationalization of industry, land reform and introduction of collective farms, provision of free education and health care, and elimination of social inequities—would be illustrative of the effectiveness of law to induce change (Eorsi and Harmathy, 1971). In China, when the Communist party came into power in 1949, virtually all vices that are ubiquitous in Western countries—prostitution, gambling, pornography, drug trafficking, and usury—were eliminated by government decree along with business operations that were dependent on profits from such activities (Brady, 1981).

Recognition of the role of law as an instrument of social change is becoming more pronounced in contemporary society. Says Friedmann: "The law—through legislative or administrative responses to new social conditions and ideas, as well as through judicial re-interpretations of constitutions, statutes or precedents—increasingly not only articulates but sets the course for major social changes" (1972:513). Thus, "[a]ttempted social change, through law, is a basic trait of the modern world" (Friedman, 1975:277). In the same vein, Yehezkel Dror (1968:673) contends that "[t]he growing use of law as a device of organized social action directed toward achieving social change seems to be one of the characteristics of modern society. . . . " Many authors, such as Joel B. Grossman and Mary H. Grossman (1971:2), consider law as a desirable, necessary, and a highly efficient means of inducing change, preferable to other instruments of change.

In modern societies, the role of law in social change is of more than theoretical interest. In many areas of social life, such as education, race relations, housing, transportation, energy utilization, and the protection of the environment, the law has been relied on as an important instrument of change. In the United States, the law has been used as the principal mechanism for improving the political and social position of blacks. Since the 1960s, the courts and Congress dismantled a racial caste system embedded in the law and in practice for generations. The old order was swept away by legislation, including the Civil Rights Act of 1964 and the Voting Rights Act of 1965, as well as by the commitment of billions of dollars to social welfare programs. In a relatively short time, these policies have produced notable effects. For example, the immediate results of the Voting Rights Act of 1965 were dramatic, particularly in states that have successfully resisted earlier attempts to end voting discrimination. The percentage of potential black voters registered in Alabama increased from 23 to 52 percent between 1964 and 1967. By 1969, it went up to 61 percent. In Mississippi, the increase was most significant, from 7 percent in 1964 to 60 percent in 1967, and 67 percent by 1969. Between the 1964 and 1968 presidential elections, overall black registration in the South increased by nearly one million voters. About 75 percent of the increase came in the six states that were fully covered by the Act—Alabama, Georgia, Louisiana, Mississippi, North Carolina, and South Carolina. This effectively doubled the number of registered blacks in these states (Logan and Winston, 1971:27). The 1965 law through its impact on black registration and voting also had major consequences for black political power. In 1965, there were some 70 elected black officials in the South. By 1969, their number rose to 400. In 1981, there were approximately 2500 elected black officials in 11 southern states, including a black mayor in Atlanta (Scher and Button, 1984:45). It would be erroneous to assume, however, that similar changes took place in other domains. For instance, since 1964, the median family income of blacks has vacillated between 54 and 62 percent of the figure for whites.

Similarly, in Eastern European countries, the law was a principal instrument in transforming society after the Second World War from a bourgeois to a socialist one. Legal enactments initiated and legitimized rearrangements in property and power relations, transformed basic social institutions such as education and health care, and opened up new avenues of social mobility for large segments of the population. Legislation guided the reorganization of agricultural production from private ownership to collective farms, the creation of new towns, and the development of a socialist mode of economic production, distribution, and consumption. These changes, in turn, affected values, beliefs, socialization patterns, and the structure of social relationships.

There are several ways of considering the role of law in social change. In an influential article, "Law and Social Change," Dror (1968) distinguishes between the indirect and direct aspects of law in social change. Dror (1968:673) contends that "[l]aw plays an important indirect role in social change by shaping various social institutions, which in turn have a direct impact on society." He uses the illustration of the compulsory education system, which performed an important indirect role in regard to change. Mandatory school attendance upgraded the quality of the labor force, which, in turn, played a direct role in social change by contributing to an increased rate of industrialization and modernization. He emphasizes that law interacts in many cases directly with basic social institutions, constituting a direct relationship between law and social change. For example, laws prohibiting racial discrimination in education have a direct influence on social change by enabling previously excluded groups to attend schools of their choice. He warns, however, that "[t]he distinction is not an absolute but a relative one: in some cases the emphasis is more on the direct and less on the indirect impact of social change, while in other cases the opposite is true" (Dror, 1968:674).

Dror argues that law exerts an indirect influence on social change in general by influencing the possibilities of change in various social institutions. For example, the existence of a patent law protecting the rights of inventors encourages inventions, and furthers change in the technological institutions which, in turn, may bring about other types of social change.

For all modern societies, every collection of statutes and delegated legislation is "full of illustrations of the direct use of law as a device for directed social change" (Dror, 1968:676). A good example of social change directly induced by law was the enactment of prohibition in the United States to shape social behavior. (It was also one of the more conspicuous failures, showing that there are limits to the efficacy of law to bring about social change, as I will discuss later.) Other illustrations of comparable magnitude would include the abolition of slavery in the United States and the passage of the 1964 Civil Rights Act (Horowitz and Karst, 1969).

Another way of considering the role of law in social change is in the context of Leon H. Mayhew's (1971:195) notion of the possibility of either redefining the normative order or creating new procedural opportunities within the legal apparatus. He designates the former as an "extension of formal rights," illustrated by the pronouncement of the Supreme Court that defendants accused of serious crimes have the right to legal representation. The second is termed the "extension of formal facilities," and is exemplified by the establishment of a system of public defenders who provide the required legal representation. The extension of formal rights and of formal facilities has definite implications for the criminal justice system in the form of greater protection of individual rights.

A rather different perspective on law in social change is presented by Lawrence M. Friedman. He refers to change through law in terms of two types: "planning" and "disruption." Planning "refers to architectural construction of new forms of social order and social interaction. Disruption refers to the blocking or amelioration of existing social forms and relations" (Friedman, 1973:25). Planning through law is an omnipresent feature of the modern world. Although it is most pronounced in socialist countries (for example, five-year plans of social and economic development), all nations are committed to planning to a greater or lesser extent. Both planning and disruption operate within the existing legal system and can bring about "positive" or "negative" social change, depending on one's perspective.

Although revolution is the most distinct and obvious form of disruption,

> milder forms are everywhere. Judicial review is frequently disruptive. American courts have smashed programs and institutions from the Missouri Compromise to the Alaska pipeline. Activist reformers have played a sensational role in American life in the last decade. Ralph Nader is the most well-known example. . . . He stimulates use of legal process as a lever of social change. Much of his work is technically disruptive; it focuses on litigation and injunctions, on stopping government dead in its tracks, when it fails to meet his ethical and policies standards. Legal disruption can . . . include lawsuits; particularly after *Brown* v. *Board of Education,* reformers have frequently gone to court to upset many old and established arrangements (Friedman, 1975:277).

Social change through litigation has always been an important feature in the United States. Whether the change produced by such action is considered "destructive" or "constructive," the fact remains that law can be a highly effective device for producing social change. For example, when the California Supreme Court destroyed the legal basis for the system of financing schools in the state, Friedman (1973:27) succinctly observed: "Many a *coup d'état* in small countries have achieved less social change than this quiet *coup d'état* in the courts."

Friedman considers social change through litigation as an American phenomenon and raises the question: Will this spread to other countries? His response is that creative disruption of the judicial type presupposes a number of conditions which rarely coincide and are apparently not present in other countries to the same degree. These conditions include an activist legal profession, financial resources, activist judges, a genuine social movement, and what he describes as "[t]he strongest condition," the fact that in the United States "[e]lites—the power holders—must accept the results of disruptive litigation, like it or not" (Friedman, 1975:278). Clearly, no socialist or authoritarian country will tolerate anything like the American form of judicial review. Their legal structures are not designed to accommodate these patterns.

The Efficacy of Law as an Instrument of Social Change

As an instrument of social change, law entails two interrelated processes: the institutionalization and internalization of patterns of behavior. Institutionalization of a pattern of behavior refers to the establishment of a norm with provisions of its enforcement (such as desegregation of public schools), and internalization of a pattern of behavior means the incorporation of the value or values implicit in a law (for example, integrated public schools are "good"). Evan notes: "Law ... can affect behavior directly only through the process of institutionalization; if, however, the institutionalization process is successful, it, in turn, facilitates the internalization of attitudes or beliefs" (1965:287).

In many instances law is an effective mechanism in the promotion or reinforcement of social change. However, the extent to which law can provide an effective impetus for social change varies according to the conditions present in a particular situation. William M. Evan (1965:288–291) suggests that a law is likely to be successful to induce change if it meets the following seven conditions: (1) the law must emanate from an authoritative and prestigious source; (2) the law must introduce its rationale in terms which are understandable and compatible with existing values; (3) the advocates of the change should make reference to other communities or countries with which the population identifies and where the law is already in effect; (4) the enforcement of the law must be aimed toward making the change in a relatively short time; (5) those enforcing the law must themselves be very much committed to the change intended by the law; (6) the implementation of the law should include positive as well as negative sanctions; and (7) the enforcement of the law should be reasonable, not only in terms of the sanctions used, but also in the protection of the rights of those who stand to lose by violation of the law.

As an agent of social change law has both advantages and limitations. The efficacy of law, that is, its ability to produce change, is determined in a large part by public acceptance. In a pluralistic democratic society—in which people tend to belong to many groups and publics—change through the law is typically met by a variety of reactions; some are opposed, some are favorable, but most are indifferent or only mildly hostile. If the majority of opinion leaders are behind the change, the opposition remains a minority and most of the people gradually accommodate themselves to the change (Rose and Rose, 1969:537).

The efficacy of law as an instrument of social change is conditioned by a number of factors. One is the amount of information available about a given piece of legislation, decision, or ruling. When there is insufficient transmission of information about these matters, the law will not produce its intended effect. Ignorance of the law is not considered as an excuse for disobedience, but ignorance obviously limits the law's effectiveness. In the same vein, law is limited to the extent that rules are not stated precisely, and not only because people are uncertain about what the rules mean. Vague rules permit multiple perceptions and interpretations (what does the expression "all deliberate speed" mean?). Consequently, the language of the law should be free of ambiguity, and care should be exercised to prevent multiple interpretations and loopholes (Carter, 1979:27-37).

Legal regulations and the required behavior of people to whom the law is addressed must be clearly known, and the sanctions for noncompliance need to be precisely enunciated. The effectiveness of the law is directly related to the extent and nature of perception of officially sanctioned rules. Perceptions of rules, in turn, vary with their sources. Rules are more likely to be accepted if they reflect a notion of fairness and justice that is prevalent in society and when their source is considered legitimate (Jacob, 1986:24-25). It should be noted, however, that the contrast between legitimacy and legality at times remains confused. As Carl J. Friedrich (1958:202) observes: "Law must not be seen as operating only in one dimension of the state, but in the many dimensions of the community if we are to comprehend legitimacy as an objective pattern. Legitimacy is related to right and justice; without a clarification of what is to be understood by the rightness and justice of law, legitimacy cannot be comprehended either. Hitler's rule was legal but it was not legitimate. It had a basis in law but not in right and justice."

The responsiveness of enforcement agencies to a law also has an impact on its effectiveness. Law enforcement agents not only communicate rules, they also show that the rules are taken seriously and punishment for their violation is likely. But for a law to be enforceable, the behavior to be changed must be observable. For example, it is more difficult to enforce a law against homosexual behavior than a law against racial discrimination in public housing. Moreover, law enforcement agents need to be fully committed to enforcing a new law. One reason for the failure of prohibition, for example, was the unwillingness of law enforcement agents to implement the law. Selective enforcement of a law also hinders its effectiveness. The more high status individuals are arrested and punished, the greater will be the likelihood that a particular law will achieve its intended objective (Zimring and Hawkins, 1975:337-338). Laws regularly and uniformly enforced across class and group lines tend to be perceived as more binding than they would have been if they were seldom and selectively enforced, because enforcement establishes behavioral norms, and in time, as E. Adamson Hoebel (1954:15) puts it: "The *norm* takes on the quality of the *normative*. What the most do, others should do."

As a strategy of social change, law has certain unique advantages and limitations as compared to other agents of change. Although these advantages and limitations go hand in hand and represent the opposite sides of the same coin, for analytical purposes I will examine them separately. The following discussion will focus on some of the more obvious reasons why law can facilitate change in society.

ADVANTAGES OF LAW
IN CREATING SOCIAL CHANGE

As I have emphasized earlier, identifying the perimeters of change and attributing change to a particular causal variable or a set of variables should always be undertaken with prudence. In many instances, the state of art of social change endeavors is not methodologically sophisticated enough to distinguish clearly among causal, necessary, sufficient, or contributory conditions to produce desired effects in society. Social change is a complex, multifaceted phenomenon brought about by a host of social forces. At times, change is slow, uneven and can be brought about by different factors to differing degrees. Change in society may be initiated by a number of means. Of these, the most drastic is revolution, aimed at fundamental changes in the power relation of classes within society. Others include rebellion, riot, *coup d'état,* various forms of violent protest movements, sit-ins, boycotts, strikes, demonstrations, social movements, education, mass media, technological innovations, ideology, and various forms of planned but nonlegal social change efforts dealing with various behaviors and practices at different levels in society.

As compared to this incomplete list of change inducing forces, the law has certain advantages. Change efforts through law tend to be more focused and specific. Change through law is a deliberate, rational, and conscious effort to alter a specific behavior or practice. The intentions of legal norms are clearly stated with a concomitant outline of the means of implementation and enforcement and sanction provisions. Essentially, change through law aims at rectifying, improving, ameliorating, or controlling behaviors and practices in precisely defined social situations—as identified by the proponents of a particular change. The advantages of law as an instrument of social change are attributed to the fact that law in society is seen as legitimate, more or less rational, authoritative, institutionalized, generally not disruptive, and backed by mechanisms of enforcement and sanctions.

Legitimate Authority

A major advantage of law as an instrument of social change is the general feeling in society that legal commands or prohibitions ought to be observed even by those critical of the law in question. To a great extent, this feeling of obligation depends on respect for legitimate authority (Andenaes, 1977:52).

The classic treatment of legitimate authority is that of Max Weber (1947). Weber defines "imperative coordination" as the probability that specific commands from a given source would be obeyed by given groups of persons. Obedience to commands can rest on a variety of considerations, from simple habituation to a purely rational calculation of advantage. But there is always a minimum of voluntary submission based on an interest in obedience. Obedience to authority can be based on custom, affectual ties, or on a purely material complex of interests, or by what Weber calls ideal motives. These purely material interests result in a relatively unstable situation, and must therefore be supplemented by other elements, both affectual and ideal. But even this complex of motives does not form a sufficiently reliable basis for a system of imperative cooperation, so that another important element must be added, the belief in legitimacy.

Following Max Weber, there are three types of legitimate authority—traditional, charismatic, and rational-legal. *Traditional* authority bases its claims to legitimacy on an established belief in the sanctity of traditions and the legitimacy of the status of those exercising authority. The obligation of obedience is not a matter of acceptance of the legality of an impersonal order, but rather as a matter of personal loyalty. The "rule of elders" would be illustrative of traditional authority.

Charismatic authority bases its claim to legitimacy on devotion to the specific and unusual sanctity, heroism, or exemplary character of an individual and the normative patterns that are revealed or ordained. The charismatic leader is obeyed by virtue of personal trust and in his or her revelation, or in his or her exemplary qualities. Illustrations of individuals with charismatic authority would include Moses, Christ, Mohammed, or Ghandi.

Rational-legal authority bases its claims to legitimacy on a belief in the legality of normative rules and in the right of those elevated to authority to issue commands under such rules. In such authority, obedience is owed to a legally established impersonal order. The individuals who exercise authority of office are shown obedience only by virtue of the formal legality of their commands, and only within the scope of authority of their office. Legal authority is not entirely conceptually distinct from traditional authority, although the distinction is nonetheless worth having. In modern society, "legality" suggests a component of rationality which traditional authority seems to lack. Indeed, during the transition to modernity, especially in the sixteenth and seventeenth centuries, authority tends more and more to be rationalized in distinctively legalistic and voluntaristic terms. "Rational" people "voluntarily" make a "contract," which generates the impersonal legal order.

Theory and empirical research tend to indicate that legitimate authority can wield considerable influence over both action and attitudes. It can be the result of both the coercive processes involved and the individual's internalized values regarding legitimate authority. There is a tendency on the part of individuals to assume that the law has the right to regulate behavior and then to justify conformity to the law. To an extent, obedience to the law stems from respect for the underlying process: "People obey the law, 'because it is the law.' This means they have general respect for procedures and for the system. They feel, for some reason, that they should obey, if Congress passes a law, if a judge makes a decision, if the city council passes an ordinance. If they were forced to explain why, they might refer to some concept of democracy, or the rule of law, or some other popular theory sustaining the political system" (Friedman, 1975:114).

Acceptance of legitimate authority can also minimize the possibility of cognitive dissonance (discrepancies between action and cognition) by interpreting or construing legally prohibited action as "wrong" or morally bad. The law then not only represents accepted modes of behavior, but also enforces and reinforces these accepted modes of behavior. Moreover, it defines the "correct" way of behaving and ordering in our everyday lives. This effect is ingrained and institutionalized and is present even without the sanctions which are part of the enforcement machinery. In fact, most people in most situations tend to comply with the law without consciously assessing the possibility of legal sanctions or punishment. The legal definitions of proper conduct become to a large extent subsumed in individual attitudes toward everyday life and become part of internalized values. As Talcott Parsons (1949:206) points out, "The well integrated personality ... has and feels obligations to respect legitimate authority. ... " The felt obligation, Parsons argues, is "disinterested," and the individual adheres to the prescribed code of conduct because it is considered "right." Something like the following may take place in the case of a person for whom a newly passed law represents legitimate authority:

> First, he believes the law has the right to regulate his behavior. Then, to justify his conformity to the law and lessen any cognitive dissonance he may feel, he may interpret the legally forbidden action as "wrong," or morally bad. In the course of time, with several repetitions of this process, behaviors disapproved by legitimate authority may perhaps come to be seen as morally improper without the intermediate behavioral compliance (Berkowitz and Walker, 1975:376).

The origin of a law can play an important role in perceptions of legitimate authority. The Supreme Court is considered the most vulnerable branch of the government when questions of legitimacy are raised because the public does not perceive the court as a policy-making agency (Rodgers and Bullock, 1972:188). Individuals expect that law as an instrument of change should be used by popularly elected officials such as legislators, and there is less doubt about the legitimacy of a law if Congress or the President is the agent. Possibly, school desegregation would have been more effective and abortion less controversial had they been initiated by Congress rather han decided by the Supreme Court.

The Binding Force of Law

There are several reasons why law is binding. They range from an assertion that laws are ordained by nature to the belief that law results from the consensus of its subjects to be bound. The immediate and simplest answer is that law is binding because most people in society consider it to be. The awareness and consciousness of law by most people serve as the foundation for its existence. People generally submit their behavior to its regulations, although they may have many different reasons for doing so. Some may believe that in obeying the law, they obey the higher authority of the law: God, nature, or the will of the people (Negley, 1965).

Others consider the content of the law to command obedience which, in turn, is seen as an obligation (Ladd, 1970). The law achieves its claim to obedience, and at least part of its morally obligatory force, from a recognition that it receives from those, or from most of those, to whom it is supposed to apply. In addition to agencies that encourage obedience through the application of law, other ingredients are normally present and essential. They include an inner desire of people to obey, reinforced by a belief that a particular law is fair and just because it is applied equally, a feeling of trust in the effectiveness and legitimacy of the government, and a sense of civic mindedness. They also include self-interest and the knowledge that most people obey the law and recognize it as having a certain morally rightful claim upon their behavior, or at the very least, that they behave as though they felt this way.

Even when laws go against accepted morality, they are often obeyed. The extermination of over 6 million Jews in Nazi Germany, clearly the most extreme instance of abhorrent immoral acts, was carried out by thousands of people in the name of obedience to the law. Stanley Milgram (1975:xii) contends that the essence of obedience lies in the fact that individuals come to see themselves instruments for implementing someone else's wishes, and they therefore no longer view themselves as responsible for their actions. In many instances, the acceptance of authority results in obedience. For example, Milgram, interested in the phenomena of obedience and authority, has shown that people of a wide range of backgrounds will do morally objectionable things to other people if they are told to do so by a clearly designated authority. Under the guise of conducting experiments on the "effects of punishment on memory," he found that about two-thirds of his laboratory subjects willingly behaved in a manner *they* believed was painful or harmful to others. Even though "victims" cried out in pain, feigned heart attacks, and literally begged for the experiment to be terminated, most subjects continued to obey authority and deliver what they believed to be high levels of electric shock (Milgram, 1975). The study, in addition to showing that under certain conditions many people will violate their own moral norms and inflict pain on other human beings, succinctly underlines the notion that most people willingly submit to authority and, by extension, the law.

Another reason for the binding force of the law may be that people prefer order over disorder and predictability of behavior. Individuals are creatures of habit because the habitual way of life requires less personal effort than any other and caters well to a sense of security. Obedience to the law guarantees that way. It also pays to follow the law, it saves effort and risk, a motivation sufficient to produce obedience. Obedience to the law is also related to the socialization process. People in general are brought up to obey the law. The legal way of life becomes the habitual way of life. From an early age, a child increasingly gains insight into the meaning of parental orders and regulations and becomes socialized. This process repeats itself in school and in the larger society. All such discourse increasingly provides—or should provide—for participation of the maturing person. The individual, so to speak, shapes these regulations and makes them his or her own. In the process, discipline is replaced by self-discipline.

Sanctions

Sanctions for disobedience to the law are surely among the reasons why laws have binding force. Hoebel says: "The law has teeth, teeth that can bite if need be, although they need not necessarily be bared" (1954:26). Sanctions are related to legal efficacy and are provided in order to guarantee the observance and execution of legal mandates, to enforce behavior. The sanctions recognized and used by legal systems are usually of a diversified character. In primitive societies, they may take the form of cruel punishments or social ostracism. In developed legal systems, the administration of sanctions is, as a general rule, entrusted to the organs of political government. Among the means of coercive law enforcement are punishment by fine or imprisonment, the imposition of damage awards which may be carried out by executions into the property of the judgment-debtor, the ordering by a court of specific acts or forbearances at the threat of a penalty, and the impeachment and removal of a public officer for dereliction of duty. As Hans Kelsen (1967:35) notes, the sanctions characteristic of modern legal systems go beyond the exercise of merely psychological pressure, and authorize the performance of disadvantageous coercive acts, namely, "[t]he forceable deprivation of life, freedom, economics and other values as a consequence of certain conditions."

Robert B. Seidman (1978:100) points out that "[l]aws more or less consistent with the existing social order need not rely upon the threat of legal sanction to induce behavior." However, not all laws are consistent with the existing social order, and an advantage of the law as an agent of social change is that potential law violation is often deterred by actual or perceived risk and by the severity of sanctions attached to noncompliance. Even the threat of sanctions can deter people from disobedience. Perhaps sanctions also play a part by inducing a moralistic attitude toward compliance (Schwartz and Orleans, 1970).

The types of sanctions used obviously vary with the purposes and goals of a law or legal policy. An essential distinction is whether the main purpose of a law is to prevent individuals from doing things which others in society oppose as being harmful or immoral, or whether the purpose of the law is to create new types of relationships between groups or individuals—essentially the difference between proscriptive and positive policy (Grossman and Grossman, 1971:70). The distinction is not always perfect. Positive policy-making often involves negative sanctions as well as positive rewards, although proscriptive policy-making usually involves only negative sanctions. Rewards such as federal contracts or subsidies are frequently a part of regulatory statutes attempting to change established patterns of economic behavior and have been used widely as an incentive to compliance with desegregation laws. Those who violate such laws not only lose prospective rewards but may also be liable for fines or criminal penalties. Grossman and Grossman point out: "Laws or statutes which seek positive societal changes of major proportions must rely as much on education and persuasion as on negative sanctions. For the carrot and stick approach to be successful, the latter must be visible and occasionally used" (1971:70).

The situation is different where the changes sought through the law are the reduction or elimination of deviant behaviors. In such instances, the law does not provide rewards or incentives to dissuade individuals from committing such acts—only the possibility, if not the certainty, of detection and punishment. In such instances, the emphasis is on deterence, punishment, and vengeance, and the objective is the elimination or reduction of a particular type of behavior considered harmful.

There are, of course, additional discernible advantages of the law in creating social change. For example, the law as an instrument of change can effectively be involved in the context of John Stuart Mills' notion of the law:

> (i) to achieve common purposes which cannot be left to the forces of supply and demand—such as education; (ii) to protect the immature and helpless; (iii) to control the power of associations, managed not only by the persons directly interested but by delegated agencies; (iv) to protect individuals acting in concert in cases where such action cannot be effective without legal sanctions; (v) to achieve objects of importance to society, present and future, which are beyond the powers of individuals or voluntary associations or which, if within their powers, would not normally be undertaken by them (Ginsberg, 1965:230).

The list of conceivable advantages of the law as an instrument of social change is indeed incomplete. What has been said so far is intended simply to demonstrate that the law has a peculiar and unparalleled position among agents of social change. At the same time, it has certain limitations. A knowledge and awareness of the limitations will help to understand more fully the role of the law in social change, and they need to be taken into account for the use of the law in change efforts.

LIMITATIONS OF LAW
IN CREATING SOCIAL CHANGE

In a period when alienation from virtually all social institutions proceeds swiftly, when people are suffering from a "crisis of confidence," it would seem a bit absurd to advance the idea that the law is an expression of the will of the people. For the great majority of individuals the law originates externally to them, and is imposed upon them in a manner that can be considered coercive. In reality, very few individuals actually participate in the formation of new laws and legislation. Consequently, one of the limitations of the law as an instrument of social change is the possibility of prevailing conflict of interests which tends to determine which laws are promulgated and which alternatives are rejected. Other limitations bearing on the efficacy of the law as an instrument of social change include the divergent views on the law as a tool of directed social change and the prevailing morality and values. In the following pages, I will consider these limitations separately, and then examine a number of conditions conducive to resistance to change from sociological, psychological, cultural, and economic perspectives.

Conflicting interests arise out of scarcity. Access to scarce resources and highly cherished objects is limited in every society. In the struggle for achieving them, some individuals and groups win, others lose. Several decades ago, Max Weber had already recognized, as did Karl Marx before him, that many laws are created to serve special economic interests. Individuals with the control of ownership of material goods are generally favored by laws since " . . . economic interests are among the strongest factors influencing the creation of law" (Weber, 1968:334). Weber further recognized that other special interests, in addition to the economic ones, influence the formation of law. Says Weber: "Law guarantees by no means only economic interest, but rather the most diverse interests ranging from the most elementary ones of protection of personal security to such purely ideal goods as personal honor or the honor of the divine powers. Above all, it guarantees political, ecclesiastical, familial and other positions of authority as well as positions of social preeminence of any kind. . . . " (1968:333).

There are two important insights contained in Weber's points. The first is that conflict of interest provides the framework in which laws are framed and change is brought about. Consequently, social stratification in a society will determine to a large extent the part laws will play in bringing about change based on the selectiveness and preferences exercised by those who promulgate those changes. The second point concerns the significance of the use of power to back up these changes. Studies of the legislative, judicial, and administrative processes in a society could lead very quickly to a discovery of not only who wills the power in society, but also what interests are significant and influential in that group. Thus, the law as an instrument of a change can be viewed in the context of the organization of power and the processes by which interests are established in everyday social life; the resulting changes might very well be evaluated in these terms.

In a sense it is obvious, understandable, and even tautological that the powerful make and administer the laws in society. If anything gets done, it is because somebody had the power to do it. At the same time, those who are powerful and influential tend to use the law to protect their advantageous position in society and for them " . . . the law in effect structures the power (superordinate-subordinate) relationships in a society; it maintains the status quo and protects the various strata against each other" (Hertzler, 1961:421).

Many legislative enactments, administrative rulings, and judicial decisions reflect the power configurations in society. Some groups and associations are more powerful than others, and by virtue of being at the center of power they are better able to reinforce their interests than those at the periphery. Even members of the legal profession are considered as "professional go-betweens" for the principal political, corporate, and other interest groups, and hence serve to "unify the power elite" (Mills, 1957:289). Furthermore, as I noted in Chapter Three, many people are often apathetic or unaware of an issue, but even when they are concerned, they are frequently unable to organize and thus successfully impose their preference on the legislature. According to Marxist writers, it results in a sense of alienation and powerlessness coupled with a feeling of oppression and exploitation (see, for example, Szymanski and Goertzel, 1979).

Curiously, however, those who are supposed to be coerced or oppressed by a system of laws imposed upon them by a ruling minority often seem unaware of their coercion or oppression. Indeed, they are frequently among the strongest partisans of the existing legal system. It may be argued that they have been "indoctrinated" by the ruling establishment who uses its power to confuse them as to their true interests. But this requires that we distinguish between what people define as their interests and what their "true interests" are, a distinction that has given rise to a great deal of complex, subtle, and inconclusive polemics.

There are numerous instances when racial and ethnic minorities, workers, and farmers organized to promote what they conceived to be their interests. Blacks have been instrumental in the passage of a variety of civil rights laws. In recent years, Spanish Americans have effectively managed the introduction of bilingual education in high schools in areas with a large proportion of Hispanics. Labor was instrumental in the enactment of a series of legislations dealing, for example, with occupational safety and health, flexitime work schedules, collective bargaining, and unemployment compensation. Similarly, farmers have succeeded in furthering their interests through legal measures dealing, for example, with migrant workers, the importation of certain food items, such as citrus fruits, and favorable export provisions. Does this not mean that racial and ethnic minorities, workers, and farmers are too a part of the power structure? And if they are, does this not mean that the distribution of power in society is more widespread and complicated than is suggested by writers who speak of a simple division of society into "the powerful" and the "powerless"?

It is debatable whether the existence of conflicting interests could really be construed as pointing to a major limitation of the law as an instrument of change. The points raised concerning the power of certain interest groups are valid, but the actual mechanics of change through the law would in any case preclude inclusion of large segments of the population. Large-scale participation of the citizenry in legal change, even in a democratic society, is seldom feasible. But lack of participation does not necessarily mean lack of representation. In the United States and Western European countries, people do have access (although of varying rates) to lawmakers and to the legal apparatus, and their aspirations for change through the law are often realized.

Law as a Policy Instrument

Another school of thought on the limits of the law as an instrument of social change is epitomized by Yehezkel Dror. He contends that "law by itself is only one component of a large set of policy instruments and usually cannot and is not used by itself. Therefore, focusing of exclusive attention on law as a tool of directed social change is a case of tunnel vision, which lacks the minimum perspective necessary for making sense from the observed phenomena" (Dror, 1970:554). He suggests that it is necessary to redefine the subject of "law as a tool of directed social change" and to consider it as part of other social policy instruments, since the law is but one of many policy instruments which must be used in combination. In the context of social problems such as race relations, public safety, drug abuse, pollution, and the like, "the necessity to use law as a policy instrument should be quite convincing" (Dror, 1970:555). This view certainly has merits. At times, change through the law can and should be construed as an ingredient of a larger policy. For example, the passage of the Economic Opportunity Act took place in the context of a broader policy which attempted to alleviate poverty in the United States.

However, the law is often used as an instrument of change outside of the context of a broad policy-making framework. This is typically the situation in reform-oriented litigation where the objective is to alter a particular institutionalized practice. For example, the Supreme Court decision to overrule state abortion statutes was not carried out within specific policy considerations, and yet it obviously had a tremendous impact on women seeking to terminate pregnancy legally. Although judicial decisions are generally not rendered as a policy instrument, due to the adversary nature of litigation, legislative and administrative reforms dealing with larger social issues should take place in a broader social policy-making framework. Such an approach would greatly enhance the efficacy of the law as an instrument of change. To this end, Dror advocates the establishment of interdisciplinary teams of lawyers, social scientists, and policy analysts to engage in relevant studies and prepare policy recommendations.

Morality and Values

The sociological literature recognizes, as James P. Levine (1970:592) notes, that the ability of the law to produce social change is probabilistic, contingent, and sequential. If a law is enacted or a court decision is rendered, it is probable that certain changes will follow, but the degree of change is contingent on certain prevailing circumstances. The law is sequential to the degree that it must precede certain desired changes, but because a large number of factors influence change, the time lag is not obvious. Moreover, a number of factors other than the law may have an effect on change in a particular area, which means that the cause and effect relationship between the law and change is very difficult to identify. Some of these factors are related to the prevailing morality and values in society.

Patrick Devlin (1965) argues that a society owes its existence less to its institutions than to the shared morality that binds it together. Although his thesis is only partly true, morality and values affect the efficacy of the law in social change. Obviously, society could not exist without accepting certain basic values, principles, and standards. On certain issues, such as violence, truth, individual liberty, and human dignity, a shared morality is essential. But this does not mean, however, that all the values in our shared morality are basic and essential, or that decline in one value spells decline in all the rest. Moreover, not all our values are essential. Rules about property, for example, are not: Some principles about property are essential, but no society needs to have those very property principles that are characteristics of, for example, the United States—the principle of private ownership. A society could own all property in common without ceasing to count as a society.

In general, when the law is used as an instrument of social change it needs the support of society. Says Schur: "A good illustration of the systematic ineffectiveness of unsupported law is provided by the utter failure of legislation designed to enforce private morality" (1968:132). Thus, an obvious limitation of the law in social change appears when it tries to deal with what may be called moral issues in society. Laws prohibiting adultery, for example, have existed for centuries, but adultery remains a favorite indoor sport in the United States and elsewhere. Similarly, laws dealing with homosexuality or prostitution, have generally been ineffective. The well-known failure of the prohibition of alcohol through constitutional amendment and legislation to produce a truly "dry" society, or to keep most people from drinking, is another example of the limitation of the law to bring about social change in public "morals."

A similar situation exists with regard to the prohibition of several kinds of drugs, especially marijuana. Interestingly, the marijuana laws have been called the "new prohibition," to underline the similarity to alcohol prohibition and the futility of legal control of consumption of these substances (Kaplan, 1971). Clearly, "Behavior that is perceived of as satisfying important drives is more difficult to extinguish than behavior that satisfies less compelling drives" (Zimring and Hawkins, 1975:332). In fact, some argue that marijuana at least should be a source of pleasure, not pain or shame: "We should be free to cultivate and sell and buy this 'euphoriant.' The only controls should be those imposed to protect from bogus or polluted merchandise. With the dreadful example of Prohibition before us, it seems nearly unthinkable that we should have done it again.... When will we learn that in a democracy it is for the people to tell the government, not for the government to tell the people, what makes them happy?" (Goldman, quoted in Behavior Today, 1979:8).

The link between law and morality in the making and unmaking of law raises two questions: (1) What needs to be done in considering a change in the law when moral opinion is divided? Are there criteria other than individual likes and dislikes to which appeal can be made? (2) How to draw the line between that part of morality or immorality which needs legal enforcement and that which the law ought to leave alone (Ginsberg, 1965:232). In response to these questions, Morris Ginsberg suggests that the law ought to deal only with what can be ascertained on reliable evidence and with acts that can be precisely defined; with primarily overt or external observable acts; and the law must, as far as possible, respect privacy. He contends that these are "[p]rinciples of demarcation arising from the limitations inherent in the machinery of the law" (Ginsberg, 1965:238).

Thus, laws are more likely to bring about changes in what may be called external behavior. However, changes in external behavior are after a while usually followed by changes in values, morals and attitudes. As Morroe Berger (1952:172) emphasizes: "While it is true that the province of law is 'external' behavior, it is also true that in an urban, secular society an increasing number of relations fall within this province. Thus the range of behavior that can be called 'external' is enlarged. At the same time, law can influence 'external' acts which affect or constitute the conditions for the exercise of the private inclinations and tastes that are said to be beyond the realm of law." The fact that a change in attitude is only partial at first does not make it any the less of a change. This is contrary to the arguments advanced several decades ago by William Graham Sumner (1906), which since have been echoed by many, that "stateways cannot change folkways."

What Sumner contended was that the law is limited to the regulation of individual behavior, and it cannot be used to alter attitudes, values, and morality. There are many examples both to support and refute this contention. There are several instances where the promulgation of laws did not result in widespread acceptance by the population. For example, the U.S. Constitution asserted the equality of persons before the law without much effect upon increased opportunities for blacks or upon the prejudicial attitudes of many whites for generations. Similarly, the Indian Constitution purportedly outlawed discrimination against untouchables that has not significantly changed the values and attitudes of most Indians (Seidman, 1978:156).

On the other side of the debate regarding the power of law to change attitudes, there are several studies suggesting that law can, indeed, alter values and attitudes. For example, studies on the effects of desegregation in situations such as "armed forces units, housing projects, and employment situations indicate that change required by law has lessened prejudice" (Greenberg, 1959:26). Essentially, the purpose of the law is to change behavior, and in some measure the laws requiring whites to change their behavior in dealing with blacks has changed attitudes (Harris, 1977:168). However, it should be noted that there is no simple way to describe white attitudes toward black people. Although there has been a massive shift toward more favorable racial attitudes, resistance to change in race relations is still widespread. Some forms of change, such as acceptance of blacks in work situations, are accepted. Other more private kinds of change (for example, interracial marriage) are resisted. The idea of racial superiority is no longer characteristic of white attitudes. This conventional sign of racial doctrine seems to have changed for the better. This is reflected, in part, in the relative disuse of derogatory and stereotyped language. In the early 1900s, derogatory words and expressions were commonly used to describe blacks—and one hardly thought it was wrong to do so. While such language is still used today, its use has greatly diminished. Finally, those Americans who went to college after World War II are clearly more positive in their attitudes toward blacks than those who did not go to college or who went to college before the war (Campbell, 1971).

But the law can change morality and values only under some conditions, and those conditions need to be specified. As Robert B. Seidman (1978:156) notes, "[t]he literature contains little more than speculations," and there is a void of empirical studies. In general, the law will more readily change morality and values where it first changes behavior. Such a change is usually followed by a justification of the new activity. To a great extent, however, the efficacy of the law depends much upon its adaptation to morality and values if it is intended to induce change (Fuller, 1969:38–91).

There is still much to be learned about when and under what conditions the law can "not only *codify* existing customs, morals, or mores, but also ... *modify* the behavior and values presently existing in a particular society" (Evan, 1965:286). In change efforts through the law, the prevalence and intensity of moral feelings and values need to be taken into account in both preserving and altering the status quo.

RESISTANCE TO CHANGE

In addition to the limitations of law as an instrument of social change discussed in the preceding section, the efficacy of the law (as well as other mechanisms of change) is further hindered by a variety of forces. In the modern world, situations of resistance to change are much more numerous than situations of acceptance. Members of a society can always find a justification in some more or less practical and rational terms for active resistance to change. Often change is resisted because it conflicts with traditional values and beliefs, or a particular change may simply cost too much money, and sometimes people resist change because it interferes with their habits or makes them feel frightened or threatened. Although the law has certain advantages over other agents of change, for a greater appreciation of the role of law in change, it is helpful to identify some general conditions of resistance which have a bearing on the law. The awareness of these conditions is a prerequisite for a more efficient use of law as a method of social engineering.

The sociological literature recognizes a variety of tendencies to ward off change which directly or indirectly have an effect on law as an instrument of change. The intent of this section is to discuss briefly, rather than to analyze in depth, a series of forces that act as barriers to change. For the sake of clarity, I shall consider resistance to change through law in the context of social, psychological, cultural, and economic factors. The categories are only illustrative, and this distinction is made only for analytical purposes, for many of these factors operate in various combinations and intensity, depending on the magnitude and scope of a particular change effort. Obviously, there is a fair amount of overlapping among these factors. They are not mutually exclusive, and many of them, depending on the purpose, may be subsumed under different categories.

Social Factors

There are several social factors that may be construed as potential barriers to change. They include vested interests, ideological resistance, moral sentiments, and organized opposition.

Vested Interests   Change may be resisted by individuals or groups that fear a loss of power, prestige, or wealth, should a new proposal gain acceptance. There are many different types of vested interests for whom the status quo is profitable and preferable. Students attending state universities have a vested interest in tax-supported higher education. Divorce lawyers constitute a vested interest, and for a long time have fought efforts to reform the divorce laws. Physicians opposing various forms of "socialized medicine" constitute a vested interest. Residents in a community often develop vested interests in their neighborhood. They often organize to resist zoning changes, interstate highways, the construction of correctional facilities, or the busing of their children. In fact, nearly everyone has some vested interests—from the rich with their tax-exempt bonds to the poor with their welfare checks.

The acceptance of almost any change through law will adversely affect the status of some individuals or groups in society, and to the degree that those whose status is threatened consciously recognize the danger they will oppose the change. For example, Gregory Massell (1973) reports that Soviet efforts in the early 1920s in central Asia to induce Moslem women to assert their independence of male domination was perceived by men as threatening to traditional status interests. The men reacted by forming counter-revolutionary bands and murdering some of the women who obeyed the new laws.

Social Class   Rigid class and caste patterns in general tend to hinder the acceptance of change. In highly stratified societies, persons are expected to obey and take orders from those in superior positions of authority or power. The prerogatives of the upper strata are jealously guarded and attempts to infringe upon them by members of lower socioeconomic groups are often resented and repulsed. For instance, under the traditional Indian and Pakistani rigid caste system, members of different castes could not draw water from the same well, go to the same schools, eat together, or otherwise mingle. In most cases, for the upper classes there is a tendency to cherish the old ways of doing things and to adhere to the status quo.

In the United States, those who identify themselves as working-class people tend more readily to agree that legal intervention is necessary to rectify deleterious social conditions such as guaranteeing employment opportunities and providing adequate medical care (Beeghley, 1978:114). By contrast, middle- and upper-class people tend to oppose government intervention in these domains. For other government programs (such as aid to education), class-related differences tend to diminish.

Ideological Resistance   Resistance to change through law on ideological grounds is quite prevalent. A good example of this is the opposition of the Catholic Church to legislation and court decisions dealing with the removal of some of the restrictions on birth control and abortion. Another illustration of ideological resistance (which goes hand in hand with vested interests) is that by the medical profession to anything suggesting socialized medicine, including the enactment of the Medicare Law of 1965 (Allen, 1971:278–279). In general, the basic intellectual and religious assumptions and interpretations concerning existing power, morality, welfare, and security tend to be rather consistent and adversely disposed to change (Vago, 1980:229).

Moral Sentiments Fear and apprehension is often related to the moral consequences of accepting something novel. Notes La Piere: "Here resistance usually has as its rationale the claim that the new violates and so jeopardizes a valued moral principle or precept, one that is considered essential to the survival of the social system or of mankind in general" (1965:179). For example, laws making contraception available are resisted in some circles because they violate the sanctity of life. Resistance to change on moral grounds is based on the fact that in every society individuals are more or less effectively socialized into considering that the established forms of conduct, especially those of an organizational nature, are the only ones that are right and proper. In this sense, the ideas of right and proper are emotionally incorporated into the personality. Change that would result in emotional disturbances is resisted.

Organized Opposition Occasionally, widespread individual resistance to change may become mobilized into organized opposition which can assume formal organizational structure, for example, the National Rifle Association opposing gun control, or it may be channeled through a social movement, for instance, the recent pro-life activities. In modern societies, with the multiplicity of informal and formal organizations often in conflict with each other, a variety of new organizations have developed to combat specific threats to the status quo. For example, members of the John Birch Society decry a whole range of social changes from racial integration to the acceptance and legal protection of pornography. As with the John Birch Society, the reemergence of the Ku Klux Klan is based on public opposition to social change, but focuses mainly on changing race relations. These and similar organizations have resisted change that was under way, and while most of them have fought a losing battle, their delaying effects have often been considerable. At times, however, when organized opposition to change through law is not forthcoming, the consequences can be disastrous. For instance, over 6 million Jews were slaughtered in concentration camps during the Second World War in part because they did not organize resistance to the changes beginning in the early 1930s in Nazi Germany.

Psychological Factors

Goodwin Watson (1969:488) remarks that "[a]ll of the forces which contribute to stability in personality or in social systems can be perceived as resisting change." Any detailed discussion of these forces is obviously beyond the scope of this book. For the present purpose I shall only consider habit, motivation, ignorance, selective perception, and moral development.

Habit   From a psychological perspective, an initial impediment to change is the matter of habit. Once a habit is established, its operation often becomes satisfying to the individual. People become accustomed to behaving or acting in a certain manner and they feel comfortable with it. Once a particular form of behavior becomes routinized and habitual, it will resist change. Meyer F. Nimkoff (1957:62) suggests that the customs of a society are collective habits; in particular, where sentiment pervades custom, custom is slow to change when challenged by new ideas and practices. To cite but a single illustration, attempts to introduce the metric system have met with considerable resistance in the United States. We are accustomed to miles and feel uncomfortable with kilometers; we prefer a quart of something, rather than a liter. When the law is used as an instrument of social change to alter established customs, it is more likely that the achievement of acceptable rates of compliance will require an active reorientation of the values and behaviors of a significant part of the target population (Zimring and Hawkins, 1975:331).

Motivation   The acceptance of change through law is also conditioned by motivational forces. Some motivations are culture bound, in the sense that their presence or absence is characteristic of a particular culture. For instance, religious beliefs in some cultures offer motivations to certain kinds of change, while in other cultures these motivations center on the preservation of the status quo. Other kinds of motivations tend to be universal, or nearly universal, in that they cut across societies and cultures (Foster, 1973:152). Examples of these motivations include the desire for prestige or for economic gain and the wish to comply with friendship obligations. Changes that may threaten the desire for economic gain or the attraction of prestige and high status will in general be considered threatening and likely resisted.

Ignorance   Ignorance is another psychological factor generally associated with resistance to change. At times, ignorance goes hand in hand with fear of the new. This is often true in the case with new foods. Not too long ago many individuals assumed that citrus fruit brought an acid condition to the digestive tract. Once it was proved otherwise, resistance based on the acid matter has faded. Ignorance can also be a factor in noncompliance with laws designed to reduce discriminatory practices. For example, employers often make observations about nonwhites as a group relative to whites and then on that basis hesitate to hire individual nonwhites (Beeghley, 1978:242). Ignorance is obviously an important factor in prejudice when a preexisting attitude is so strong and inflexible that it seriously distorts perception and judgment.

Perception   Law, by design and intent, tends to be universal. The perception of the intent of the law, however, is selective and varies with socioeconomic, cultural, and demographic variables. The unique pattern of people's needs, attitudes, habits, and values derived through socialization determines what they will selectively attend to, what they will selectively interpret, and what they will selectively act upon. People in general will be more receptive to new ideas if they are related to their interests, consistent with their attitudes, congruent with their beliefs, and supportive of their values. Differing perceptions of the purpose of a law may hinder change. For example, in India the law provides for widespread distribution of family-planning information and supplies. But the use of contraceptive devices has been rejected by many Indian villagers because they perceived the law's intent to stop birth completely. In the United States, the early attempts to fluoridate city water supplies met with perceptions of "communist conspiracy" being behind these efforts, and as a result they were resisted in many communities.

The way a law is written, as I noted earlier, also affects perception. For example, in their early stages most civil rights laws have been ambiguous and weak. The *Brown* decision is a good illustration. Calling for desegregation "with all deliberate speed" is too vague, too indefinite to bring about meaningful change. "Ambiguity always lends itself to individualized perceptions" (Rodgers and Bullock, 1972:199), and the individuals will interpret and perceive the meaning of the law in a way they consider most advantageous.

Moral Development   To a great extent, obedience to the law stems from a sense of moral obligation, which is the product of socialization. Only relatively recently, however, has there been some awareness of moral codes which are not necessarily linked to conventional external standards of right and wrong behavior, but represent internally consistent principles by which people govern their lives.

Perhaps the most extensive work on moral development was carried out by Lawrence Kohlberg (1964, 1967). He defines six stages in moral development. The first stage is described as an "obedience and punishment" orientation. This stage involves a "deference to superior power or prestige" and an orientation toward avoiding trouble. The second stage, "instrumental relativism," is characterized by naive notions of reciprocity. With this orientation, people will attempt to satisfy their own needs by simple negotiation with others or by a primitive form of equalitarianism. He calls these two stages "premoral." The third stage, "personal concordance," is an orientation based on approval and pleasing others. It is characterized by conformity to perceived majority beliefs. Such people adhere to what they consider to be prevailing norms. Stage four is the "law and order" stage. People with such orientations are committed to "doing their duty," and being respectful to those in authority. Stages three and four combine to form a conventional moral orientation.

Stages five and six indicate the internalized-principle orientation. Kohlberg calls stage five the "social contract" stage; it involves a legalistic orientation. Commitments are viewed in contractual terms, and people at this stage will avoid efforts to break implicit or explicit agreements. The final and highest stage of moral development is "individual principles." This emphasizes conscience, mutual trust, and respect as the guiding principles of behavior.

If the developmental theory proposed by Kohlberg is correct, the law is more or less limited depending on the stage of moral development of members of a society. In this context, David J. Danelski (1974:14–15) suggests that both qualitative and quantitative considerations are important. We would need to know the modal stage of the moral development of elites, of "average" citizens, and of deprived groups. If most members of a society were at the first and second stages, institutional enforcement would be essential to maintain order and security. Law would be least limited in a society in which most people were at the third and fourth stages of development. Law at the last two stages is probably more limited than at stages three and four, "but it might be otherwise if it is perceived as democratically agreed upon and consistent with individual principles of conscience. If it is not, it is likely to be more limited" (Danelski, 1974:15). The limits of law, in other words, appear to be curvilinear in terms of moral development.

Cultural Factors

When long-established practices or behaviors are threatened, resistance to change is usually strong, often on the basis of traditional beliefs and values. The status quo is protected and change resisted. For example, the Mormons, on the basis of traditional religious beliefs, opposed laws threatening their polygamous marriage. Similarly, in India, where malnutrition is a problem of considerable magnitude, over 3 million cows sacred to Hindus are not only exempt from being slaughtered for food but are also allowed to roam through villages and farm lands, often causing extensive damages to crops. Eating beef runs counter to long-held religious beliefs, and as a result it is unlikely that the raising of cattle for food will be acceptable in India. Other cultural factors also act often as obstacles to change. They include fatalism, ethnocentrism, notions of incompatability, and superstitions.

Fatalism   States Mead: "In many parts of the world we find cultures adhering to the belief that man has no causal effect upon his future or the future of the land; God, not man, can improve man's lot.... It is difficult to persuade such people to use fertilizers, or to save the best seed for planting, since man is responsible only for the performance, and the divine for the success of the act" (1953:201). Basically, fatalism entails a feeling of a lack of mastery over nature. People have no control over their lives and everything that happens to them is caused by God or evil spirits. Such a fatalistic outlook undoubtedly results in resistance to change, for change is seen as human-initiated rather than having a divine origin.

Ethnocentrism   Some groups in society consider themselves "superior," possessing the only "right" way of thinking about the world and of coping with the environment. Feelings of superiority about one's group are likely to make people unreceptive to the ideas and methods used in other groups. As a result, ethnocentrism often constitutes a bulwark against change. For example, such feelings of superiority by whites have hindered integration efforts in housing, employment, and education.

Incompatibility   Resistance to change is often due to the presence in the target group of material and systems which are, or considered to be, irreconcilable with the new proposal. When such incompatibility exists in a culture, change comes about with difficulty. An illustration is the marriage age law enacted in Israel in an attempt to induce changes in the immigrant population through legal norms. The law sets seventeen as the minimum age for marriage with the exception of pregnancy and imposes a criminal sanction on anyone who marries a girl below the age of seventeen without permission of the district court. By setting the minimum age at seventeen, the law attempted to impose a rule of behavior which was incompatible to the customs and habits of some of the sections of the Jewish population of Israel which came from Arab and Oriental countries, where marriage was usually contracted at a lower age. The act only had limited effect, and communities which formerly permitted marriage of females at an early age continue to do so (Dror, 1968:678).

Superstition   Superstition is defined as an uncritical acceptance of a belief which is not substantiated by facts. At times, superstitions act as barriers to change. For example, in one situation in Zimbabwe (formerly Rhodesia), nutrition education efforts were hampered due to the fact that many women would not eat eggs. According to widespread belief, eggs cause infertility, make babies bald, and cause women to be promiscuous. Similarly, in the Philippines, it is a widely accepted idea that squash and chicken eaten at the same time produce leprosy. In some places, women are not given milk during late pregnancy because of the belief that it produces a fetus too large for easy delivery, and in other places, a baby may not be given water for several months after birth because water's "cold" quality will upset the infant's heat equilibrium. In some parts of Ghana children are not given meat or fish because it is believed that they cause intestinal worms (Foster, 1973:103–104). Obviously, where such superstitious beliefs prevail, change efforts through law or other agents will meet some resistance.

Economic Factors

Even in affluent societies, limited economic resources constitute a barrier to changes that might otherwise be readily adopted. For instance, in the United States, almost everyone would readily accept the desirability of more effective controls on pollution, cheaper and more convenient systems of public transportation, effective welfare programs, and adequate health care for all. The fact that changes in these areas come very slowly is a matter of not only priorities, but also of cost. Cost and limited economic resources in a society do in effect provide a source of resistance to change.

It is a truism that like everything else, change through law has its costs. In most instances, the implementation of legislation, administrative ruling, or court decision carries a price tag. For example, the economic impact of federal regulations on institutions of higher education has been significant. The various affirmative action programs carry sanctions providing for the cutoff of *all* federal funding to institutions which do not comply with anti-bias laws. Compliance, in turn, results in increased administrative costs for postsecondary institutions. Philip Boffey (1975) discusses a study of six institutions to determine the economic impact of federal regulations on their operating budget. The study considered the impact and financial cost of the equal employment opportunity provisions of the Civil Rights Act, Equal Pay Act, the Affirmative Action Program based on a 1965 executive order, age discrimination in employment, the Occupational Safety and Health Act of 1970, minimum wage law, unemployment insurance, and the Environmental Protection Law on university operating expenses. Although the impact of a small number of these and related regulations would be minimal on the university, collectively, however, the effect is substantial. Of the six colleges and universities studied, the increase in the total operating budget over the decade from 1965 to 1975 relating to federal regulations ranged from 1 to 4 percent. These costs may seem small in comparison to the total institutional operational budgets, but are substantial relative to the operating deficits experienced by some institutions in recent years, and are greater than the budgets of some academic departments that may face extinction through shifts in institutional budget priorities. During the ten-year period of the study, the cost of complying with federal regulations increased twenty-fold (Boffey, 1975:445). The increased economic costs associated with compliance are resisted in many academic circles, and have contributed to the demands for modification of a variety of laws affecting higher education.

In addition to the direct cost of a particular change effort, the way costs and benefits are distributed also affects resistance. For example, when costs and benefits are widely distributed (as in Social Security), there is minimal resistance to programs. The cost to each taxpayer is relatively small, the benefits are so widely distributed "that they are almost like collective goods; beneficiaries will enjoy the benefits, but only make small contributions to their retention or growth" (Handler, 1978:15). Resistance will be forthcoming in situations where benefits are distributed while costs are concentrated. For example, automakers resist (although not too successfully) legal attempts to impose pollution control measures on cars.

Although a particular change through the law may be desirable (such as an effective and comprehensive universal health insurance plan in the United States), limited economic resources often act as barriers to such change efforts. Of the four sources of resistance to change, the economic factors are perhaps the most decisive. Regardless of the desirability of a proposed change, its compatibility with the values and beliefs of the recipients and many other considerations, it will be resisted if the economic sacrifice is too great. Simply stated, regardless of how much people in a society want something, if they cannot afford it, chances are they will not be able to get it. As George M. Foster (1973:78) suggests: "Cultural, social and psychological barriers and stimulants to change exist in an economic setting ... (and) economic factors ... seem to set the absolute limits to change."

SUMMARY

Social change occurs constantly—although at varying rates—in contemporary societies, and it affects the lives of individuals in different ways. Changes in society are a product of a multitude of factors and in many cases of the interrelationships among them. In addition to law, there are a number of other mechanisms of social change. All these mechanisms are in many ways interrelated, and one should be careful not to assign undue weight to any one of these "causes" in isolation.

Law is both a dependent and independent variable in social change. The relationship between law and change is still controversial. Some maintain that law is a reactor to social change, others argue that it increasingly is an initiator of change. These two views represent the extremes of a continuum dealing with the relationship between law and social change. In modern society, law does play a large part in social change and vice versa.

Increasingly, law is being considered as an instrument of social change. Today the role of law in change is of more than theoretical interest. In many areas of social life, such as education, race relations, housing, transportation, energy utilization, and the protection of the environment, the law has been relied on as an important instrument of change. Law influences social change directly and indirectly. It redefines the normative order, extends formal rights, and is used for planning purposes.

As compared to other agents of change, the law has several distinct advantages. The advantages of law as an agent of change are attributed to the fact that the law in society is seen as legitimate, more or less rational, authoritative, institutionalized, generally not disruptive, and backed by mechanisms of enforcement and sanctions.

At the same time, the law has certain limitations in creating social change. It is not always able to resolve conflicting interests, and generally the powerful in society fare better than the less privileged and the unorganized. Law alone cannot deal effectively with social problems such as drug addiction, overpopulation, or corruption in government. These problems still defy adequate solution. Each is not a single problem but a complex of problems: each generates a host of countervailing considerations—moral, economic, and otherwise—that compound the complexities. Further limitations flow from the inherent clumsiness of the instrument of the rule of law. One cannot easily foresee and take into account the situations to which a rule might apply. How many advocates of rent control for the poor would have anticipated the extent to which it would contribute to the perpetuation of the ghetto? How many legislators would have foreseen that subsidies to help farmers would result in reducing the number of farmers? The law is further limited by the divergencies in values and moral codes, the difficulty of the enforceability of some laws, the occasional lack of clarity of law, and by the questionable diligence of enforcement of certain laws.

In addition to these limits on the law in social change, a variety of social, psychological, cultural, and economic forces may provide direct or indirect resistance to change efforts. The social factors include vested interests, social class, moral sentiments, and organized opposition. Psychological resistance may be triggered by habit, motivation, ignorance, selective perception, and the complexities inherent in moral development. Cultural barriers to change include fatalism, ethnocentrism, and notions of incompatibility and superstitions. But the economic factors are perhaps the most decisive. Cost and limited economic resources effectively set a limit to change.

SUGGESTED FURTHER READINGS

A. ALLOTT, *The Limits of Law*. London: Butterworths, 1980. A critical analysis of the role and limits of law in social change.

LAWRENCE M. FRIEDMAN, *American Law: An Introduction*. New York: W.W. Norton and Company, 1984. See in particular Chapter fourteen on law and social change.

WOLFGANG FRIEDMANN, *Law in a Changing Society*, 2nd ed. New York: Columbia University Press, 1972. An analysis of the dual function of the law as a reactor to and initiator of social change.

JOEL B. GROSSMAN and MARY H. GROSSMAN, eds., *Law and Change in Modern America*, Pacific Palisades, Santa Monica, CA: Goodyear, 1971. An outstanding collection of articles on law as an instrument of social change and on the functions of law in the process of change.

P. P. GUREYEV and P. I. SEDUGIN, eds., *Legislation in the U.S.S.R.* Moscow: Progress Publishers, 1977, translated by Denis Ogden. A detailed analysis of how the law is being used as a form of social engineering in the Soviet Union.

JOEL F. HANDLER, *Social Movements and the Legal System, A Theory of Law Reform and Social Change*. New York: Academic Press, 1978. An analysis of the conditions under which the law and the courts can be used to accomplish changes in the domains of environmental protection, consumer protection, civil rights, and social welfare.

ARTHUR SELWYN MILLER, *Social Change and Fundamental Law, America's Evolving Constitution*. Westport, CT: Greenwood Press, 1979. An examination of the impact of science and technological change on the law from a lawyer's perspective.

ROBERT B. SEIDMAN, *The State, Law and Development*. New York: St. Martin's Press, 1978. A detailed investigation of the uses and limitations of the law in promoting third-world development.

STEVEN VAGO, *Social Change*. New York: Holt, Rinehart & Winston, 1980. A comprehensive text on social change.

ALAN WATSON, *The Evolution of Law*. Baltimore: Johns Hopkins University Press, 1985. An historical analysis of the relationship between law and social and economic variables with illustrative material from Roman and seventeenth-century Scots private law.

REFERENCES

ALLEN, FRANCIS R. 1971. *Socio-Cultural Dynamics, An Introduction to Social Change*. New York: Macmillan.

ANDENAES, JOHANNES. 1977. "The Moral or Educative Influence of Criminal Law," Pp. 50–59 in June Louis Tapp and Felice J. Levine, eds., Law, Justice, and the Individual in Society, Psychological and Legal Issues. New York: Holt, Rinehart & Winston.

AUBERT, VILHELM, ed. 1969. *Sociology of Law*. Harmondsworth, England: Penguin Books, Ltd.

BEEGHLEY, LEONARD. 1978. *Social Stratification in America, A Critical Analysis of Theory and Research*. Santa Monica, CA: Goodyear.

Behavior Today. 1979. "New Roundup," 10 (26)(July 9):8.

BERGER, MORROE. 1952. *Equality by Statute*. New York: Columbia University Press.

BERKOWITZ, LEONARD and NIGEL WALKER. 1975. "Laws and Moral Judgements," Pp. 374–383 in Ronald L. Akers and Richard Hawkins, eds., Law and Social Control. Englewood Cliffs, NJ: Prentice-Hall.

BOFFEY, PHILIP. 1975. "Higher Education and Regulation: Counting the Costs of Compliance," Science 190 (October-December):444–446.

BRADY, JAMES P. 1981. "A Season of Startling Alliance: Chinese Law and Justice in the New Order," International Journal of the Sociology of Law 9:41–67.

CAMPBELL, ANGUS. 1971. *White Attitudes Toward Black People.* Ann Arbor, MI: Institute for Social Research, University of Michigan.

CARTER, LIEF H. 1979. *Reason in Law.* Boston: Little, Brown.

DANELSKI, DAVID J. 1974. "The Limits of Law," Pp. 8–27 in J. Roland Pennock and John W. Chapman, eds., The Limits of Law. New York: Lieber-Atherton.

DEVLIN, PATRICK. 1965. *The Enforcement of Morals.* New York: Oxford University Press.

DROR, YEHEZKEL. 1968. "Law and Social Change," Pp. 663–680 in Rita James Simon, ed., The Sociology of Law. San Francisco: Chandler Publishing Company; 1970. "Law as a Tool of Directed Social Change," American Behavioral Scientist, 13:553–559.

EORSI, GYULA and ATTILA HARMATHY. 1971. *Law and Economic Reform in Socialistic Countries.* Budapest: Akademiai Kiado.

EVAN, WILLIAM M. 1965. "Law as an Instrument of Social Change," Pp. 285–293 in Alvin W. Gouldner and S. M. Miller, ed., Applied Sociology, Opportunities and Problems. New York: Free Press.

FOSTER, GEORGE M. 1973. *Traditional Societies and Technological Change,* 2nd ed. New York: Harper and Row Pub.

FRIEDMAN, LAWRENCE M. 1969. "Legal Culture and Social Development," Law and Society Review, 4 (1):29–44; 1973. "General Theory of Law and Social Change," Pp. 17–33 in J. S. Ziegel, ed., Law and Social Change. Toronto: Osgoode Hall Law School, York University; 1975. *The Legal System, A Social Science Perspective.* New York: Russell Sage Foundation.

FRIEDMANN, WOLFGANG. 1972. *Law in a Changing Society,* 2nd ed. New York: Columbia University Press.

FRIEDRICH, CARL J. 1958 *The Philosophy of Law in Historical Perspective.* Chicago: University of Chicago Press.

FULLER, LON L. 1969. *The Morality of Law,* rev. ed. New Haven: Yale University Press.

GINSBERG, MORRIS. 1965. *On Justice in Society.* Ithaca, NY: Cornell University Press.

GREENBERG, JACK. 1959. *Race Relations and American Law.* New York: Columbia University Press.

GROSSMAN, JOEL B. and MARY H. GROSSMAN, eds. 1971. *Law and Change in Modern America.* Pacific Palisades, CA: Goodyear.

GUREYEV, P. P. and P. I. SEDUGIN, eds. 1977. *Legislation in the USSR,* translated by Denis Ogden. Moscow: Progress Publishers.

HANDLER, JOEL F. 1978. *Social Movements and the Legal System, A Theory of Law Reform and Social Change.* New York: Academic Press.

HARRIS, PATRICIA ROBERTS. 1977. "Freedom and the Native-Born Stranger," Pp. 160–174 in Norman A. Graebner, ed., Freedom in America, A 200-Year Perspective. University Park: The Pennsylvania University Press.

HAUSER, PHILIP M. 1976. "Demographic Changes and the Legal System," Pp. 15–29 in Murray L. Schwartz, ed., Law and the American Future. Englewood Cliffs, NJ: Prentice-Hall.

HERTZLER, J. O. 1961. *American Social Institutions.* Boston: Allyn and Bacon.

HOEBEL, E. ADAMSON. 1954. *The Law of Primitive Man, A Study in Comparative Legal Dynamics.* Cambridge, MA: Harvard University Press.

HOROWITZ, HAROLD W. and KENNETH L. KARST. 1969. *Law, Lawyers and Social Change.* Indianapolis: Bobbs-Merrill.

JACOB, HERBERT. 1986. *Law and Politics in the United States.* Boston: Little, Brown and Company.

KAPLAN, JOHN. 1971. *Marijuana: The New Prohibition.* New York: Pocket Books.

KELSEN, HANS. 1967. *The Pure Theory of Law,* 2nd ed., translated by M. Knight. Berkeley: University of California Press.

KOHLBERG, LAWRENCE. 1964. "Development of Moral Character and Ideology," Pp. 383–431 in L. Hoffman and M. Hoffman, eds., Review of Child Development Research, Vol. I. New York: Russell Sage; 1967. "Moral Education, Religious Education, and the Public Schools: A Developmental Approach," Pp. 164–183 in T. Sizer, ed., Religion and Public Education. Boston: Houghton Mifflin.

LADD, JOHN. 1970. "Legal and Moral Obligation," Pp. 3–45 in Roland Pennock and John W. Chapman, eds., Political and Legal Obligation. New York: Lieber-Atherton Inc.

LA PIERE, RICHARD T. 1965 *Social Change.* New York: McGraw-Hill.

LEVINE, JAMES P. 1970. "Methodological Concerns in Studying Supreme Court Efficacy," Law and Society Review, 4 (1)(May):583–592.

LOGAN, RAYFORD W., and MICHAEL WINSTON. 1971. *The Negro in the United States, Vol. 2, The Ordeal of Democracy.* Princeton, NJ: Van Nostrand Reinhold.

LOTH, DAVID and MORRIS L. ERNST. 1972. *The Taming of Technology.* New York: Simon & Schuster.

MASSELL, GREGORY. 1973. "Revolutionary Law in Soviet Central Asia," Pp. 226–261 in Donald Black and Maureen Mileski, eds., The Social Organization of Law. New York: Seminar Press.

MAYHEW, LEON H. 1971. "Stability and Change in Legal Systems," Pp. 187–210 in Bernard Barber and Alex Inkeles, eds., Stability and Social Change. Boston: Little, Brown.

MEAD, MARGARET, ed. 1953. *Cultural Patterns and Technical Change.* Paris: UNESCO.

MILGRAM, STANLEY. 1975. *Obedience to Authority.* New York: Harper Colophon Books.

MILLER, ARTHUR SELWYN. 1979. *Social Change and Fundamental Law, America's Evolving Constitution.* Westport, CT: Greenwood Press.

MILLS, C. WRIGHT. 1957. *The Power Elite.* New York: Oxford University Press.

NAGEL, STUART S., ed. 1970. *Law and Social Change.* Beverly Hills: Sage Publications.

NEGLEY, GLENN. 1965. *Political Authority and Moral Judgement.* Durham, NC: Duke University Press.

NIMKOFF, MEYER F. 1957. "Obstacles to Innovation," Pp. 56–71 in Francis R. Allen, Hornell Hart, Delbert C. Miller, William F. Ogburn, and Meyer F. Nimkoff, Technology and Social Change. New York: Appleton-Century-Crofts, Inc.

NISBET, ROBERT. 1975. *Twilight of Authority.* New York: Oxford University Press.

PARSONS, TALCOTT. 1949. *Essays in Sociological Theory.* Glencoe, IL: Free Press.

RODGERS, HARRELL R. JR. and CHARLES S. BULLOCK III. 1972. *Law and Social Change: Civil Rights Laws and Their Consequences.* New York: McGraw-Hill.

ROSE, ARNOLD M. and CAROLINE B. ROSE. 1969. *Sociology: The Study of Human Relations.* New York: Knopf.

SCHER, R., and J. BUTTON. 1984. "Voting Rights Act: Implementation and Impact," Pp. 20–54 in Charles Bullock and Charles Lamb, eds., Implementation of Civil Rights Policy. Monterey, CA: Brooks/Cole Publishing Co.

SCHUR, EDWIN M. 1968. *Law and Society, A Sociological View.* New York: Random House.

SCHWARTZ, RICHARD D. and SONYA ORLEANS. 1970. "On Legal Sanctions," Pp. 533–547 in Richard D. Schwartz and Jerome A. Skolnick, eds., Society and the Legal Order. New York: Basic Books.

SEIDMAN, ROBERT B. 1978. *The State, Law and Development.* New York: St. Martin's Press.

SUMNER, WILLIAM GRAHAM. 1906. *Folkways.* Boston: Ginn.

SZYMANSKI, ALBERT J. and TED GEORGE GOERTZEL. 1979. *Sociology: Class, Consciousness, and Contradictions.* New York: D. Van Nostrand Company.

TOFFLER, ALVIN. 1970. *Future Shock.* New York: Random House.

VAGO, STEVEN. 1980. *Social Change.* New York: Holt, Rinehart & Winston.

WATSON, GOODWIN. 1969. "Resistance to Change," Pp. 488–498 in Warren G. Bennis, Kenneth D. Benne, and Robert Chin, eds., The Planning of Change, 2nd ed. New York: Holt, Rinehart & Winston.

WEBER, MAX. 1947. *The Theory of Social Economic Organizations,* edited by Talcott Parsons, Glencoe, IL: Free Press; 1968. *Economy and Society,* Vol. I., edited by Roph Guenther and Claus Wittich. New York: Badminster Press.

ZIMRING, FRANKLIN and GORDON HAWKINS. 1975. "The Legal Threat as an Instrument of Social Change." Pp. 329–339 in Ronald L. Akers and Richard Hawkins, eds., Law and Control in Society. Englewood Cliffs, NJ: Prentice-Hall.

8

The Profession
and Practice of Law

An analysis of the legal profession and its role in society touches on central issues in sociological theory—issues involving power, social control, stratification, socialization, and the social organization of law work. This chapter examines the character of the legal profession and the conditions shaping it. It begins with a discussion of the practice of law in an historical context: the professionalization of lawyers and the emergence of the legal profession in America. Next, the chapter describes the legal profession today: what lawyers do, their income, and how they compete for business. Then emphasis is placed on the availability of legal services to the needy and not so needy, followed by an analysis of the training of lawyers and their socialization into the profession. Finally, admission to the bar, bar associations as interest groups, and professional discipline are considered.

AN HISTORICAL SKETCH OF LAW PRACTICE

In primitive societies, as I discussed in Chapter Two, custom and law coincided. The laws of a primitive legal system are unwritten and comparatively undifferentiated. Such societies have courts and judges but no lawyers. The courts are temporary, and when a violation of a law has occurred, the defendant is not represented by a "lawyer." Each individual is his or her own "lawyer," and everyone more or less knows the law. Although some individuals may be wiser than others and more skilled in social affairs, this skill is not considered a *legal* skill.

The development of the legal profession has been intimately connected with the rise and development of legal systems. The origins of the legal profession can be traced back to Rome (Friedman, 1977:21). Initially, Roman law allowed individuals to argue cases on behalf of others. But these persons were trained not in law but in rhetoric. They were called orators and were not allowed to take fees. Later on, by Cicero's time, there were jurists as well—individuals who were knowledgeable about the law and people went to them for legal opinions. They were called *juris prudentes,* but these men learned in the law did not yet constitute a profession. Only during the Imperial Period did lawyers begin to practice law for a living and schools of law emerged. By this time, the law became exceedingly complex in Rome. The occupation of lawyers arose together with a sophisticated legal system, and the complexity of that system made the Roman lawyer indispensable.

C. Ray Jeffery (1962:314–315) points out that by the Middle Ages, the lawyer had three functions—agent, advocate, and jurisconsult. The word "attorney" originally meant an agent, a person who acts or appears on behalf of someone else. In this role of agent, the lawyer appeared in court to handle legal matters in place of his client. In ancient Athens and Rome, an agent was allowed to appear in the place of another person. In France, however, he had to appear in court himself, and in England, a person needed special permission from the king to be represented in court by an agent. In France, by 1356, there were 105 *legistes* (men of law) representing clients in court (Jacoby, 1973:14).

The difference between an agent and an advocate appeared when the lawyer went to court with his client to assist the client in presenting his case. In addition to law, the advocate was trained in the art of oratory and persuasion. In England, the function of the agent was taken over by solicitors and attorneys; the advocate became the barrister (trial lawyer). The function of a lawyer as a jurisconsult was both as legal advisor and as a writer and teacher. Although contemporary lawyers perform essentially the same functions, the modern legal profession is fundamentally different. Friedman notes: "It is organized. It is lucrative. It is closed except to those who have undergone training or apprenticeship. It holds a monopoly of courtroom work and the giving of 'legal' advice" (1977:21).

THE PROFESSIONALIZATION OF LAWYERS

In the sociological literature, professionalization implies the transformation of some nonprofessional occupation into a vocation with the attributes of a profession, and the specification of these could be discussed in great detail. Says Foote: "As a modicum, the possession (1) of a specialized technique supported by a body of theory, (2) of a career supported by an association of colleagues, and (3) of a status supported by community recognition may be mentioned as constituting an occupation as a profession" (1953:371–372). Also usually included in the discussion of professions are the ideas of a client-practitioner relationship and a high degree of autonomy in the execution of one's work tasks. Harold L. Wilensky (1964:143) has studied those occupations that are now viewed as professions such as law, medicine, ministry, and so on, and notes that they have passed through the following general stages in their professionalization:

1 Became full-time occupations;
2a Training schools established;

2b   University affiliation of training schools;
3a   Local professional associations started;
3b   National professional associations evolved;
4   State licensing laws;
5   Formal codes of ethics established.

Magali Sarfatti Larson (1977) provides additional insights into the process of professionalization as the process by which producers of special services seek to constitute and *control* a market for their expertise. Because marketable expertise is an important element in the structure of inequality, professionalization also appears as a collective assertion of special social status and as a collective process of upward mobility. She considers professionalization an attempt to translate one type of scarce resources—special knowledge and skills—into another—social and economic rewards. The attempt by professions to maintain scarcity implies a tendency toward monopoly: monopoly of expertise in the market and monopoly of status in a system of stratification. She contends that: "Viewed in the larger perspective of the occupational and class structures, it would appear that the model of professional passes from a predominantly economic function—organizing the linkage between education and the marketplace—to a predominantly ideological one—justifying inequality of status and closure of access in the occupational order" (Larson, 1977:xviii). For Larson, the following elements in the professionalization process are inseparably related: differentiation and standardization of professional services; formalization of the conditions for entry; persuasion of the public that they need services only professionals can provide; and state protection (in the form of licensing) of the professional market against those who lack formal qualifications and against competing occupations. She contends that educational institutions and professional associations play a central role in attaining each of these goals.

An essential element in the professionalization process is market control, the successful assertion of unchallenged authority over some area of knowledge. Until the body of legal knowledge, including procedure, had become too much for the ordinary person to handle, there was no need for a legal profession. Before the thirteenth century, it was possible for a litigant to appoint someone to do his or her technical pleading. This person was not a member of a separate profession, for apparently anyone could act in that capacity. The person who did the technical pleading eventually developed into, or was superseded by, the attorney who was appointed in court and had the power to bind his employer to a plea.

"The profession of advocate," writes Michael E. Tigar (1977:157), "in the sense of a regulated group of (law) practitioners with some formal training, emerged in the late 1200s." Both the English and the French sovereigns legislated with respect to the profession, limiting the practice of law to those who had been approved by judicial officers. The profession of full-time specialists in the law and in legal procedures appeared initially as officers of the king's court. The first professional lawyers were judges who trained their successors by apprenticeship. The apprentices took on functions in the courtroom and gradually came to monopolize pleading before the royal judges. In England, training moved out of the courtroom and into the Inns of Court, which were the residences of the judges and practicing attorneys. The attorneys, after several reorganizations of their own ranks, finally became a group known as barristers. Members of the Inns became organized and came to monopolize training in the law as well as control of official access to the government. Signs of the professionalization of lawyers began to appear.

In England, the complexity of court procedures required technical pleading with the aid of an attorney, and oral argument eventually required special skills. By the time of Henry III (1216–1272), judges had become professionals, and the courts started to create a body of substantive legal knowledge as well as technical procedure. The king needed individuals to represent his interests in the courts. In the early fourteenth century, he appointed sergeants of the king to take care of his legal business. When not engaged in the king's business, these fabled sergeants-at-law of the Common Pleas Court could serve individuals in the capacity of lawyers.

A crucial event in the beginning of the legal profession was an edict issued in 1292 by Edward I. During this period, legal business had increased enormously, yet there were no schools of common law and the universities considered law too vulgar a subject for scholarly investigation. The universities were, at that time, agencies of the church, and the civil law taught there was essentially codified Roman law, the instrument of bureaucratic centralization. Edward's order, which directed Common Pleas to choose certain "attorneys and learners" who alone would be allowed to follow the court and to take part in court business, created a monopoly of the legal profession.

The effect of placing the education of lawyers into the hands of the court cannot be overestimated. It resulted in the relative isolation of English lawyers from Continental, Roman, and ecclesiastical influences. Lawyer taught lawyer, and each learned from the processes of the courts, so that the law had to grow by drawing on its own resources and not by borrowing from others. But the court itself was no place for the training for these attorneys and learners. It did, however, provide aid in the form of an observation post, called the crib, in which students could sit and take notes, and from which occasionally they might ask questions during the course of a trial.

Training for lawyers was provided by the Inns of Court. A small self-selecting group of barristers gave informal training and monopolized practice before the government courts of London, as well as judgeships in those courts. The barristers' monopoly of court functions helped to create a second group within the legal profession—the solicitors, who advised clients, prepared cases for trial, and handled matters outside of the courtroom. This group arose to meet the needs of clients, since barristers were too involved as officers of the court to be very responsible to outsiders. The barristers outranked solicitors, both by virtue of their monopoly over access to the court and through their control of training. Originally, solicitors were drawn from the ranks of those who attended the Inns of Court, and later they came to be trained almost entirely by apprenticeships or through schools of their own. At first, in the Inns of Court, lawyers lived together during the terms of court, and for them the Inns represented law school, a professional organization, and a tightly knit social club, all in one.

Initially, universities such as Oxford and Cambridge saw little reason to include training such as it was practiced in the Inns into their teaching programs. Only subjects such as legal history, jurisprudence, and Roman and ecclesiastical law were considered part of a liberal education to be provided by the universities (Kearney, 1970). University education was sought by "gentlemen," while legal training at the Inns of Court became the cheapest and the easiest route of social mobility for those who aspired to become gentlemen. Many sons of prosperous yeomen and merchants chose to opt for legal apprenticeship in an attempt to adopt a lifestyle associated with a gentleman. The appointment of Sir William Blackstone to the Vinerian chair of jurisprudence in 1758 at Cambridge, marked the first effort to make English law a university subject. Blackstone thought it would help both would-be lawyers and educated people generally, to have a "system of legal education" (as he called it), which would be far broader than the practical legal training offered in the Inns of Court. Blackstone may thus be considered the founder of the modern English system of university education in law (Berman, 1958:5).

By the end of the eighteenth century, law in England became a full-fledged profession. Members of the profession considered the law as a full-time occupation, training schools were established, universities began to offer degrees in law, and a professional association evolved in the form of a lawyers' guild. The practice of law required licensing, and formal codes of ethics were established. Knowledge of law and skills of legal procedures became a marketable commodity, and lawyers had a monopoly over them. The practice of law in royal courts was limited to members of the lawyers' guild, which in turn enhanced their political power, their monopoly of expertise in the market, and their monopoly of status in a system of stratification. Access to the profession became controlled, and social mobility for those admitted assured. By the end of the eighteenth century, the name "attorney" was dropped in favor of the term "solicitor," with the formation of the Society of Gentlemen Practicers in the Courts of Law and Equity, which was their professional society until 1903, when the Law Society came into being. In the following section I shall examine the rise of legal profession in the United States.

EMERGENCE OF THE LEGAL PROFESSION IN AMERICA

Like American government, the American legal profession has its roots in the history of English government organization. Colonial America was a transplant of English institutions, but with an emphasis toward even greater decentralization. The practice of law in the prerevolutionary period was virtually monopolized by the upper class of merchants and planters who did their best to emulate the English pattern of closed legal castes. In the South, wealthy planters tended to send their sons to the Inns of Court in London for legal training. In the northern colonies bar associations developed in most of the populous places after 1750, beginning originally as social clubs, but gradually coming to control admission to practice. The colonial legislatures delegated to the courts the power of admission to practice before them. In the late eighteenth century, the local bar associations, in particular in New York and Massachusetts, had in turn been delegated responsibility for recommending lawyers for admittance, amounting to de facto control; their numbers comprised a powerful political elite (Hurst, 1950:249–311).

Prior to the revolution, lawyers were unpopular. Both the Puritans and planters feared a secularized legal profession. The Puritans felt that the Bible was all the "law" needed and wished to combine their religion with law. The planters opposed lawyers because of the threat they posed to their political power. Lawyers became even more unpopular during the American Revolution than they had been before (Friedman, 1973:265). Since many lawyers were closely associated with the upper class in background and in interests, it was among this group that British sympathizers were most concentrated. As a result, a substantial proportion of lawyers emigrated to England during wartime persecutions of Tories. The prevailing custom of the bar to limit practice to a small group of elites also contributed to lawyers' unpopularity, as did their efforts to collect wealthy creditors' claims in the period following the revolution.

After the revolution, the legal profession became more egalitarian, the distinction between barristers and attorneys—in imitation of the English system—disappeared with democratization of the legal profession, standards of admission to the bar became loosened, and bar associations crumbled and disappeared as their powers waned. Between 1800 and 1870, the power of admission to the bar was granted by local courts. In its most extreme form, this meant that admission in one court conferred no right to practice before others, although it was more usual for the right to practice in one to enable one to practice before any other court in the same state. Centralized admission (more in theory than practice) was prevalent only in a handful of states and territories.

Neither college education nor a law degree was absolutely required for admission to the bar. The bar examination itself was usually oral and administered in a casual fashion. Legal education throughout the nineteenth century was similarly informal. The principal method of education was apprenticeship in a lawyer's office, during which the student did small services, served papers, and copied legal documents. In his spare time, he read what law, history, and general books were available. Students in the offices of leading lawyers were often charged fees for apprenticeship.

The first law schools grew out of specialized law offices offering apprentice programs. They used much of the same techniques as the offices. The earliest such school was founded in Litchfield, Connecticut in 1784. It proved successful and grew rapidly in size. In time, it gained national reputation and attracted students from all over the country. It offered a four-teen-month course, but the school gave no diploma. At that time, law degrees were of little worth. The system was not one of formal certification. The egalitarian caste of political power in nineteenth-century America extended to legal practice as well. The school taught law by the lecture method. The lectures were never published; to publish would have meant to perish, since students would have no reason to pay tuition and attend classes.

Eventually, university law schools replaced the Litchfield type as the major alternative to office training, but legal training at universities was rare. There were a few university professorships of law established as far back as 1779 at William and Mary, and 1793 at Columbia, as well as Harvard in 1816 and Yale in 1824. But attendance was spotty, the courses given were short and informal, covering the same materials as apprenticeship programs, and allowing students to drop in and out as suited their own convenience. Legal standards of passing the course were minimal, and only a single final oral examination was required at some universities. Even at Harvard in the mid-nineteenth century, the standards were very low and "There were absolutely no examinations to get in, or to proceed, or to get out. All that was required was the lapse of time, two years, and the payment of the fees" (Friedman, 1984:242).

After 1870, a number of interrelated changes took place which established stratification within the legal profession and brought university law schools to an important position. A nationally prominent group of lawyers developed, and the bar (or the lawyers' union, although never called by that name) fought vigorously to protect the boundaries of the calling (Friedman, 1973:550). Simultaneously, university professors of law began to make claims for the scientific status of law. The bar association movement started and spread at the same time when farmers and workers were also organizing. The new establishment of bar associations led to efforts to restrict admission to the bar. In 1878, the American Bar Association was formed (Friedman, 1973:563). After 1878, boards of examiners normally controlled by the local bar associations replaced the state supreme courts as the examining authority. Statewide boards were established which financed themselves out of applicants' fees. The boards were almost invariably controlled by the state bar associations. Professional self-regulation had taken another important step forward (Stevens, 1971:458–459).

Starting in 1870, the teaching of law began with the use of the case method at Harvard University. Instead of using the older system of text reading and lectures, the instructor carried on a discussion of assigned cases designed to bring out their general principles. The proponent of the case method, Harvard Law Dean Christopher Columbus Langdell, believed that law was a general science and that its principles could be experimentally induced from the examination of case materials. He rejected the use of textbooks and instead used case books as teaching materials; these were collections of reports of actual cases carefully selected and arranged to illustrate the meaning and development of principles of law. The teacher became a Socratic guide, leading the student to an understanding of concepts and principles hidden as essences among the cases. Langdell also made it more difficult for students to gain admission. If an applicant did not have a college degree, he had to pass an entrance examination. A student was required to show a knowledge of Latin by translating from Virgil or Cicero; on occasion, a skill in French was acceptable as a substitute for Latin. Langdell likewise made it harder for a student to get out. The length of legal education was increased to two years in 1871, then to three years in 1876. The lax oral examinations for the law degree were replaced by a series of written exams with increasingly formal standards. By 1896, Harvard required a college degree as a prerequisite for admission to law school (Friedman, 1973:530–532). Prior to it, in fact, there were more lawyers than college graduates in America (Stevens, 1983:73).

But the method remained attractive and suited the needs of the legal profession. It enabled the size of classes to expand with one professor to every seventy-five students (Stevens, 1983:63). It exalted the prestige of law and legal training and affirmed that legal science stood apart as an independent entity distinct from politics, legislation, and from ordinary people. Langdell provided grounds for certain important claims of the legal profession. Law, he maintained, was a science that demanded rigorous formal training. There was justification, then, for the lawyers' monopoly of practice. The bar association movement coincided with Langdell's rise to power. The two supplemented and complemented each other and further strengthened the lawyers' monopoly of practice.

The increased emphasis on professionalization and monopoly on the practice of law brought about major efforts to improve the quality of legal education, to raise admission standards, and to intensify the power of bar associations. Attempts to improve legal education meant, in practice, the adoption of the standards of the leading law schools. The adoption of formal education requirements for admission to bar exams further strengthened the schools, and by 1940, three years of law school study were required by forty states. At the same time, efforts were made to incorporate the standards of the leading law schools into the bar exam prerequisites by calling for the requirement of two years of college as preparation before law studies in 1921, a requirement which was adopted by two-thirds of the states by 1940. By 1950, three years of college became the norm and by the 1960s, four years of college was required. A law student of today would find it hard to believe that until the 1950s the number of lawyers who had not been in college exceeded the number of those who had been (Stevens, 1983:209). The Law School Admission Test (LSAT) was ready for general use in 1948. The American Bar Association, in 1929, established law school accreditation standards, and the bar-admitting authorities encouraged the ABA's accreditation efforts. Today, graduation from an ABA-approved law school satisfies the legal education requirement for admission to the bar (after passing the bar exam) in all jurisdictions in the United States.

For much of its history, the profession was dominated by white males. Not a single woman was admitted to the bar before the 1870s, and very few blacks (Friedman, 1984:238). Women, particularly married women, were not considered suitable for the practice of law. They were seen as delicate creatures, and just like children and lunatics, lacked full legal rights. By allowing women to practice law, the traditional order of the family would be upset.

In a notorious opinion of a justice of the U.S. Supreme Court in 1873, " ... the natural and proper timidity and delicacy which belongs to the female sex evidently unfits it for many of the occupations of civil life.... The paramount destiny and mission of women are to fulfill the noble and benign offices of wife and mother. This is the law of the creator" (Stevens, 1983:82). Not until 1878 did federal courts open the door to women attorneys. Law schools began to admit women in 1869, although in many places the courses of instruction were "open to the male sex only." As of 1880, there were 75 women lawyers and 1,010 by 1900 (Stevens, 1983:83). By 1984, of the 649,000 lawyers, over 83,000 were women (Curran, 1986:20,25).

The profession explicitly discriminated against blacks (Abel, 1986). They were excluded from the American Bar Association until the 1950s and from many law schools. As recently as 1965, blacks made up 11 percent of the population, but less than 2 percent of lawyers and only 1.3 percent of law students, half of them in all-black law schools. Even in 1977, only 5 percent of the country's law students were black (Friedman, 1984:239).

Law firms were about as discriminatory as law schools. Many excluded Jews, Catholics, blacks, and women. Through the 1950s, most firms were solidly WASP. Legal politicians argued that the profession was a means by which Jews, immigrants, and basically non-WASPs "might undermine the American way of life" (Stevens, 1983:100–101). By the 1960s, discriminatory hiring practices started to decrease, but they have not yet fully disappeared. There are still signs of tokenism for blacks and women, and Jews are excluded from high prestige fields (Heinz and Laumann, 1982:112).

There have also been noticeable changes in the practice of law. Prior to the Civil War, much of legal business concerned land and commerce, primarily representing speculative interests in the West. After the middle of the nineteenth century, the most lucrative business came to center around the big corporations, beginning first with the railroads. Following the Civil War, the position of general counsel for the railroads was the most highly esteemed legal position, and, during the same period, lawyers became closely involved with the major banks and began to sit on boards of directors. By the turn of the century, corporate law firms were edging to the pinnacle of professional aspiration and power (Auerbach, 1976:22). Lawyers were instrumental in the growth of corporations, devising new forms of charters, assisting companies to organize national business, while taking maximum advantage of variable state laws concerning incorporation and taxation. The emergence and proliferation of corporation law firms at the turn of the century provided those lawyers who possessed appropriate social, religious, and ethnic credentials with an opportunity to secure personal power and to shape the future of their profession. But only lawyers who possessed what Gerald S. Auerbach (1976:21) calls "considerable social capital" could inhabit the corporate law firm world.

Through corporate law firms, the large modern style law firm came into existence. Prior to the middle of the nineteenth century, law practice was individual or carried on in two-man partnerships. After 1850, partnerships dealing with business interests began to specialize internally with one person handling the court appearances and the other taking care of office details. At the same time, business clients started to solicit opinions from law firms on legal aspects of prospective policies, a practice that gradually led to the establishment of permanent relationships between law firms and corporations. The size of major law firms began to grow. The prominence of the "Wall Street law firm," allied to major corporations, originated in the late nineteenth century, growing along with the corporations whose economic dominance they helped make possible. Notes Friedman: "By and large, the leading lawyers of the big Wall Street firms were solid Republicans, conservative in outlook, standard Protestant in faith, old English in heritage" (1973:553). It should be noted, however, that such large firms were, and are today, an exception. Close to half of all lawyers in private practice continue to practice alone, usually in a particular ethnic community, and this has undoubtedly been the case throughout history (Carlin, 1962). Generally, individual practitioners of law use the legal profession more as an avenue for social mobility than their counterparts in large firms.

In addition to changes in the structure and functions of the profession, there have been substantial changes in its numbers. In 1850, there were approximately 24,000 lawyers in the United States. In the next fifty years, after the Civil War and the transformation of the American economy, there were major changes in supply and demand. The number of lawyers increased to approximately 60,000 by 1880, and to 115,000 by 1900 (Halliday, 1986:62).

THE LEGAL PROFESSION TODAY

Since the 1960s, law has become the fastest growing of all professions in the United States. The number of lawyers increased from 285,933 in 1960 to 355,242 in 1970 and reached 649,000 in 1984 when already one out of every 364 people was a lawyer (Curran, 1986:20). (But only one attorney seems to be available for every 7,000 *poor* Americans and the ratio is 1 to 14,000 in the Chicano community [Spangler, 1986:6].) By contrast, the population to lawyer ratios are much higher in other countries. In the early 1980s, for example, there was one lawyer for 1,431 people in Belgium, 1 for 963 in Scotland, and 1 for 599 in Ontario, Canada (Lewis, 1986:82). Japan has less than 12,000 lawyers and only one law school and fewer than 2 percent of the some 30,000 applicants pass the school's entrance exam (Easton, 1984). China, with a population in excess of 1 billion, has about 5,000 lawyers. Today there are over 750,000 lawyers in the United States, and their number is expected to reach 1 million by the end of this century. The number of lawyers in any society is a function of the social role assigned to lawyers (Friedman, 1977:24; Halliday, 1986). The role of lawyers in society is conditioned by a variety of factors, such as the degree of industrialization, bureaucratization, complexity of business transactions, expansion of legal entitlements, the growth of regulation, crime rates, and attitudes toward and availability of nonlegal methods of conflict resolution.

Members of the profession have never been popular and "lawyers, on the whole, have a terrible image" (Friedman, 1984:249). Plato spoke of their "small and unrighteous" souls, and Keats said, "I think we may class the lawyer in the natural history of monsters." Thomas More left lawyers out of his Utopia, and Shakespeare made his feelings known in that famous line from *Henry VI, Part II:* "The first thing we do, let's kill all the lawyers." Undoubtedly, the adversarial system is costly not only in money but also in trust. Polls show that the public has limited confidence in the profession (*U.S. News & World Report,* 1985:53). Similar attitudes prevail towards lawyers in other countries. For example, in the Soviet Union (despite the fact that Lenin himself was trained as a lawyer and actually practiced for a short time), lawyers are considered as one of the most unnecessary parasitic and exploitative groups, ranking in esteem with priests and capitalists (Cameron, 1978:50). In India, the profession "has lost the social and moral prestige" and lawyers "go all out for money with little qualms about the image and morality of the profession" (Gandhi, 1982:33).

In fairness to lawyers, much of their negative image is exaggerated, and they are probably no worse than members of other professions. Some of the charges are due to guilt by association. They often deal with people in trouble: criminals, politicians, business persons and those seeking a divorce. At times, they articulate strong partisan interests, and it is no surprise that they are the object of strong sentiments. Although lawyers play a useful role and are sometimes admired, they are rarely loved. Probably no other legitimate profession has been subjected to extremes of homage and vilification as have lawyers (Bonsignore, et al., 1979:177–178).

There are four major subgroups in the legal profession: lawyers in private practice, lawyers in government service, lawyers in private employment, and the judiciary. In the United States, 68 percent of lawyers are in private practice, 10 percent work for the government, 10 percent are in salaried positions in private industry, and 4 percent are in the judiciary. Of the remaining 8 percent, 5 percent are retired or otherwise inactive, and 3 percent are employees of educational institutions, legal aid programs, private associations such as unions, or other special interest organizations (Curran, 1986:25–27). It is interesting to note, by contrast, that in Germany slightly over one-fifth of the bar are in private practice, while another fifth are employed by the judiciary. Proportionately three times as many lawyers work for the government and twice as many are in private employment in Germany than in the United States (Rueschemeyer, 1973:32).

In career patterns, self-image, and sheer numbers, lawyers in private practice constitute the central group of the American legal profession from which other types of practice are branching out. These lawyers generally work as either individual practitioners or members of law firms. Of the lawyers in private practice, some 180,000 work as individual practitioners (Curran, 1986:28). The next section will consider the private practice of law in the context of solo and firm practitioners.

WHAT LAWYERS DO

Law is big business in the United States, and legal work now accounts for nearly 2 percent of the gross national product, more than steel or electric power. Each year thousands of young adults graduate from law school, pass the bar, and enter into the profession. They engage in a variety of activities in diverse settings. Some go into private practice, others find jobs in government or private industry. A few even decide not to stay in law.

Lawyers in Private Practice

The majority of lawyers in the United States are in private practice. In 1980, about 180,000 worked alone and 190,000 were associated with law firms. Over 27,000 were employed in firms of 50 or more lawyers (Curran, 1986:28). Contrary to the popular image that is reinforced by television, only a small proportion of lawyers engage in litigation. In private practice, lawyers perform a number of significant roles. One is *counseling*. Attorneys spend about a third of their time advising their clients about the proper course of action in anticipation of the reactions of courts, agencies, or third parties. Another is *negotiating* both in criminal and civil cases. Plea bargaining is an example of negotiation and is widely used in criminal cases. Pretrial hearings and conferences in attempts to reach a settlement and thus avoid a costly trial are illustrative of the negotiating role of lawyers in civil cases. *Drafting*, the writing and revision of legal documents such as contracts, wills, deeds, and leases, is the "most legal" of a lawyer's role, although the availability of standardized forms for many kinds of legal problems often limits the lawyer to filling in the blanks. *Litigating* is a specialty, and relatively few lawyers engage in actual trial work. Much of the litigation in the United States is generally uncontested in cases such as debt, divorce, civil commitment, and criminal charges. Some lawyers also engage in *investigating*. In a criminal case, for example, the defense attorney may search for the facts and gather background information in support of the client's plea. Finally, lawyers take part in *researching*—searching, for example, for precedents, adopting legal doctrine to specific cases, and anticipating court or agency rulings in particular situations. Much of such research activity is carried out by lawyers in large firms and appellate specialists. Experienced lawyers working in their specialty (or those working for a small fee) usually do little research (Klein, 1984:74–76).

The two extremes in private practice are represented by solo practitioners and big law firms, often referred to as Wall Street firms. Solo practitioners are generalists; they operate in small offices and are "the jacks-of-all-trades of the legal profession" (Jacob, 1986:131). Many of these lawyers engage in marginal areas of law, such as collections, personal injury cases, rent cases, and evictions. They face competition from other professions, such as accountants and real estate brokers, who are increasingly handling the tax and real estate work traditionally carried out by the solo practitioner. Jerome E. Carlin (1962:209) points out that the pressures to make a living may force individual practitioners to submit to pressures to violate legal ethics, and in a later study he suggests that indeed this is the case (Carlin, 1966). Lawyers in solo practice often act, Carlin notes, as intermediaries between clients and other lawyers in order to receive referral fees. In such an instance, the individual practitioner may become a businessperson rather than a lawyer, thus defeating his or her original purpose of becoming a professional in the first place. As Carlin concludes:

In considering the work of the individual lawyer in Chicago, one is drawn to the conclusion that he is rarely called upon to exercise a high level of professional skill. This arises in part from the generally low quality of his professional training, but even more from the character of the demands placed upon him by the kinds of work and clients he is likely to encounter. Most matters that reach the individual practitioner—the small residential closing, the simple uncontested divorce, drawing up a will or probating a small estate, routing filings for a small business, negotiating a personal injury claim, or collecting on a debt—do not require very much technical knowledge, and what technical problems there are are generally simplified by use of standardized forms and procedures (1962:206–207).

Carlin notes that these lawyers attempt to justify their low status in the profession by emphasizing their independence and the fact that they are general practitioners and thus knowledgeable about all facets of the law. This notion of autonomy, however, does not compensate for the fact that these lawyers also feel insignificant in the overall legal structure and are frustrated because their initial high ambitions have not been realized, although they are professionals. Carlin (1962:206) suggests that these individual practitioners, like their counterparts in general practice in medicine, are "most likely to be found at the margin of (their) profession, enjoying little freedom in choice of clients, type of work, or conditions of practice."

Jack Ladinsky (1963), in a study of a sample of 207 Detroit area lawyers of which 100 were solo and 107 were medium- to large-firm practitioners, reinforced Carlin's findings on individual practitioners. Ladinsky also found that individual practitioners come from minority religious and ethnic backgrounds, have parents of entrepreneurial or small business status, and receive qualitatively and quantitatively inferior educations more often than the lawyers in law-firm practice he included in the study (1963:49). Ladinsky suggests that social background (religious preference of mother and occupation of father) is the strongest determinant of whether a lawyer goes into firm or solo practice. The quality of the law school is an important intervening variable. Ladinsky notes: "Social background describes two major career contingencies: level of technical skill and access to clients" (1963:53). Socioeconomic considerations and ethnic and cultural factors force solo lawyers toward local night school or Catholic university law schools. Ladinsky further points out that after graduation, relatively poor training and discrimination in firm recruitment make it difficult to get a prestigious firm job, and so solo lawyers end up doing low-paying, low-status work, that is, injury suits, divorce, petty criminal, and debt collection. They often develop a clientele of people of similar class, ethnic, and religious background.

There are also differences between individual and firm practitioners in acceptance of and compliance with ethical norms. Jerome Carlin (1966) found that the individual practitioner was the most likely to violate ethical norms (for example, soliciting kickbacks or making or arranging police payoffs), with the nature of the client and type of case being important contributing factors in the violations. Since solo practitioners often represent individuals, as contrasted to corporations which are represented by larger firms, the quality of the lawyers involved adversely affects the legal representation that many individuals receive. Since these lawyers are often from minority groups, minority clients are the ones who are adversely affected. Moreover, many of the larger, more prestigious, and more ethical firms will not accept the kinds of cases the individual practitioner confronts, and in fact refer these cases to him or her, so that the organization of the bar is such that ethical violations and ineffective practice are almost built into certain situations.

In a survey of the Chicago bar's attitudes toward a specific problem in professional ethics (ambulance chasing), Kenneth F. Reichstein (1965) documents essentially the same relationship between professional status and notions of professional ethics found by Carlin in New York. Despite the fact that selecting personal injury cases is prohibited by the canons of ethics, an elaborate social structure (that is, legitimating values, specialist practitioners, techniques, etc.) exists around this type of practice. Reichstein found that high-status lawyers (high income, corporate practice, large firm, etc.) were almost unanimous in strongly disapproving of personal injury practice (and those lawyers engaged in it), on the grounds that "it brings disrepute on the profession." On the other hand, low-status lawyers (low income, solo practitioners, lack of established clientele) were more likely to give qualified approval of personal injury practice. Low-status lawyers based their attitudes on the rationale that "it is necessary to make a living," or "it prevents poor people from being taken advantage of." Reichstein also notes that "deviance" in this case is in no small part a product of elite control of the rule-making and enforcement machinery of the organized bar, which will be discussed later in this chapter.

Practicing in large law firms is very different from solo practice. About 70 law firms in the United States now have more than 200 lawyers—Chicago based Baker & MacKenzie is the largest firm in the world, with some 750—along with hundreds of persons in the supporting staff, including paralegals, business-trained administrators, librarians, and technicians (The Lawyer's Almanac, 1986:2). Many of these large firms are becoming national and international in scope by opening up offices in several cities in the United States and abroad. These firms shy away from less profitable business—individual legal problems such as wills and divorces—in favor of corporate clients. Unlike solo practitioners, firms maintain long-term relationships with their clients and many are on retainers by large corporations. Large firms offer a variety of specialized services with departments specializing in a number of fields such as tax law, mergers, antitrust suits, or certain types of government regulations (Jacob, 1986:130). These firms deal generally with repeat players and provide the best possible information and legal remedies to their clients along with creative and innovative solutions for the clients' problems (Jacob, 1986:136–137).

Large law firms have a pronounced hierarchical structure. Young lawyers are hired as associates. Beginning associates are viewed as having limited skills even with their elite education and are assigned the task of preparing briefs and engaging in legal research under the supervision of a partner or senior associate. In seven or eight years, they either become junior partners or leave the firm. For a new associate who has a strong desire to move into a partnership position, the competition with cohorts is very strong. Nowadays, it is almost as difficult for an associate in a good firm to attain partnership as for an assistant professor in sociology to get tenure and promotion.

Associates are on a fixed salary while partners' incomes are based on profits. In most firms, law partners earn profits largely on hourly billings of associates: the more associates per partner, the higher the profits. How profits are divided among partners is usually decided by a small committee that looks at such factors as work brought in, hours billed, and seniority. The traditional rule is that associates should produce billings of about three times that of their salaries—a third goes to the associate, a third to overhead, and a third to the firm's profit. For example, an associate who earns $50,000 and whose time is billed at $75 an hour would have to put in 2,000 billable hours, or 38½ billable hours a week, 52 weeks a year. That may not sound like much, but 2,000 billable hours usually means 50 hours or more at the office a week. (On the average, lawyers work 46.5 hours a week [Reidinger, 1986b:44].) At most firms, lawyers' time is billed in six-minute units, with each nonbusiness conversation, personal phone call, and vacation day cutting into billable hours. No wonder many associates are workaholics and spend evenings and weekends in their offices.

One of the most complete analyses of law firms is Erwin O. Smigel's (1964) *The Wall Street Lawyer.* Although the Wall Street law firm is not typical of the majority of law firms in the Unites States because of its size and type of practice, the contrast between this type of law practice and that of the individual practitioner illustrates the immense diversity within the legal profession.

The law firms investigated by Smigel perform a variety of functions. They are spokespersons for much of big business in the United States. But they not only represent business, many members of the firms serve as members of the boards of directors of corporations they represent. These law firms also act as recruiting centers for high-level government service. Members of the firm are appointed to important government positions and seek national political offices. Many of their members are also active in various capacities in national, state, and local governmental agencies. Wall Street lawyers also participate in civic and philanthropic activities, such as the Metropolitan Opera, various museums, and other cultural and charitable affairs.

The Wall Street law firms are large, ranging from 50 to several hundred lawyers on the staff. Over 70 percent of the lawyers had attended Harvard, Yale, or Columbia Law School—the elite schools of the nation—and had been top students. The Wall Street law firms actively recruit these top individuals, and would prefer all their lawyers to have these credentials. In addition, the firms also look for the "correct" family background, which is considered important in order to make contacts that would bring business in the future. As might be expected, Smigel found very few black or women attorneys in the Wall Street firms. Similarly, relatively few Catholic lawyers were found in the Wall Street firms because of what are considered to be lower-class origins, poorer education, and immigrant parents. As compared to individual practitioners, the Wall Street lawyers have a superior education, both quantitatively and qualitatively. It should be noted, however, that not every graduate of prestige law schools desires the kind of law practiced by the Wall Street lawyers. Smigel notes that many students feel that the specialization in the large law office is so great that they would soon become limited in their abilities. Others feel that they would be lost in such a setting, and their mobility opportunities impaired. Some law school graduates look upon the Wall Street firm as a postgraduate training period, using it as a springboard for future positions in industry and government.

The observations of Carlin and Ladinsky on solo practitioners and Smigel on large law firms are supplemented by the conclusions of John P. Heinz and Edward O. Laumann's (1982) seminal study of the Chicago bar. They note that much of the "differentiation within the legal profession is secondary to one fundamental distinction—the distinction between lawyers who represent large organizations (corporations, labor unions, or government) and those who represent individuals. The two kinds of law practice are the two hemispheres of the profession." Most lawyers, they add, "reside exclusively in one hemisphere or the other and seldom, if ever, cross the equator" (1982:319). The two sectors of the profession are separated by the social origins of lawyers, the schools where they were trained, the types of clients they serve, office environment, frequency and type of litigation, values, different circles of acquaintance; the two sectors "rest their claims to professionalism on different sorts of social power" (1982:384). Large cities, Heinz and Laumann conclude, have two legal professions, one that is recruited from more privileged social origins where lawyers serve wealthy and powerful corporate clients, and the other, from less prestigious backgrounds where lawyers serve individuals and small businesses. Thus, "the hierarchy of lawyers suggests a corresponding stratification of law into two systems of justice, separate and unequal" (1982:385).

Lawyers in Government

Approximately 10 percent of the members of the bar in the United States are now employees of the federal, state, county, and municipal governments, exclusive of the judiciary. Malcom Spector (1972) suggests that taking positions in government agencies may be a strategy used by young lawyers for upward professional mobility. He considers employment with the government a mobility route into a more prestigious practice situation for the young lawyer handicapped by mediocre education or stigmatized by sex, religion, or ethnic background. Spector maintains that by pursuing a short-term career in a government agency, the young lawyer not able to initially break into "big league" firms gains valuable trial experience, specialized knowledge of regulatory law, and government contacts that eventually might be parlayed into a move to Wall Street or to private industry. Many of those entering public service are recent law school graduates who find government salaries sufficiently attractive at this stage of their careers, and seek the training which such service may offer as a prelude to private practice. Limitations on top salaries discourage some from continuing with the government, although in recent years, public service has become more attractive as a career.

The majority of lawyers serve by appointment in legal departments of a variety of federal and state agencies and local entities. The various departments and regulatory agencies, such as the Justice or Treasury Departments or the Interstate Commerce Commission, employ thousands of attorneys. Others work in the various legal departments in cities. Still others are engaged as public prosecutors. Federal prosecutors, the United States attorneys, and their assistants are appointed by the President and are subordinate to the Attorney General of the United States. State prosecutors, sometimes known as district attorneys, are commonly elected by each county, and are not under the control of the state attorney general. As a rule, lawyers in government are directly engaged in legal work, since law training is infrequently sought as preparation for general government service. However, a small but important minority, which is considered an exception to this rule, consists of those who have been appointed to high executive positions and those who have been elected to political office.

Lawyers in Private Employment

About 10 percent of lawyers are in private employment. These lawyers (often referred to as house counsels) are salaried employees of private business concerns, usually industrial corporations, insurance companies, and banks. The growth of corporations, the complexity of business, and the multitude of problems posed by government regulation make it desirable, if not imperative, for some firms to have lawyers and legal departments familiar with the particular problems and conditions of the firm. In view of the increased complexity of business transactions and the growth of federal regulations, the proportion of the profession engaged in this kind of activity can be expected to increase in coming years. In addition to legal work, lawyers often serve as officers of the company, and may serve on important policy-making committees, perhaps even on the board of directors. Although lawyers in legal departments are members of the bar and entitled to appear in court, because of their lack of trial experience, usually an outside lawyer is retained for litigation and for court appearances. Lawyers in legal departments of business firms do not tend to move to other branches of legal work after a number of years. Many of these lawyers have been in private practice or in government service. There is some horizontal mobility between government work and private employment, but not to the same extent as between government and law firms (Jenkins, 1977).

Judges

Approximately 4 percent of lawyers are federal, state, county, or municipal court judges. Except for some inferior courts, judges are generally required to be admitted to the bar to practice, but do not practice while on the bench. There is so little uniformity that it is difficult to generalize further about judges, other than to point out three salient characteristics which relate to the ranks from which judges are drawn, to the method of their selection, and to their tenure.

Judges are drawn from the practicing bar and less frequently from government service or the teaching profession. In the United States, there is no career judiciary such as is found in many other countries, and there is no prescribed route for the young law graduate who aspires to be a judge, no apprenticeship which he or she must serve, no service which he or she must enter. (In Norway, for example, the judiciary relies heavily on the institution of "judge-apprentice" for the training and preparation of judges [Aubert, 1969:292].) The outstanding young law graduates who act for a year or two as law clerks to distinguished judges of the federal and state courts have only the reward of the experience to take with them into practice, not the promise of a judicial career. While it is not uncommon for a vacancy on a higher court to be filled by a judge from a lower court, even this cannot be said to be the rule. The legal profession is not entirely unaware of the advantages of a career judiciary, but it is generally thought that they are outweighed by the experience and independence which lawyers bring to the bench. Many of the outstanding judges of the country's highest courts have had no prior judicial experience. Criticism has centered instead about the prevalent method of the selection of judges.

As I indicated in Chapter Three, in over two-thirds of the states, judges are elected usually by popular vote, and occasionally by the legislature. Since 1937, the American Bar Association has advocated a system (the Missouri Plan) under which the governor appoints judges from a list submitted by a special nominating board, and the judge then periodically stands unopposed for reelection by popular vote on the basis of his or her record. Such a system is now in effect in several states. In a small group of states, judges are appointed by the governor, subject to legislative confirmation. This is also the method of selection of federal judges who are appointed by the President, subject to confirmation by the Senate. The selection of judges is not immune from political influence and pressures.

A third characteristic is that judges commonly serve for a term of years rather than for life. For courts of general jurisdiction, it is typically four or six years, and for appellate courts, six to eight years. In a few state courts and in the federal courts, the judges sit for life. Whether on the bench for a term of years or for life, a judge may be removed from office only for gross misconduct and only by formal procedures.

LAWYERS AND MONEY

One out of nine lawyers is a millionaire. The rest of them have average annual incomes of $121,913 and average net worths of $500,000 (*The Wall Street Journal*, 1986:23). After physicians, lawyers as a group are the highest paid professionals. Not surprisingly, a recent poll showed that almost half of the lawyers chose law because its income potential appealed to them (but only 21 percent wanted "to see justice done" and 23 percent had a desire to improve society) (Reidinger, 1986b:44). There is an unusually large range of income among lawyers, and a high proportion of income goes to elites. A study found that 5 percent of law firm partners earned 35 percent of all income while the bottom 19 percent of individual practitioners earned only 5 percent (York and Hale, 1973:16). There are several factors that account for the variation in lawyers' income. They include the type of practice (firm or solo); the type of clientele (corporations or individuals with "minor" problems); reputation of law school; achievement in law school; the age and length of practice; degree of specialization; and the region and population of the place of practice (generally, the larger the community, the greater the average income).

According to a survey of 36,687 law students graduated in 1984, there is a substantial variation in starting salaries. Those who obtained employment with firms of more than 100 attorneys in New York City reported an average starting salary of $45,966 (Texas Bar Journal, 1986:490). Starting salaries in New York City for new associates ranged between $38,000 and $52,000; in Boston between $33,000 and $40,000; in Kansas City between $34,500 and $42,500; and in Pittsburgh between $27,000 and $38,000 in 1984 dollars. (The Lawyer's Almanac, 1986:126). Average starting salaries in very small firms varied from city to city from $8,733 in Morgantown, West Virginia to $37,000 in Glendale, California. Graduates who became solo practitioners had the greatest range of salaries from $5,000 to $100,000 (Texas Bar Journal, 1986:490). To put these figures in some kind of perspective, in 1984 the median family income was $26,433 and new assistant professors in state colleges and universities started at an average salary of $23,590. For their counterparts in private colleges and universities, the figure was $22,705. The average pay for full professors in public institutions was $35,840 and $37,715 in private institutions (*The Chronicle of Higher Education*, 1985:30). While on the topic of starting salaries, it is worth noting that the average debt on graduation from law school is $25,000 and $10,000 for new Ph.D.'s (Fiske, 1986:34) which is, of course, not a significant consideration in the subsequent salary discrepancy.

Some unusually high starting salaries in New York City got a lot of publicity in the media in 1986. Some firms offered new associates fresh from law school $65,000 and anywhere from $10,000 to $20,000 in additional bonuses if they have spent a year or two clerking for a judge. Investment firms were luring away highly qualified law school graduates with starting salaries in excess of $100,000 (Reidinger, 1986a:42). But there were few such openings and they were filled by top graduates of elite law schools. Still, such high initial salaries jolted the legal profession, especially the expanding megafirms that compete with each other for a relatively stable pool of top graduates. Shortly after the publicity, a ripple effect pushed up salaries at major firms across the country. This is good news for young associates who work in some cases up to nine years in the hope of joining the full partners, who split a firm's profit.

In 1985, partners in a top law firm earned an average of $770,000. In less profitable firms, partners averaged about $200,000 and senior associates $100,000 (Lewin, 1986:18).

Lawyers in private employment do not fare as well as their colleagues in private practice. In 1984, recent graduates started at an average salary of $29,369. Chief legal officers in corporations had an annual average compensation of $122,624, exclusive of bonuses. In the upper quartile, they received $181,000 plus a bonus of $41,560. Deputy chiefs at the top made $145,250 with a bonus of $29,297. Nonsupervisory attorneys received $53,666 on the average with a bonus of $7,954 (The Lawyer's Almanac, 1986:129).

In general, the compensation of judges is lower than attorneys in private practice and employment. Some examples: In 1985 salaries of associate justices of the highest courts ranged from $47,300 to $92,500 with an average of $64,430; for intermediate appellate court justices was $46,300 to $87,500 with an average of $63,985; and general trial court judges were paid between $42,735 and $82,000 and their average was $56,977 (The Lawyer's Almanac, 1986:759).

The average salary of recent graduates in 1984 working for government agencies was $21,598 and chief legal officers earned $47,433. In the upper quartile, the highest average salary was paid to division counsels, $59,833. In the same quartile, attorneys earned $49,883 (Lawyer's Almanac, 1986:142).

In private practice, there are several ways lawyers generate income. Some lawyers charge by the hour for services rendered. For top firms, the hourly rates billed by senior partners can be in excess of $500 and good firms averaged about $250 an hour in 1986. That was also the going rate for established trial attorneys. To most Americans, legal fees for justice seem almost criminal: about $2000 for misdemeanors; $3000 to $6000 for nontrial felonies; and $5000 and above for felony trials. Similarly, the legal fees in estate and probate provide the opportunity for large profits from legal work. Few people understand why a lawyer who fills out mostly standard forms for two hours at the closing of a $200,000 house deserves 1 percent, or $2000, for his or her effort. In probate, legal fees are determined usually as a percentage of the worth of the transaction—in this case, the value of the estate. Typical charges are 7 percent for the first $7,000 of the estate, 5 percent on the next $4,000, 4 percent on the next $10,000, 3 percent on the next $60,000 and 2.5 percent on the remainder. Once again, the amount of the fee is not necessarily related to the amount of work expended by lawyers, especially in cases where the value of an estate exceeds several million dollars. Nowadays, it is not unusual to hear of multimillion-dollar fees lawyers receive, especially in large class-action suits such as the one against the Manville Corporation which was sued by those who were exposed to the asbestos it manufactured. Mergers provide another avenue for lucrative fees. In addition to fees, percentages, and hourly charges, some lawyers and law firms are on retainers. A wealthy individual or a corporation pays a certain sum a year to a lawyer or firm for a predetermined amount of legal work, for example, a maximum of eighty hours of consultation.

Lawyers also take on cases on a contingency fee basis. This is an arrangement whereby a lawyer receives a percentage of any damages collected. Contingency fees are used primarily in medical malpractice, personal injury, and in some product liability and wrongful death cases. If the plaintiff loses, there is no payment required for legal services; if he or she wins, the lawyer takes his or her expenses off the top, then gets a percentage of the remainder—from 10 to 15 percent on big airline-crash suits to 35 percent on smaller suits. For example, when an individual is awarded $100,000 in damages, the lawyer may get from $10,000 to $35,000. The system has its merits. It allows individuals to retain the services of an attorney who could not otherwise afford it. It encourages lawyers to screen out weak cases because they share the risk of litigation—if they do not win, they do not collect.

At the same time, the contingency fee arrangement provides a motivation to seek out high damages. Lawyers make substantial investments by hiring investigators, expert witnesses, and consultants to augment their chances of winning. Often, they invest a considerable amount of their time in cases that can drag on literally for years. But the payoff can be substantial. It is not unusual to hear of a jury award of $14.7 million in a personal injury case, and there have been over 367 verdicts of a million dollars or more in medical malpractice suits (*U.S. News & World Report*, 1986:35–36). In 1984, the average medical malpractice verdict was $954,858. For product liability, it was $1,069,037 (The Lawyer's Almanac, 1986:836–837) and the number of suits increased from 1,600 in 1974 to 13,554 in 1985. Personal injury cases have also increased substantially, and in 1985 alone there were 401 verdicts exceeding $1 million (*U.S. New & World Report*, 1986:35).

In spite of the fact that the contingency fee arrangement does influence the amount of efforts lawyers devote to a given case (Kritzer et al., 1985), the high legal fees and high damage awards created a number of problems. Medical fees are increasing to cover the cost of malpractice insurance. Some obstetricians and surgeons are walking away from their practices rather than paying insurance premiums of $50,000 or more per year. States, cities, and school districts are faced with substantial increases in their liability insurances and have started to phase out high-risk services such as recreation programs. Corporations are passing on to the consumers the cost of higher insurance premiums for product liability.

As a result, several states are considering measures to limit both the size of damage awards and lawyers' fees. Some states have already imposed caps on the size of medical malpractice awards to $250,000. A few states are also imposing price control on what a lawyer can charge. In general, the new laws allow the traditional fees for prosecuting minor lawsuits but reduce them sharply for certain big-money cases that are costly and complicated to bring. Lawyers, of course, do not like these limitations. They contend that the contingency fee is the victim's key to the courthouse. It allows the poor to obtain the same high-caliber legal services as the rich. Many of the cases require much expense and preparation. In case of losing, the lawyer gets nothing, therefore the one-third contingency fee is most reasonable. But it does not seem that cutting contingency fees would reduce the number of malpractice and other damage suits filed. Because of the high level of competition for business, if top lawyers bow out, others will still handle these cases. In states without caps on verdict size, there will be still huge damage awards and logjams in the courts.

COMPETITION FOR BUSINESS

But the days of exorbitant legal fees for the profession may be numbered. Many lawyers may enjoy less prestige, less interesting work, and lower pay scales in the future. For years now, law schools have been turning out more lawyers than the profession can afford. (In Scandinavian countries, by contrast, the bar is declining in size, and there is also a decrease in the proportion of law students relative to other students in Western Europe [Friedman, 1977:24].) In the unflattering words of former U.S. Chief Justice Warren E. Burger, "We may well be on our way to a society overrun by hordes of lawyers, hungry as locusts. . . . " (*Time*, 1978:56). As a result, there is a growing competition among lawyers for the consumer's dollars.

Two recent Supreme Court decisions have contributed to competition among lawyers for business. In 1975, as I noted above, the court ruled that lawyers, like others in business, should not be allowed to fix prices. Until then, it had been standard procedure for lawyers' associations to issue "minimum-fee schedules," lists of the lowest fees members should charge for handling divorces, wills, and so on. Another important case gave lawyers the right to advertise. Two Arizona lawyers placed an ad for their firm in a local newspaper that violated the model code of professional responsibility formulated in 1969 by the American Bar Association and adopted in Arizona by the state's supreme court. The lawyers were censured for their ad. They appealed the case to the U.S. Supreme Court, which decided in 1977 that state laws and bar associations prohibiting lawyers' advertising were in conflict with the Constitution's guarantee of free speech. At the prodding of the Supreme Court, bar associations have been developing guidelines to allow lawyers to advertise. Typically, these guidelines allow lawyers to indicate their education, specialties, public offices, teaching positions held, and memberships in professional organizations. They may also, with their clients' permission, indicate other clients represented, tell what credit arrangements are acceptable, and indicate fees for initial consultations and other services.

The number of lawyers currently advertising has risen sharply, nearly doubling from 10 percent in 1984 to 17 percent in 1985. Another 18 percent of lawyers intend to advertise in the future. Young, small-town, small-firm, or solo practitioners who earn less than $35,000 are the most likely to try it. Older, big-city lawyers still shy away from advertising: 30 percent of lawyers aged 24–34 have tried it, compared to 11 percent in the 55 and older age bracket, and 14 percent in the 45–54 age group. Lawyers are more likely to advertise in cities with fewer than 50,000 residents and less likely in cities with 1 million or more. Large legal clinics advertise heavily, especially on television with slogans such as "no frill will—$25." Large law firms are least likely to advertise (ABA Journal, 1986:44).

Members of the legal profession have not unanimously welcomed the changes. The profession has traditionally considered unethical the more obvious forms of competition—advertising and soliciting clients. The underlying belief of traditionalists is that increased competition leads to a decreased quality of service. The implication is that high fees indicate high quality. In fact, the U.S. Supreme Court said that lawyers had wrongly over-charged clients for decades, under the rationale that the dignity of the profession required it (Green, 1975:55). Many people avoid going to lawyers because they do not have the necessary information about specialization, and because they believe that lawyers charge too much. To reach a larger segment of the population, lawyers could advertise the types of cases they handle and lower their fees. However, most bar associations, although they are developing guidelines, still treat advertising as something that is just not done. Attempts to lower fees are usually met with the old arguments about ethics and the quality of service. As a result, with some exceptions, the fees are steadily increasing, and few lawyers allow themselves anything more than the traditional one-line listing in the yellow pages—name, address, and phone number.

Some large law firms are becoming more competitive by adopting modern cost-management techniques and strategic planning. Others are starting to experiment with public relations firms to handle new contacts. Virtually every major law firm in the country has a partner for whom management has become a major preoccupation. Many firms are also increasing the number and size of specialized departments, and there is a growth of "specialty firms," such as the type that specializes in labor law work on the side of management (Heinz and Laumann, 1982:358). The business of law in large firms, in fact, is turning out to be much like business in any field.

Competition for law business is not limited to the United States. In India, for example, there is excessive and unconstrained competition among lawyers for clients. The author of an excellent study on lawyers bitterly complains that the profession has turned into a commercial business "bereft of all ideals, principles ... there are no sacrosanct ground rules" and "the ruling passion of the Bar is greed and maximisation of economic gains" (Gandhi, 1982:153, 155–156). Many lawyers rely on "touts" or brokers to get business and "touting" is a widely used, albeit highly unprofessional, form of activity. A tout may be a government clerk, typist in the courtroom, policeman, village headman, or anyone with some prestige and visibility in the community. A tout befriends a potential client and refers him to a lawyer. He gets a commission from the lawyer, the seller of legal services, whom he brings business. A tout may get up to 50 percent of the fee the lawyer collects from the client, but receives no commission from the client. A tout works only for one lawyer, and good touts are sought after by lawyers. Successful lawyers have several touts "procuring" for them and about two-thirds of criminal and one-third of civil cases are obtained through touts (Gandhi, 1982:108).

In this highly competitive climate, the clients are often cheated by unscrupulous touts and lawyers who know they are vulnerable and expendable. The clients are helpless because they are ignorant of the law and unfamiliar with the legal arena. They do not know where to find adequate and reasonable legal services and welcome the advances of touts with the promise of professional help. Once entrapped, they are passed on "among the various actors of the drama as a nutritious morsel and each has his mouthful of bite." Clients have no recourse, or even a chance to protest, because lawyers do not give them receipts for services rendered. Lawyers view clients as exclusive trading commodities and nonrepeat business and extract whatever they can from them the first time. The touts associated with lawyers are equally ruthless and exploitative and, like lawyers, do not develop continuing relationships with the clients. Even the most notorious "shysters," "ambulance chasers," and "ticket-fixers" hungry for legal business in the United States do not come close to their counterparts in India when it comes to violating ethical codes and professional standards.

LEGAL SERVICES FOR THE NEEDY AND NOT SO NEEDY

About 37 percent of the U.S. population encounters a legal problem in a year, but only 10 percent consults an attorney (Waldman, 1986). A major reason is that law and lawyers are expensive. Many people who need or want a lawyer have trouble paying the price. But as Friedman comments: "Justice is for sale; but in a just society it should not be totally for sale" (1984:251). Consequently, under a 1963 Supreme Court decision, people who tell the court in a serious criminal case that they are too poor to pay a lawyer must be represented, usually by public defenders on the state's payroll or by court-appointed attorneys. Such defendants are now involved in more than half the felony cases in the country.

The practice of the court appointing attorneys for the defense is unpopular among lawyers. It is damaging to their pocketbook for they receive only a nominal amount of compensation for their services and it interferes with their regular activities. Even though the compensation is modest, $15 to $20 per hour in Missouri for example, from time to time states run out of money to pay court-appointed lawyers for defending indigents. In Missouri, when the state ran out of money to pay court-appointed lawyers and the legislature refused to appropriate any more, the Missouri Supreme Court upheld compulsory service without compensation rather than see the criminal justice system come to a halt. As a result, all lawyers in the state, including real estate and merger specialists, were faced with compulsory service in criminal courts. Obviously, many of these attorneys were not specialists in criminal proceedings, which had a bearing on the quality of legal help defendants received.

At times lawyers provide legal services *pro bono publico* (for the public good) for indigents. From time to time, various bar associations have recommended that all lawyers engage in such endeavors. But many cannot afford it, and others, particularly those who work for large firms, are discouraged from doing so. Many large firms are reluctant to take on *pro bono* criminal law work, divorce, housing disputes, and consumer problems because they would be regarded as unseemly by their corporate clients. A principal reason for the reluctance of large firms to represent "the poor, downtrodden, friendless, and despised" or to engage in public interest causes is that such sort of legal work "would give offense to their regular clientele" (Heinz and Laumann, 1982:371).

In civil cases, the poor can gain access to lawyers through public or private legal aid programs. As part of the "War on Poverty" program in the 1960s, the Office of Economic Opportunity established neighborhood law offices to serve the indigents. In 1974, much of legal aid work was assumed by the Legal Services Corporation. Due to the number of activist lawyers in the program who fought and antagonized city hall, the corporation soon became controversial. There were attempts by President Reagan in the early 1980s to phase the program out, but Congress balked. Although the program is still viable, it was subjected to a drastic budget cut.

The work of Legal Services attorneys is concentrated in five main areas: family, consumer, housing, landlord-tenant, and welfare. To qualify, applicants must have proof of indigency and have a case that falls within the mandate of Legal Services. Cases that involve, for example, contingency fees are not accepted because private attorneys would handle them even for poor clients. Divorce cases are also rejected for fear that the agency would become a divorce mill.

For those who lack both proof of indigency and the means (or the will) to hire a private attorney, there are two relatively low-cost ways of obtaining legal services. They are legal clinics and prepaid legal plans.

A legal clinic is simply a high-volume, high-efficiency law firm. Because the cost per case is low, the firm can afford to set lower fees. Legal clinics build case volume primarily through advertising and publicity. They achieve efficiency by using systematic procedures, by relying heavily on standard forms, and by delegating much of the routine work to paralegals (nonlawyers trained to handle routine aspects of legal work). They concentrate on legal problems that are fairly common such as wills, personal bankruptcy, divorces, and traffic offenses (Muris and McChesney, 1979).

Some clinics have established chain operations with more than a hundred offices in various states and advertise heavily on late-night television. Two-thirds of the clients have problems that do not require formal legal action. They are mostly money claims—rent deposits, suits by collections companies, and the like. When a case does not warrant the services of a lawyer, the client is informed how to go to small-claims court or how to negotiate with bill collectors. Of the cases that go beyond the first meeting, about half are divorces, wills, name changes, and adoptions. The fees are usually set in advance and are based on a published schedule. For example, they charge a flat fee of $200 (plus court costs) for a simple uncontested divorce as contrasted to $500 at a conventional firm. The offices are often located in shopping centers or other heavy traffic areas with easy access and plenty of parking. Attorneys are available during the day and the evening, and on Saturdays. Credit cards are accepted along with installment payments (Sullivan, 1979:9).

A second way of providing low-cost legal services is through prepaid legal plans which work very much like medical insurance (Waldman, 1986). There are currently two basic ways used to finance such a plan. The organizer can sign up a group of people—a labor union or credit union—and charge so many dollars per person per year. The other way is to sign up individuals one by one. Obviously, individuals who sign up are those who think they will be likely to use the service. Since more legal services will be used, the cost per person will be higher compared with the group method.

There are two general ways of selecting lawyers in prepaid legal plans. There is either a designated lawyer or a group of lawyers from which a client may select, or a client may pick any lawyer he or she prefers. In the latter case, there are usually limits on how much of the fee will be covered by the plan. In recent years, unions have been the prime movers in organizing prepaid plans. For example, a plan set up by the United Auto Workers is probably the largest in the country. It covers 150,000 Chrysler employees, retired workers and their immediate families. Thus far, though, prepaid plans have not grown as fast as the proponents expected. Individuals in general consider the need for legal insurance as less urgent than the need for medical insurance. Another impediment to widespread prepaid legal plans may be the legal clinic. If many more legal clinics are established, fees for routine services are likely to decline throughout the profession. As a result, there will be less of a need for protection against problems that may come up. In other countries, however, the idea of legal insurance seems more appealing. In West Germany, prepaid legal plans are widely accepted and about 40 percent of the households carry legal expense insurance.

THE TRAINING OF LAWYERS

Although applications to law schools have fallen nearly 20 percent from their peak in 1982 (Evangelauf, 1986:1), many college graduates still aspire to become lawyers. Today 175 law schools are approved by the American Bar Association. Since 1960, enrollment in law schools more than tripled from 40,381 to 125,698 in 1984 (The Official Guide, 1986:13). For the same period, the number of graduates almost quadrupled to about 37,000.

For many years, the first degree in almost all law schools was the Bachelor of Law (LL.B.). A few gave their Juris Doctor (J.D.) to all students, while others reserved the J.D. for students graduating with honors. In recent years, all schools have changed to granting the J.D. There is no difference in the nature of the course of study for the two degrees. The Master's degree (LL.M.) usually involves a one-year program combining coursework and research beyond the J.D.; the Doctorate of Juridicial Sciences (S.J.D.) is a graduate academic research degree that involves major advanced academic publishable work; and the Master's in Comparative Law (M.C.L.) involves advanced work for foreign-educated lawyers. In addition, a number of law schools offer "joint degrees," that is, a law school in conjunction with some other college or school offers a combined program leading to a joint degree, such as Juris-Doctor–Master of Public Administration degree.

Over the years there have been substantial changes in the composition and characteristics of law students. Women have been dramatically under-represented in the past both in law schools and in the profession. As late as 1970, women comprised only 2.8 percent of the population of lawyers in the United States. More recently, women have been entering the profession in unprecedented numbers and by 1984 almost 13 percent of lawyers were women (Curran, 1986:25). In 1970, 8.5 percent of law school students were women, in 1984, 38 percent. Of the 40,747 first-year law students in 1984, 16,233, or 38 percent were women (The Lawyer's Almanac, 1986:339).

Minorities, like women, historically have been extremely underrepresented in the legal profession. In 1970, black lawyers comprised slightly over 1 percent of all lawyers—3845, of whom 600 were located in the South (Leonard, 1977:4–5). The various minority recruitment programs implemented by most law schools in the late 1960s have increased the enrollment of minority-group students substantially over earlier years, but still, these groups do not have representations within the law school populations anywhere near the percentage of the total population. Between 1970 and 1984, the percentage of minority students enrolled in law schools increased from 3.3 to 9.4 percent. In 1984, 5 percent of all law students were black American; 2.7 percent Hispanic-American; 1.6 percent Asian-American; and 0.03 percent Native-American (The Official Guide, 1986:20). The number of minority-group law students remains disappointingly low, and there are discouraging indications that this is the group most likely to drop in numbers as the total registration slackens or even declines (McKay, 1976:272–273).

Lawyers in the United States established a monopoly on the instrumentalities of the law and the right to practice in the courts. Similarly, law schools have a monopoly on the training of lawyers. They are the gatekeepers for the legal profession. Entry into the profession is conditioned by socioeconomic status and academic standing. Robert Stevens (1973), in a sample of eight law schools studied in 1960, 1970, and 1972, reconfirms the notion that law schools tend to draw students from more affluent families. Students in general come from better educated and richer families than the general population, and there is increasing homogenization of the college background of law students. In 1960, Stevens found that law schools recruited primarily humanists; by 1970, however, they were recruiting social scientists. By 1970, the numbers majoring in social sciences had doubled to more than a majority (Stevens, 1973:574–575).

Although more people apply to law school than can be accepted, about 70 percent of all applicants are accepted to at least one school. Admission to law school is competitive. The higher the reputation of a law school, the greater the competition among students for the number of places. The status of a law school is related to the placement of its graduates. Graduates of law schools attached to elite colleges and universities (for example, Harvard, Yale, Columbia, Chicago) are more likely to be employed in firms, whereas graduates of Catholic or commercial law schools are more likely to be found in solo practice (Ladinsky, 1967:222–232). The elite Wall Street firms have been most educationally selective in this regard, choosing not only from ivy league law schools but also from a group whose backgrounds include attendance at elite prep schools and colleges (Smigel, 1964:73–74).

Moreover, many lawyers graduating from high-status law schools do not practice in the lower-status specialties of criminal law, family, poverty, and debtor-creditor law (Zemans, 1977). Since many students are motivated by a desire for financial rewards (Stevens, 1973:577), competition for admission in high-status law schools is further heightened. As a result, only a small proportion of applicants are accepted in elite national law schools. For example, in 1985 the Official Guide to U.S. Law Schools (1986) shows that of the 6000 applicants, 780 (13 percent) were accepted at Harvard and of the 3316 applicants, 470 (14 percent) were accepted at Stanford. The percentage of those admitted at state schools is much higher. For example, Ohio Northern University admitted 79 percent, Mississippi College 69 percent, and William Mitchell College of Law 81 percent. Similarly, in Catholic universities, the acceptance rate is moderately high: St. Louis University accepts 74 percent of the applicants and Loyola University of New Orleans 60 percent. But in addition to the quality and reputation of law school, other factors enter into a decision to apply to a particular school, such as the desire to practice in the school's state, job opportunities upon graduation, the school's orientation toward social sciences, availability and extent of financial aid, job opportunities for spouse while in school, attraction to the community or area where the school is located, and not the least, tuition.

Law school education is expensive. At the higher end, annual tuition at elite schools such as Harvard was $10,305, at Yale $10,700, and at Stanford $10,776 in 1985. The minimum budget required at these schools is around $17,800 a year. At the lower end, tuition for in-state residents at University of Alabama is $876 and at Louisiana State University $891. Law schools generally admit only those with a college degree, which itself restricts the profession to those who can afford seven years of education beyond high school. If one goes to a state university where the cost of an undergraduate degree is a reasonable $5,000 a year, the direct cost is $20,000. If the modest yearly "income" of $10,000 is added (the amount a student might have earned had he or she not gone to college), the total "cost" of college education is $60,000. Add to this the cost of law school and foregone earnings, another $60,000, and a law degree from a state university will cost at least $120,000. For those who cannot afford such expenses, the alternative is to attend a less expensive college, then go to law school part-time at night. But this option will take longer and will provide a lower quality legal education than full-time enrollment (Jacob, 1986:126).

Law school admission is determined to a great extent by the combined scores of grade point averages in college and Law School Admission Test (LSAT) scores. LSAT is a nationally administered, standardized test taken by all law school applicants. In 1986–1987 the test alone cost $90. Virtually all law schools also require that applicants submit the Law School Data Assembly Service Report, a summary of their college transcript that the Law School Admission Council/Law School Admission Services prepare. The LSAT test and the transcript service, with unlimited reports to law schools cost $145. Letters of recommendation in support of one's application are submitted separately to law schools.

The LSAT has been used in various forms since 1948. The current version was administered for the first time in June, 1982. In 1985, 95,129 persons took the test, down from the all-time high of 135,397 in 1974. The test consists of six 35-minute sections, two of which are not scored. The four scored sections, consisting of 110 to 120 questions, are designed to measure the ability to read with understanding and insight, the ability to structure relationships and to make deductions from them, the ability to evaluate reading, the ability to apply reasoning to rules and facts, and the ability to think analytically. There is also a 30-minute writing sample which is sent directly to the applicant's law school. The score is reported on a scale of 10 to 48 with 48 as the highest possible score. Approximately two-thirds of the test takers score between 22 and 38 (The Official Guide, 1986:21).

The test repeatedly came under criticism and questions have been raised concerning the extent to which the LSAT can predict success in law school. Performance criteria of success in law school have traditionally been and continue to be grades obtained in formal course work. More and more studies conclude that the LSAT, or a combination of LSAT and grade point average, do not predict law school grades for practical purposes of selection, placement, or advisement for candidates seeking entrance into law school (Leonard, 1977:204). Despite the fact that there are questions about the validity and reliability of the LSAT to predict success in law school, all law schools require it as part of the admission process. It should be noted though, that law schools are not alone in their dependence on some form of admissions (or exclusionary) device. Americans have come to expect testing. The fact that some definitive scientific answer about the best way or ways to measure human abilities and potentials is still remote will not stop the process.

Socialization into the Profession

The purpose of "law school is to transform individuals into novice lawyers, providing them with competency in the law, and instilling in them a nascent self-concept as a professional, a commitment to the values of the calling, and that esoteric mental style called "thinking like a lawyer" (Bonsignore et al., 1979:209). Chambliss and Seidman note: "The American law school education is a classic example of an education in which the subject matter formally studied is ridiculously simple, but the process of socialization into the profession is very difficult" (1971:97). The study of law is a tedious although not a challenging undertaking. After the first year, the work load in law schools tends to be light. The popular conception of law students' life as a mixture of long hours, poring over case books, and endless discussions of the contents of those books is more myth than reality. For many students, law school is a part-time commitment, and by the fifth semester, they have the equivalent of a two-day work week and discuss their studies rarely if at all. Says Stevens: "At least intellectually law school appears to be a part-time operation" (1973:653).

The key to an understanding of the socialization of law students is

best found through an examination of their principal method of instruction, the case or Socratic method. As I noted earlier, the case method was
initiated by Langdell in 1870 at Harvard, and it has since become the dominant form of instruction in American law schools.

This method of education "generally involves an intensive interrogation by the teacher of individual students concerning the facts and principles presumed to be operative" in a particular case. The method is intended to accomplish two objectives. The first is informational: instruction
in the substantive rules of law. The second

> is to develop in the student a cognitive restructuring for the style analysis
> generally called "thinking like a lawyer." In that analysis, a student is trained
> to account for the factual 'details' as well as legal issues determined by the
> court to be at the core of the dispute which may allow an intelligent predic-
> tion of what another court would do with a similar set of facts. The technique
> is learner centered: students are closely questioned and their responses are
> often taken to direct the dialogue (Bonsignore et al., 1979:213).

This method of learning the law through court decisions, appellate
opinions, and attempts to justify these opinions predominates at virtually
every law school in the country and has not changed since its introduction
in 1870. Historically, as well as today, the first year of legal education is the
most dramatic of the law school's three years. The curriculum of the first
year has become as well-established in the past century as the teaching
method. Nearly all of the over 42,000 people who begin their legal educations every fall are required to take what are generally thought of as the
basic subjects—contracts, torts, property, criminal law, and civil procedure.
And for all of them, the effects of that education are considered to be
equally predictable and far-reaching. It is during the first year that law students learn to read a case, frame a legal argument, and distinguish between
seemingly indistinguishable ideas; then they start absorbing the mysterious
language of the law, full of words like "estoppel" and "replevin." It is during
the first year that a law student learns "to think like a lawyer," to develop
the habits and perspectives that will stay with him or her throughout a legal
career (Turow, 1977:60).

The ratio of the number of students to the number of faculty in law
schools is markedly higher than that of any other field of graduate training.
A 1 to 25 faculty-student ratio is rather common at the best law schools,
compared with about a 1 to 6 ratio in graduate schools (Loh, 1984:735).
The ratio is predicated on the assumption that law students, unlike other
graduate students, are handled in large classes and that law professors, unlike other academicians, "have no research work to be done" (Manning,
1968:4). Although the emphasis on research is on the increase among law
professors, students, especially during the first year, are taught in large
classes. One striking advantage of the case method noted by educational
administrators is its adaptability to large classes; indeed, there is an argument to be made for the proposition that the impersonality of the large
class is helpful to the student called upon to perform under attack for the

first time in his or her life. As stated by a law professor at Yale, "I prefer a hundred, I will work for a hundred and put on a good show; I'll go to sleep with ten or twelve. After you've taught a subject to a class of a hundred for two or three years, you can anticipate the questions and their timing. When I started, I was told, 'Pick four or five points and keep coming back to them; find the bright students and play them like a piano!' It works" (Mayer, 1967:83–84). This method requires the student to do his or her own work and to prepare regularly for classes. When a professor has a gift for posing hypothetical questions, invents cases to supplement the real ones, the method can be extremely stimulating, pointing out to a student that the rule, as he or she has stated it, would produce a different result under other circumstances. The method also focuses attention to subtleties, and provides a good background for logical reasoning.

Although the processes of legal education continue to produce lawyers to fill the present institutional roles calling for them, through methods that have worked and proved themselves consistently over the last century, a feeling of malaise and discontent has been growing among students and faculty at many of the nation's law schools. Many students deplore the Socratic method's inconclusiveness, its failure to encourage creativeness, and its lack of intellectual stimulation (Stevens, 1973:636–638). The class atmosphere is considered to be a hostile one, with the hostility directed from the icily distant law professor toward the student on the spot. Law professors often ignore the emotional and connotative level of communication. As a result, there is an intense emotional climate in the classroom in which the student may suffer a severe loss of self-respect and possibly an identity crisis. This result of the Socratic method of teaching is generally rationalized by explaining that the method is meant to acclimate the students to "legal reasoning," or "thinking like a lawyer." But it is difficult to see the relationship between the psychic damage and these stated goals, "and one often gets the feeling that the recitation of 'thinking like a lawyer' has become more a talismanic justification for what is going on than an articulated educational program" (Packer and Ehrlich, 1972:30). In addition to the fact that the Socratic method provokes anxiety, hostility, and aggression in the classroom, the domination by the law professor as an authority figure suggests that another aspect of law school training is to enforce a respect for authoritative power (Bonsignore et al., 1979:214). Yet, the method has proved to be remarkably resilient, and in spite of all the criticism against it, there has been no serious competitor (Stevens, 1983:xiv).

Essentially, the objective of law school education is to indoctrinate students into the legal profession. Questions that challenge the basis of the system are seldom raised and law students define the problems presented to them within the framework of the existing system. The socialization of law students tends to make them intellectually independent, but at the same time it restrains them from looking for radical solutions, "for throughout their law school education they are taught to define problems in the way they have always been defined" (Chambliss and Seidman, 1971:99). During law school, students change their political orientation in a conservative direction (Erlanger and Klegon, 1978). It is not surprising that "[l]egal education seems to socialize students toward an entrepreneurial value position in which the law is presumed to be primarily a conflict-resolving mechanism and the lawyer a facilitator of client interests. The experience seems to move students away from the social welfarist value in which the law is seen as a social change mechanism, and the lawyer a facilitator of group or societal interests" (Kay, 1978:347).

Political values are often fused with the learning of law, and "[s]tudents are conditioned to react to questions and issues which they have no role in forming or stimulating. Such teaching *forms* have been crucial in perpetuating the status quo in teaching *content*. For decades, the law school curriculum reflected with remarkable fidelity the commercial demands of law firm practice" (Nader, 1969:21). Students anticipate and law professors reinforce the notion that successful lawyers tend to be conservative and use conservative solutions. A financially successful lawyer needs clients who are able to pay fees. Businesspersons and rich people in general pay larger fees than wage earners and poor people. Successful lawyers represent successful clients, and such a lawyer "if not already attuned to the value-sets of his client, tends to adopt them" (Chambliss and Seidman, 1971:99).

Another critic of law school education argues that the stamp of reality is missing from the case method. David N. Rockwell "suggests that the reliance of the case method on appellate opinions, which are produced primarily by those legal interests who are sufficiently affluent to pursue costly appeals, biases the instruction" (Rockwell, quoted in Bonsignore et al., 1979:215). He points out that:

> The emphasis placed on the study of appellate decisions omits consideration of the actual problems of trial work, such as the prejudices of judges and juries, the deals which are made in criminal courts, or the political focus affecting various classes of interested parties, such as tenants. This coincides with the insistence of many law schools that emphasis be placed on a supposedly value-free theoretical approach to law. In practice this means that law students draw only from theory heavily tinged with corporate values. They will thus be able to offer solutions for corporate problems, but not for the problems posed by injustices in the judicial system or other injustices caused by the corporate interests (Rockwell, quoted in Bonsignore et al., 1979:215).

In response to the escalating criticism of the socialization process of law students, there is a growing emphasis on interdisciplinary work in law schools, and on joint degrees such as law and sociology, law and psychiatry, law and business, and law and just about anything. There is also a trend toward "clinical" programs. The idea is to remove law students from classroom situations and place them during their second and third years in real situations, such as criminal defense offices and poverty-related neighborhood legal aid offices. For many law students, clinical education is considered to be more "relevant" to perceived social needs, and they believe that it should contribute to providing better legal services for the poor and other unrepresented groups in society. Clinical education lends itself to being a separate activity, and is by nature removed from the law school. Since active participation is fundamental in clinical education, in addition to learning "how to think like a lawyer" students also learn "how to work like lawyers." Other than these attempts, however, law schools oppose efforts to reform the traditional curriculum, such as the establishment of comprehensive programs (similar to medical internships) to provide students with a more practical grounding in courtroom skills and other aspects of law practice (Jacobson, 1979:10).

ADMISSION TO THE BAR

The legal profession has defined the perimeters of the practice of law and carefully excluded all who cannot utter the password of bar membership. Recall the lockstep of the profession as it now operates. The process begins after college where the performance of the aspiring lawyer is carefully measured by more or less standard grading processes, as further refined by the Law School Admission Test. Nowadays, only the strongest, as measured by those two criteria, have been allowed to enter the portals of legal education. There the refining process continues with study and examinations designed to test the same qualities that were measured on the LSAT. Finally, at the end of law school—again a graded performance—there is for nearly all a bar examination, which reviews fitness to practice by testing for the same qualities as did the LSAT and the law school examinations.

In the United States, the possession of a law degree does not entitle one to practice law. Since a lawyer is technically a court official, he or she must, in addition to legal training, be admitted to practice by a court. Historically, there were no standards and criteria for admission to the bar, and it depended a great deal on the charity or leniency of a local judge. In most instances, to be admitted by one court was sufficient to practice before any court in a state, for each judge respected his or her colleagues' actions in admission proceedings. As a result, the standards of the most lenient judge in a state became the minimum standard for admission (Hurst, 1950:276–285).

The practice of lack of standards attracted the attention of the American Bar Association and state bars. Their concern was two-fold. Easy admission permitted the entry of unqualified and unscrupulous lawyers whose work blemished the reputation of all lawyers. Furthermore, easy entrance into the legal profession allowed more lawyers to compete for the available legal business and depressed the income of lawyers.

There were several efforts by the ABA and state bar associations to restrict entry into the legal profession. They obtained legislation to lengthen the required training before application for admission could be accepted. Most efforts to restrict entry into the bar, however, were focused on requiring applicants to pass a standardized bar examination. Bar examinations have had their desired impact in reducing admission to the legal profession and increasing the standards of the profession. Today, "No person who is not a member of the bar of another American or common-law jurisdiction should be admitted to practice until he has successfully undergone a written examination accomplished under terms and conditions equivalent to those applicable to all other candidates for bar admission" (American Bar Association, 1979:83).

Over time, bar examinations have had some unanticipated consequences. Since bar examinations follow a content pattern substantially identical to that borrowed from the law school curriculum, the pattern of the local bar examination in turn strongly inhibits change in educational programs. The extent to which a school introduces innovative programs or markedly deviates in its curriculum from traditional programs places its graduates at a competitive disadvantage in taking a bar examination. Moreover, because law schools are accredited according to, among other criteria, the number of students who pass the bar exam, and are often rated by students according to this standard, legal education has become very much examination-oriented in many states. Subjects included in the examination are required of the students and courses in these subjects are often molded according to the questions asked on the examinations.

Many law school graduates, in preparation for the local bar examination, take cram courses and sit through six hours of daily lectures for six to twelve solid weeks, memorizing endless outlines and gimmicks of local examinationship—which will be erased from their minds within months after examination date. Whatever improvement is made in law schools greatly increases the necessity of this type of cramming unless the bar examinations change too.

In addition to educational qualifications of would-be lawyers, bar associations also restrict admission procedures to those who are morally fit to become lawyers. Applicants for admission to the bar must have "good moral character." But the definition of this standard is weak. Basically, it means that no one who has a serious criminal record can be admitted to the practice of law. In some cases, it has led to the refusal of a board of examiners to admit someone who has held (or still holds) unpopular political views, and during the McCarthy era the ABA urged that all those who would become lawyers should take a loyalty oath as a condition of practice (Green, 1976:5). Although the standards are vague, historically the U.S. Supreme Court often upheld the authority of state courts to refuse admission to individuals the state deemed unworthy to practice law. Admission is a privilege which a court may withhold. Through such actions, bar associations effectively control the entry of some individuals who could potentially damage the image of the legal profession.

BAR ASSOCIATIONS AS INTEREST GROUPS

In addition to restricting entry into the profession and seeking to control the activity of their members, bar associations are also interest groups actively engaged in the promotion of activities that the bar considers vital to its interests.

Much of the bar's activity concerns the organization and personnel of the courts. Bar associations attempted repeatedly to devise and to promote court reorganization schemes. Much of these efforts went into the elimination of nonprofessional elements from the judicial process. The bar has also been active in seeking to influence the selection of judges. On the state level, where judges are often elected on a partisan or nonpartisan ballot, the bar association has frequently lobbied for a change in selection procedures that would give the bar a greater voice. The bar also influences the selection of federal judges, and it is now a standard procedure for the Attorney General to seek the ABA's opinion about political nominees when choosing a name for submission by the President to the Senate. The bar is also active in promoting legislation that will benefit lawyers and the administrations of justice. For example, the bar actively promoted legislation against the unauthorized practice of the law in an attempt to safeguard its monopoly over legal services.

In addition to taking a leading part in shaping laws (especially on criminal and regulatory matters), structuring the legal system, and making recommendations for judicial positions, the national and state bar associations have often turned to politics to promote their professional and economic interests. Such efforts, among other things, have resulted in state regulations which limit the number of lawyers and raise the income of those who do practice. Associations of trial lawyers have also sought to influence state and national legislation or regulations which are regarded as affecting their economic interests. A recent example has been the opposition of trial lawyers to no-fault automobile insurance, whereby people in an automobile accident can collect from their own insurance companies without having to hire a lawyer, go to court, and establish liability. Other attempts of the bar to enhance the economic status of its members included the promotion of continued benefits for self-employed lawyers; permission for lawyers to practice before federal agencies without having to obtain special admission or take a special admission examination; promotion of a bill to remove ceilings on attorneys' fees in federal departments and agencies; opposition to bankruptcy reform that would remove lawyers from the proceedings; and opposition to the extension of the role of title companies in home closings at the expense of lawyers (Green, 1976:7).

Of course, the bar associations, like all professional associations (and unions), have, as one of their major functions, the promotion of the social, political, and economic interests of their members. Ideally, at least, however, there is a fundamental difference between the legal profession and other professions. Fred Rodell of Yale is quoted as stating that "[w]hile law is supposed to be a device to serve society . . . it is pretty hard to find a group less concerned with serving society and more concerned with serving themselves than lawyers" (Green, 1976:19). Thus, it is not surprising that the most discernible common cause of bar associations is the needs of their lawyers and those clients whose interests they regularly attend.

PROFESSIONAL DISCIPLINE

One of the characteristics of a profession is a code of ethics. A profession, among other things, involves a sense of service and responsibility to the community, and the conduct required of a professional is delineated in a code of ethics for that profession. A lawyer's code of ethics deals with his or her relations with clients, other lawyers, the court, and the public.

The legal profession has long been concerned with the ethical forms under which lawyers operate. In 1908, the American Bar Association published its *Canons of Ethics*. In 1969, it was revised and called the *Model Code of Professional Responsibility*. The standards of professional conduct promulgated by the Code were adopted by most states. The Code covered a variety of important rules from representation of conflicting interests and preservation of clients' confidences to matters of professional etiquette. In 1977, the ABA decided that the Code was insufficient in view of the changing nature of the profession and established a commission to come up with a new, more realistic, and practical set of ethical rules.

In 1983, the ABA adopted the *Model Rules of Professional Conduct and Code of Judicial Conduct* (1983). It deals with a series of rules on, for example, fees, confidentiality of information, various types of conflict of interest, safekeeping property, unauthorized practice of law, advertising, and reporting professional misconduct.

A major weakness of the codes and model rules is that adoption of them is not required by local groups. The ABA exerts no control over state bars in this process. Furthermore, enforcement is not obligatory. Although the ABA advocates uniform standards in disciplinary procedures, it is unable to implement uniform adherence.

Generally, disciplinary sanctions are imposed only for serious instances of misconduct, such as criminal acts, mishandling of client's property, and flagrant violation of certain rules of professional conduct such as breach of confidentiality. Other rule violations rarely evoke formal disciplinary action, although there is informal discipline in the form of expressed disapproval, which carries its own practical penalties such as questions about one's professional reputation.

Generally, the highest ethical standards are found among attorneys who work for large firms (Carlin, 1966:47–48) and represent big business clients in more traditional fields such as patents and admiralty. Those who represent individuals in cases that are characterized "unsavory" such as personal injury plaintiffs' work, divorce, and criminal defense tend to have lower ethical standards (Heinz and Laumann, 1982:107). These are usually lower status solo practitioners who practice before state courts. As Herbert Jacob (1984:62) notes, the more contact such attorneys have with lower courts, the less likely they are to comply with legal ethics: "The culture of lower courts—waiting around, exchanging gossip, litigating petty criminal and civil cases" promotes unethical conduct.

Violations of legal ethics may be punished by a reprimand, a temporary suspension of license to practice law, or the revocation of the license. Jerome E. Carlin (1966:170) found that only about 2 percent of the lawyers who violated ethical norms were even processed by the bar's disciplinary machine, and only 0.2 percent were officially sanctioned. In 1972, bar associations disciplined 357 lawyers, roughly one-tenth of 1 percent of practicing lawyers at that time (Garbus and Seligman, 1976:48). In 1984, 59,862 complaints were received by the disciplinary boards in 48 states.

That number represents about 8 percent of all practicing attorneys. During the same year, 1,408 lawyers received public sanctions (disbarment, suspension, and public reprimand) and 1,833 received private sanctions (reprimand and formal admonition) (Austern, 1986:17). Although the bar spent more than $30 million for lawyer discipline, the enforcement of the ethical standards it has promulgated for the guidance of its members leaves something to be desired when only 5.4 percent of those who had complaints against them were subjected to either public or private sanctions.

How serious are lawyers about professional responsibility? A 1985 poll conducted for the ABA Journal Reskin (1985:41) finds that professional responsibility is important to most lawyers; most are familiar with ethical codes in effect in their jurisdiction. Lack of familiarity with the code of professional responsibility is highest (15 percent) among lawyers who are not in private practice—law professors and government, legal aid, and corporate law department lawyers.

Ethics are emphasized and considered extremely important among partners according to 66 percent of the respondents. The group that places the greatest accent on ethics consists of lawyers earning more than $75,000 from the practice of law (76 percent). Ethics are not discussed or emphasized especially among sole practitioners (22 percent) and lawyers not in private practice (27 percent). These findings are consistent with studies on lawyers' ethics (see, for example, Carlin, 1966 and Heinz and Laumann, 1982) that suggest that high-status lawyers in firms are more likely to adhere to the ethical norms of the profession than their lower status-counterparts in solo practice.

Seven out of ten lawyers say that they would report a lawyer outside of their firm who acted unethically, and six out of ten would report a colleague in their own firm. Since 71 percent say they have occasionally encountered dishonest opposing counsel, it is obvious that lawyers should be doing a lot more reporting. But they are not. Most complaints against lawyers are filed by clients or initiated by the bar council. It is rare that lawyers or judges report lawyer or judicial misconduct. The reasons for not reporting vary from "no use" because nothing would happen and it is not their responsibility to not wanting to ruin someone's career. About 40 percent of the lawyers who do not report misconduct fear that too much time would be taken up testifying in a disciplinary proceeding, do not know where to report the misconduct, or they are afraid of being subjected to a lawsuit. Although lawyers claim that ethical conduct is important and the majority are willing to report violation of professional norms, in reality, they are reluctant to do it—which raises serious concerns about the efficacy of the internal modes of control of the profession.

There are also external modes of control of the profession, primarily from the federal government. Both the Federal Trade Commission and the Justice Department are concerned with the delivery of legal services in matters of monopolistic restrictions (curbing the provision of legal services to the poor and moderate income people) and practices constituting restraint of trade (such as, real estate agents filling out legal forms in closing a deal, which is considered "unauthorized" practice of law). The Securities and

Exchange Commission also has authority to discipline lawyers who practice before it and engage in fraudulent activities by temporarily suspending or disbarring them.

Finally, there is the delicate and difficult problem of monitoring judicial conduct. How can judges be protected from unfair attacks so they can maintain their judicial independence and have, at the same time, effective mechanisms for the retirement or removal of those who do not perform their duties properly? In some states, the only procedure for removal of judges before the end of their term is impeachment by a vote of legislators. In others, committees of judges are empowered to investigate judicial incompetence and compel the retirement of a judge found unable to carry out his or her duties (Flood, 1985:42).

The problem is further compounded by the fact that most lawyers who have witnessed judicial misconduct have not reported it (Reskin, 1985:41). So far the most dramatic measure for rooting out judicial corruption has been Operation Greylord (Flood, 1985:42). The Federal Bureau of Investigation for three and a half years investigated the largest court system in the country with over 300 judges—the Cook County system which includes Chicago. It uncovered a variety of corrupt practices by some judges, such as favorable rulings, case referrals, and lighter criminal sentences in return for bribes. Judges also gave permission to attorneys to solicit clients in the courthouse. The FBI relied on agents to represent attorneys and criminals to infiltrate the court and in one instance a judge was wired to record conversations between corrupt lawyers and judges. As a result of the FBI investigation, several judges, lawyers, and court officials have been indicted for corruption, four judges so far have been convicted, and one acquitted.

SUMMARY

In all societies, the legal profession has been intimately connected with the rise and development of legal systems. Primitive societies had courts and judges, but no lawyers. In such societies, custom and law coincided. No special legal skills were required before a court. With the development of court procedures, a class of skilled advocates emerged. The origins of the legal profession can be traced back to Rome. Lawyers, in the sense of a regulated group of practitioners, emerged in the late 1200s. By that time the body of legal knowledge, including procedure, had become too much for the ordinary person to handle alone. Technical pleadings required the aid of an attorney, and legal business increased tremendously. In the fourteenth and fifteenth centuries, a secular class of lawyers emerged in England, and the law administered by the royal courts became independent, in some important respects at least, from Roman and canon law. To a large extent, English lawyers received their training in the Inns of Court, at the hands of the legal profession itself and not in the universities. Blackstone's appointment to the Vinerian Chair of Jurisprudence in 1758 marked the first effort to make English law a university subject.

Initially in the United States, legal education was modeled after the British system. Many of the early upper-class American lawyers obtained their training in the Inns of Court. In the late eighteenth and early nineteenth centuries, general courses in law were established in many American universities. However, these courses were in time superseded by the development of university law schools—a form of professional legal education which, strictly speaking, has no counterpart either in England or on the continent of Europe.

Lawyers have established a monopoly on legal business, and the profession of law has become the fastest growing of all professions in the United States during the last two decades. Although members of the profession have never been popular, lawyers rank high in prestige in the United States. There are four major subgroups in the legal profession: lawyers in private practice, in government service, in private employment, and in the judiciary. The American legal profession is highly stratified. Lawyers in private practice who are solo practitioners in general tend to have a lower status in the profession than their counterparts working in law firms. The relatively low status of solo practitioners is attributed to their socioeconomic background and to the quality of education they have received. Many solo practitioners use the legal profession as a form of social mobility. Employment with the government is often considered a mobility route into a more prestigious practice situation for young lawyers. The proportion of lawyers in private employment is on the increase, and they handle only the work of their corporate employer. Some larger corporations today have legal departments that compare in size and excellence with those of the largest law firms. In the United States, there is no career judiciary, and there is no prescribed route for the young law graduate to become a judge. Judges are elected or appointed.

There is a substantial variation in income by types of lawyers. Those in law firms and in private employment generally earn more than their counterparts in solo practice or in the judiciary. Income is related to the type of practice, the type of clientele, the degree of specialization, the size of the firm, the quality of education and achievement in law school, the age and length of practice, and the size and location of the place of practice. In recent years, there is a growing competition for legal business. Although the minimum fee schedules have been abolished (at least in principle) and lawyers are now able to advertise, the cost of legal services is still beyond the reach of many people.

Law and lawyers are expensive. In criminal cases, the poor are either represented by public defenders or by court-appointed attorneys. In civil cases, the poor can gain access to lawyers through public or private legal aid programs. Others with less limited finances resort to legal clinics or prepaid legal plans as a way of obtaining legal representation.

Contemporary lawyers must submit to a long period of training before becoming eligible to practice. This, however, is a recent development in the United States. Throughout the nineteenth century, legal training was haphazard. Most lawyers received their training in the office of a practicing attorney. They worked for him as a clerk, and by doing so learned the trade themselves. University training of lawyers in the United States did not really begin until after 1870. Today there are 169 law schools approved by the American Bar Association. Entry into a law school requires a college degree, and applicants must have a high grade point average in addition to a moderately high LSAT score. The number of law students tripled during the past two decades and the number of women in law schools increased almost twenty-fold. However, minority students still represent a smaller proportion in law schools than their percentage of the total population. Law school education still relies heavily on the case or Socratic method which has remained virtually unchanged during the past 110 years. The method is meant to acclimate the students to "legal reasoning," or to "thinking like a lawyer," but lately it has been subjected to criticisms such as its failure to encourage creativeness and its lack of intellectual stimulation. It also provokes anxiety, hostility, and aggression in the classroom. Law schools seem to socialize students toward an entrepreneurial value position and questions that challenge the basis of the legal system are seldom raised. During law school, students tend to change their political orientation in a conservative direction. In response to the growing criticism of the socialization process of law students, law schools in recent years began to emphasize interdisciplinary work and clinical programs. However, major efforts to reform curriculum are still opposed.

To maintain standards and to control entry into the bar, law school graduates are required to pass a standardized bar examination in the state where they wish to practice. Bar examinations have stifled changes in legal education. Many students are preoccupied with passing the bar, which forces law schools to mold courses according to the questions asked on the examinations. Bar associations further restrict admission procedures to those who are morally fit to become lawyers. Applicants for admission to the bar must have "good moral character." Bar associations also act as interest groups in promoting social, economic, and political activities that the bar considers vital to its interests. They often act like other interest groups in pressing for adoption of measures desired by their members.

In an attempt to improve the negative public image of lawyers, and to assist the courts in rendering justice, the legal profession adopted a code of ethics in 1908. Although violation of the code of legal ethics may be punished by reprimand, suspension from the bar, or disbarment, only a very small proportion of lawyers who violate the ethical standards are ever subjected to disciplinary action. Ethical codes seem to be more enforced when the profession, rather than the clients or society at large, is threatened.

SUGGESTED FURTHER READINGS

RICHARD L. ABEL, "The Transformation of the American Legal Profession." *Law & Society Review* 20 (1), 1986:7–17. A good analysis of the changes in the American legal profession.

GEORGE DANA CAMERON, III, *The Soviet Lawyer and His System.* Ann Arbor, MI: The University of Michigan, Division of Research, Graduate School of Business Administration, 1978. A rare study of the profession and practice of law in the Soviet Union. It provides the most comprehensive picture of Soviet lawyers available from any single source.

JEROME E. CARLIN, *Lawyers On Their Own*. New Brunswick, NJ: Rutgers University Press, 1962. A now classic study of individual practitioners in Chicago.

BARBARA A. CURRAN, "American Lawyers in the 1980s: A Profession in Transition." *Law & Society Review* 20 (1), 1986:19–52. A current statistical profile of the legal profession.

J. S. GANDHI, *Lawyers and Touts: A Study in the Sociology of the Legal Profession*. Delhi, India: Hindustan Publishing Corporation. 1982. A fascinating study of the various undesirable legal practices such as the exploitation of clients and the use of business agents or touts who procure clients for a share of the fee.

JOHN P. HEINZ and EDWARD O. LAUMANN, *Chicago Lawyers: The Social Structure of the Bar*. New York: Russel Sage Foundation AND American Bar Foundation. 1982. A seminal study of the profession in Chicago based on 777 personal interviews with lawyers.

EVE SPANGLER, *Lawyers for Hire: Salaried Professionals at Work*. New Haven: Yale University Press. 1986. An excellent discussion of how salaried attorneys do their work in a variety of settings.

ROBERT STEVENS, *Law School: Legal Education in America from the 1850s to the 1980s*. Chapel Hill: The University of North Carolina Press. 1983. A well-written and detailed history of legal education and American law schools.

SCOTT TUROW, *One L*. New York: Putnam's, 1977. A personal account of the author's first year as a student at the Harvard Law School. The book is a rather devastating statement against the still popular case method of legal education.

PAUL B. WICE, *Criminal Lawyers, An Endangered Species*. Beverly Hills, CA: Sage Publications, 1978. An empirical study of a national sample of private criminal lawyers.

REFERENCES

ABA Journal, 1986. "Lawyer Advertising Is On The Rise," 72 (April):44.

ABEL, RICHARD L. 1986. "The Transformation of the American Legal Profession," Law & Society Review 20 (1):7–17.

American Bar Association. 1979. A Review of Legal Education in the United States—Fall 1978. Chicago: American Bar Association.

AUBERT, VILHELM. 1969. "Law as a Way of Resolving Conflicts: The Case of a Small Industrialized Society," Pp. 282–303 in Laura Nader, ed., Law in Culture and Society. Chicago: Aldine.

AUERBACH, JEROLD S. 1976. *Unequal Justice, Lawyers and Social Change in Modern America*. New York: Oxford University Press.

AUSTERN, DAVID. 1986. "How Lawyers Police Themselves," Trial 22 4(April):17.

BERMAN, HAROLD J. 1958. *The Nature and Functions of Law*. Mineola, NY: The Foundation Press.

BONSIGNORE, JOHN J., ETHAN KATSH, PETER d'ERRICO, RONALD M. PIPKIN, STEPHEN ARONS, and JANET RIFKIN. 1979. *Before the Law, An Introduction to the Legal Process*, 2nd ed. Boston: Houghton Mifflin Company.

CAMERON, GEORGE DANA III. 1978. *The Soviet Lawyer and His System*. Ann Arbor, MI: Division of Research, Graduate School of Business Administration, The University of Michigan.

CARLIN, JEROME E. 1962. *Lawyers on Their Own*. New Brunswick, NJ: Rutgers University Press; 1966. *Lawyers' Ethics*. New York: Russell Sage Foundation.

CHAMBLISS, WILLIAM J. and ROBERT B. SEIDMAN. 1971. *Law, Order, and Power*. Reading, MA: Addison-Wesley.

CURRAN, BARBARA. 1986. "American Lawyers in the 1980s: A Profession in Transition," Law & Society Review 20 (1):19–52.

EASTON, STEPHEN D. 1984. "Fewer Lawyers? Try Getting Your Day in Court," The Wall Street Journal (November 27):34.

ERLANGER, HOWARD S. and DOUGLAS A. KLEGON. 1978. "Socialization Effects of Professional School, The Law School Experience and Student Orientations to Public Interest Concerns," Law and Society Review 13 (1)(Fall):11–35.

EVANGELAUF, JEAN. 1986. "Law Schools Boost Recruiting to Offset Application Slump," The Chronicle of Higher Education (March 5):1,18.

FISKE, EDWARD B. 1986 "Student Debts Reshaping Colleges and Careers," The New York Times Education Life (Section 12, August 3):34–41.

FLOOD, JOHN. 1985. *The Legal Profession in the United States,* 3rd ed. Chicago: American Bar Foundation.

FOOTE, NELSON N. 1953. "The Professionalization of Labor in Detroit," American Journal of Sociology, 58 (4)(January):371–380.

FRIEDMAN, LAWRENCE M. 1973 *A History of American Law.* New York: Simon & Schuster; 1977. Law and Society, An Introduction. Englewood Cliffs, NJ: Prentice-Hall; 1984. *American Law: An Introduction.* New York: W.W. Norton & Company.

GANDHI, J. S. 1982 *Lawyers and Touts: A Study in the Sociology of Legal Profession.* Delhi, India: Hindustan Publishing Corporation.

GARBUS, MARTIN and JOEL SELIGMAN. 1976. "Sanctions and Disbarment: They Sit in Judgement," Pp. 47–60 in Ralph Nader and Mark Green, eds., Verdicts on Lawyers. New York: Thomas Y. Crowell Company.

GREEN, MARK J. 1975. "The High Cost of Lawyers," The New York Times Magazine (August 10):8–9; 53–56.

GREEN, MARK. 1976. "The ABA as Trade Association," Pp. 3–19 in Ralph Nader and Mark Green, eds., Verdicts on Lawyers. New York: Thomas Y. Crowell Company.

HALLIDAY, TERENCE C. 1986. "Six Score Years and Ten: Demographic Transitions in the American Legal Profession, 1850–1980," Law & Society Review 20 (1):53–78.

HEINZ, JOHN P. and EDWARD O. LAUMANN. 1982. *Chicago Lawyers: The Social Structure of the Bar.* New York: Russell Sage Foundation.

HURST, J. WILLARD. 1950. *The Growth of American Law.* Boston: Little, Brown.

JACOB, HERBERT. 1984. *Justice in America: Courts, Lawyers, and the Judicial Process,* 4th ed. Boston: Little, Brown and Company; 1986. *Law and Politics in the United States.* Boston: Little, Brown and Company.

JACOBSON, ROBERT L. 1979. "Law Schools are Cool to Chief Justice's Ideas on Reforming Curriculum," The Chronicle of Higher Education 17 (18)(January 15):10.

JACOBY, HENRY. 1973. *The Bureaucratization of the Word,* trans. by Eveline L. Kanes. Berkeley: University of California Press.

JEFFERY, C. RAY. 1962. "The Legal Profession," Pp. 313–356 in F. James Davis, Henry H. Foster, Jr., C. Ray Jeffery, and E. Eugene Davis, Society and the Law, New Meanings for an Old Profession. New York: Free Press.

JENKINS, JOHN A. 1977. "The Revolving Door Between Government and the Law Firms," The Washington Monthly 8 (11)(January):36–44.

KAY, SUSAN ANN. 1978. "Socializing the Future Elite: The Nonimpact of a Law School," Social Science Quarterly 59 (2)(September):347–356.

KEARNEY, HUGH. 1970. *Scholars and Gentlemen, Universities and Society in Pre-Industrial Britain.* Ithaca, NY: Cornell University Press.

KLEIN, MITCHELL S.G. 1984. *Law, Courts, and Policy.* Englewood Cliffs, NJ: Prentice-Hall.

KRITZER, HERBERT M., WILLIAM L.F. FELSTINER, AUSTIN SARAT, and DAVID M. TRUBEK. 1985. "The Impact of Fee Arrangement on Lawyer Effort," Law & Society Review 19 (2):251–278.

LADINSKY, JACK. 1963. "Careers of Lawyers, Law Practice, and Legal Institutions.," American Sociological Review 28 (1)(February):47–54; 1967. "Higher Education and Work Achievement Among Lawyers," Sociological Quarterly 8 (2):222–232.

LARSON, MAGALI SARFATTI. 1977. *The Rise of Professionalism: A Sociological Analysis.* Berkeley: University of California Press.

LEONARD, WALTER J. 1977. *Black Lawyers.* Boston: Senna and Shih.

LEWIN, TAMAR. 1983. "A Gentlemanly Profession Enters a Tough New Era." The New York Times (January 16):1F, 10F; 1986. "Leaving the Law For Wall Street, The Faster Track," The New York Times Magazine (August 10):14–19,42,50–53.

LEWIS, P.S.C. 1986. "A Comparative Perspective on the Legal Profession in the 1980s," Law & Society Review 20 (1):79–91.

LOH, WALLACE D. 1984. *Social Research in the Judicial Process: Cases, Readings, and Text.* New York: Russel Sage Foundation.

McKAY, ROBERT B. 1976. "Legal Education," Pp. 261–276 in Bernard Schwartz, ed., American Law: The Third Century. South Hackensack, NJ: Published for New York University School of Law by Fred B. Rothman & Company.

MANNING, BAYLESS. 1968. "Introduction: New Tasks for Lawyers," Pp. 1–11 in Geoffrey C. Hazard, Jr., ed., Law in a Changing America. Englewood Cliffs, NJ: Prentice-Hall.

MAYER, MARTIN. 1967. *The Lawyers*. New York: Harper & Row.

Model Rules of Professional Conduct and Code of Judicial Conduct. 1983. Chicago: American Bar Association.

MURIS, TIMOTHY J. and FRED S. MCCHESNEY. 1979. "Advertising and the Price and Quality of Legal Services: The Case for Legal Clinics," American Bar Foundation Research Journal. (1)(Winter):179–207.

NADER, RALPH. 1969. "Law Schools and Law Firms," The New Republic (October 11):21–23.

PACKER, HERBERT L. and THOMAS EHRLICH. 1972. *New Directions in Legal Education*. New York: McGraw-Hill.

REICHSTEIN, KENNETH J. 1965. "Ambulance Chasing: A Case Study of Deviation and Control Within the Legal Profession," Social Problems 13 (1)(Summer):3–17.

REIDINGER, PAUL. 1986A. "Salary Wars," ABA Journal 72 (August 1):42; 1986b. "It's 46.5 Hours a Week in Law," ABA Journal 72 (September 1):44.

RESKIN, LAUREN RUBENSTEIN. 1985. "Lawyers Are Serious About Professional Responsibility," ABA Journal 71 (December):41.

RUESCHEMEYER, DIETRICH. 1985. Lawyers and Their Society. Cambridge, MA: Harvard University Press.

SMIGEL, ERWIN O. 1964. *The Wall Street Lawyer*. New York: Free Press.

SPANGLER, EVE. 1986. *Lawyers for Hire, Salaried Professionals at Work*. New Haven: Yale University Press.

SPECTOR, MALCOLM. 1972. "The Rise and Fall of a Mobility Route," Social Problems 20 (2)(Fall):173–185.

STEVENS, ROBERT. 1971. "Two Cheers for 1870: The American Law School," Pp. 405–548 in Donald Fleming and Bernard Bailyn, eds., Law in American History. Boston: Little, Brown; 1973. "Law Schools and Law Students," Virginia Law Review 59 (4)(April):51–707; 1983. *Law School: Legal Education in America From the 1850s to the 1980s*. Chapel Hill: The University of North Carolina Press.

SULLIVAN, COLLEEN. 1979. "The Upstart Lawyers Who Market the Law," The New York Times (August 26)(Section 3):1;9.

Texas Bar Journal. 1986. "Employment Patterns of Law School Graduates," 49 (5)(May):490.

The Chronicle of Higher Education. 1985. "Average Faculty Salaries by Rank in Selected Fields, 1984–85," (May 1):30.

The Lawyer's Almanac 1986. 1986. Clifton, NJ: Law and Business, Inc. Harcourt Brace Jovanich, Publishers.

The Official Guide to U.S. Law Schools 1986–87. 1986. Prelaw Handbook. Newtown, PA: Law School Admission Council/Law School Admission Services.

The Wall Street Journal. 1986. "Parties, Polls and Pejoratives: Lawyers Meet," (August 13):23.

TIGAR, MICHAEL E. 1977. *Law and the Rise of Capitalism*. New York: Monthly Review Press.

Time. 1978. "Those # * X ! ! ! Lawyers" (April 10):56–66.

TUROW, SCOTT. 1977. "The Trouble with Law School," Harvard Magazine 80 (1)(September-October):60–64.

U.S. News & World Report. 1985. "Morality," (December 9):52–57; 1986. "Sky-High Damage Suits," (January 27):35–43.

WALDMAN, PETER. 1986. "Pre-Paid Legal Plans Offer Consultations, Follow-Up Calls and Referrals at Low Cost," The Wall Street Journal (February):33.

WILENSKY, HAROLD L. 1964. "The Professionalization of Everyone?" American Journal of Sociology 70 (2)(September):137–158.

YORK, JOHN C. and ROSEMARY D. HALE. 1973. "Too Many Lawyers? The Legal Service Industry: Its Structure and Outlook," Journal of Legal Education 26 (1):1–31.

ZEMANS, FRANCES K. 1977. *Law School and Law Practice: Credentials for Professional Status*. Chicago: American Bar Foundation.

9

Sociological Research of Law in Society

Many of the generalizations and conclusions about law in society in the preceding chapters were based on empirical studies. The purpose of this chapter is to impart an analytical perspective on the interrelationship between law and society by looking at the ways sociologists research law and the methods they use to arrive at their findings. The chapter also demonstrates the relevance and applicability of sociological research to the formulation, implementation, and evaluation of social policy. The general comments on methodological tools for research on law are not intended to replace the more detailed technical discussions found in books on methods of social research. They are intended to provide an exposure to the strategies utilized in the study of law in society, and to illuminate the methodological concerns and complexities inherent in such endeavors.

METHODS OF INQUIRY

Several methods can be applied in researching law in society, and more than a single method is usually involved in such a study. However, there are four commonly used methods of data collection in sociology: All other methods are variations and combinations of these four methods. These four methods that will be considered are: the historical, observational, experimental, and survey methods.

Actual research is much more complicated than these methods indicate. All research is essentially a process in which choices are made at many stages. The methods are many and are combined in various ways during research. Methodological decisions are made on such diverse matters as the kind of research design to be used, the type of research population and sample, the sources of data collection, the techniques of gathering data, and the methods of analyzing the research findings. The differences among the four methods are more a matter of emphasis on a particular data collection strategy to obtain observable data for a particular research purpose than a clear-cut "either/or" distinction. For example, in the observational method, while the emphasis is on the researcher's ability to observe and record social activities as they occur, the researcher may interview the participants—a technique associated with the survey and experimental methods. Similarly, in the experimental method, the subjects are usually under the observation of the researcher and his or her collaborators. The information gained in such observations also plays a crucial role in the final analysis and interpretation of the data. Furthermore, historical evidence is often used in observational, survey, and experimental studies.

At all stages of sociological research, there is an interplay between theory and method. In fact, it is often the theory chosen by the researcher that determines which methods will be used in the research. The selection of the method is to a great extent dependent on the type of information desired.

To study a sequence of events and explanations of the meanings of the events by the participants and other observers before, during, and after their occurrence, observation (especially participant observation) seems to be the best method of data collection. The researcher directly observes and participates in the study system with which he or she has established a meaningful and durable relationship as did, for example, Jerome H. Skolnick (1975:30–37) in his study of police officers. While the observer may or may not play an active role in the events, he or she observes them firsthand and can record the events and the participants' experiences as they unfold. No other data collection method can provide such a detailed description of social events. Thus, observation is best suited for studies intended to understand a particular group and certain social processes within that group. When these events are not available for observation as they occurred in the past, the historical approach is the logical choice of method for collecting data.

If an investigator wishes to study norms, rules, and status in a particular group, intensive interviewing of "key" persons and informants in or outside the group is the best method of data collection. For example, Jerome E. Carlin (1966) interviewed approximately 800 lawyers in New York City for his study of legal ethics and their enforcement. Those who set and enforce norms, rules, and status, because of their position in the group or relations with persons in the group, are the ones who are the most knowledgeable about the information the researcher wishes to obtain. Intensive interviews (especially with open-ended questioning) with these persons allow the researcher to probe for such information.

When an investigator wishes to determine the numbers, proportions, ratios, and other quantitative information about the subjects in his or her study possessing certain characteristics, opinions, beliefs, and other categories of various variables, then the best method of data collection is the survey. The survey relies on a representative sample of the population cases to which a standardized instrument can be administered.

Finally, the experiment is the best method of data collection when the researcher wants to measure the effect of certain independent variables on some dependent variables. The experimental situation provides control over the responses and the variables, and gives the researcher the opportunity to manipulate the independent variables. In the following pages, I will examine and illustrate these methods in greater detail.

Historical Methods

Sociologists are largely accustomed to studying social phenomena at one point in time—the present. But social phenomena do not appear spontaneously and autonomously. Historical analysis can indicate the possibility that certain consequences can issue from events which are comparable to other events of the past: history as something more than a simple compilation of facts. It can generate an understanding of the processes of social change and document how a multitude of factors have served to shape the present. The study of history also has an existential function. It informs us who we are, and that we are links that connect the past with the present and future (Inciardi, Block, and Hallowell, 1977:27–28).

Historical research carried out by sociologists is a critical investigation of events, developments, and experiences of the past; a careful weighing of evidence of the validity of sources of information on the past; and the interpretation of the evidence. Historical research is important and valuable in sociology because the origins and roots of the discipline have to be understood if contemporary theories and research are to be understood. As a substitute for direct data from the participants, contents from documents and historical materials are used as a method of data collection. These documents and materials can range from census data, archives of various types, official files such as court records, records of property transactions, records of poor relief administration, tax records, business accounts to personal diaries, witness accounts, propaganda literature, and numerous other personal accounts and letters. The researcher uses these available data sources to carry out what is generally referred to as secondary analysis, that is, the data were not generated or collected for the specific purpose of the study formulated by the researcher. Of course, the usefulness of the historical method depends to a large extent on the accuracy and thoroughness of the documents and materials. With accurate and thorough data, the researcher may be able to gain insights, generate hypotheses, and even test hypotheses.

Official records and public documents have provided the data for sociological analyses attempting to establish long-term legal trends. For example, William J. Chambliss (1964), as I mentioned in Chapter One, has shown how the vagrancy statutes changed in England according to emerging social interests. The first full-fledged vagrancy law, enacted in 1349, regulated the giving of alms to ablebodied, unemployed persons. After the Black Death and the flight of workers from landowners, the law was reformulated in order to force laborers to accept employment at a low wage. By the sixteenth century, with an increased emphasis on commerce and industry, the vagrancy statutes were revived and strengthened. Eventually, vagrancy laws came to serve, as they do today, the purpose of controlling persons and activities regarded as undesirable to the community. Similarly, Jerome Hall (1952) has shown, on the basis of historical records, how changing social conditions and emerging social interests brought about the formulation of trespass laws in fifteenth century England.

The historical method is also used to test theories. For example, Mary P. Baumgartner (1978) was interested in the relationship between the social status of the defendant and the litigant and the verdicts and sanctions awarded them. She analyzed data based on 389 cases (148 civil and 241 criminal) heard in the colony of New Haven between 1639 and 1665. She found, not unexpectedly, that in both the civil and criminal cases, individuals who enjoyed high status were more likely to receive favorable treatment by the court than their lower-status counterparts. Another example to test theories is Lawrence M. Friedman and Robert V. Percival's survey of the case loads of two California trial courts at five points in time between 1890 and 1970 (1978). As I described in Chapter Six, the authors hypothesized that over time, trial courts have come to do less work in settling disputes and more work of a routine administrative nature. They concluded that the dispute settlement function of the trial courts has declined noticeably over time, a conclusion which has since been repeatedly questioned.

In addition to relying on official documents, the historical method may also be based on narrations of personal experiences generally known as the *life-histories* method. This technique requires that the researcher rely solely on a person's reporting of life experiences relevant to the research interest with minimal commentary. Often life histories are part of ethnographic reports. In such instances, they are referred to as "memory cases" (Nader and Todd, 1978:7). This method is useful to learn about events such as conflict or dispute which occurred in the past, particularly in instances when there are no written records available. Obviously, this method has certain pitfalls, for life histories tend to be tainted by selective recall: Subjects tend to remember events which have impressed them in some way and tend to forget others. Although the life-history method has been little used in recent years, it serves several functions. First, it provides insights into a world usually overlooked by the objective methods of data collection. Second, life histories can serve as the basis for making assumptions necessary for more systematic data collection. Third, life histories, because of their details, provide insights into new or different perspectives for research. When an area has been studied extensively and has grown "sterile," life histories may break new grounds for research studies. Finally, they offer an opportunity to view and study the dynamic process of social interactions and events not available with many other kinds of data.

A major difficulty of the historical method lies in the limited accuracy and thoroughness of the documents and materials involved. As the data are "compiled" by others with no supervision or control by the researcher, the researcher is, in fact, at the mercy of those who record the information.

The recorders use their own definitions of situations, define and select events as important for recording, and introduce subjective perceptions, interpretations, and insights into their recordings. For example, how do the recorders define a dispute? In many instances, a dispute enters officially into the court records when it is adjudicated, and a settlement is imposed after full trial. But as I noted in Chapter Six, not all disputes are adjudicated. Many are settled informally in pretrial conferences, or judges may intervene in other less formal ways as well. Therefore, a researcher must ascertain the reliability and validity of documents. They should be verified for internal consistency (consistency between each portion of the document and other portions) and external consistency (consistency with empirical evidence, other documents or both). Although the historical method provides details, and in certain cases presents a processual view of events, often unmatched by other methods of data collection, it is desirable (when possible, of course) to combine this method with other data collection methods.

Observational Methods

Observational methods can be divided into two types, those utilizing either human observers (participant observers or judges) or mechanical observers (cameras, tape recorders, etc.), and those directly eliciting responses from subjects by questioning (questionnaires, schedules, and interview guides). Observational methods can be carried out both in laboratory or controlled situations and in field or natural settings.

Participant observation has a long history of use in anthropological research. Thus, there is justification if the term conjures up the image of a social scientist living with some preliterate tribe perhaps for several years. Indeed, much of our knowledge of primitive law comes from anthropologists who lived in traditional societies such as Bronislaw Malinowski or E. Adamson Hoebel. Of course, for anthropologists, the opportunity to observe ongoing legal phenomena (outside of an institutional setting such as a court) depends on a combination of circumstances and luck: It means that the anthropologists have to be in the right place at the right time. Anthropological (and sociological) field researchers generally proceed by way of a kind of methodological eclecticism, choosing the method that suits the purpose and present circumstances at any given point in time. In summary: "Hence, unobtrusive measurement, life history studies, documentary and historical analysis, statistical enumeration, in-depth interviewing, imaginative role-taking, and personal introspection are all important complements of direct observation in the field worker's repertoire" (Williamson, Karp, and Dalphin, 1977:200).

Many of the observational techniques are used in laboratory or controlled situations. For example, comparatively little empirical research has been performed with actual juries because of the legal requirements of private deliberations. Consequently, mock trials in which jurors or juries respond to simulated case materials have become a primary research vehicle. The mock trial permits both manipulation of important variables and replication of cases (Davis, Bray and Holt, 1977:327). Many of the laboratory jury studies deal with the deliberation processes preceding the verdict and how the verdict is reached by juries of diverse composition deliberating under various conditions (Loh, 1984:460–461). One method of analyzing deliberations is to audio tape or video tape the deliberations and then analyze their content (Kessler, 1975:73).

Observational methods have been used by sociologists extensively in field settings which involve direct contact with subjects and takes place in relatively natural social situations (McCall, 1978:1). For example, in attempts to find out and understand how the law typically works on a day-to-day basis, sociologists have focused on various aspects of the criminal justice system. The study of the public defender's office by David Sudnow (1965); studies of the police by Jerome H. Skolnick (1975) and others; Frank W. Miller's (1969) study of prosecution; Donald J. Newman's (1966) study of conviction; and Abraham S. Blumberg's (1979) work on the entire criminal justice system, all point to the day-to-day working of law. These studies have also noted the role of discretion in the application or nonapplication of the law in legally equivocal and unequivocal situations. At each step in the criminal justice system, from the citizen's decision to lodge a complaint or to define the situation as one in which it is necessary to summon the police, to the judge's decision as to what sentence a convicted person should receive, decisions are made that are not prescribed by statutory law.

There are both advantages and limitations of observational methods. The advantages include the opportunity to record information as the event unfolds or shortly thereafter. Thus, the validity of the recorded information can be high. Often observations are made and information is recorded independently of the observed person's abilities to record events. At times, when verbal or written communication between the researcher and the subjects is difficult, for example, in studying primitive tribes, observation is the only method by which the researcher can obtain information. Finally, the observer need not rely on the willingness of the observed persons to report events.

There are also several limitations of observational research. The method is not applicable to the investigation of large social settings. The context investigated must be small enough to be dealt with exhaustively by one or few researchers. In the case of field work, there is a great likelihood of the researcher's selective perception and selective memory possibly biasing the results of the study. There is also the problem of selectivity in data collection. In any social situation, there are literally thousands of possible pieces of data. No one researcher, in other words, can account for every aspect of a situation. The researcher inevitably pulls out only a segment of the data that exist, and the question inevitably arises as to whether the selected data are really representative of the situation. Finally, there is no way to easily assess the reliability and validity of the interpretations made by the researcher. As long as data are collected and presented by one or a few researchers with their own distinctive talents, faults, and idiosyncracies, there will remain suspicion concerning the validity of their rendering of the phenomena studied. Researchers often respond to these criticisms by suggesting that the cost of imprecision is more than compensated for by the in-depth quality of the data produced.

Experimental Methods

The prevailing method for testing causal relations by social scientists, especially psychologists, is the experiment. An experiment may be carried out in a laboratory or a field setting, and it ideally begins with two or more equivalent groups with an experimental variable introduced into only the experimental group. The researcher measures the phenomenon under study before the introduction of the experimental variable and after, thus getting a measure of the change presumably caused by the variable.

There are two common ways of setting up experimental and control groups. One is the matched-pair technique. For each person in the experimental group another person similar in all important variables (such as age, religion, education, occupation, or anything important to the research) is found and placed in the control group. Another technique is the random-assignment technique, in which statistically random assignments of persons to experimental and control groups are made—such as assigning the first person to the experimental group and the next to the control group, and so on.

Experiments in sociology face certain difficulties. An experiment involving thousands of people may be prohibitively expensive. It may take years to complete a prospective study. Ethical and legal considerations prohibit the use of people in any experiments which may injure them. The scientific community reacts strongly in those infrequent instances where human subjects have been used in a hazardous or harmful manner (Mintz and Cohen, 1976). When people are unwilling to cooperate in an experiment, they cannot be forced to do so (although occasionally they are tricked into unconscious cooperation). Moreover, when individuals realize that they are experimental subjects, they begin to act differently and the experiment may be spoiled. Almost any kind of experimental or observational study upon people who know they are being studied will give some interesting findings which may vanish soon after the study is terminated. Experiments with human subjects are most reliable when the subjects do not know the true object of the experiment. But the use of deception in social research poses the ethical question of distinguishing between harmless deception and intellectual dishonesty.

Moreover, the law does not allow experiments in the United States that involve elimination of a right which the due process clause guarantees under all circumstances. For example, there would be legal and ethical questions involved in the use of experimental methods in the study of legal services, welfare payments, or incarcerations. There are however, exceptions, and one is the New Jersey Guaranteed Income Experiments, a rare example of government-sponsored policy experimentation. These experiments involve the systematic selection of experimental and control groups, the application of the policy under study to the experimental groups only, and a careful comparison of differences between the experimental and the control group after the application of the policy.

The experiment was designed to resolve some serious questions about the impact of welfare payments on the incentives for poor people to work. Debates over welfare reform have generated certain questions which social science could presumably answer with careful, controlled experimentation. Would a guaranteed family income reduce the incentive to work? If payments are made to poor families with employable male heads, will the men drop out of the labor force? Would the level of the income guarantee, or the steepness of the reductions of payments with increases in earnings, make any difference in working behavior? Since current welfare programs do not provide a guaranteed minimum family income, or make payments to families with employable males, or graduate payments in relation to earnings, these questions could only be answered through experimentation.

To assess the impact of guaranteed incomes on families with able-bodied men, the Office of Economic Opportunity sponsored a three-year social experiment involving 1350 families in New Jersey and Pennsylvania. The research was undertaken by the University of Wisconsin's Institute of Research on Poverty. To ascertain the effects of different levels of guaranteed income, four guarantee levels were established. Some families were chosen to receive 50 percent of the Social Security Administration's poverty line income, others 75 percent, others 100 percent, and still others 125 percent. In order to ascertain the effects of graduated payments in relation to earnings, some families had their payments reduced by 30 percent of their outside earnings, others 50 percent, and still others 70 percent. Finally, a control sample was observed—families who received no payments at all in the experiment, but were matched in every way with families who were receiving payments.

The experiment began in 1968, and a preliminary report issued by the U.S. Office of Economic Opportunity (1970) showed that there were no differences in the outside earnings of families receiving guaranteed incomes (experimental groups) and those who were not (control group). More importantly, the experiment raised a series of questions (Rossi and Lyall, 1976). Do researchers have the right to withhold public services from some individuals simply to provide a control for experimentation? In the medical area where the giving or withholding of treatment may result in death or injury, the problem is obvious, and many attempts have been made to formulate a code of ethics. In the area of social experimentation, what can be said to control groups who are chosen to be similar to experimental groups but denied benefits in order to serve as a basis for comparison? Setting aside the legal and moral issues, it will be politically difficult to provide services for some people and not for others. Moreover, as noted earlier, people behave differently when they know they are being watched. Students, for example, generally perform at a higher level when something—anything new and different—is introduced into the classroom routine. This "Hawthorne effect" may cause a new program or reform to appear more successful than the old, but it is the newness itself which produces improvement rather than the program or the reform. Another problem in such experimentation is that results obtained with small-scale experiments may differ substantially from what would occur if a large-scale nationwide program were adopted. In the New Jersey experiments, if only one family receives income maintenance payments in a neighborhood, its members may continue to behave as the neighbors do. But if everyone in the nation is guaranteed a minimum income, community standards may change and affect the behavior of all recipient families (Kershaw, 1969).

On a smaller scale, experimental methods have been used, for example, in the study of jury deliberations (Simon, 1975), allocation of scarce criminal justice resources (Nagel and Neef, 1977), and in determining the effectiveness of pretrial hearings. In the latter case, to find out whether pretrial hearings were time savers or time wasters, a controlled experiment was carried out. Sociologists developed a design calling for a random assignment of cases by court clerks to one of two procedures: obligatory pretrial hearing in one group of cases and optional pretrial in the control group, where it was held only if one or both of the litigants requested it. The conclusion was that the obligatory pretrial hearing did not save court time; in fact, it wasted it (Zeisel, 1967:84). Persuaded by the experiment, the State of New Jersey changed its rules and made pretrial hearings optional.

Many experiments, however, are conducted in a laboratory situation. The National Commission on the Causes and Prevention of Violence (1969), for example, relied heavily, although not exclusively, on the results of laboratory experiments for its final report. In one group of experiments, young children who were shown acts of violence and then later observed at play committed more acts of violence in their play than children who did not witness acts of violence. In another group of experiments, college students were told that they were participating in a "learning experiment" in which they must apply mild electric shocks at whatever level of intensity they wished to other "learners" if and when the "learners" made a mistake. The "learning experiment" was interrupted and some students were shown a violent film while others were shown a nonviolent one. When the "learning experiment" was resumed, the students who saw the violent film used slightly stronger shocks on their "learners" than those who had watched the nonviolent film.

Laboratory experiments, as important as they may be in revealing insights in the human behavior, achieve rigorous and controlled observation at the price of unreality. The subjects are isolated from the outside and from their normal environment. The laboratory experiment has been criticized for its unnaturalness and questioned as to is generalizability. By contrast, experimental methods that are used in nonlaboratory settings increase the generalizability of results and lend greater credence to the findings, but concomitantly increase the difficulty of controlling relevant variables.

Survey Methods

Survey research aims for a systematic and comprehensive collection of information about the attitudes, beliefs, and behavior of people. The most common means of data collection are face-to-face interviews, self-administered questionnaires (for example, mail questionnaires), and telephone interviews. Typically the questionnaire or interview schedule is set up so that the same questions are asked of each respondent in the same order with exactly the same wording. A survey deals with a representative sample of a population. Probablistic sampling is essential to survey studies. Survey studies tend to be larger than is typically the case in observational or experimental studies. Usually, data are collected at one point in time, although survey approach can be used to study trends in opinion and behavior over time. Because of its ability to cover large areas and many respondents, the survey method has become the dominant method of data collection in sociology.

Survey methods, like other research methods, have their pitfalls. Probably foremost among them is the response rate or the nonresponse rate. Since one of the important reasons for conducting a survey is that it deals with a large representative sample from a population and thus permits inference from the sampled data to the population, it is essential that the sample maintain its representativeness, which may be affected severely when a substantial number of the respondents fail to participate in the study. The return rate for mail questionnaires is generally low, a 60 percent rate or higher return rate is considered good. Of course, for the interview survey, the expected response rate is higher than that of the questionnaire survey. In both cases, in addition to the subject's refusal to participate, other factors affect the response rate. They include the inability of the subject to understand the question, the possibility that the subject may have moved or died, or the physical or mental incapacitation of the participants. Although questionnaire and interview studies have a margin of error, they are still useful. For example, public officials seldom take a position on a public issue without first reviewing public opinion polls, and legislators often delay casting a vote on an important bill until they receive the latest survey of voter opinion from their districts.

An illustration of the use of survey methods can be seen in the efforts of the Department of Justice to gain a more accurate measure of the extent of crime in the United States. For years both law enforcement agencies and sociologists have had to rely on official records compiled by such agencies as the Federal Bureau of Investigation in order to measure the amount of crime. However, there have been concerns with the accuracy of these reports, and many sociologists have suggested that officially recorded crime statistics are a far better indicator of police activity than they are of criminal activity.

Since 1970, the U.S. Department of Justice (1985) has conducted sophisticated victimization surveys for the nation and several major cities in an attempt to both supplement and overcome some of the problems of accuracy in official crime records. In victimization surveys, subjects in a large sample of the population are systematically interviewed to determine how many crimes have been committed against them. In addition to determining the volume of crime, the surveys are also used in developing a variety of information on crime characteristics and the effects of crime on the victims: victim injury and medical care, economic losses, time lost from work, victim self protection, and reporting of crime to the police. There are three advantages of victimization surveys that make them superior to self-report studies and the FBI's *Uniform Crime Reports*. First, people are more willing to discuss crimes committed against them than the ones they have committed. Second, victimization surveys by design seek out information about crimes rather than wait for victims to report them as is the case with the *Uniform Crime Reports*. Third, victimization surveys rely on more representative samples than the other sources of crime data. There are also some disadvantages to these surveys. They are rather expensive—costing about $40 per interview—and since they deal primarily with major cities, information is lacking for the majority of local areas in the United States.

At times, large-scale surveys are carried out at the behest of the Congress. For example, the 93rd Congress passed an amendment to an educational bill in 1974 requiring the Secretary of the Department of Health, Education and Welfare to conduct a survey to determine the extent and seriousness of school crime. This extensive study included 4,014 school principals, 31,373 students, and 23,895 teachers in 642 junior and senior high schools throughout the country who received questionnaires from Washington (Toby, 1980). The study reconfirmed the general belief that schools are plagued with real crime and showed, unexpectedly, that the crime problem was worse in junior than in senior high schools. The findings prompted a series of hearings in Congress, but surprisingly little in the way of systematic national effort to reduce school crime. In other instances, however, the results of such massive surveys, such as the studies by James S. Coleman (1966) and his colleagues on the effects of a large number of variables on educational achievement, which will be discussed shortly, contribute significantly to policy decisions.

Survey methods have been widely used also in a variety of cross-cultural studies dealing with knowledge and opinion about law (Tomasic, 1985:116–126), evaluation of the effectiveness of the law, prestige of the law, and legal and moral attitudes (Podgorecki, 1974:83–124). Some of these studies reveal important and unexpected findings. For example, a European study asked people of Poland, Holland, and West Germany whether they thought people should obey the law. They found significant national variations; more Germans (66 percent) than Poles (45 percent) or Dutchmen (47 percent) answered "yes" to this general question (Friedman and Macaulay, 1977:216). Several surveys have also found that the public knowledge in a number of European countries concerning legal topics is considerably poorer than assumed by the legal authorities and by many scholars. But lack of knowledge about the law is not limited to European countries. For example, many respondents in an Oregon study did not know that Oregon law provides minors with the right to venereal disease treatment, birth control information, and medical treatment without parental knowledge (Friedman and Macaulay, 1977:607–608).

THE IMPACT OF SOCIOLOGY ON SOCIAL POLICY

A distinction between pure and applied science is drawn in every scientific field. *Pure* science is a search for knowledge, without primary concern for its practical use. *Applied* science is the search for ways of using scientific knowledge to solve practical problems. For example, a sociologist making a study of the social structure of a slum neighborhood is working as a pure scientist. If this is followed by a study of how to prevent crime in a slum neighborhood, this is applied science.

Essentially, however, sociology is both a pure and an applied science. For unless a science is constantly searching for more basic knowledge, its practical applications of knowledge are not likely to be very practical. This explains, in part, why a substantial amount of sociological work is still generated for academic purposes and executed with disciplinary concerns in mind. Much of sociological knowledge remains within the boundaries of the discipline. Often, the consumers of this knowledge are other sociologists and their students. But simultaneously with the continuing development of scientific knowledge, sociologists are also concerned with the generation of knowledge and information with potential applied or policy implications. Sociological knowledge and methodology can be useful in the formulation and implementation of social policy and in the evaluation of current policies or proposed policy alternatives. Contemporary sociologists are attempting to contribute toward improving conditions of life in society in a number of ways, and policy-relevant work is a major activity in American sociology today (Scott and Shore, 1979:12).

The purpose of this section is to demonstrate how sociological knowledge and expertise can have an impact on social policy. But what is "social policy?" Although there is no consensus in the sociological literature on the term "social policy" (Morris, 1979:1–13), it generally refers to purposive legal measures that are adopted and pursued by representatives of government who are responsible for dealing with particular social conditions in society. The term "policy-making" refers to the process of identifying alternative courses of action that may be followed and choosing among them (Scott and Shore, 1979:XIV). Following Robert A. Scott and Arnold R. Shore (1979:13–33), the impact of sociology on social policy can be ascertained in terms of sociology's contributions to policy recommendations and in terms of sociology's contributions to enacted policy. The former deals with specific sociological research endeavors carried out on social problems that have been used for the development of specific policy recommendations for governmental programs to diminish and ameliorate these conditions, and the latter has had a direct impact on enacted policy.

Contributions of Sociology to Policy Recommendations

There have been instances in which sociological knowledge, perspectives, concepts, theories, and methods have been useful in connection with the development of policy recommendations. Perhaps the best known illustrations of this are the various uses made of sociology in Presidential Commissions. These Commissions include the Commission on Law Enforcement and Administration of Justice, the Commission on the Causes and Prevention of Violence, the Commission on Obscenity and Pornography, and the Commission on Population Growth and the American Future. Sociologists were active in these commissions and disciplinary research and knowledge were incorporated in the recommendations.

Sociology played an important role in the Commission on Law Enforcement and Administration of Justice. Social science concepts, theories, and general perspectives were of great utility to the Commission in forming final recommendations, and "existing social science theories and data were drawn upon to formulate broad general strategies in the prevention and control of crime" (Ohlin, 1975:108). Sociologists also provided sensitizing concepts and theories which oriented the search for solutions of the crime problem. For example, studies of the correctional system and the operation of law enforcement in the courts raised doubts about the effectiveness of existing criminal justice policies or of rehabilitation and treatment efforts. On the basis of sociological data, the Commission accepted the view that alternative systems of social control should be used in place of the criminal justice system when possible, and recommended the possibility of decriminalizing certain offenses against moral or public order and called for a reconsideration of consensual crimes, or "crimes without victims" (Ohlin, 1975:109).

James F. Short points out that sociologists made similar contributions to the work of the National Commission on the Causes and Prevention of Violence. The specific recommendations provided by sociologists were incorporated in the Commission's progress report and "marked the high point of social science input to the Commission" (Short, 1975:84). Specific recommendations included the "relativity of attributions of legitimacy or illegitimacy to violence"; that the nature of violence is essentially social as opposed to biological or psychological; that there is a connection between perceived legitimacy of the law and effective legal control of violence; and that the notions of responsibility for violence and of "relative deprivation" often lie in the unresponsiveness of social institutions (Short, 1975:85).

One of the final recommendations of the Commission on Obscenity and Pornography resulted directly from sociological and other social science research on the personal, psychological, and social consequences of exposure to explicit sexual materials. The Commission recommended that federal, state, and local laws prohibiting the sale, exhibition, and distribution of sexual material to consenting adults be repealed (Scott and Shore, 1979:17).

This recommendation was based upon extensive sociological investigation that provided

> ... no evidence that exposure to or use of explicit sexual materials plays a significant role in the causation of social or individual harm such as crime, delinquency, sexual and nonsexual deviancy, or severe emotional disturbance—Empirical investigations thus support the opinion of a substantial majority of persons professionally engaged in the treatment of deviancy, delinquency and anti-social behavior, that exposure to sexually explicit material has no harmful causal role in these areas (Report of the Commission, quoted by Scott and Shore, 1979:17).

A similar conclusion was reached by Berl Kutchinsky (1973) in his study of the effects of liberalizing pornography in Denmark. In fact, he found that concurrent with the increasing availability of pornography, there was a significant decrease in the number of sex offenses registered by the police in Copenhagen. He adds: "The unexpected outcome of this analysis is that the high availability of hard-core pornography in Denmark was most probably the very direct cause of a considerable decrease in at least one type of serious sex offense, namely, child molestation" (Kutchinsky, 1973:179). In a later study, Kutchinsky found a similar decrease in child molestation in West Germany which he attributed to an increased availability of pornographic material (U.S. Department of Justice, 1986:974). By contrast, the recently completed report of the Attorney General's Commission on Pornography (U.S. Department of Justice, 1986) negates many of the conclusions of earlier studies and that of the 1970 Commission report partly because, in the words of the commission chairman, "If we relied exclusively on scientific data for every one of our findings, I'm afraid all our work would be inconclusive" (Newsweek, 1986:18). No doubt many of the "proofs" in support of the report's conclusions were less than compelling.

Sociological research also had an appreciable impact on the substance of the final report of the President's Commission on Population Growth and the American Future. The Commission recognized that although population growth played a minor role in the short run (thirty to fifty years) as compared with technological, economic, and government policy considerations, "[i]n the longer run, population growth would become increasingly important. The message for population policy, therefore, was that resource and environmental considerations implied prudence rather than crisis; that there were no benefits to be realized from continued growth, but that population was an indirect and ineffectual policy lever for environmental problems" (Westoff, 1975:54).

Demographic research contributed importantly to other Commission deliberations and recommendations. For example, it was shown that if women averaged 2.0 rather than 2.1 births, zero population growth could be achieved near the same level while immigration remains at the current volume. Notes Westoff: "Although not a world-shaking scientific discovery, this bit of demographic intelligence was extremely important in the debate over immigration policy and was influential in defeating a recommendation to reduce the volume" (1975:55).

But one of the most important applications of social science research to policy formation resulted from the National Fertility Studies of 1965 and 1970. It makes a major difference in the nature of population policy whether the stabilization of population can be achieved largely through the prevention of unwanted births or whether more radical social changes are necessary to change the number of children desired. These two studies estimated that the elimination of unwanted pregnancy would result in a population growth rate that would be below replacement level. The policy significance of this finding cannot be overestimated. By concentrating on the improvement and distribution of methods of fertility control, a solution to the problems of population growth can be reached within politically acceptable means.

Sociological research also discovered an appalling amount of ignorance among the general public about population (for example, 60 percent did not know or could not guess the size of the United States population within plus or minus 50 million) which provided a ground for recommendations about population education. A research finding that only 20 percent of sexually active unmarried teen-age girls report using any contraception regularly dramatized the recommendation of the provision of such information and service to minors (Westoff, 1975:55–56). There were other contributions as well. Studies showing a negative relationship between income and unwanted births served as a rationale for governmental subsidization of family planning for the poor. An opinion poll taken by the Commission has shown that about half of the American people felt that abortion is a private matter and should be decided solely between individuals and their physicians, a finding that was subsequently used to support a policy recommendation for liberal abortion (Scott and Shore, 1979:19).

On the basis of the involvement of sociologists in Presidential Commissions, Scott and Shore conclude that sociology has made a contribution to recommendations for policy in three ways:

> The first is through the use of sociological concepts that are said to provide new or unique perspectives on social conditions—perspectives that are based upon more than common sense and that may in fact be inconsistent with basic notions upon which existing policies are based.... Second, prescriptions for policy are sometimes suggested by the findings of sociological research undertaken primarily to advance scientific understanding of society.... The third is the use of sociological methods and techniques of research to obtain information about specific questions central to the deliberations of Commissions (1979:20–21).

Of these three uses of sociology, the third is by far the most common. However, it should be noted that there is no way of precisely determining the extent to which sociology can or does contribute to policy recommendations. For example, in many instances the methods of empirical research, not the knowledge and concepts of sociology, have been directly responsible for policy prescriptions. Obviously, conducting research is not a skill possessed exclusively by sociologists. Moreover, there is no way of distinguishing between the contributions of intelligent and insightful individuals who happened to be trained as sociologists, and the contributions of sociological knowledge and perspective as such. Consequently, care needs to be exercised in crediting the discipline's knowledge in all cases in which sociology has had an impact on policy.

Despite these qualifications, it is fair to state that sociological knowledge can and at times does have an impact on developing recommendations for social policy. "For this reason," as Scott and Shore observe (1979:23), "sociologists can legitimately claim that their discipline has been and is relevant to the development of policy recommendations."

Contributions of Sociology to Enacted Policy

Although the extent of impact in some instances remains controversial, in certain cases, sociology is considered to have had a direct impact on enacted policy. A most widely cited illustration of this is the social science contribution to the 1954 Supreme Court decision outlawing segregation in public schools. Other examples of impact on social policy would include sociological studies that resulted in the reduction of delay in the courts, changes in testimony procedures, in selection of judges, provision of council to the indigent, and releasing indigent criminal defendants without bail pending trial. The last study, for example, showed that a careful screening and notifying of defendants released without any bond produced a higher percentage of court appearances than did the traditional bail bond system (Nagel, 1969:31–32).

A number of other examples may be cited to support the view that sociology has had an impact on enacted policy. They include the involvement of sociologists in programs to combat juvenile delinquency (U.S. Department of Justice, 1980), to reduce school drop-out rates, and to prevent narcotics addiction (in particular, studies dealing with attempts to reduce youth crime and delinquency problems contributed to legislation which became the Juvenile Delinquency and Youth Offenses Control Act of 1961 [Katz, 1978:137]); and sociological research on talent loss as a consequence of inadequate educational opportunities for minority groups and persons of low socioeconomic status led to the enactment of remedial measures such as the establishment of new scholarships and loan resources, and the creation of federal programs like Outward Bound, Talent Search, and Vista. In each instance, sociologists have contributed research and conceptual skills toward the "formulation of programs and policies that were eventually enacted to ameliorate social conditions deemed harmful to society" (Scott and Shore, 1979:24).

In social policy research, sociologists doing scientific work are often confronted with problems and issues which have an impact on many people whose lives may be substantially altered or changed. To illustrate, a study which had a significant impact on the lives of many people in the United States is the so-called Coleman Report. In 1964, the U.S. Office of Education was authorized by the Civil Rights Act to undertake a survey and to make a report to the President and Congress in two years concerning the lack of availability of equal educational opportunities for individuals by reason of race, color, religion, or national origin in public educational institutions at all levels in the United States. Subsequently, a social survey on a massive scale was carried out by a social science team led by James S. Coleman, Ernest Q. Campbell (1966), and their associates. The survey included 570,000 school pupils, 60,000 teachers, and 4,000 schools. The final report is a 737-page document.

Following this monumental study, efforts at the national and regional levels involving financial support and structural changes on a large scale have been made for the purpose of achieving a better mix of students in schools and continuity of research activities in this area. One far-reaching policy outcome of the study was the decision of the federal government to implement busing for the purpose of achieving integrated schools. The issue of busing, as I noted in Chapter Four, remains a controversial policy and has generated many protests, counterprotests, and even violence. While the researchers involved in the original study may not agree with all the policies which have been formulated and implemented, the study's policy influence has been substantial.

The above illustrations show some of the contributions of sociology to enacted policy. However, a great deal of applied sociological research has no discernible policy implications of any kind. Many of the recommendations are pragmatically useless (that is, too expensive to implement) or considered politically unrealistic or implausible by policy-makers. Furthermore, policy questions are fundamentally political and not sociological questions. Often, policies are formulated and *then* relevant research is sought to support, legitimize, and dramatize (or even propagandize) these policies. Thus, it would be erroneous to assume that research generally precedes and determines policy actions. Furthermore, some sociologists feel that they should not be directly involved through research in the development and implementation of social policy, and this position is epitomized by Daniel P. Moynihan (1969:193), who contends that "the role of social sciences lies not in the formation of social policy but in the measurement of its results." In the next section I shall consider evaluation research and impact studies.

EVALUATION RESEARCH AND IMPACT STUDIES

Evaluation of enacted policy is as old as policy itself. Policy-makers have always made judgments concerning the worth or effects of particular policies, programs, and projects. Many of these judgements have been impressionistic, often influenced by ideological, partisan self-interest, and valuational criteria. For example, a tax cut may be considered necessary and desirable because it enhances the electoral chances of the evaluator's political party, or unemployment compensation may be deemed "bad" because the evaluator "knows a lot of people" who improperly receive benefits. Undoubtedly, much conflict may result from this sort of evaluation because different evaluators, employing different value criteria, reach different conclusions concerning the merits of the same policy.

Another type of evaluation has centered on the operation of specific policies or programs. Questions that are asked may include: Is the program honestly run? What are its financial costs? Who receives benefits (payments or services) and in what amounts? Is there any overlap or duplication with other programs? Were legal standards and procedures followed? This kind of evaluation may provide information about the honesty or efficiency in the conduct of a program, but like the impressionistic kind of evaluation, it will probably yield little if anything in the way of hard information on the societal effects of a program. A welfare program, for instance, may be carried out honestly and efficiently, and it may be politically and ideologically satisfying to a given evaluator. However, such an evaluation will tell very little about the impact of the program on the poor, or whether it is achieving its officially stated objectives.

Since the late 1960s, a third type of policy evaluation is receiving increasing attention among policy-makers. It is the systematic objective evaluation of programs to measure their societal impact and the extent to which they are achieving stated objectives. In 1967 and 1968, Congress altered some of the central pieces of President Johnson' Great Society legislation so that mandatory evaluation would be included in all programs, such as the Economic Opportunity Act. The intention was to monitor the progress of programs and to terminate those that did not seem to yield the desired level of results. There were also political benefits to be obtained by emphasizing evaluation. Low-cost experiments on social problems and rigid evaluation requirements could be used to subvert attempts to solve social problems through (expensive) direct social change or action programs. The contrast between the evaluation components required for War on Poverty programs and those required for such "welfare" programs as urban renewal, railroad subsidies, and agribusiness subsidies points this up dramatically. Notes Morehouse: "None of the older, well-established, and 'safe' domestic programs have evaluation requirements. . . . Program evaluation requirements were an important by-product of a general policy of bringing controversial programs under control" (1972:873).

For many, evaluation research quickly became a proper use of sociology in policy-related work (Scott and Shore, 1979:43). Rapidly, this use of social research in policy analysis became widespread and an entire field of specialization has developed about methods and procedures for conducting evaluation research. Technically speaking, however, there are no formal methodological differences between evaluation and nonevaluation research. Both have in common the same techniques and the same basic steps that must be followed in the research process. The difference lies in the following: (1) evaluation research uses deliberate planned intervention of some independent variable; (2) the programs it assesses assume some objective or goal as desirable; and (3) it attempts to determine the extent to which this desired goal has been reached. As Edward A Suchman (1967:15) puts it, "evaluative research asks about the *kind* of change the program views as desirable, the *means* by which this change is to be brought about, and the *signs* according to which such change can be recognized." Thus, the major distinction between evaluation and nonevaluation research is one of objectives.

Carol Weiss (1972:6–8) proposes several additional criteria that distinguish evaluation research from other types of research:

1. Evaluation research is generally conducted for a client who intends to use the research as a basis for decision making;

2. The investigator deals with his or her client's questions as to whether the client's program is accomplishing what the client wishes it to accomplish;

3. The objective of evaluation research is to ascertain whether the program goals are being reached;

4. The investigator works in a situation where priority goes to the program as opposed to the evaluation;

5. There is always a possibility of conflicts between the researcher and the program staff because of the divergences of loyalties and objectives; and

6. In evaluation research there is an emphasis on results that are useful for policy decisions.

Social policy evaluation is essentially concerned with attempts to determine the impact of policy on real-life conditions. As a minimum, policy evaluation requires a specification of policy objectives (what we want to accomplish with a given policy), the means of realizing it (programs), and what has been accomplished toward the attainment of the objectives (impacts or outcomes). In measuring objectives, there is a need to determine not only that some change in real life conditions has occurred, such as a reduction in the unemployment rate, but also that it was due to policy actions and not to other factors such as private economic decisions.

Thomas R. Dye (1972:291–295) suggests that the impact of a policy has several dimensions, all of which must be taken into account in the course of evaluation. These include the impact on the social problem at which a policy is directed and the people involved. Those whom the policy is intended to affect must be clearly defined, that is, the poor, disadvantaged, school children, or unwed mothers. The intended effect of the policy must then be determined. If, for example, it is an antipoverty program, is its purpose to raise the income of the poor, to increase the opportunities for employment, or to change their attitudes and behavior? If some combination of such objectives is intended, the evaluation of impact becomes more complicated since priorities must be assigned to the various intended effects.

At times, as Friedman and Macaulay (1977:501) note, it is difficult to determine the purpose of a law or a program of regulation. They suggest that the determination of intent is complicated because many individuals with diverse purposes participate in the policy-making. Will consideration be given to the intention or intentions of the persons who drafted the statute or the judge who wrote the opinion creating the rule? To that of the majority of the legislature or court who voted for it? To that of the lobbyists who worked for the bill? To that purpose openly discussed or to the purpose which is implicit but never mentioned? They add that sometimes one can only conclude that a law has multiple and perhaps even conflicting purposes, but this is not to say that one can never be sure of the purpose of a law. However, one must be aware of the complexities of determining "purpose."

It should also be noted that a law may have either intended or unintended consequences or even both. A guaranteed income program, for example, may improve the income situation of the benefited groups, as intended. But what impact does it also have on their initiative to seek employment? Does it decrease this, as some have contended? Similarly, an agricultural price support program intended to improve farmers' incomes, may lead to overproduction of the supported commodities.

The difficulties of measurement of impact are most acute for those areas of conduct where the behavior in question is hard to quantify and where it is hard to tell what the behavior *would* have been without the intervention of the law. The laws against murder illustrate the difficulties here. There is a fairly good idea about the murder rate in most countries; but no information at all exists about the contribution which the *law* makes to this rate. In other words, there is no way of determining how high the murder rate would be if there were, for example, no capital punishment for murder.

Knowledge of a new law by members of the legal profession also plays a role in the study impact. For example, the Magnuson-Moss Warranty Act of 1975 was heralded as a major piece of legislation intended to protect the consumers against defective products. Did the new law help consumers with specific complaints about faulty products? Not much, according to research findings. Two years after the passage of the new law, one study concluded that "most lawyers in Wisconsin knew next to nothing about the Magnuson-Moss Warranty Act" and "many had never heard of it . . . " (Macaulay, 1979:118). The fact that many lawyers know little about laws that are intended to protect consumers obviously impairs the effectiveness of such laws. As this example shows, another problem confronting impact research is the assessment of knowledge of a particular law on the part of those who are involved in its interpretation and application.

The study of impact is further complicated by the fact that policies may have effects on groups or situations other than those at which they are directed. These are called spillover effects (Wade, 1972). These spillover effects may be positive or negative. An illustration of the negative effects would be the testing of nuclear devices, which may provide data for the design of nuclear power plants but may also generate hazards for the population. An illustration of a positive spillover effect would be that when tariffs are lowered at the request of American exporters to increase their sales abroad, consumers in the United States may benefit from lower prices caused by increased imports that lower tariffs stimulate. Obviously, in the evaluation of impact, attention must also be paid to the spillover effects.

A given legislation may also have impact on future as well as current conditions. Is a particular policy designed to improve an immediate short-term situation or is it intended to have effects over a longer time period? For example, was the Head Start program supposed to improve the cognitive abilities of disadvantaged children in the short run or was it to have an impact on their long-range development and earning capacity? The determination of long-term effects stemming from a policy is much more difficult than the assessment of short-term impacts. For example, it will be next to impossible to determine if the regulation of the price of natural gas at the wellhead, a policy which began in the 1950s, really contributed to the controversial energy shortage in the late 1970s, as some now contend. If so, this would be a long-term effect of a policy with a negative spillover effect.

A fairly rich literature of evaluation of actual and proposed programs of law has developed, using criteria derived from economics as its standard. This literature takes certain economic goals as its basic values and assesses legal programs as good or bad depending upon whether they most efficiently or rationally achieve the economic goals or make use of theoretically correct economic means. Of course, it is fairly easy to calculate the dollar costs of a particular policy when it is stated as the actual number of dollars spent on a program, its share of total government expenditures, how efficiently the funds are allocated, and so on. Other economic costs are, however, difficult to measure. For example, it is difficult to discover the expenditures by the private sector for pollution control devices that are necessitated by air pollution control policy. Moreover, economic standards are hardly applicable to the measurement of social costs of inconvenience, dislocation, and social disruption resulting, for instance, from an urban renewal project. At the same time, it is also difficult to measure the indirect benefits of particular policies for the community. For example, the social security program may contribute to social stability as well as the retirement incomes of recipients. The problem of measurement is again apparent.

In addition to the difficulties inherent in the measurement of indirect costs and benefits, other complexities arise from the fact that the effects of a particular law may be symbolic (intangible) as well as material (tangible). Intended symbolic effects capitalize on popular beliefs, attitudes and aspirations for their effectiveness. For example, taken at face value, the graduated income tax is a symbol of equality and progressivity in taxation and draws wide support on that basis. In reality, the impact of income tax on many people, particularly the wealthy, is greatly reduced by provisions such as those for tax shelters. The result is that effective tax rates for the rich are considerably lower than imagined. What is symbolically promised is quite different from what materially results. There are other laws that appear to promise more symbolically than their implementation actually yields in material benefits. They include antitrust activity, public utility rate regulation, and various antipoverty efforts. These endeavors attempt to assure people that policy-makers are concerned with their welfare, although the real tangible benefits are limited.

These are some of the difficulties that need to be taken into consideration in measuring the impact of a particular law. There are several possible research approaches that can be used for measuring impact. One approach might be the study of a group of individuals from the target population after it has been exposed to a program that had been developed to cause change. This approach is referred to as the *one-shot study*. Another possible approach is to study a group of individuals both *before and after* exposure to a particular program. Still, another possibility would be the use of some kind of *controlled experiment*. But as I noted earlier in this chapter, in measuring the impact of law, one major problem is the absence of control groups. As a result, one is rarely able to say with confidence what behavior would have been had a law not been passed or had a different law been passed. Outside of a laboratory setting, it is difficult to apply an experimental treatment to a group which one has matched in all significant respects to another group which does not receive the treatment, so as to control for all possible sources of distortion or error. This difficulty is further accentuated by ethical problems which often arise from such research methods as the random assignment of persons to different legal remedies.

The final consideration of evaluation research involves the utilization of results. As James S. Coleman (1972:6) states, "the ultimate product is not a 'contribution to existing knowledge' in the literature, but a social policy modified by the research result." In many instances, however, those who mandate and request evaluation research fail to utilize the results of that research. These people may feel committed to particular ways of doing things despite evidence that a program is ineffective. This is particularly true in instances when programs were instigated by political pressures such as the various endeavors in model city programs, war against poverty, corrections, and drug and alcohol rehabilitation. As public interest waned in the later stages of these programs, there was no real pressure to incorporate the results of evaluation studies into the ongoing activities (Vago, 1980:403). There are, of course, a number of other ways initiators of evaluation research can respond to the results. They include the manipulation of research outcomes for their own interests, rationalization of negative results, or in some instances when the findings are negative, dismissal of results.

It is apparent that sociological expertise can be made relevant to social policy. Of course, it is a question of choice whether one would want to pursue primarily disciplinary or a policy-oriented applied sociology, although the two are not mutually exclusive. Sociology undoubtedly has a good potential to play an active, creative, and significant role in the formulation, implementation and evaluation of social policy. At the same time, as sociological knowledge and methods become relevant to and influential on policy, they become part of politics by definition. In such a situation, the contributions of sociology can become a tool for immediate political ends and propaganda purposes by justifying and legitimizing a particular position. Ideally, the objective should be to insulate, but not isolate, sociological inputs from the immediate vagaries of day-to-day politics, and to strike some sort of balance between political and sociological considerations, permitting neither to dominate.

SUMMARY

This chapter examined procedures that are useful for advancing our understanding of law in society and considered the impact of sociological research on law and the applicability of such research to social policy. Several methods can be applied in studying law in society and more than a single method is usually involved in an investigation. The methods of sociological research include the historical, observational, experimental, and survey studies. Historical analysis relies on secondary sources collected for purposes other than the researcher's intentions. Thus, a major difficulty of the historical method lies in the limited accuracy and thoroughness of the documents and materials involved. In addition to relying on official documents, the historical method may also be based on narrations of personal experiences generally known as the life-histories method. Although there are difficulties with the use of historical methods, they provide an aid in understanding long-term developments and change processes involved in the study of law.

Observational methods utilize either human observers or mechanical devices and procedures to elicit responses directly from the subjects by questioning. Many of the observational techniques are used in laboratory situations as, for example, the studies on jury deliberations. Observational methods are also used by sociologists in field settings, which involve direct contact with subjects and take place in relatively natural social situations. Observational methods have been used extensively to study the various facets of the criminal justice system and the legal profession.

Experimental methods are used to test causal relationships either in a laboratory or a field setting. Experiments in sociology face certain difficulties such as ethical, legal, and financial considerations. Although there have been several large-scale experiments dealing with law and a large number of laboratory studies, questions of generalizability of results still plague the researchers. The use of experimental methods also raises questions about the legitimacy of "manipulating" human subjects.

Survey methods are widely used in sociological research and they generally involve a reasonably representative cross section of the population under study. Survey studies tend to be larger than is typically the case in observational and experimental studies, and data may be collected at one point in time or over time. Policy-makers tend to rely on the results of surveys more than other methods of sociological inquiry.

Sociology, like all sciences, may be either pure or applied. Pure sociology searches for new knowledge, while applied sociology tries to apply sociological knowledge to practical problems. Although this distinction is often used in the sociological literature, sociology is both a pure and applied science. Sociological knowledge and expertise have demonstrable relevance and influence on social policy in terms of the discipline's contributions to policy recommendations and to enacted policy. Sociological knowledge, methods, and concepts have been used in a number of Presidential Commissions as grounds for policy recommendations, and a number of sociological studies have had a direct impact on enacted policy, such as the Coleman study on school desegregation.

There is an increasing involvement of sociologists in evaluation research and impact studies. There are specific requirements for the evaluation of many federal programs and activities designed to induce change in some area. The object of evaluation research is to determine how successful a particular change effort is in achieving its goals. Impact studies are concerned with the intent of those who formulated a legal rule or policy, whether or not a legal rule was responsible for the change, knowledge of a law by its interpreters, and spillover effects. Evaluation research allows policy-makers to determine the effectiveness of a program, whether or not it should be continued or phased out, and what in-course adjustments, if any, are needed to make it more effective. In some cases, however, when the results of the evaluation are negative, the client might attempt to dismiss or rationalize the findings.

SUGGESTED FURTHER READINGS

WALLACE D. LOH, *Social Research in the Judicial Process: Cases, Readings, and Text.* New York: Russell Sage Foundation, 1984. An excellent and detailed treatment of empirical legal studies and the application of social research in the judicial process.

R. LUCKHAM, ed. *Law and Social Inquiry: Case Studies of Research.* Uppsala: Scandinavian Institute of African Studies, 1981. An enlightening collection of nine articles discussing the problems of socio-legal research in different parts of the world.

GEORGE J. McCALL, *Observing the Law, Field Methods in the Study of Crime and the Criminal Justice System.* New York: Free Press, 1978. A discussion of a variety of methods, their use, and the results obtained in studying crime and the criminal justice system.

STUART S. NAGEL, ed., *Policy Studies in America and Elsewhere.* Lexington, MA: D.C. Heath and Company, Lexington Books, 1975. A collection of cross-cultural articles on social policy.

STUART S. NAGEL, and MARIAN NEEF, *The Legal Process, Modeling the System.* Beverly Hills, CA: Sage Publications, 1977. A somewhat technical study on how modeling can be used to study various legal processes.

JAMES B. RULE, *Insight and Social Betterment, A Preface to Applied Social Science.* New York: Oxford University Press, 1978. A brief book about the relationship between the study of social conditions and effective ways to improve them.

ROBERT A. SCOTT and ARNOLD R. SHORE, *Why Sociology Does Not Apply: A Study of the Use of Sociology in Public Policy.* New York: Elsevier, 1979. A provocative essay on the role of sociology in social policy. The book provided much of the background for parts of this chapter.

RITA J. SIMON, ed., *Research in Law and Sociology, Vol. 1.* Greenwich, CT: Jay Press, Inc., 1978. A collection of fourteen articles written by scholars representing five disciplines which covers a wide range of methodological concerns.

RITA J. SIMON, *The Jury: Its Role in American Society.* Lexington, MA: Lexington Books, D.C. Heath and Company, 1980. A review of much of the major research that has been done on the American jury between 1950 and 1979.

REFERENCES

BAUMGARTNER, MARY P. 1978. "Law and Social Status in Colonial New Haven, 1639–1665," Pp. 153–174 in Rita J. Simon, ed., Research in Law and Sociology, Vol. 1. Greenwich, CT: Jay Press Inc.

BLUMBERG, ABRAHAM, S. 1979. *Criminal Justice: Issues & Ironies,* 2nd ed. New York: New Viewpoints.

CARLIN, JEROME E. 1966. *Lawyers' Ethics. A Survey of the New York City Bar.* New York: Russell Sage Foundation.

CHAMBLISS, WILLIAM J. 1964. "A Sociological Analysis of the Law of Vagrancy," Social Problems 12 (1)(Summer):67–77.

COLEMAN, JAMES S., ERNEST Q. CAMPBELL, CAROL J. HOBSON, et al. 1966. *Equality of Educational Opportunity.* Washington, D.C.: U.S. Government Printing Office.

COLEMAN, JAMES S. 1972. *Policy Research in Social Science.* Morristown, NJ: General Learning Press.

DAVIS, JAMES H., ROBERT M. BRAY, and ROBERT W. HOLT. 1977. "The Empirical Study of Decision Processes in Juries, A Critical Review," Pp. 326–361 in June Louin Tapp and Felice J. Levine, eds., Law, Justice, and the Individual in Society, Psychological and Legal Issues. New York: Holt, Rinehart & Winston.

DYE, THOMAS. 1972. *Understanding Public Policy.* Englewood Cliffs, NJ: Prentice-Hall.

FRIEDMAN, LAWRENCE M. and STEWART MACAULAY. 1977. *Law and the Behavioral Sciences,* 2nd ed. Indianapolis: Bobbs-Merrill.

FRIEDMAN, LAWRENCE M. and ROBERT V. PERCIVAL. 1978. "A Tale of Two Courts: Litigation in Alameda and San Benito Counties," Pp. 69–79 in Sheldon Goldman and Austin Sarat, eds., American Court Systems, Readings in Judicial Process and Behavior. San Francisco: W. H. Freeman and Company.

HALL, JEROME. 1952. *Theft, Law and Society,* 2nd ed. Indianapolis: Bobbs-Merrill.

INCIARDI, JAMES A., ALAN A. BLOCK, and LYLE A. HALLOWELL. 1977. *Historical Approaches to Crime: Research Strategies and Issues.* Beverly Hills, CA: Sage Publications.

KATZ, JAMES EVERETT. 1978. *Presidential Politics and Science Policy.* New York: Praeger Publishers.

KERSHAW, DAVID N. 1969. *The Negative Income Tax Experiment in New Jersey.* Princeton, NJ: Mathematica.

KESSLER, JOAN B. 1975. "The Social Psychology of Jury Deliberations," Pp. 69–93 in Rita James Simon, ed., The Jury System in America, A Critical Overview. Beverly Hills, CA: Sage Publications.

KUTCHINSKY, BERL. 1973. "The Effects of Easy Availability of Pornography on the Incidence of Sex Crimes: The Danish Experience," Journal of Social Issues 29 (3):163–181.

LOH, WALLACE D., 1984. *Social Research in the Judicial Process: Cases, Readings, and Text.* New York: Russell Sage Foundation.

MACAULY, STEWART, 1979. "Lawyers and Consumer Protection Laws," Law & Society Review 14 (1):115–171.

McCALL, GEORGE J. 1978. *Observing the Law: Field Methods in the Study of Crime and the Criminal Justice System.* New York: Free Press.

MILLER, FRANK W. 1969. *Prosecution: The Decision to Charge a Suspect with a Crime.* Boston: Little, Brown.

MINTZ, MORTON and JERRY S. COHEN. 1976. "Human Guinea Pigs," The Progressive 40 (12)(December):32–36.

MOREHOUSE, THOMAS. 1972. "Program Evaluation: Social Research Versus Public Policy," Public Administration Review 32 (6)(November/December):868–874.

MORRIS, ROBERT. 1979. *Social Policy of the American Welfare State: An Introduction to Policy Analysis.* New York: Harper & Row, Pub.

MOYNIHAN, DANIEL P. 1969. *Maximum Feasible Misunderstanding.* New York: Free Press.

NADER, LAURA and HARRY F. TODD, JR. 1978. "Introduction: The Disputing Process," Pp. 1–40 in Laura Nader and Harry F. Todd, Jr., eds., The Disputing Process–Law in Ten Societies. New York: Columbia University Press.

NAGEL, STUART S. 1969. *The Legal Process From a Behavioral Perspective.* Homewood, IL: The Dorsey Press.

NAGEL, STUART S. and MARIAN NEEF. 1977. *The Legal Process: Modeling the System.* Beverly Hills, CA: Sage Publications.

National Commission on the Causes and Prevention of Violence. 1969. To Establish Justice, To Insure Domestic Tranquility. Final Report. Washington, D.C.: U.S. Government Printing Office.

NEWMAN, DONALD J. 1966. *Conviction: The Determination of Guilt or Innocence Without Trial.* Boston: Little, Brown.

Newsweek, 1986. "A Salvo in the Porn War." (July 21):18.

OHLIN, LLOYD E. 1975. "Report on the President's Commission on Law Enforcement and Administration of Justice," Pp. 93–115 in Mirra Komarovsky, ed., Sociology and Public Policy, The Case of Presidential Commissions. New York: Elsevier.

PODGORECKI, ADAM. 1974. *Law and Society.* London: Routledge & Kegan Paul.

ROSSI, RICHARD H. and KATHERINE LYALL. 1976. *Reforming Public Welfare: A Critique of the Negative Income Tax Experiment.* New York: Russell Sage Foundation.

SCOTT, ROBERT A. AND ARNOLD R. SHORE. 1979. *Why Sociology Does Not Apply: A Study of the Use of Sociology in Public Policy.* New York: Elsevier.

SHORT, JAMES F., JR. 1975. "The National Commission on the Causes and Prevention of Violence, Reflections on the Contributions of Sociology and Sociologists," Pp. 61–91 in Mirra Komarovsky, ed., Sociology and Public Policy, The Case of Presidential Commissions. New York. Elsevier.

SIMON, RITA JAMES, ed. 1975. *The Jury System in America: A Critical Overview.* Beverly Hills, CA: Sage Publications.

SKOLNICK, JEROME H. 1975. *Justice Without Trial: Law Enforcement in Democratic Society,* 2nd ed. New York: John Wiley.

SUCHMAN, EDWARD A. 1967. *Evaluative Research: Principles and Practice in Public Service and Social Action Programs.* New York: Russell Sage.

SUDNOW, DAVID. 1975. "Normal Crimes: Sociological Features of the Penal Code in a Public Defender Office," Social Problems 12 (3)(Winter):255–276.

TOBY, JACKSON. 1980. "Crime in American Public Schools," The Public Interest (58)(Winter):18–42.

TOMASIC, ROMAN. 1985. *The Sociology of Law.* London: Sage Publications.

U.S. Department of Justice. 1980. Annual Report of NIJJDP, Fiscal Year 1979. National Institute for Juvenile Justice and Delinquency Prevention. Office of Juvenile Justice and Delinquency Prevention. Law Enforcement Assistance Administration (March). Washington, D.C.: U.S. Government Printing Office; 1985. Criminal Victimization in the United States, 1983. A National Crime Survey Report NCJ-96459 (August). Washington, D.C.: U.S. Government Printing Office; 1986. Attorney General's Commission on Pornography. Final Report. vols. 1 and 2 (July). Washington, D.C.: U.S. Government Printing Office.

U.S. Office of Economic Opportunity. 1970. Preliminary Results of the New Jersey Graduated

Work Incentive Experiment, February 18. Washington, D.C.: U.S. Government Printing Office.

VAGO, STEVEN. 1980. *Social Change.* New York: Holt, Rinehart & Winston.

WADE, LARRY L. 1972. *The Elements of Public Policy.* Columbus, OH: Merrill Company.

WEISS, CAROL. 1972. *Evaluation Research: Methods of Assessing Program Effectiveness.* Englewood Cliffs, NJ: Prentice-Hall.

WESTOFF, CHARLES F. 1975. "The Commission on Population Growth and the American Future, Its Origins, Operations, and Aftermath," Pp. 43–49 in Mirra Komarovsky, ed., Sociology and Public Policy, The Case of Presidential Commissions. New York: Elsevier.

WILLIAMSON, JOHN B., DAVID A. KARP and JOHN R. DALPHIN. 1977. *The Research Craft: An Introduction to Social Science Methods.* Boston: Little, Brown.

ZEISEL, HANS. 1967. "The Law," Pp. 81–99 in Paul F. Lazarsfeld, William H. Sewell and Harold Wilensky, eds., The Uses of Sociology. New York: Basic Books.

Index*

*Page numbers in italics refer to pages where reference is to be found.